Date Due

DE 12 '97	

Growing Pains

Children in the Industrial Age, 1850–1890

Twayne's History of American Childhood Series

Series Editors
Joseph M. Hawes, University of Memphis
N. Ray Hiner, University of Kansas

Growing Pains

Children in the Industrial Age, 1850–1890

Priscilla Ferguson Clement

Twayne Publishers
An Imprint of Simon & Schuster Macmillan
New York
Prentice Hall International
London   Mexico City   New Delhi   Singapore   Sydney   Toronto

Growing Pains: Children in the Industrial Age, 1850–1890
Priscilla Ferguson Clement

Copyright © 1997 by Twayne Publishers

Twayne Publishers
An Imprint of Simon & Schuster Macmillan
1633 Broadway
New York, NY 10019

Library of Congress Cataloging-in-Publication Data

Clement, Priscilla Ferguson, 1942–
    Growing pains : children in the industrial age, 1850–1890 /
  Priscilla Ferguson Clement.
       p. cm.—(Twayne's history of American childhood series)
    Includes bibliographical references and index.
    ISBN 0-8057-4109-7 (alk. paper)
  1. Children—United States—History—19th century.   I. Title.
II. Series.
HQ792.U5C565   1997
305.23—dc20
                                           96-41085
                                               CIP

10 9 8 7 6 5 4 3 2 1

Printed in the United States of America

This book is dedicated to my mother,
Isabel Thomson Ferguson,
and to my three children:
John Andrew Clement
Jennifer Ann Clement
Laura Thomson Clement

Contents

Series Editors' Note

The history of children is coming of age. What began in the 1960s as a spontaneous response by some historians to the highly visible and sometimes unsettling effects of the baby boom has emerged as a vigorous and broad-based inquiry into the lives of American children in all generations. As this series on American childhood attests, this new field is robust and includes the work of scholars from a variety of disciplines.

Our goal for this series is to introduce this rich and expanding field to undergraduate students as well as nonspecialists in related fields. Thus, books in this series are more synthetic than monographic in nature, although some areas are so little known that original research was necessary. All of the books provide important insight into the changing shape and character of children's lives in America. Finally, this series demonstrates very clearly that children are and always have been influential historical actors in their own right. Children play an essential role in the American story that this series is designed to illuminate.

In telling the story of the variety of American childhoods that emerged in the nineteenth century, Priscilla Ferguson Clement reminds us of the enormous social impact of the Civil War, rapid industrialization and urbanization, and the growth of immigration in the second half of the nineteenth century. In a comprehensive but succinct treatment, Clement highlights the ways in which the variables of race, class, and gender all significantly influenced child-rearing patterns and schooling. As a consequence of American economic expansion in the late nineteenth century, working-class children swelled the ranks of the American workforce, while middle- and upper-class children came to enjoy the fruits of industrial capitalism: a greater variety of clothing, a plethora of toys and, even for young children, a room of one's own. A new sensitivity to the importance of children and childhood emerged from the chaos of the late nineteenth century, yet that sensitivity competed with a new focus on consumption and continuing pressure for expansion. While the century to come might be labeled the century of the child at its birth, it would take more than an increased social sentimentality about children to transform that ideal into reality.

N. Ray Hiner   Joseph M. Hawes
University of Kansas   University of Memphis

Preface

I began this book with the goal of writing the history of all children in the United States between 1850 and 1890. I soon discovered the obvious: that this is impossible. I have compromised by trying to analyze various life experiences of the majority of American children. I have left out the stories of upper-class youngsters and of Native American children: the former because there were so few of them and their life experiences are so distinct from those of other children and the latter because another book in the series of which this study is a part will cover Native American youth.

Overall, this book has been a real pleasure to write. I have learned a lot in the process and have been able, through it, to clarify my thinking on various aspects of American social and family history. There are many people who have made this project a pleasurable one. I am most grateful to three librarians at Penn State, Delaware County Campus, who have tirelessly helped in my search for materials on the history of children. They are Sara Whildin, Head Librarian, Susan Ware, Research Librarian, and Jean Sphar, Staff Assistant. Various colleagues, including Carol Kessler, Sally McMurry, Gary Cross, Susan Porter, Eric Schneider, and Janet Golden, read parts of the manuscript and made useful comments on it. Of most help have been my editors, N. Ray Hiner and especially Joseph Hawes. He has been both a good friend and an excellent critic.

A sabbatical from Penn State helped me get started on this project. I finished it thanks to summers at our home in Eagles Mere, where the peace and quiet of the weekdays promoted productivity and the joyful noise of the weekends with my family provided a needed respite from my books, notes, and word processor.

It seems appropriate that this book in particular should be dedicated to a mother and to children. Without the love and support of my mother, I wouldn't be here to write at all. As for my children, they are well beyond the age of youngsters I write about, yet their childhoods are fresh in my memory and continue to inspire me to understand earlier childhoods than theirs or my own. This dedication is one way of thanking them for how they have encouraged me and how they have loved and understood me as both mother and historian.

1

The United States and Its Children, 1850–1890

Between 1850 and 1890 the United States was a youthful nation. At midcentury, 52 percent of the population were younger than 19 years of age, and 41 percent were under the age of 15. Forty years later, the proportion of young people in the population, though smaller, was still sizable: 46 percent of Americans were younger than 19, and 35 percent were younger than 15. Close to 50 percent of both whites and African-Americans were children.[1] The history of children in this period is the history not of a minority, but of half of all Americans.

That history is marked by division. There was no common experience of childhood in the United States between 1850 and 1890; there were many childhoods. This complexity is a consequence of widening disparities in social-class status and in the life experiences of whites and blacks, natives and immigrants, females and males, city dwellers and farmers, and inhabitants of the North, Midwest, Far West, and the South. Regardless of the rhetoric of equality that had long distinguished American society from European society, American childhoods became more distinct in this era.

In the second half of the nineteenth century, two huge changes in the United States promoted class, race, and gender divisions that affected all American children and adults. One was an economic transformation, the other, political, but both reverberated throughout American society. The first was industrialization, accompanied by urbanization and immigration, which will be discussed in this chapter. The second was the Civil War and Reconstruction, which form the subject of the next chapter.

Industrialization began before midcentury with the mechanization of production of textiles and shoes, which were no longer fabricated in the shops of small artisans but in factories. After 1850, factory production of consumer items accelerated. So too did iron and steel making, petroleum refining, and the manufacture of machinery. All were items purchased by producers, who in turn used them in ways that enhanced economic productivity. For example, railroads bought steel to make stronger, more durable rail lines and locomotives; construction companies bought it to build sturdier bridges and taller buildings; and smaller companies bought it to improve products such as wire, nails, and screws sold to ordinary Americans. All these industries (and others) grew thanks to technological innovation, new sources of power, and improved transportation. Steel production benefited from the Bessemer process (developed in Great Britain and adopted in the United States by the 1870s) of converting iron ore to steel; petroleum production, from methods of changing the molecular structure of crude oil to yield a variety of products; textile production, from faster machinery; clothing and shoe manufacture, from the sewing machine; meat packing, from mechanical refrigeration. Water power gave way to steam power with the discovery of large deposits of anthracite coal and the enlargement of the mining industry. The vast expansion of railroads made it possible for industries to obtain raw materials quickly and to transport finished products to consumers. In 1860, there were just 30,000 miles of railroad tracks in the United States, but by 1890 there were 166,703. At the end of the century, four transcontinental railroads connected the East to the West, and smaller lines joined most towns to nearby cities.[2]

Several profound changes accompanied industrialization. One was the increased size of business firms: by 1890, railroads, textile mills, and iron and steel companies employed hundreds of workers. Large factories became the norm, and machines took the place of many skilled workers. Most manufacturing jobs could be filled by any unskilled worker. As businesses grew in size and complexity, managerial tasks proliferated: accurate record keeping and accounting, as well as efficient organization of widespread enterprises, were essential. Large industrial firms were commonly located in cities near workers, markets, and railroad connections. After 1850, older East Coast cities such as New York, Philadelphia, and Boston grew rapidly, but so did river cities in the Midwest, including Pittsburgh, Cincinnati, and St. Louis; lake cities such as Buffalo, Cleveland, Detroit, and Chicago; and West Coast cities such as San Francisco and Los Angeles.[3]

Immigration coincided with urbanization and industrialization. Between 1847 and 1854, 1.2 million Irish immigrants arrived in the United States. Impoverished by the potato famine and accustomed chiefly to farm labor, they could not afford to move beyond the slums of New York, Baltimore, Philadelphia, and Boston. In these cities, most Irish ended up in low-paying jobs because they lacked industrial skills and because of prejudice against them. The Civil War interrupted immigration, but after the war, between 1870 and 1900, more than 11 million immigrants poured into the United

States. Most were peasants from Italy, Poland, Austria-Hungary, and Russia, and they too swelled the ranks of unskilled industrial workers.[4] Among the immigrants, only a small number were middle-class. They were usually landlords and shopkeepers who lived in ethnic neighborhoods and shared the "class and cultural characteristics" of the areas in which they lived. They did not resemble the native-born middle class.[5] In eastern and Midwestern cities most immigrants were European-born, but in Western cities many were of Mexican descent. In the West, Mexican-Americans were actually the "host" culture, but when Anglos dominated the regional economy, "Chicanos sought work in the Anglo-dominated sphere, they 'immigrated' to a new economy, an Anglo world whose very structure was, to an extent, formed by and dependent on their presence as laborers."[6]

Between the 1850s and 1890s, several business downturns impacted on wage workers and employers. There were economic depressions in 1857–59, 1873–79, 1885–87, and 1893–97. As new industries grew, so did the number of firms competing with one another for sales. More firms produced more products, and ultimately markets became saturated. Companies then reduced production, cut wages, and fired workers. More businesses and farmers were affected as the unemployed purchased less, and the economy spiraled downward. Hundreds of firms went bankrupt. Eventually the economy reached its low point, and businesses began again to hire workers and increase production. There was no federal government intervention to assist either workers or employers. By the 1870s, railroad and oil companies led the way in trying to prevent price wars and overproduction by buying up competitors or driving them out of business. Such measures were largely successful, and the number of competing firms in these and other industries diminished substantially by 1900.[7]

Tensions between employers and workers escalated in the depression of the 1870s when employers cut wages and fired workers. Workers totally dependent on wages for their livelihood grew angry and struck back in several large and violent strikes. In 1877 anthracite coal miners staged a bloody strike against mine owners in Pennsylvania and were defeated. Twenty Irish miners, known as the Molly Maguires, were tried, convicted, and hanged. Later in 1877, when several railroads cut wages 10 percent, workers struck in cities across the nation. Fierce fighting erupted in several places. Anxious businessmen supported the establishment of National Guard units, led by officers from the middle classes, in all the states. During the economic downturn of the 1880s, there were further strikes against railroads. In 1886 an effort by workers to achieve the eight-hour day resulted in a riot at Haymarket Square in Chicago when someone threw a bomb at police. Eight anarchists were arrested, and although trial testimony indicated six were not at Haymarket when the bomb was thrown, all were convicted and seven sentenced to death.[8] These terrible labor-management confrontations were the most obvious sign that divisions between business-men and salaried professional persons and wage workers had intensified with industrialization.

As class divisions within the United States deepened, children from prosperous middle-class families grew up in very different circumstances than youngsters born to poorer, working-class parents. Larger, more complex businesses required more engineers, bookkeepers, accountants, architects, lawyers, salesmen, clerks, and typists. Companies hired men for most of these jobs and paid them fairly well. Consequently, middle-class men were able to support their families on their salaries alone. They could afford to purchase large homes on the outskirts of cities, staff them with a few servants, and themselves ride to work on the new streetcars. Middle-class wives managed households and devoted much of their time to child rearing. Eventually, some middle-class occupations opened to women as well, including teaching, clerking, and typing, but these jobs paid considerably less than did those reserved for men and usually only unmarried women took them. Middle-class family life seemed relatively secure, but parents agonized over the present and future dangers posed by turbulent working-class youth. The high rate of business failure in this period also meant that family heads, their wives, and children might face financial setbacks and had to be prepared to adapt to changing economic circumstances.[9]

The sons and daughters of working-class parents had little in common with the children of more prosperous families. In every industry there were a small number of skilled workers (about 10 percent of the total nonagricultural workforce), most of whom were native born, who could usually earn enough to support their families. Yet because of continuous changes in industry, which eliminated many craft jobs, first in shoemaking and weaving and later in other crafts as well, few could be sure they would be able to pass on their skills and economic and social status to their children. To protect their jobs, skilled workers organized unions. The American Federation of Labor, founded in 1886, furthered their interests, although its greatest successes did not come until the twentieth century.[10]

The majority of the urban working class were foreign-born, unskilled workers. The wages of such laborers increased about 31 percent between 1860 and 1900, but most were also frequently unemployed or underemployed. During economic depressions, workers' jobs were most at risk. In Massachusetts, for which the best records of employment exist, in 1885 and in 1895, 30 percent of the state's workers were out of work for three to four months at some time in each year. Even in prosperous years such as 1890, 20 percent of Massachusetts workers were unemployed at some time.[11] Few urban, working-class fathers could earn enough to support their families. In 1883 a laborer with a wife and two young children described to a congressional committee how he earned wages of $1 per day and was out of work at least three weeks in a year. Despite the fact he had taken a second job, practiced every economy he could, and even borrowed $60, on the day he testified, his family had nothing to eat except a loaf of bread borrowed from a neighbor.[12] White working-class wives sometimes took in boarders or sewing or piecework to earn extra dollars, but rarely did they work outside the home. In the absence of labor-saving household appliances, working-class housewives sewed for long hours to keep their husbands and children clothed, shopped daily for food bargains, and made all meals from scratch. Among working-class women, principally those who were young and unmarried worked outside the home, sometimes in factories, more often as domestic servants.[13] Urban laborers and their children usually lived in small apartments in crowded neighborhoods. Youngsters enjoyed little privacy and protection from the larger world. They lived always with the specter of poverty and family breakup. Their childhoods were short, for as soon as boys were able, parents expected them to go to work to help supplement the family economy, and girls either had to do the same or helped their mothers with child care and housework. (See chapters 3 and 5.)

Despite many similarities, the experiences of working-class children and their parents varied because of racial and ethnic divisions. Among ethnic groups there were differences that impacted on how quickly the foreign born were accepted and how easily they adapted to the American industrial system. English and Scots immigrants were often skilled workers who faced no language barriers and, like most native-born Americans, were Protestant in faith. They and their children often advanced into the middle class. Despite the language barrier, German immigrants also often prospered because so many were skilled workers. Irish immigrants spoke English, but their lack of industrial skills and the prejudice of native American Protestants against the Irish workers' Catholicism consigned them to low-wage, unskilled industrial jobs. Language and religious differences and low skills also handicapped Polish, Italian, and Russian-Jewish immigrants.[14] As for African-Americans, racial prejudice against them and their lack of industrial skills meant that in Northern and Southern cities black men, who were denied most factory jobs, often worked as day laborers and typically earned even less than white native-born and immigrant workers. Partly because their husbands earned so little, African-American wives were more likely than white working-class married women to labor outside the home, usually as domestics.[15] Whereas those working-class persons with the lowest-wage industrial jobs benefited little from the industrial system, African-Americans, who were virtually excluded from the system, profited much less.

Industrialism also impacted on a totally different part of the United States economy: agriculture. In 1870, 53 percent of all employed persons labored on farms, and by 1890, 42 percent. Between 1850 and 1890, more persons worked on farms than in cities, and more children lived in rural areas than in urban ones. Rural folk too felt the impact of industrial change. As the railroad companies extended their lines, they encouraged farmers to move on to the Great Plains and to other parts of the West and Far West. There, by means of the new transportation system, farmers became a part of the commercial system, producing not just for their own needs but for a larger market. Just like other businessmen, farmers suffered when railroads charged high rates and profited when rate wars drove rates down. The huge output of farm produce helped make possible the concentration of people in cities and the manufacture of new products. Those products in turn became available to farmers and widened their horizons and those of their children.

As corn production in the Midwest and wheat production on the Great Plains increased, farmers in the Northeast turned increasingly to providing nearby city folk with dairy products, vegetables, and fruit. Specialization proceeded apace in farming as in manufacturing.[16] This was also true in the South, where before the Civil War most white plantation owners grew cotton. After the war, when former slaves refused to work as wage laborers for whites and insisted upon a greater degree of independence, sharecropping, tenantry, and the crop lien system developed. African-Americans, who as slaves had been unable to accumulate any savings, could not purchase farmland. So black families agreed to work 30 to 50 acres of land supplied by white owners or merchants (as were seeds, tools, and housing) in return for half the crop raised—a system known as sharecropping. Some blacks and many Southern whites became tenant farmers and themselves supplied seeds and tools in return for one-fourth the cotton crop they raised. White owners usually insisted that sharecroppers or tenants raise only cotton because it, unlike other farm products, had a guaranteed market. Such specialization precluded the raising of food crops, so sharecroppers and tenants had to borrow or take crop liens at ruinously high interest rates from local merchants in order to supply themselves with food during the year. If sharecroppers or tenants could not raise enough from the sale of their share of the crop to pay off their debts in a year, they committed to paying them off the next. In this way, most black and many white farmers in the South fell further and further into debt.[17]

Increasing debt and lack of savings help to explain why most Southern blacks and poor whites were unable to take advantage of an important benefit to farmers of industrialization—new, efficient farm machinery. By the mid-1850s some Midwestern farmers began to replace simpler farm tools with mechanical reapers, mowers, threshers, and seed drills. During the Civil War, high farm prices and conscription of farmers in the Midwest resulted in the introduction of even more machines to increase production. Work that had previously taken five men to perform now took only two. Farmers who purchased new machines often bought more land as well. They grew richer, and other farmers who did not purchase machinery grew poorer. Class divisions developed on farms as in cities. Children of prosperous men who mechanized their farms experienced childhood more like youngsters in middle-class urban and suburban homes did, while boys and girls who grew up on the frontier or on small farms without much machinery had more in common with working-class youngsters in cities.[18]

For the history of children, the chief legacy of industrialization was the hardening of class lines. Subsequent chapters will demonstrate that the class status of young people's parents strongly influenced what kind of a home they would live in, how much attention they would get from their mothers, how long they would live under maternal care, the likelihood of their family's breaking up and their moving to an orphanage or foster home, the kind of toys they would have and books they would read, the amount and duration of their schooling, the kind of employment they would obtain, and the age when they would go to work.

But class divisions alone do not account for all the differences in children's experiences. Race, gender, and the part of the country in which a child grew up are also crucial. Prejudice against African-Americans precluded nearly all of them from ever obtaining middle-class status. Yet if we focus exclusively on working-class white and black children, we find their educational and employment experiences and even the fictional stories each group preferred to read diverged strikingly. Gender also impacted childhood. Parents of all classes, races, and ethnicities were more protective of daughters than of sons, although the form and effectiveness of that protection varied. Last, the place children lived, whether it was a city or a farm, the North or the South, influenced their education, employment, and the degree to which the Civil War and Reconstruction altered their lives. This most divisive and destructive war and its impact on the nation's children forms the subject of chapter 2.

The remaining chapters of the book are topical. Each will explore how differences in class, race, gender, and geographical locale interacted in unique ways to influence various aspects of children's lives. Chapter 3 focuses on both the four distinct patterns of child rearing of the Victorian era and the common worries of all parents—particularly for their children's health. The subject of chapter 4 is schooling: what most boys and girls learned and how they learned it, as well as the manner in which schooling differed for youngsters depending on their geographical location, race, ethnicity, religion, and gender. Chapter 5 deals with what most youngsters did when they were not in school: labor. Employment varied most by class, but race, ethnicity, gender, and locale also played a part in determining which youngsters would go to work early and what kind of jobs they would take. The topic of chapter 6 is the play, toys, games, and stories enjoyed by white and black, middle- and working-class boys and girls. Last, chapter 7 concerns impoverished and delinquent children, the child welfare programs created for them by middle-class reformers, and the reactions of poor families and young people to these welfare measures. The conclusion summarizes the childhood experiences of various groups of young people in the late nineteenth century and makes some comparisons to children growing up in the late twentieth century.

2

The Civil War, Reconstruction, and America's Youth

The most divisive events of the second half of the nine-teenth century, and probably of all American history, were the Civil War and Reconstruction. Among the many causes of the war were familial issues including parental concern about the current and future prospects of their own and other Americans' children. During the war, some young people served in the military, but many more felt the impact of the war in the tempo-rary or even permanent loss of a father or brother. In wartime, children took on new responsibilities to help support their families. Children also experi-enced more poverty and physical danger because parents were less able to protect youngsters from deprivation and military encounters. The war affected all boys and girls, but it altered the lives of children in the South, especially African-American children freed from slavery, most dramatically. During Reconstruction, wartime poverty diminished for most children in the North, and life returned, if not exactly to the way it had been previously, to at least a close approximation of the prewar pattern. The war also lessened discrimination against free African-American children in the North. Con-versely, during Reconstruction, many Southern white children continued to live in poverty and to shoulder work responsibilities they had assumed in wartime, although eventually the postwar era brought Southern white chil-dren new access to schooling. As for former slaves, whereas Reconstruction did not mitigate poverty, end violence and discrimination against them, and preclude the need for most to labor at a young age, Reconstruction did bring wonderful benefits. These included the chance to live and work within a fam-ily context that could no longer be broken by sale, and the opportunity to obtain an education.

Henry Alexander Field Hoyt. One of the many teenagers who enlisted in the military during the Civil War. Hoyt served with the 57th Massachusetts Infantry. (Courtesy of Trevis Young and St. John's Episcopal Church of Lower Merion, Pennsylvania)

The Civil War began in 1861, but the deep divisions that caused it had a long history. From the time English colonists founded Virginia and Massachusetts in the seventeenth century, differences existed between the South and the North. A common language, history, religion, and culture bound the sections, but North and South divided over the issue of slavery, especially after the Revolutionary War, when the Northern states abolished involuntary servitude. In the nineteenth century, Northerners excluded slavery from the lands they moved into north of the Ohio River and west to the Mississippi. At the same time, slavery became more entrenched in the South with the introduction of cotton as a staple crop. The economies of the two sections diverged as the South concentrated on agriculture and raising cotton, rice, tobacco, and sugar by means of slave labor, while the North industrialized and relied on free wage labor in both factories and farms. Slavery became an increasingly troublesome issue when the United States acquired California and New Mexico after the Mexican War in 1848–49. Would slavery be permitted in the new territories of the United States? Southerners answered yes, but Northerners, especially those influenced by the abolition movement, which called for an end to slavery entirely, said no. Not all Northerners agreed with the abolitionist desire to free slaves everywhere in the United States, but reformers did raise troubling issues about families and children. These issues are of special import to this study. At a time when Northern middle-class parents increasingly valued their children and attempted to raise them in a protected environment managed by their mothers (see chapter 3), abolitionists demonstrated how slavery prevented black families from doing the same. Harriet Beecher Stowe's *Uncle Tom's Cabin*, published in 1854, graphically described to Northerners how wrenching slavery could be when masters separated children from their mothers in order to sell one or both for a profit. After the 1860 election to the presidency of Abraham Lincoln, who sympathized with the antislavery movement, supported free labor over slave labor, and opposed the extension of slavery into the territories, Southern states seceded from the Union. Shortly thereafter, the Civil War began. At first, the North fought the war to reunite the nation, but by 1863, when Lincoln issued the Emancipation Proclamation, the North was fighting a war against slavery.

This is a much abbreviated version of the events leading up to the Civil War. The war had many causes, but for this study, the most relevant are those pertaining to children and families. In both the North and the South, many whites and blacks, women and men, interpreted the great issues that divided the nation, slavery and its extension into the territories, from a familial perspective. Many Northern white men objected to slavery in the territories because its expansion prevented them and their children from moving west. Free labor could not compete with slave labor, so wherever the government permitted slavery, white farmers who did not own slaves and hoped to farm land with their families and pass some of it on to their children were disadvantaged. Many Northern white women condemned slavery in the territories and in the South because slavery challenged a right they presumed common to all women: to nurture their own children and to protect them from exploitation and abuse. Victims of economic and social discrimination, free African-Americans living in the North and in Southern cities welcomed the war because it might free their relatives and friends and allow all African-Americans the opportunity to earn respect for themselves and new rights for their children. White Southern planters regarded Northern determination to keep slavery out of the territories as an unfair, unconstitutional way of preventing planters from carrying their slave property west as they sought new opportunities for themselves and their children. Southern white men also opposed abolitionism because it challenged their patriarchal right to control slave children. Southern white women agreed with their menfolk in order to safeguard their own and their children's material well-being. For white women, slavery was a mixed blessing: it provided them with servants, but it also granted their husbands enormous power and license to sire black children with impunity. Southern slaves of both genders looked forward to a war that might end slavery and thereby allow them for the first time to reunite their families and control and protect their own children.[1] All these groups explained the Civil War, at least in part, with reference to children.

The war affected both Northern and Southern children, but it most disrupted the lives of white and black children living in the South. So too did Reconstruction. Wherever the Union army invaded the Southern states, Reconstruction began. When the war ended in 1865, the North commenced rebuilding all Southern states, a process that continued until 1877, when Southern whites resumed control of Southern state governments. During Reconstruction, the Southern states reentered the Union only after they had ratified the Thirteenth Amendment, which ended slavery, and the Fourteenth Amendment, which granted citizenship to freed slaves. The Southern states also agreed to the Fifteenth Amendment, giving African-American men the right to vote.[2] During the Civil War, the issues that most affected children were military enlistment of themselves or their fathers, the experience of battle, new employment responsibilities, poverty, and, especially in the South, homelessness and military invasion. During Reconstruction, the matters that most impacted children were pension legislation, continued economic dislocation and violence, orphanage, poverty, apprenticeship, and schooling.

Because the experiences of children during the Civil War and Reconstruction were so much determined by where they lived, this study examines the war and its aftermath from a sectional perspective: first that of children growing up in the North, and second that of youngsters whose homeland was the South.

When the war began in 1861, some young people joined the Union army. Two-fifths of all Northern soldiers who served in the war were 21 years of age or younger.[3] Early on, many young men rushed to enlist, with or without the permission of their parents. In 1861, the single largest group of soldiers was 18 years of age.[4] In August 1861, the military required boys under 18 to secure their parents' consent before enlisting, and in 1862 barred enlistment of all such young teens entirely. Nonetheless, young men often managed to get into the army throughout the war by lying about their age. Sixteen-year-old Chauncey H. Cook reported that he was not even asked his age because "the mustering officer saw my whiskers." Historian Bell Irvin Wiley estimated that between 1 percent and 2 percent of all Union soldiers were under the age of 18.[5]

For boys without whiskers, the easiest way to enter the Union army was to sign up as a drummer or bugler, positions for which there was no minimum age until March 1864, when military officials set it at 16. In the Union army, there were 40,000 slots for musicians, whose task was communication: they called soldiers to meals and to muster. In camp the boys also performed various services for soldiers, including running errands, collecting wood, and cooking. During battles, the boys marched with the regular troops, and their drumbeats communicated to soldiers how to maneuver on a smoke-filled field of combat. Drumming was not necessarily a safe position, as 14-year-old Orion P. Howe discovered in 1863. He was wounded several times during the Battle of Vicksburg, yet continued to perform the job assigned him: to carry messages to General William T. Sherman. For his bravery, Howe earned the Medal of Honor. In the heat of battle, some drummer and bugler boys gave up their instruments and took up muskets instead. Whether boys fought or not, all saw some horrible sights. At Manassas, Thomas Galway reported seeing knees, toes, and skulls protruding from shallow graves. Some young soldiers became ill from the carnage they witnessed, and others deserted and fled home. Those who served the longest became somewhat inured to the terrible sights.[6]

Some children who were not soldiers also experienced firsthand the carnage of war. When the Battle of Gettysburg began, 18-year-old Daniel Skelly, one of the 2,500 residents of the town, and some friends went out to observe the fighting until "shot and shell began to fly over our heads. There was then a general stampede toward town." During the three days of battle, many Gettysburg families took refuge in their cellars, including 17-year-old Jennie McCreary, who remembered, "To know the rebels were in town, to hear the shells bursting and expecting every minute they would fall on the house, was indeed horrible." When the battle ended, children and their families emerged to find dead and dying soldiers everywhere and much of their familiar town landscape destroyed. Fifteen-year-old Tillie Pierce observed amputations and "a pile of limbs higher than the fence" in a makeshift hospital created for some of the 16,000 wounded men. One couple housed in their barn injured soldiers who played with and made toys for the children in the family. Unfortunately the youngsters "broke out with sores, were infested with vermin," and the five-year-old died of an illness contracted from the ailing men. "The rest of Gettysburg's children would struggle for the remainder of their lives to make personal peace with their memories."[7]

The Union soldiers who fought at Gettysburg and other battles, no matter what their age, viewed the war through the lens of family. Soldiers fought the Civil War to protect their families and expected to return to their families when the fighting ceased. Because most served in volunteer regiments organized by persons in their home communities, soldiers often served with family members, or at least with persons who knew their folks back home. Not surprisingly, Northern soldiers rarely criticized their families.[8] Most soldiers successfully maintained their family roles by keeping in close touch by writing letters and spending furloughs at home. During the 29 months that teenager J. L. Smith was in the army, he sent 184 letters to his mother. Fathers continued to be concerned about their children and wrote home to advise their wives about child rearing. Mothers and sons remained especially close, and some mothers actually came to the battlefront to nurse their own sons and remained to care for the sons of other women.[9]

Some officers even brought their children to the battlefront. Ulysses S. Grant kept his 11-year-old son Fred with him near Cairo, Illinois, in 1861, and Ellen Sherman accompanied her children to several military camps to visit their father, General William T. Sherman, until the oldest boy, Willy, died of typhoid fever he contracted at Vicksburg in 1863. Men willingly took such risks with the lives of their children because the presence of family was so central to "this generation's sense of well-being." Officers liked their sons to be with them so that they could express their love for the boys, "exert a gentle control" over them, and teach them "the lessons of manhood."[10]

Northern soldiers sometimes interpreted the Civil War itself in terms of family. Rarely did persons in power view the war as one against "the South the disobedient child," but many Northern soldiers did. They understood the political world in familial terms. Such Northerners argued that children should obey their parents, not only their natural ones but also the national government. It too was a parent and thus deserving of loyalty. This "parental metaphor made rebellion a primal sin." Only bad sons disobeyed their mothers, fathers, or their government, and in any case, disobedient sons deserved punishment. From this perspective, the North was the teacher; the army, her weapon; and the misbehaving child to be whipped, the South.[11]

Although a few young people in the North fought in the war or experienced battle near their hometowns, most youngsters felt the deprivation of war in another way, through the absence of their fathers. Between 1861 and 1863, the Union army accepted only whites. Those who volunteered in 1861 did so without benefit of financial incentives. Privates received just $11 a month, which the army did not always pay to them on time and was not, in any case, a living wage for a family man.[12] As the war dragged on, their families were especially likely to become destitute because of the long absence of the chief breadwinner. However, the families of soldiers who enlisted later profited from bounties (cash payments) paid by the federal government, cities, counties, and local citizens. Beginning in 1862, volunteers became scarce as casualties mounted and it became clear that the war would be a prolonged and bloody one. In March 1863, for the first time in U.S. history, the Union army began to draft men between the ages of 20 and 45. Prospective soldiers could avoid service by paying a commutation fee of $300 or hiring a substitute. Most Americans, long accustomed to a volunteer army, opposed the draft, and endorsed the concept of enlarging the pool of volunteers by accepting blacks, now that the war had become one to free slaves. Throughout the North, free blacks, who had long been anxious to fight, joined special black regiments. Unfortunately, until 1864, black soldiers received even less pay than did whites, which put the families of African-American fighting men in greater jeopardy of impoverishment. Beginning in 1863, Northern citizens opposed to the draft also organized to pay bounties to encourage men to volunteer. Manpower needs did not abate, and by the end of the war, both white and black enlistees could earn over $1,000 in national, city, and local bounties, a very large sum in a day when the average laborer earned about $1.50 a day. Bonuses reduced the likelihood that the families of such soldiers would become impoverished in their absence. Substitution did not benefit rich white men only, because cities, counties, and employers of drafted men helped workers pay for substitutes. In addition, "draft insurance societies sprang up everywhere to offer a $300 policy for premiums of a few dollars a month."[13]

When fathers went off to war, children and their mothers assumed new responsibilities. Although bounties certainly helped the families of Northern soldiers, bounties rarely obviated the necessity for employment by one or more members of a man's family. On farms, boys and girls and their mothers took up the chores that fathers customarily performed, including planting, cultivating, and harvesting crops. Thanks to the introduction of farm machines such as mowers and reapers, youngsters found it easier to perform these tasks. During the Civil War, upstate New York dairy-farming families also centralized cheese making in small factories, partly to permit women and children more time to replace men's labor in haying and harvesting field crops. Because a large agricultural output was essential for the success of the Union, it was vital that children and mothers replace farmers in Northern fields. As one rural New York newspaper reported in 1863, "the incessant rattle of the mowing machine, the busy activity of every man and boy that can wield a fork or rake, declare how important to the farmer is the present crisis."[14]

Many children who lived in cities also went to work to help replace family income lost when a father went to war. During the recession of 1861, wage work for children and their mothers and for men who did not go to war was scarce, but for the remaining three years of the war the expansion of government contracts and military needs fueled a growing economy. Urban, working-class youngsters did not ordinarily enter the labor force until their early teens (see chapter 5), but during wartime, Northern textile mills recruited boys and girls as young as seven. By 1865, 13 percent of textile-mill workers in Massachusetts and 22 percent of textile-mill workers in Pennsylvania were under the age of 16. Soldiers' wives also sought wage-earning jobs during the war. Many took up sewing for the government or for government contractors, although wages for such labor were very low. In fact, in all jobs, women earned less than did men.

Even when Northern children and mothers worked, they often found their standard of living declining because prices went up so much faster than wages. "Eggs rose from 15 cents per dozen in 1861 to 25 cents in late 1863; potatoes rose from $1.50 per bushel to $2.25 per bushel in the same period." The rate of inflation in the North, although much less than in the South, was still 80 percent. Consequently, even though their wages rose in wartime, because of inflation Northern workers suffered on average a decline of 20 percent in real wages by 1863 or 1864.[15]

In the North, because of the loss of paternal income, inflation, and low wages paid to youngsters and women, poverty increased. Throughout the North, existing charities and new soldiers' aid associations labored to raise funds to help the needy families of soldiers. Payments were minimal. They varied "from about $5 a week for a wife and four children in New York City to about $4 per month in the rural West . . . and these modest payments stopped when soldiers were discharged or killed." Because families of this size in New York City required at least $15 a week for necessities, wartime poor relief was obviously insufficient.

Many mothers and their children took refuge in public almshouses or poorhouses. The child population in New York almshouses rose 300 percent during the Civil War. Children took to the streets in search of work to help support their families. Absent fathers and working mothers could provide little supervision of their sons and daughters. Juvenile delinquency increased, and more children entered institutions for juveniles during the war. "The inspector of prisons in Massachusetts observed, 'I have talked with many boys in Jails and Houses of Correction who were either sons or brothers of soldiers or sailors in the service. It may not be extravagant to say that one out of four of the many children in our prisons have near relatives in the army.' "[16] Youngsters who were employed or seeking work rarely went to school. School attendance declined substantially between 1860 and 1870.[17] Children in the streets also got caught up in mob protests. During July 1863, when workers protested the new draft law by rioting for three days in New York City, children were amid the protesters. Of the 261 rioters arrested for whom information on age exists, 27 percent were between the ages of seven and twenty years old.[18]

At the war's end, seemingly the most disadvantaged of Northern children were those whose fathers were among either the 17 percent of all Union soldiers killed or the 13 percent disabled by the war. However, the economic suffering of such youngsters was considerably mitigated by the federal government, which provided them and their mothers with generous pension payments. In 1862 Congress passed the first law providing pensions to soldiers disabled due to military service. Payments varied depending on rank and on type of disability. Widows and orphans of soldiers who were killed received pensions "at the rates their relatives would have gotten for total disabilities." In subsequent years, Congress improved benefits. By 1873 widows received extra payments monthly for dependent children, and by 1879, no matter when they originally applied for pensions (up until July 1880), veterans, their widows, and orphans received not only regular monthly pension payments but also a lump sum that covered benefits from the time of the veteran's actual death or disability. In 1881, on the average, widows and their children received a first payment of $1,021.51—a lordly sum at a time when the average annual wage of workers was $400.[19] In addition to receiving pensions, veterans' children made homeless by the war who had no other relatives to care for them might in many states enter orphan asylums designed especially for them. (See chapter 7.)

As for youngsters in the North whose fathers had either never served in the war or survived it in good health, during Reconstruction their lives returned to much the way they had been before the war. The number of youngsters in almshouses and juvenile reformatories diminished, and so too did crime among the young. In Philadelphia the rate of arrests of young people between 10 and 20 years of age declined in 1866 and 1867 to between 6 percent and 7 percent, which was less than half the rate of prewar years.

School attendance rates improved in the postwar era, and free African-American children benefited disproportionately from changes made in Northern education. Before the Civil War, only Massachusetts had integrated schools. In all other Northern states, schools were segregated, and those for blacks were less well equipped than those for whites. After this war to free African-American slaves, a war in which black soldiers from the North and the South fought valiantly for the Union, officials in most Northern states recognized the justice of extending greater rights to black citizens. One of those rights was desegregated schools. Nonetheless, not all Northern states equalized education for blacks and whites. Indiana was especially hostile to blacks and kept its public schools entirely closed to them.[20]

The problems of Northern children during the Civil War—greater poverty, homelessness, crime, lower levels of school attendance, and higher levels of labor—were largely artifacts of wartime. There is little evidence that the Civil War substantially changed the lives of large numbers of children, nor did it irrevocably alter patterns of child rearing among any group of Northern families. (See chapter 3.)

The Civil War and Reconstruction more indelibly marked the lives of children born and raised in the South. Within the Confederacy, the impact of these events on white and African-American youngsters was somewhat similar, yet the effects were distinct enough that each group's experiences merit attention.

A larger proportion of white boys in the South than in the North enlisted in the military, at least in the first year of the war. In 1861–62, 5 percent of Confederate soldiers, in contrast to 1 percent or 2 percent of Union soldiers, were under the age of 18. Because there were fewer white men of all ages in the South than in the North, it is not surprising that a higher percentage of young white men (or men of any age, for that matter) served in the Confederate army than in the Union army. As in the North, Southern boys under 18 had to obtain their parents' permission to serve. In the early years of the war, when optimism about a quick victory ran high, most boys who sought parental permission to serve secured it or circumvented it somehow. Because friends and relatives formed volunteer regiments in the South as in the North, a boy might have many fellow soldiers willing to attest he was of age to enlist. However, after 1862, fewer teens under the age of 18 joined the army, probably because they were more reluctant to serve and their families were more unwilling to have them go. By this time, the death toll in the war was very high, and many families had already lost a male breadwinner. In addition, food shortages, inflation, and the prospect of Union invasion produced family hardship that would only worsen if an able-bodied son went off to fight.[21]

Just as in the Union army, many of the young white boys who served in the Confederate army were drummers or buglers. There were a total of 20,000 in the Southern army. Some came under enemy fire. " 'A ball hit my drum and bounced off and I fell over,' a Confederate drummer at the Battle of Cedar Creek recalled. 'When I got up, another ball tore a hole in the drum and another came so close to my ear that I heard it sing.' " In addition, the Confederacy called on teen boys from the many military schools in the South to serve as drillmasters for the regular troops. By the end of the war, the Confederacy was so desperate for soldiers that officials required students in these military schools to act as a reserve army, and some engaged in combat in 1864. Unlike the North, the South never forbade young men under 18 to enlist.[22]

There were many more battles fought in the South than in the North, and thus more Southern than Northern youngsters coped with the problems faced by boys and girls at Gettysburg. During the Battle of Fredericksburg in December 1862, one woman and her children spent 13 hours in a damp basement as shells destroyed their home overhead. For weeks thereafter the children remained frightened of the smallest noise. Families who lived in Vicksburg during the long Union siege of that city lived in damp basements or caves in the city walls. Youngsters coped with infestations of mosquitoes and rattlesnakes and went hungry when soldiers appropriated their food.[23]

Unlike Northern soldiers, those who fought for the South did not understand the war to be a family squabble. They did not see themselves as disobedient children, nor did they perceive Northerners in this light. Instead, white Southerners believed they were fighting to preserve the original American republic forged in the Revolution—a government of limited powers that protected property (as in slaves). Yet when it came to individual, personal reasons for fighting, soldiers who fought for the Confederacy, like Northern soldiers, enlisted to protect their families and tried to remain in close touch with them during the war. As in the North, Southern fathers wrote home to advise mothers on how to manage children, and mothers kept in close touch with their sons by mail and willingly journeyed to military hospitals to nurse their boys when necessary.

However, Southern white soldiers had a much more difficult time than did Northerners protecting their families from poverty and want. Southern soldiers earned the same inadequate wages as did Northern soldiers, and Southern soldiers were much less likely to receive bounties. Southern communities simply lacked the financial resources to provide such benefits to volunteers. In the Civil War, Southern white families lost their male breadwinners and had no nest egg from the government to tide them over until he returned. Southern white men found it harder than did Northerners to stay home and care for their families. The South instituted a draft in April 1862, earlier than the North, and while almost all Northern men drafted could manage to hire a substitute with financial aid from various sources, the same was not true in the South. By 1863, when the Confederacy abolished substitutes, to hire one cost $6,000, or three years' wages of a skilled worker.[24]

The lack of bounties and the high price of substitutes combined with the poor home-front economy to make the Civil War much tougher on ordinary white yeoman farmers and their families in the Confederacy than in the Union states. In the South, economic problems developed quickly and worsened steadily throughout the conflict. Both the war and the Union navy's blockade precluded Southern families from obtaining manufactured items from the North and from abroad as they had previously. The South's poor transportation network prevented food and other items from reaching families in many parts of the South. Necessities were scarce from the beginning of the war, and inflation was much worse than in the North. The overall rate of inflation in the South was 9,000 percent. In 1862 alone, wages rose 55 percent, but prices soared 300 percent. By then there were serious food shortages, and flour rose to $75 a barrel. Mothers fasted to ensure their children had enough to eat. Hungry youngsters grew emaciated and listless. Parents' tempers flared, and they found it difficult to discipline starving boys and girls.

Farm families in the South did their best to produce food crops but had only marginal success. In white yeoman farm families, mothers and children toiled in the fields to replace the labor of soldier fathers, but the absence of farm machinery made it almost impossible for women and children to replicate the work of fathers. A Georgia woman told the War Department, "I can't manage the farm well enough to make a surporte." She needed her husband at home. On large plantations, when white men went off to fight and left their wives and children behind, slaves often either departed or stopped working for the mistress and farmed for their own needs. Planter women and children began to perform the household and field work that blacks had done before, but inevitably, the women and children produced less food and cotton. Sometimes, a white woman and her children took advantage of the large kin networks characteristic of Southern white families (see chapter 3) and relied on a father, brother, or cousin to help manage the farm. However, if the man many families depended on was drafted, all suffered.[25]

Southern white children and their mothers often moved to cities in search of wage-labor jobs to replace the earnings of absent fathers, but there were not many such jobs in the Confederacy. Moreover, in Southern cities crowded with refugees fleeing the invading Union army, there was fierce competition for the little paid work available. Like their Northern counterparts, Southern women earned less than did men. White boys and girls who moved about seeking employment or who labored on family farms or plantations rarely attended school. There were few schools in the South when the war began, and during the war, many closed due to lack of pupils and of books and other supplies.

As in the North, desperately poor white women and their children appealed to the government and to charities for assistance. Southern state and county governments purchased food and clothing for indigent soldiers' families, but although states and counties spent $10 million by 1864, they could not provide all that impoverished children and women required. "A woman with four children who received ten dollars a month, which was about average, could buy a pound of bacon, a bushel of potatoes, and a dozen eggs. Even combined with an army private's pay of eleven dollars a month, shoes and flour were beyond reach." In some cities, charitable persons set up "free markets" where the children and wives of soldiers could come once a week to obtain free foodstuffs. Yet such aid proved insufficient, and mothers and children grew angry at inflated prices that they could ill afford to pay for food. In Richmond and other cities, needy mothers and children took the law into their own hands and looted the warehouses of speculators who hoarded precious food.[26]

While in wartime Southern white children assumed new work roles and grappled with parental loss and poverty to a greater degree than did their Northern counterparts, Southern white boys and girls also coped with unique and serious problems. For example, only in the South did large numbers of children find their homes invaded by enemy troops. As the Union army advanced, first in Northern Virginia and later in New Orleans, the sea islands off South Carolina, Tennessee, and eventually through the heart of the South with Sherman's march to Atlanta, Southern white women and children had to decide if they would flee or stay to face the invaders. More fled early in the war than later, when families realized they were at greater risk of losing their homes if they abandoned them. Those who became refugees often moved more than once to avoid the invaders. Ultimately one-quarter million Southerners became refugees. For children, it was very frightening to leave comfortable surroundings for unfamiliar accommodations, often in densely populated cities. Refugee families "slept on church pews, in stables, carriage houses, tents, and caves." Most Southern families were willing to take in relatives but not anyone else. The Confederate government provided no assistance to refugees, and they got "only sporadic aid from the Confederate Army, local organizations, a few organized groups, and interested civilians."[27]

Southern white mothers and children who stuck it out in their homes faced Union army troops, even the best behaved of whom "wanted to cow Southern civilians." Northern soldiers first appropriated Southerners' precious and limited supplies of food. Soldiers often swore at children and their mothers and scrawled graffiti on the walls of their homes. During Sherman's March, Union soldiers snatched personal items, smashed children's toys, and burned down Southerners' homes. Southern white boys and girls lost virtually all physical objects that gave them a sense of security and place. Rarely did Northern troops do violence to Southern women and children, but "soldiers regularly intimidated mothers by threatening to rape their adolescent daughters, and even if they had not such intentions, rumors and scattered reports of sexual assaults struck fear in many households." One New York officer described white children in Virginia in 1864: "They look so sad with so much astonishment wondering, I presume, why we are all armed, filling their little hearts with terror, & why they are all so destitute & why Papa is not at home attending to their wants in this bleak cold winter weather."[28]

Ultimately the terrible devastation to white Southern family homes and the terror experienced by children and their mothers led both to plead with their menfolk to leave the army and return home. With every year the war dragged on, the desertion rate mounted. One of the major reasons the Civil War ended was because of the crises in Southern family life the war caused.[29]

Because the death rate among Confederate soldiers was 20 percent, higher than among Union troops, a larger proportion of Southern white children than Northern white children became war orphans. There were no federal government pensions for Confederate soldiers or their widows or orphans, so Southern white boys and girls were probably more impoverished during Reconstruction than were Northern youngsters. By the late 1880s and 1890s, 11 Southern states offered pensions, but only to very poor veterans and their widows. Benefits were much lower than for Northern pensions. Some impoverished widows and orphans obtained aid from private charities, mostly in Southern cities, but poor relief was much less available and less generous in the physically devastated former Confederacy than in the North.[30]

The absence of adequate pensions and poor relief most harmed the neediest white Confederates: yeoman farmers and their families. Such men were more likely to serve in the military and thus to die or be disabled in the war. The families of both men who perished and those who survived the conflict found their small farms devastated by war. " 'The Yankees came through Franklin and Hart counties [in Georgia], and just tore up everything as they came along,' a resident later recalled. 'They took all the cows, horses, and mules. They killed the hogs in the pens, and carried them off for their own food.' " Without savings, pensions, or even much charitable aid, "yeoman farmers and their families were in the worst position to start over. . . ."[31] During Reconstruction they coped with crop failures, high taxes, and, in the

1870s, a sharp decline in agricultural prices. Many white Southern small farmers, their widows, and orphans went into debt, and by 1880, one-third of small farmers in cotton areas had become tenants. Children in yeoman farm families worked at home and in the fields as soon as they were physically able, just as did farm children elsewhere in the country, but regardless of their hard work and that of their parents, debts led to displacement from their old family homes to other, rented farmhouses. By the 1880s, poverty and tenantry forced many Southern white farm boys and girls and their families off farms entirely and into cotton mill villages where they labored in factories in a very different context than previously. (See chapter 5.)

White planter families in the South emerged from the war "in a state of shock." Thousands of their men had died, and planter families lost their investment in slaves and in Confederate bonds. "In Dallas County, in the heart of Alabama's plantation belt, whites' per capita wealth fell from $19,000 in 1860 to one sixth that amount ten years later." Crop failures in 1865 and natural disasters in 1866 also translated into big losses for planters. Some were so impoverished that they abandoned their homes, but most cotton and tobacco farmers retained their land.[32] The children of white planters continued as they had in wartime to replace the labor of freed slaves: daughters, in homes, and sons, in fields. These "children could not count on family position, inheritance, or marriage" to provide them with security.[33]

The impact of the Civil War and Reconstruction on Southern white children was much greater and longer lasting than on Northern boys and girls. A larger proportion of Southern white children served in the military, confronted the devastation of battle, lost their homes and their fathers, labored fruitlessly to support their families, and endured poverty without charitable or public assistance. These were wrenching changes for Southern white children, but some aspects of life remained the same and at least one improved. Gender roles did not alter much. Southern white parents still expected their daughters to marry, raise large families, and assume responsibility for managing homes, and parents expected sons to seek permanent employment in either agriculture or the cotton mills or, if they could afford it, one of the professions (see chapter 3). Finally, by the end of Reconstruction, state governments, under pressure from Congress, created new opportunities for education for white and black children in public schools. Before the Civil War, public education had been a rarity, and although afterward it left much to be desired, at least it had become accessible to Southern youth for the first time. (See chapter 4.)

The Civil War and Reconstruction altered the lives of African-American slaves more than any other group of children in the country. At the beginning, the war was a mysterious event to slave children, for their masters often tried to conceal knowledge of it from them. "A Tennessee ex-slave recalled how during the war she and the other children 'would go round to the win-

Contrabands coming into Fortress Monroe.

Slave children and their families (labeled contraband by the Union military during the Civil War) who fled Southern plantations and sought refuge with the Union Army at Fortress Monroe, Virginia. Here in 1861 Mary Peake, an African-American woman, set up a school for freed slave children. (Historical Society of Pennsylvania)

dows and listen to what the white folks would say when they was reading their papers and talking after supper.' " Once whites began to enlist and to drill, it proved more difficult to hide the war from blacks. A teenage slave girl remembered accompanying white children to watch the soldiers march. "The drums was playin' and the next thing I heerd, the war was gwine on. You could hear the guns just as plain."[34] Some young slave boys themselves went to war when they became body servants to their white masters.[35]

In slavery, sale frequently split families, and the Civil War forced additional separations of slave children from their fathers. Early in the war, requirements of the Confederate military and the actions of white owners broke up slave families in various ways. Some planters volunteered male slaves to do physical labor for the military. Masters quickly realized that this practice was a waste of valuable property, but by then the Confederate army began seizing slaves even without their masters' consent. Angry at this practice and fearful that invading Union armies might free their slaves, some masters began "refugeeing" their most valuable slave property away from the battlefront, often as far as Texas.[36] Some slaves and their masters were on the road for years. "Elvira Boles, who had been a slave in Mississippi, left her baby buried 'somewhere on dat road to Texas.' " Slave men impressed into Southern labor battalions or refugeed far from their home plantations soon lost touch with their children and other family members. Owners most commonly left children and women slaves behind and expected them to do the absent men's work. "Lee Guidon's summary of his wartime experience is typical: 'Yes maam I sho was in the Cibil War. I plowed all day and me and my sister helped take care of the baby at night.' "[37] Resentful at the forced removal of their fathers, remaining family members sometimes refused to work for their masters and instead raised food crops for their own use. When masters were away fighting and only white women and children were left on plantations, it was probably easier for slave children and women to gain a degree of independence. Eventually, white planter families had to negotiate with their former slaves to get them to work. Often slave mothers and children refused to labor unless owners agreed to keep their families intact. The Civil War led to hardship for black youngsters by removing their fathers, as well as to greater autonomy for many youngsters and mothers on Southern plantations.

Beginning in 1861, when the Union army invaded parts of the South, Southern slave families sometimes separated voluntarily until they could regroup under the protection of the Northern military. Slave men forced to labor for the Confederacy often ran away to work for the Union army. Slaves were determined to initiate their own freedom. Army officers welcomed the men, but not their children and wives, for whom little military work was available. Slave youngsters often trailed behind the army as it marched or, with their mothers, set up makeshift camps near military bases. After fall 1862, when the national government guaranteed freedom to all who reached Union lines, many more slaves fled in family groups. Army officers continued to welcome the men but not their families. Some black men refused employment unless the army provided housing for their families. A few Northern military commanders ignored this demand and banned women and children from army camps, but other commanders set up contraband camps for black families in several places in the South. The camps were often makeshift and overcrowded, but they did permit black families to reunite in freedom without the threat of sale and without the necessity to perform unpaid labor for whites. African-Americans maintained the contraband camps themselves; children attended school and church within them. Contraband camps were also one of the few places where ex-slaves obtained charitable aid. Abolitionists in the North organized freedmen's aid societies, which collected clothing, Bibles, schoolbooks, and medicine and distributed them to ex-slave children and their families in the camps.

In early 1863, shortly after President Lincoln issued the Emancipation Proclamation freeing all slaves in the Confederacy, the Union encouraged both free blacks in the North and newly freed slaves in the South to enlist as soldiers. Many former slave men willingly enrolled, but they sought to avoid family separation by continuing to insist that their children and wives, rendered homeless by the fathers' decision to leave Southern plantations and join the Union army, be provided for by the army. The Northern military responded by setting up contraband camps at recruitment stations in the South and by leasing plantations seized from Confederates to Northerners, who employed former slave children and women to work the plantations. These efforts were never enough, and contraband camps could not accommodate all soldiers' children. Neither were black fathers able to support their children on army pay. Until 1864, blacks earned less than whites, and the Union army never permitted more than a few blacks to command an officer's salary. Moreover, in July 1864, when Northern states frequently could not fill their draft quotas, the army sent recruiters south to offer slave men bounties to serve in Northern state regiments. If the men refused, recruiters sometimes put them in uniform and forcibly removed them from their families.[38]

The Union army offered slave children and their families in the Confederacy freedom, but at a price. Black fathers could not earn enough as either laborers or soldiers in the Union army to support children and their mothers satisfactorily unless they were among the lucky few to receive bounties. Once a slave father signed up with the Northern army, whether voluntarily or not, he had to leave his family behind on a plantation or bring them with him to freedom behind Union lines. Many slave men and their families ultimately elected freedom and the uncertainty of temporary housing in contraband camps. Slave children in such families gained freedom from their masters' control and the opportunity to live with their families, but in an uncertain environment. Children also gained admiration for their soldier fathers, who not only escaped their abusive masters but fought to free all other slaves.

In the border states that remained within the Union (Delaware, Maryland, Kentucky, and Missouri), African-American children and their parents endured slavery on plantations much longer than did many blacks in the Confederacy. Slaves in the border states were not freed by the Emancipation Proclamation, which applied only to slaves in the states that had seceded. In 1863 the army began to recruit slaves in the border states as well as in the Confederacy and by fall promised freedom to those who enlisted in Maryland, Delaware, and Missouri. This promise did not extend to recruits' families, however. When thousands of border-state slaves rushed to volunteer, most left their families behind because there were no contraband camps in the border states. Slave children suffered when angry masters retaliated by whipping and abusing the youngsters, sometimes locking them up to prevent flight and other times driving them off plantations altogether. Not until 1865 were slave children in the border states freed to join their soldier fathers.

Because the Civil War was fought in the South, black slave children, like many white youngsters, encountered war close up. James Goings, who was ten years old when the war ended, noted, "In dem days it wuzn't nuthin' to fin' a dead man in de woods." He remembered Appomattox: "De dead wuz laying all long de road an' dey stayed dere, too." A former Louisiana slave recalled, "During the war all the children had fear." Slave children who remained on plantations in the South, like many Southern white children, faced the invading Union army. Masters often warned slave children that the Northern soldiers were devils.[39] In some cases this description proved accurate. Northern soldiers on occasion took out their anger about the war on slaves, whom the soldiers blamed for causing the fighting. One Union sergeant locked black slave children in a dark storage room and enjoyed their shrieks of terror. When he let them out, he fed them a pot of burned beans. "The children plunged their hands into the narrow-mouthed pot and, unable to pull them out because of the crowding, burned their hands . . ." Union soldiers usually only threatened to rape white women but more frequently assaulted black girls and women, sometimes in front of white women and their children.[40] When Union soldiers ransacked and burned down plantations, they destroyed the homes not only of white children but also of slave youngsters.

The ordeal of African-American slave children in the South, although somewhat similar to that of other children in the Civil War, was also distinct. Like other youngsters in both the North and South, many slave children endured separation from fathers who left home to labor or to fight. As with other youngsters, the absence of their fathers sometimes meant that African-American children had to work harder. Yet their attitude toward work diverged from that of other children because of their slave status. Slave boys and girls customarily began to labor at younger ages than did other youngsters (see chapter 4), so toil in trying conditions was not as new to them as it was to many other young people. In addition, the laboring conditions of Southern black children often improved during wartime. Many black children on plantations labored more for their families than for their masters, and black children in contraband camps worked exclusively among their own people and not for a white master at all. Slave children also endured greater poverty than any other group of youngsters. Unlike most Southern and Northern white youngsters, slave children's parents owned no family farms, held no wage-labor jobs, and possessed virtually no savings. For most of the war, black fathers earned less than whites in either army and probably did not benefit much from bounties until the end of the war. Because of blacks' low earnings, inflation especially hurt black families. Many slave children, like Southern whites, became refugees, and few if any of them received adequate relief. However, the only sources of poor relief for black children and their families were outside the South: Northern freedmen's aid societies and the Northern army. Some slave children took refuge in contraband camps, a form of shelter unavailable to whites. No matter how dilapidated, those camps allowed slave children a measure of freedom to live and work among the black community that they had never had before. As did other youngsters, especially in the South, slave children witnessed much bloodshed, but they probably also experienced more physical attacks from whites, whether angry masters or invading Union troops. Black children were also more likely to be orphaned by the war. Almost 38 percent of blacks who fought for the Union died, most of them from disease, which was also the chief killer of whites.[41] The death rate of blacks was almost twice as high as that of whites who served in either the Union or Confederate armies.

When the war ended and Reconstruction began, the first priority of most freed slave mothers, fathers, and children was to reunite their families. For them, the opportunity to have a genuine family life was a sign of freedom. Some had been separated only during the war, as was the case of slaves refugeed to Texas, but others had lost relatives to sale years previously. "Mary Armstrong, a seventeen-year-old Missouri youth, went in search of her mother, who had been sold and taken to Texas. Several years later, she tracked her down in Wharton County. 'Law me, talk 'bout cryin' and singin' and cryin' some more, we sure done it,' she recalled of their reunion." This search proved successful, but many others did not. Freed slaves often had no idea where their mothers or fathers might be and searched in vain for them, sometimes for decades. Reunions were not always happy. Slave children who had been sold away from their natural mothers and raised by other women were not always delighted to be claimed. One child recalled of her mother, "At firs' I was scared o' her 'cause I didn' know who she was."[42]

Not only did time and distance complicate blacks' efforts to rebuild their families, but so did whites. As soon as the war ended, many former slave owners took advantage of both the nature of slavery and apprenticeship laws in order to retain control of black children. Apprenticeship laws originated in England. Americans had long used them to provide for orphaned children or children whose parents could not support them adequately. Local judges could remove children from their natural families and apprentice them to other families for whom the youngsters worked in exchange for food, housing, and clothing until 18 or 21 years of age. Masters took advantage of the fact that in slavery no black parent could really provide for his or her child. Before former slave parents could secure employment, masters rushed black children to local courts to have them apprenticed on the pretense that their parents were too poor to care for them. In Maryland and North Carolina, whites had used apprenticeship before the war as a way of controlling free blacks, and continued to do so afterward, but in Texas and Alabama legislators instituted apprenticeship for the first time at the war's end.[43] In some cases, the children had no known living relatives, in which case apprenticeship became an extension of slavery. Silas Dothrun, who was 10 when slavery ended and could not remember his parents, was apprenticed in Arkansas. He reported, "They kept me in bondage and a girl that used to be with them. We were bound to them that we would have to stay with them. They kept me just the same as under bondage. I wasn't allowed no kind of say-so." In most cases, children had parents who wanted them. However, in Maryland, "judges did not even bother to hear testimony concerning the parents' ability to care for the children." Whites beat and swore at black parents who objected to apprenticeship. The system was a powerful control not only over children but also over their parents, who might be persuaded to stay and work for an old master if he had their children as apprentices.[44]

To cope with this injustice, freed slaves turned to the federal government, which, in March 1865, created the Freedmen's Bureau in the Department of War under Major General Oliver Otis Howard. The bureau was in charge of refugees, freedmen, and abandoned lands. Agents of the bureau responded to freedmen's complaints about apprenticing and, in various states, attempted to influence the courts to stop the practice with varying results. Once Congress took control of Reconstruction in the Southern states and ensured freed slaves access to the polls, state legislatures banned apprenticeship.

Whites not only attempted to subvert black family life with apprenticeships but also challenged it with violence. Any signs that black parents controlled their own children and taught them their own values angered former slave owners, who were long accustomed to managing blacks and educating them to obey whites. Planters preferred themselves to define freedom for African-American children rather than let their parents do it. Whites often attacked black institutions such as churches and schools that had a role in socializing children. Whites also challenged black parents' right to discipline their own children. One freedman was beaten for claiming the right to whip his own child and not letting his former master and employer do so. Blacks rarely retaliated for the violence done to them. They preferred to avoid it by moving from isolated rural areas, where they had little protection from whites, to Southern cities, where they could live in black communities and more safely send their children to black churches and schools.

The Freedmen's Bureau intervened where it could to stop violence against former slaves, but the bureau's main task was to alleviate poverty in a South decimated by war. When Congress created the bureau in 1865, it allotted the bureau no money, so at first the bureau appropriated food, medicines, and clothing from the army to dispense to impoverished Southern blacks and whites. When the war ended, the government promptly closed contraband camps, so freed black children and their mothers sought aid elsewhere, often in cities. There the Freedmen's Bureau concentrated much of its work. In the first 15 months after the war, the bureau gave out 13 million rations, two-thirds to blacks. A ration consisted of enough cornmeal, flour, and sugar to last one person a week.[45] The bureau also funded hospitals to provide medical care for blacks and helped establish orphanages for blacks in Richmond, Atlanta, and Nashville. Following the pattern of segregation created in the military during the Civil War, the Freedmen's Bureau supported separate welfare asylums for blacks in the postwar era. Despite the bureau's useful work in alleviating poverty among freed persons, federal government officials feared the bureau might make former slaves permanently dependent on welfare. Therefore, in 1866, the agency ceased granting rations except to orphan asylums and hospitals and attempted to turn over many of its relief functions to local governments. White Southern political leaders felt that African-Americans were the responsibility of the federal government that had freed them and proved reluctant to assist blacks. Eventually, Southerners did accept responsibility for providing poor relief to blacks, but only in segregated facilities, which were often underfunded and inferior to those provided to whites. Welfare for the many black children orphaned by the war was minimal. Of the twelve orphan asylums in the South that received public moneys, only three admitted blacks. The African-American community was financially able to support only a few orphanages; relatives and friends cared for most needy black children.[46] (See chapter 7.)

The many black children orphaned by the death of their fathers serving in the Union army were potential recipients of federal government pensions. No study has been made of how many freed persons' families benefited from this generous welfare program, but black children apparently had particular difficulty qualifying for aid because of both illiteracy and the absence of formal marriage contracts among blacks in slavery.[47]

During Reconstruction, freed slave parents worked to find and keep their children, avoid their apprenticeship, protect them from violence and poverty, and provide them with an education. Before the Civil War, educating slave children was against the law in Southern states, so there were no public or private schools open to young blacks. For African-Americans, schooling was a sign of freedom: it would advance them spiritually by allowing them to read the Bible, and economically by enabling them to read a labor contract.[48]

In 1861, Mary Peake, a free black woman, set up the first school for blacks in the South in Hampton, Virginia. Thereafter, African-Americans formed countless other schools in communities all across the South. Blacks donated their labor to build schoolhouses, boarded teachers in their homes, and, despite their poverty, expended over one million dollars on schools by 1870. In 1865, Alabama black parents paid the equivalent of one-tenth the wages of an agricultural laborer to send one child to school.[49] The Freedmen's Bureau helped finance the construction of schools, and Northern missionary societies supplied teachers. Between 1865 and 1870, 31 Northern charitable societies spent fifteen million dollars on schools in 18 Southern and border states. From 1869 to 1870, these dollars financed the education of almost 150,000 pupils in over 2,500 schools with more than 3,500 teachers. Whenever local blacks accepted assistance from Northern philanthropic groups such as the American Missionary Association, an abolitionist organization allied with the "evangelical wing of American Protestantism," blacks lost control over schools. Northern freedmen's aid groups such as the AMA preferred to manage the schools they funded.

The AMA and other missionary societies sent Northern teachers—usually white, young, female, committed Christians—to the South. These teachers had their own agenda for black schools. White teachers taught the regular subjects offered in the North, including reading, writing, spelling, grammar, diction, history, geography, and arithmetic, and emphasized the same moral values that teachers in the North taught (see chapter 4). These values, including obedience, self-control, honesty, politeness, and respect for authority, were the values of the Northern middle class. Northern teachers stressed that a free person of good character, acting on her or his own as an individual, would achieve success.[50] There was also an element of racism in these Northern-sponsored schools. The standard texts they typically used, the same as those employed in Northern classrooms, portrayed blacks in a negative manner (see chapter 4). In addition, some of the special materials and books designed for the freedmen by the American Tract Society depicted white children as well dressed and well behaved and black youngsters as "obese, grinning, poorly dressed, with houses ramshackle and neglected and yards in disarray." The texts referred to whites as babies or children but to blacks as pickaninnies. The most nonracist of the books written by Northerners for Southern black children was *The Freedmen's Book* by abolitionist Lydia Maria Child. In it she included biographies of successful blacks from all over the world, whom she described as bright and independent. However, in her conclusion, Child argued that all freedmen needed was good character to overcome all their problems, even slavery. "Ultimately, blame fell back on the victim. Failure to progress indicated lack of character, not systematic oppression."[51]

However, before we assume that these Reconstruction-era schools substantially affected Southern black children, we need to examine the extent of the schools' influence and impact. Between 1865 and 1870, when Northerners exerted considerable control over black schools in the South, in no state did the schools reach more than 15 percent of the black population. The schools were often poorly constructed, and children had trouble concentrating on their studies in them. In Southern cities, where Northern-sponsored schools were most in evidence, classes were large and children received little personalized instruction. Black youngsters did not attend the schools regularly. Around election time, parents often feared violence and kept children at home. When the yearly labor contracts that freedmen signed were renegotiated at the end of each year, youngsters often missed about six weeks of school if their parents changed farms. And any time a parent required a youngster's help around the house or in the fields, the child missed school.

Schools for freed persons run by Northern missionary associations may also have failed to achieve their desired impact because of black parents' attitudes toward the Northern-sponsored schools. Parents and children both sought education; black girls and boys attended class willingly, and if they attended school regularly, "acquired basic literacy skills quickly." But African-American parents were less enamored of Northern teachers' commitment to the idea that the moral, upright individual who worked hard would ultimately achieve monetary success. Historian Jacqueline Jones has remarked:

> The tenet of individualism was worthless, rarely if ever rewarded by the master class and potentially threatening to group solidarity. . . . The slave community had encouraged self-help and solidarity; its members thought in terms of day-to-day survival, not progress along a vague continuum to "success," defined in terms of money and moral behavior. They derived feelings of pride and self-respect from their religion and relationships with kinfolk and friends, not from the work they performed for the benefit of a white owner. . . . The irony inherent in the teachers' attempts to instill the Protestant work ethic in persons who had literally slaved their whole lives for other people is self-evident today, though it was not to the teachers in 1865.[52]

Black parents understood that white Northern teachers wanted to change black children's religion and way of life. If at all possible, black parents preferred to enroll their sons and daughters in schools where the teachers were freed persons like themselves. The Freedmen's Bureau responded to black parents and increased its expenditures on teacher training programs for black teachers. By 1871, there were 11 colleges and universities and 61 normal schools that catered to a largely black student population. The proportion of black teachers in schools for freed persons rose from 33 percent in 1867 to 53 percent in 1869.[53]

Southern whites reacted angrily to Northerners' helping blacks obtain schooling at a time when there were few schools open to whites in the South; they objected to former slaves achieving any semblance of equality with whites. Actually, the Northern missionary societies welcomed white children in their schools, but few Southern white parents were willing to send their sons and daughters to school with black boys and girls. Southern whites often threatened white male and female teachers in freed person's schools, and whites physically attacked both black pupils and black teachers. In 1868, whites beat and stoned black children who attended a Texas school taught by a white woman. Members of the Ku Klux Klan frequently attacked black teachers or any educated black.[54]

The Freedmen's Bureau attempted to protect schools for blacks, but both the bureau and the Northern missionary societies that ran so many schools for blacks in the early part of Reconstruction saw their task to be temporary: both expected Southern states would eventually assume responsibility for educating black and white pupils. After the passing of the Fifteenth Amendment allowed blacks to vote and Republicans controlled Southern state governments, the Southern states did assume responsibility for educating both whites and blacks. However, state officials found it too costly to build public school systems from scratch, so the state governments deferred to local funding and local control of the schools. In a South still impoverished and divided by war, it is not surprising that such schools were both underfunded and for the most part segregated. Southern whites never endorsed integration. Blacks as well often opposed it because integrated schools rarely employed black teachers and were not controlled by the black community. Black parents did not usually want their children to attend school with the children of their former masters. Said one black mother of integrated schools, "I don't want my children to be pounded by dem white boys. I don't send them to school to fight, I send them to learn." The new Reconstruction-era public schools substantially expanded educational opportunities for Southern boys and girls: by 1872, a majority of Texas children were in school, and by 1875 one-half of all children of both races were enrolled in Mississippi, Florida, and South Carolina schools.[55]

When Reconstruction ended and Southern white Democrats resumed control of all state programs and began to disenfranchise blacks, the new all-white state governments did not eliminate public schools for whites and blacks, but they did write segregation into law, and permitted local officials to spend much less on black schools than on white ones. Black parents opposed low levels of expenditure on their children's schools but continued to accept segregated schools if they were staffed by black rather than white teachers, as was sometimes the case. Reconstruction did not grant most black children the high-quality education they hoped for, but if freed persons themselves, the Freedmen's Bureau, and Northern missionary societies had not acted to open some schools for African-American pupils at this time, blacks would probably never have gained access to public schools later. It is extremely unlikely that Southern whites would ever have created schools for blacks had those schools not already been in place when whites resumed control of state governments after the Civil War. Southerners discovered that educating blacks did not endanger whites. Education was a conservative reform, partly because of the way white Northerners, and later, Southern whites, conducted schools for blacks and partly because economic limits placed on freed persons undercut any advantages they might have gained from schooling.[56]

At the beginning of Reconstruction, freed slaves tried to secure their children's future both educationally and economically. Blacks sought employment so that they could support their families and pay for their children's education. Most desired independence as landowning farmers. Blacks believed the federal government had promised them land to which they were entitled because of their long years of unpaid toil as slaves. Indeed, the Union Army seized land from Confederate planters, and Congress granted control of 850,000 acres to the Freedmen's Bureau. The bureau prepared to distribute this land to freed persons, but in early 1865, President Andrew Johnson began to pardon former Confederates and return their land to them. In the end, the Freedmen's Bureau distributed very little land to blacks, and Southern whites refused to extend blacks credit for land purchases or even to sell land to those former slaves who could afford to purchase it.

Instead, when the Civil War ended, white cotton and sugar planters offered blacks wage-labor jobs working in gangs in the fields. The Freedmen's Bureau endorsed such employment in order to preclude former slaves' dependence on government welfare. Because white planters possessed little cash and doubted blacks' willingness to commit to long-term employment, planters often contracted with former slaves to pay their wages just once a year, after the sale of the crop. If the crop yield was poor or prices depressed, black workers might receive very little for their labor. Sometimes whites cheated blacks out of what little compensation they earned. In 1866 and 1867, the Freedmen's Bureau acted to prevent such unfair treatment, but the bureau continued to support year-long wage-labor contracts, which ultimately benefited white landowners more than black laborers. Blacks objected to this new economic system. Gang labor in fields was too much like slave labor; it precluded blacks from working independently and permitted whites to punish black children and perhaps abuse black women. In the 1870s, white landowners and freed slaves compromised on sharecropping. Under this system, at the end of the year when the crops were harvested and sold, black families who lived and worked on farms owned by whites divided the profits with the white owners. The system allowed black parents to manage their children without white interference, permitted black mothers to spend more time with their children, and shielded those mothers and their daughters from abuse by white employers. However, sharecropping did not provide African-American parents and their children economic security. Instead, during the year, before the sale of the staple crop, black sharecroppers borrowed money, often at very high interest rates, to purchase food for themselves and their families. At year's end, their debts were often as high as or higher than their profits from the sale of the crop. Blacks could not save for their children's future. Sharecropping also required that all family members labor during much of the year, and so black children often skipped school in order to work in the fields.[57]

The Civil War and Reconstruction influenced many aspects of children's lives, including how their parents raised them, their access to schooling, the amount and type of work they performed, and the kind of assistance they received from extrafamilial sources such as government and private charity. Just how serious and long lasting these effects were on particular children depended on the youngster's race and whether the child lived in the North or the South.

During the Civil War, when teenage boys or fathers went off to fight, the role of parents in child rearing changed. Adolescent soldiers, drummers, and buglers no longer lived under parental supervision and protection. Youths believed they were fighting the war for their families and remained in touch by mail with their mothers, fathers, brothers, and sisters. Mothers continued to play the largest role in child rearing for all groups of youngsters. Although many fathers corresponded with their wives to discuss child-rearing tasks, mothers raising youngsters whose fathers were away at war inevitably assumed new burdens. Those burdens were particularly onerous for women plagued by poverty and homelessness, problems most widespread in the South.

Wartime changes in child-rearing patterns ended in Reconstruction, except for children whose fathers perished and for children freed from slavery. For newly freed slave families, changes in child rearing were most dramatic. Such families no longer lived with the threat of permanent separation. Mothers could devote more time to caring for their sons and daughters. Freed slave fathers could live with their children and assumed new obligations for feeding, clothing, and housing them. Freedmen who had served in the military earned new respect from their youngsters for their wartime sacrifices.

During the Civil War, school attendance declined in the North, but it was virtually nonexistent in the South. In Reconstruction, school attendance rates in the North rose and returned to their prewar pattern, and educators made schooling more accessible to African-American boys and girls. During Reconstruction, for the first time, freed slaves and sympathetic Northern whites opened schools in the South to black children. Ultimately, both white and black youngsters profited from the creation of free public schools in the Southern states during Reconstruction. Nonetheless these schools remained in many ways inferior to Northern schools: they were segregated and served a smaller percentage of both white and black children.

The Civil War and Reconstruction modified the work roles of children, especially in the South. During the war, boys and girls in both sections helped their mothers more on farms, and some children also obtained wage-labor jobs. Employment in cotton textile mills became more common for impoverished Northern children in wartime and for Southern white children from needy yeoman families in the postwar era. After the war, in both sections, wherever poverty did not abate, children continued to seek employment at a young age. Yet because of the continued mechanization of farming in the

North, many children there escaped backbreaking field labor. In contrast, in the agricultural South, virtually all farm children, white and black, worked as soon as they were physically able. Freed slave children no longer labored for both their white masters and their parents but worked as other white farm children long had: alongside their mothers and fathers in homes or fields.

While the Civil War and Reconstruction influenced many aspects of children's lives, these events affected children's play, game, toy, and reading preferences only marginally. The Civil War occasioned more make-believe soldier play, sometimes with toy soldiers, but such play and toys were not new. After the war, white and black youngsters in the South played together less than they had when slave youngsters served their white masters' children. Overall, the main impact of the war on child pleasures was to reduce the time most youngsters had to enjoy them.

Because the Civil War occasioned so much child poverty, public and private poor relief for youngsters gained new significance. Welfare programs for children expanded in wartime, especially for Northern children and freed slaves, but no new, permanent, truly innovative programs emerged from the experience of war. African-American children in the South received welfare for the first time through Northern freedmen's aid associations, the Freedmen's Bureau, and, beginning in Reconstruction, Southern local governments. The first two sources of aid were helpful but temporary, and the third provided no more than what needy Northern and Southern free white children had long enjoyed. African-American children in the South, so many of whom had lost contact with family during slavery, particularly needed public or private welfare but, after the demise of the Freedmen's Bureau in 1872, obtained little assistance except through a few orphanages. More white youngsters in the North and South gained access to asylums constructed for soldiers' orphans, but such orphanages were not a new form of child welfare. Neither were pensions for the orphans of war veterans; pensions had been granted after the Revolutionary War as well. Nonetheless, pensions for Union soldiers, their children, and wives were more generous than any war-related benefits granted previously and were certainly more helpful in alleviating poverty than the small pensions some needy Civil War veterans and their families received from Southern state governments.

This chapter has examined the impact of the Civil War and Reconstruction on various aspects of children's lives, and subsequent chapters will examine each of these aspects in more detail. The first is child rearing, which forms the subject of the next chapter.

3

Growing Up in a Diverse Land: Child-Rearing Patterns in Victorian America

Between 1850 and 1890, there was no single, universal method of child rearing employed by all American parents. The racial, ethnic, and geographic diversity of the country and the growing divisions between social classes were reflected in the ways parents raised their youngsters. Of course, each family had its own style of parenting, but there is enough historical evidence of similarities between families to confirm four patterns of child rearing. The first pattern is that of white, American-born, Protestant, largely middle-class parents, most of whom lived in cities. Antebellum white Southern plantation owners adopted a variation of this pattern in raising their children. The second pattern is that of white, urban, working-class families, some native born, but most foreign born. White parents who raised children on Northern and Midwestern farms and on the frontier created the third style of child rearing by adapting both middle-class and working-class methods of child rearing. The fourth pattern is that of African-American families in slavery and in freedom.

We know the most about the first group of children, for their middle-class parents were literate and articulate and left numerous letters and diaries describing their child-rearing practices. In addition, such parents constituted the readership of the many child-rearing manuals of the mid-nineteenth century. These manuals are not ideal sources of information on actual child-rearing practices, yet they do reveal the key issues relating to children in this era.[1] As for the other three styles of parenting, historians have been very creative in using plantation, court, and various government records as well as autobiographies and oral histories to flesh out the story of how white urban working-class, farm and frontier, immigrant, and African-American parents raised their young.

"The Emigrant Wagon—on the Way to the Railway Station," from *Harper's Weekly*, Oct. 25, 1873. Families that fled Europe for the United States expected their children to help out if they could. Note that an adult is carrying a very young child, but all the other children are walking. Two boys are carrying a blanket, a basket, and a bottle, and an adolescent girl is tending a toddler. (Broadside Collection, Balch Institute for Ethnic Studies Library, Philadelphia, Pennsylvania)

The evidence reveals that parents varied considerably in their attitudes toward childhood as a time of life, in the values they taught their young and the methods by which they taught them, and in their inclination and ability to shelter youngsters from the larger world around them. However, there were many similarities between families. In all, fathers played important roles, but mothers were primarily responsible for raising youngsters, especially infants and toddlers. All mothers and fathers expected obedience from their boys and girls, and all parents, to varying degrees, used corporal punishment to enforce obedience. In virtually all families, child rearing was gendered to some degree. A major concern of every parent was protecting her or his children from illness; mothers and fathers, regardless of where they lived, their backgrounds, and their wealth, watched by the bedsides of ailing children and were largely helpless to prevent their suffering and often death.

By the mid-nineteenth century, in both large northeastern cities and small towns across the country, a distinct middle class emerged.[2] "The clash of capitalists and workers always creates an intermediary zone—a safety net for those who fall from the top; a safety valve for the most talented or determined from the bottom; a group of brokers who manage the working-class or smooth over the worst excesses of the capitalists. . . ." This emerging middle class comprised "professionals, small farmers or businessmen, managers, writers, ministers, and, in the nineteenth century, clerks."[3] These nonmanual workers earned considerably more than skilled craftsmen and could support their wives and children on their incomes alone. Yet middle-class Americans worried about passing on their class status to their sons and daughters. Because the job market was so much in flux, and new job skills necessary in an industrial economy might render learning traditional crafts useless for advancement, middle-class parents agonized about how best to rear and prepare their children for the future.[4]

Parents found one solution in new ideas about childhood and child rearing. By the 1850s, most middle-class Americans believed children to be unique, valuable resources and infancy and childhood to be extremely important phases of life. In the seventeenth and eighteenth centuries, parents had usually expected children to work and contribute to the family's survival as soon as they were physically able. The new view of childhood as distinctive developed gradually. It was reinforced by the ideas of Rousseau, who argued in *Émile* that childhood was a distinct and important period of life and a time when children required a special education suited to their individual needs.[5] John Locke also emphasized the singularity of childhood. Locke asserted that children were malleable and that parents could easily mold youngsters into good human beings.[6] For middle-class Protestant parents who sought to raise morally responsible youngsters and provide them access to new middle-class careers as managers, lawyers, and educators, or as the wives of professionals, the idea that children could easily be molded to accept new values was very useful.

Material signs of the new view of childhood as special can be found in how middle-class parents dressed their infants: in long white gowns, which "gave the tiny child substance, presence, and grace."[7] By the 1860s, mothers typically had their babies photographed in very formal poses borrowed by photographers from icon portraits—in which all the clothing and artifacts reflected emblems of power—of the baroque period. Such baby portraits were public statements of the importance of infants and their families. The value ascribed to infancy is also reflected in the use of baby record books, first published in the 1880s, in which mothers recorded the growth patterns of their infants for their first 12 to 18 months.[8]

As Americans increasingly recognized childhood to be a vital period of life, the role of mothers took on new significance. They exerted the most influence on infants in their formative years. Although household chores kept middle-class mothers busy much of the day, most employed a cook or laundress and thus could themselves devote considerable time to child rearing.[9] By the mid-nineteenth century, a middle-class woman's separate sphere of expertise had become the home and her children. It was her job to teach girls and boys the values they would need both to maintain the family and to succeed in the larger world of work. Of course, by acquiring primary responsibility for child rearing, mothers also assumed blame if youngsters did not turn out well.

Conversely, the principal role of middle-class fathers was to work outside the home to maintain the status of the family. Fathers had very little time for child rearing, yet they still cared deeply for their children and were "supportive, affectionate, and even companionate."[10] As family providers, fathers were heads of families and served as the final disciplinarians in most homes, although mothers did most of the day-to-day disciplining of youngsters. Fathers also took a more active role in child rearing when youngsters were between six and ten years old.[11] This was especially true by the 1880s and 1890s, when middle-class men came to admire the animal spirits and physical prowess of boys. Fathers sought to identify and encourage in their sons a rough-and-ready masculinity. Overall, however, middle-class fathers spent too much time outside the home to be very involved in the lives of their sons or daughters. Middle-class fathers and mothers both loved their children, but fathers' roles in child rearing were secondary to those of mothers both because men had less time to spend with their youngsters and because men were not perceived to have the natural quality "born in biology" of a mother's love.[12]

The growing centrality of mothers in child rearing was reflected by which parent customarily received custody of children in divorce proceedings. "Traditionally, in Anglo-American law fathers had an almost unlimited right to the custody of their minor, legitimate children." However, by the early nineteenth century, judges in divorce cases increasingly gave custody to mothers. In 1840, John Cadwaller, a lawyer who won a custody suit for a mother in Pennsylvania, expressed the prevailing view of the time: "Everyone knows that a father is unfit to take care of an infant; physically unfit and unfit by reason of his avocations."[13]

At the same time that raising children carefully became more crucial to middle-class parents, the birthrate began to decline. In 1850, a white woman would reach menopause after an average of 5.43 births, but in 1900 she would reach menopause after an average of 3.56 births. Mothers had fewer children and spaced those they had farther apart.[14] The birthrate did not drop equally nor at the same time among all income groups; it declined first and most dramatically among the middle class in both urban and rural areas. The change in fertility was not due to improved methods of birth control.

The methods used in the late nineteenth century were the same methods that had been used previously: limiting intercourse to a woman's "safe period" before ovulation, practicing withdrawal or abstinence, douching after intercourse, using condoms, or having an abortion.[15] Even after the 1870s, when concern about lowering birthrates resulted in passage of the Comstock Law, which made it illegal to ship contraceptive devices or information about contraception in the mail, fertility continued to decline.[16] The lower birthrate resulted from disproportionately large numbers of middle-class parents choosing to have smaller families "to improve the quality of their child's upbringing by allowing them to invest more time and energy as well as more financial resources in each child."[17]

As child rearing became so much more consequential, middle-class urban mothers, many of whom had left their families behind in rural areas, looked to child-rearing manuals for guidance. Beginning with Catharine Beecher's *Treatise on Domestic Economy*, reprinted every year from 1841 to 1856, advice manuals were directed specifically at mothers. Beecher had four predecessors in this type of literature, three of whom were men and all of whom assumed that men controlled home life. Beecher and her successors in home-advice literature instead emphasized the female role in child rearing.[18]

Advice manuals indicate that many of the goals of child rearing were not so different for Protestants in the nineteenth century than in the seventeenth or eighteenth centuries: to raise obedient, loving, moral, Christian children. However, the methods for accomplishing this goal had changed as religious views altered. The old idea that children were born sinful and depraved was replaced with the concept that children were basically innocent and loving. The notion of child depravity had required parents to discipline children harshly, to break their will, and to force them by rote memory (because they were naturally stubborn) to learn their catechism if they were to be saved. In contrast, the new view of children, best articulated by Horace Bushnell in his *Views of Christian Nurture*, first published in serial form in 1847, required parents not to repress sinfulness but to encourage "the gradual unfolding of Christian character in a suitably nurturant family environment." Once children were no longer considered sinful by nature, it was no longer necessary to force them to memorize their catechism. Instead, "kindness, love, and tender care by a mother who exemplified all the virtues would adequately prepare the child for salvation and a life of moral responsibility."[19]

Late in the century, perhaps influenced by Charles Darwin's theories, many advice writers described children less in Christian terms and more as young animals who were curious, playful, and troublesome to control. But youngsters were still seen as malleable and still required a loving mother to mold and shape them in an organized fashion.[20]

A mother's loving nurture of her child began with breast feeding. Some believed "it might even supply the child with the mother's own moral virtues." From the 1840s on, doctors encouraged mothers to breast-feed their babies, as did the authors of many maternal advice books. Breast feeding was considered "an integral part of a mother's commitment to childrearing."[21] Previously, doctors had sometimes recommended wet nurses for mothers who could afford them, but by midcentury, doctors warned mothers that wet nurses might transmit moral qualities or even venereal disease through their milk.[22] Authors of advice manuals also cautioned mothers against allowing servants to care for their children. Servants might be lazy and incompetent or teach children bad habits. Only mothers could train their babies to regular habits by feeding babies at stated intervals and not on demand. Mothers also promoted health and independence in infants by not swaddling them but instead dressing them in long, loose gowns. When children were six months to three years old, middle-class mothers attired children in short coats that came only to their ankles, thus allowing children freedom to crawl and walk.[23]

Because breast feeding was so important to both mothers and babies, weaning was a trying period for both. Weaning was uncomfortable for mothers and marked the time when they could no longer be purely nurturers but had to teach children values and discipline them.[24]

Mothers taught obedience first. Many middle-class parents belonged to evangelical churches. Such churches taught that God was the lawgiver and that parents stood in his place. If children were to learn to obey God, they had to learn to obey parents. Both Evangelicals and parents of more liberal religious persuasion agreed "that children's submission to their parents' control was necessary to engender *self*-control in later life." In the mid–nineteenth century, many middle-class parents feared social instability. They believed self-control to be essential for persons growing up at a time when the democratic form of government was comparatively new, when persons from foreign lands were crowding into American port cities, and when the new industrial economy seemingly called all men to look out principally for themselves. "Only by internalizing norms of duty and responsibility could society counteract the anarchic tendencies of democracy and individualism." Self-discipline was also necessary in the working world. Self-discipline enabled young people to save and acquire capital for business; it also helped them develop "the reputation required for a responsible job." In addition to self-discipline, middle-class families taught their children other values, including thrift, duty, and punctuality, useful in professional, industrial vocations.[25]

All such values had to be internalized, and parents believed the best way to accomplish this goal was to develop a youngster's conscience. Conscience would ultimately control behavior. To develop children's conscience, mothers withdrew love from disobedient youngsters by not talking to them or depriving them of food; mothers also shamed children to make them feel guilty. Thus, one mid-nineteenth-century mother told her three-year-old daughter that she had fasted a whole day because of worry about the child's disposition. Thereafter the guilty youngster changed her behavior voluntarily. According to the standards of the day, this mother disciplined her youngster correctly; the mother used love, and not corporal punishment, to influence behavior and values.[26] Corporal punishment was to be avoided. It engendered fear in children, and fear lessened their ability to be rational and confident—qualities especially essential to boys aspiring to careers in business. Religious views were also changing. Many middle-class Protestants no longer viewed God as angry and vengeful, but rather as a loving, caring father. To them it seemed inappropriate to scare children into believing in a Supreme Being or in anything else. Moreover, in a democracy, people needed to obey voluntarily and not because they were physically coerced into doing so. "Voluntary obedience depended not on fear but on the perception that authority is legitimate."[27]

Middle-class parents did not completely abandon corporal punishment, but rather used it only as a last resort. "The first element in governing children was the use of affection; the second, the use of reason. These two alone sufficed—ideally. The parental command, or direct statement of authority followed; and next, reproof, for the child who failed to comply." If still the child did not respond, the parent could threaten a penalty, which might be a whipping, and, if necessary, carry it out.[28]

To inculcate values in this fashion was time-consuming, and middle-class parents believed it could best be done in nuclear families living in private homes somewhat separate from the disorder of the larger society. By the mid–nineteenth century, the typical middle-class urban family included parents and children and occasionally servants or lodgers whose relationship to the family was purely economic. Extended families of children, parents, grandparents, and other kin were rare among the middle class. Before the 1870s, middle-class parents rented or bought single-family homes in less congested parts of cities relatively near their city workplaces. Thereafter, when transportation by street car became more widely available and affordable, middle-class parents often moved their families to the suburbs. There families occupied fairly large homes, which, now that work and home were separate, served purely domestic purposes. Each child had his or her own bedroom and a degree of privacy that would encourage "study and self-improvement" as well as some independence.[29] Yet Victorian homes also contained communal spaces such as the dining room where parents emphasized, in a formal setting, "the subordination of each individual's desires to the unit as a whole." Middle-class youngsters remained within such homes into their late teens or early twenties to acquire the education necessary for employment and to give their parents time to save the money they needed to launch boys into middle-class occupations and girls into marriages with members of their class. By the late nineteenth century, there was also greater concern that proper maturation took a long time; rapid growth attendant with puberty was potentially disrupting, and children needed to remain within their homes through adolescence for their own protection.[30]

Middle-class parents raised sons and daughters similarly, especially when they were very young. Until boys and girls were about seven years old, mothers dressed them identically, first in long gowns, next in short coats, and, between the ages of three and seven, in "half-length petticoats and pantaloons." Middle-class boys and girls also had their hair cropped very short above the ears or wore it long and curled. In dressing young boys and girls alike, parents preserved an image of childhood as a distinct "stage of development." They also "protected a child's ignorance about sex," thereby preserving the idea of "angelic innocence" presumably characteristic only of children.[31]

Boys and girls not only dressed alike, but also learned similar values. Even as mothers taught boys principles such as thrift, industriousness, and self-control appropriate to the working world, mothers also "had to teach their daughters how to remind men of these values." In their daily lives, in their methods of discipline, mothers also represented to both their sons and daughters the importance of love. Love united families and helped men and women get over whatever differences there were in gender roles and emotional cultures. "Maternalism meant moral qualities, to be sure, but it also represented unalloyed love, from which children could take strength regardless of gender and which provided the model for the gender-free commitment to romantic intensity later in life." Boys and girls had to be educated for different roles in public and private life, but they also had to be prepared to join emotionally in the private sphere of the family.[32] Mothers succeeded in inculcating love, for throughout the nineteenth century, boys and girls wrote affectionate letters home more to their mothers than to their fathers. Although fathers were expected to assume more responsibility in raising adolescent boys, boys' continuing affection for their mothers is borne out by letters sent home by Civil War soldiers. The young men typically wrote their mothers rather than their fathers to report events and to ask for food, clothes, and other necessities.[33]

In infancy and early childhood, parents treated youngsters similarly, but as they grew older, parents had to ready boys and girls for the very different roles they would ultimately play in life. Clothing symbolized the distinctions between boys and girls. After the age of seven, youngsters no longer dressed alike: instead, boys wore short pants, and girls wore dresses. And while mothers taught boys and girls the importance of love, mothers strongly condemned anger more in girls than in boys. Parents disapproved of either sons or daughters becoming angry at parents or siblings, for family always came first, but parents taught daughters that anger was totally unacceptable and unfeminine. Because mothers prepared girls to manage a home and children, mothers proscribed anger because it was inimical to a happy home life. In contrast, boys might ultimately become better family providers if they were competitive and aggressive, so mothers permitted boys to express anger at home as long as it was in "a just cause."[34]

Boys were also free to express anger, aggression, and competitiveness in the boy culture they entered about the age of seven. Once they were old enough to dress differently from their sisters, to wear pants, middle-class boys spent much of each day roaming patches of woodland, vacant lots, and parks near their rural or suburban homes. There boys engaged in rough games and improvised athletic contests with young male friends. Boys wrestled in a good-natured fashion with their buddies, but they fought in a fierce and angry way with rivals in their neighborhoods. Boys competed with one another in physical contests of all sorts—swimming, running, sledding, skating, and hunting. Boys also learned from one another some values that were not taught in their homes. They acquired the ability to suppress "feelings that were readily exposed in the feminine world of home—grief, fear, pain," the kinds of "emotions that would make them vulnerable to predatory rivals." Boys also constantly dared one another to run faster, dive deeper, commit acts of vandalism, and challenge—usually male—authority. In this fashion boys learned to be venturesome rather than self-denying and cautious. They also exercised power—often by terrorizing physically weaker creatures such as animals (which they hunted, trapped, and sometimes tortured) and girls (whom they pelted with mud balls and snowballs). Overall, boys became more independent: with little help from adults or friends, boys acquired physical prowess, the ability to organize games, make alliances, impose their will on others, and move up the physical pecking order. Thus, boy culture was in some ways at odds with the values that middle-class mothers taught their sons at home, but most boys successfully negotiated the transition from one culture to the other. In the process, boys came to appreciate the different spheres of men and women, of home and work, and became able to move "back and forth from a domestic world of mutual dependence to a public world of independence; from an atmosphere of cooperation and nurture to one of competition and conflict; from a sphere where intimacy was encouraged to one where human relationships were treated instrumentally; from an environment that supported affectionate impulses to one that sanctioned aggressive impulses. . . ."[35]

Before puberty, middle-class girls also enjoyed considerable freedom. Autobiographies of many nineteenth-century women reveal that they, like boys, played actively outside the household. Una Hunt, who grew up in Cincinnati in the 1870s and 1880s, remembered "climbing every tree and shed in the neighborhood." There is no reason to assume that the trees and sheds were low, easy ones, either, since she also recorded that "I was often badly hurt, but after each fall, when vinegar and brown papers had been applied, [my mother's] only comment was "You must learn to climb better," and I did.' " Although mothers certainly relied on their daughters to help with the housekeeping, such chores consumed only a small portion of each day. Lucy Larcom, who grew up in New England, remembered of her childhood, "Our tether was a long one, and when, grown a little older, we occasionally asked to have it lengthened, a maternal 'I don't care' amounted to almost unlimited liberty." Nonetheless, there is little evidence that girls were as competitive, as quarrelsome, or as likely to terrorize animals as were boys. Girls may have had almost as much freedom to play outdoors as boys, but when girls were at home, parents expected daughters to provide household services to their brothers, care for ailing relatives, and acquire appropriate social graces by visiting among their family circle of friends or helping their mothers entertain. Some time between the ages of 13 and 15, middle-class girls lost the freedom of movement they had previously enjoyed. Ellen Mordecai remembered her 13th year as one that ended her "happy-go-lucky carefree childhood." Of course, girls knew about the roles they would have to assume as women, but they did not necessarily welcome the restrictions placed upon them as they matured.[36]

By the time girls reached puberty, middle-class families were especially concerned about preserving the moral purity—the virginity—of their daughters, because women were expected to have greater moral and spiritual strength than men. Because she now required protection, a young woman could no longer move about so freely and independently. If she had sex before marriage, she was labeled a fallen woman and jeopardized her chances of ever finding an appropriate mate. "A suitor who discovered that his fiancée was not a virgin had grounds to break the engagement, and a husband could file for divorce if he learned that his wife had been unchaste before marriage." Middle-class parents allowed their daughters to meet young men at community gatherings such as church socials and skating parties. However, parents preferred their daughters to entertain potential suitors within the family home, usually in the parlor. Here the young couple had a degree of privacy, but certainly not as much as they would have had they met in a more public place. Parents did not directly choose mates for their daughters. Said one mother to her children in the 1870s, "When you want to marry you are to make your own choice and not come back home afterwards with any complaints."[37] However, by circumscribing the movement especially of their daughters, and to some degree of their sons, to certain communities and schools, parents inevitably exercised a degree of control over whom their children would meet and possibly marry.

Young women and men expected to fall in love before marrying, not to develop affection after marriage. They sought a soul mate—a companion with whom they could, in all honesty, share their innermost secrets. For both young women and men, this process could be difficult, for young men had been trained to conceal rather than express their feelings, and young women had been cautioned to be pure and submissive rather than frank or assertive about expressing affection. The basis for true love was understood to be largely spiritual; sexual attraction was desirable, and sex itself was to be enjoyed after marriage, although even then Victorians believed the spiritual connection between couples was more crucial.[38]

In order to prepare to become wives and mothers, middle-class adolescent girls needed to develop their spiritual and moral virtues—a task made more difficult by puberty itself. Doctors of the late nineteenth century viewed puberty as a particularly dangerous time for girls, a time when the beginning of menstruation might cause both psychological and physiological disorders.[39] Medical opinion held that girls should stay within the home, rest, and be careful of what they ate. To eat little was a sign of morality, of the ability to reject "carnal appetites." Girls learned that those who ate too much or who consumed the wrong foods would become ugly—a bad omen for young women expected to attract suitors. "Food and femininity" were tied in Victorian culture, and appetite was "both a sign of sexuality and an indication of lack of self-restraint." Mothers had to monitor carefully the foods they fed their daughters in order to keep them morally pure. "Adolescent girls were expressly cautioned against coffee, tea, and chocolate; salted meats and spices; warm bread and pastry; confectionery; nuts and raisins; and, of course, alcohol. These sorts of foods stimulated the sensual rather than the moral nature of the girl." The most dangerous food was meat. "Doctors and patients alike shared a common perception of meat as a food that stimulated sexual development and activity." Not surprisingly, Victorian girls ate very little meat, a practice that may have contributed to the high incidence among them of chlorosis. Named for the green tinge of the skin of many of its victims, chlorosis was probably iron-deficiency anemia.[40]

In the late nineteenth century, chlorosis was a disease peculiar to middle-class teenage girls. Sufferers lacked appetite, lost weight, and often stopped menstruating. Historian Nancy Theriot believes the symptoms of chlorosis to be so like those of anorexia nervosa that the two were probably the same disease. However, Joan Jacobs Brumberg, who has studied both diseases exhaustively, argues that the two were different maladies. Chlorosis may have been a mild form of anorexia. According to Brumberg, parents and doctors did not fear chlorosis. Both felt that the disease was common in teenage girls and that it could be treated fairly easily with rest and iron salts. Parents did fear anorexia nervosa, which was less common but more serious. Girls who had anorexia refused to eat not only meat but virtually all other foods as well. Charles Lasegue, a French doctor, noted in 1873 that anorexia was most common in girls who experienced conflicts with their parents, sometimes over romance or the lack of social or educational opportunity. "Since emotional freedom was not a common prerogative of the Victorian adolescent girl, it seems reasonable to assert that unhappiness was likely to be expressed in nonverbal forms of behavior. One such behavior was refusal of food." Mothers were particularly alarmed by their daughters' not eating because mothers were responsible for managing a girl's health and diet. By refusing virtually all food, anorexic girls avoided becoming mature, full-figured women like their mothers. Anorexia was a sign of both sexual anxiety in young women and mother-daughter conflict.[41]

The breakdown in relations between adolescent girls and their mothers signaled by anorexia nervosa was atypical in the nineteenth century. As Carroll Smith-Rosenberg has shown, emotional closeness, rather than emotional conflict, was most characteristic of Victorian middle-class mothers and daughters. Girls who served as apprentices to their mothers in order to learn domestic chores, child care, and nursing "shared skills and emotional interaction." Girls also enjoyed a large female network of sisters, cousins, and aunts, with whom girls could also relate should there be any tension with their mothers. Girls carried the loving relationships they learned at home into adolescence; when many went away to school, they formed their own networks of close friends. "Young girls helped one another overcome homesickness and endure the crises of adolescence." These female friendships were often romantic and sensual, yet they were not considered abnormal. In Victorian America there was a large distance between "committed heterosexuality" and "uncompromising homosexuality," and in between, "a wide latitude of emotions and sexual feelings" were permitted. Loving female friendships formed in youth often lasted throughout women's lives.[42]

Late in the century, when the experiences of some middle-class mothers and daughters diverged because the girls did not assume the housekeeping roles of their mothers but instead attended college and took up careers as professionals, most such young women and their mothers remained close. Linda Rosenzweig's study of the writings, letters, and diaries of middle-class women and their college-educated daughters reveals that although they sometimes expressed conflict, they more often spoke of mutual caring and support. Mothers supported their daughters' aspirations, and daughters appreciated this support. Of course, the nineteenth-century proscription against female anger may account for the absence of such sentiments in the writings of mothers and daughters, but mothers also had good reason to support daughters who made untraditional choices to further their education and careers. Widowed mothers may have wanted their daughters to be more prepared for self-support than their mothers had been; mothers who had been denied higher education in their youth may have endorsed education for their daughters; and mothers who were confident in their own lives probably had no trouble encouraging their daughters to become confident in theirs.[43]

Even as middle-class parents prepared most of their daughters for familial roles, parents entertained different expectations for their sons. Late in the century, a minority of girls acquired an advanced education and prepared for a career, but for middle-class boys, such education and career preparation was the rule, not the exception. Boys lived at home at the same time that they worked outside of it preparing for the economic independence expected of them. In the world of school and work, boys learned to be ambitious, competitive, and individualistic. Such traits, although not necessarily denigrated in the home, were not always compatible with a loving family life. Middle-class boys who lived at home well into their twenties often grew restless when their independence outside the home conflicted with their dependent status within.

To reduce such restlessness, middle-class parents encouraged their sons to participate in organized sports such as baseball and cricket. Such sports were also useful as socially accepted outlets for boys' expressions of anger.[44] Sports also provided ways of channeling and encouraging certain qualities associated with manliness by the 1880s and 1890s. Darwin's theories popularized man's connection to the animal kingdom and to animals' aggressive qualities about the same time as memories of the Civil War faded, and military strength, toughness, and endurance came to be admired. Middle-class parents encouraged their sons to join organizations (precursors of the Boy Scouts) that encouraged the strenuous life within a framework of subordination, and to participate in athletic activities that built boys' physical strength and encouraged competition. Middle-class mothers, who emphasized the importance of health and physical well-being for their children, supported their sons' efforts to grow stronger physically. Medical opinion also seemingly reinforced the value of bodybuilding for boys. Doctors believed that girls became physically weaker during puberty but that boys grew physically stronger. By the late nineteenth century, adolescent boys became obsessed with exercise and building up their bodies. "Teenagers, college students, and young clerks filled their diaries with an endless list of their outdoor activities, ranging from boxing to camping, from skating to football."[45] Among middle-class young men, body image reflected late-nineteenth-century standards for maleness, as body image among young women reflected Victorian standards for femininity.

Male strength and physicality might also be expressed sexually. Popular thought and medical opinion concurred that sexual expression was more necessary for a man than for a woman. However, beginning in early childhood, middle-class boys were also taught self-control, including sexual continence, by their mothers. In other words, Victorian culture delivered mixed messages to young men. Being strong and aggressive meant being sexually active; being self-controlled and loving of mothers, wives, and family meant curbing passion. In all likelihood, many middle-class young men had sex before marriage, but probably not with young women of their own class. "Declining premarital pregnancy rates—which dropped from twenty percent of marriages in the

1830s to ten percent in the 1850s—suggest that many middle-class courting couples internalized sexual restraint, at the least removing intercourse from the realm of acceptable premarital sexual acts." Young middle-class men instead patronized prostitutes in the red-light districts that existed in every city. "College students explored vice districts together; young male migrants to the city lived in rooming-house districts where prostitution was visible; men traveling on business could learn the location of brothels before they left the train station; members of social clubs visited houses of prostitution as a group."[46]

Although the sexual experience of young middle-class men diverged from that of their sisters, close same-sex friendships were common for both young men and women. A young man usually selected from a larger group of casual friends one young man with whom he could share emotional concerns and frankly discuss women and careers. At this time of transition from childhood, when teenage boys were physically strong but did not yet possess the trappings of manhood such as careers and marriages, young men often preferred to share their concerns with male friends rather than with parents. Close friendships between adolescent males provided love and security and were "a substitute for the emotional nurture provided most often in boyhood by a mother." Like their sisters' friendships, the friendships of young men were sometimes romantic and included "kisses, caresses, verbal expressions of physical longing, and the sharing of beds." As with girls, such expressions were perfectly normal at a time when there was as yet no word or concept for homosexuality. Kissing a male did not mean to a Victorian boy that he was becoming homosexual; "it was a gesture of strong affection at least as much as it was an act of sexual expression." Unlike the friendships of adolescent girls, those of boys did not last beyond youth. As boys entered careers and became more individualistic, independent, tough, and competitive, tender and compassionate friendships with men no longer seemed appropriate.[47]

Ideally, the end result of middle-class child rearing was to prepare children for Victorian adulthood. Mothers taught both boys and girls the value of love so that they could replicate it in the families they built. Girls learned to hide their anger in the interest of preserving peace in families they would oversee. Girls learned from their mothers how to manage homes; girls preserved their moral and religious superiority by avoiding sex and even by watching their diet; and they developed networks of female friends with whom, throughout their lives, they could share common concerns about family, children, and religion. In contrast, boys learned through boy culture and athletic activity to express the anger they would need to fuel competitiveness in the working world. Although parents urged boys to practice self-control, they lost no status by sexual adventuring. They spent a good deal of time in school or at work preparing to become providers, and the individualism they had to develop in their work roles made the friendships they formed with other young men temporary rather than lifelong. Thus, in most ways, middle-class boys and girls were trained dissimilarly to prepare them for the very distinct gender roles of men and women in Victorian America. These differences were reflected in their physical attributes, for the ideal Victorian girl was thin and prone to illness whereas the ideal Victorian male was physically strong and in robust health.

Many white Southern antebellum plantation families adopted an approach to child rearing similar to that of the Northern urban middle class. Some Southern white planters took a more child-centered approach to rearing youngsters in the eighteenth century, and by the mid-nineteenth century, Southern plantation mistresses read child-rearing manuals and attempted to follow their advice just as did Northern mothers.[48] Yet the uniqueness of the antebellum Southern economy and culture, its dynastic tradition and its reliance on slavery, inevitably also resulted in child-rearing patterns that were distinct from those in the North.

On Southern plantations, as in Northern cities and farms, mothers assumed the primary role in child rearing. "Motherhood became middle- and upper-class women's primary occupation, which society elevated not merely to a duty but to an enviable vocation." In Northern middle-class families, children were so precious that mothers began loving nurture at birth by breast-feeding their infants. Historians agree that many Southern white mothers did the same, but historians disagree over what percentage relied on slaves to nurse infants. Catherine Clinton and Elizabeth Fox-Genovese assert that most Southern planter women employed wet nurses to nurse children at least part of the time. In contrast, Sally McMillen, using comments from the journals of well-off women from various parts of the South, found that only 20 percent used a wet nurse, 10 percent hand-fed (bottle-fed), but 85 percent breast-fed their infants. The women did so because breast feeding was traditional, they liked being close to their infants, and they felt it was healthy for the children. Women may have breast-fed to delay having another child, for "current studies indicate breast-feeding can help space births about two years apart." However, there is little indication in the letters of Southern women that they employed breast feeding as a means of birth control, and if they did, they were not particularly successful as the birthrate remained high in the South. McMillen believes Southern white mothers employed wet nurses only when the mothers were ill or did not have enough milk; few relied on slaves to wet-nurse infants. Personal narratives of slaves mention the practice only occasionally. McMillen also argues that nineteenth-century visitors to the South made particular note of those few black women who did breast-feed white children or who at least carried them around because the practice was so unusual to visitors. Because white women did not nurse in public, visitors could not have observed the more common pattern of white mothers nursing their own children. Jane Censer agrees that the North Carolina planter families she studied preferred mothers to breast-feed and infrequently relied on wet nurses. "Planter families rarely mentioned their nursemaids or mammies; and even when they did, the nurse's importance often was questionable."[49]

In all probability, the majority of Southern planter mothers valued infancy as much as did Northern middle-class mothers and hence chose to breast-feed. Yet a minority took advantage of the presence of nursing mothers, usually among slaves (some wet nurses were white). Inevitably, slavery offered Southern white women a child-care choice that Northern women did not have. What is surprising and reflective of a new view of the significance of infancy and childhood is that so many Southern white women did not use slave nurses. Historians agree that Southern white mothers worried about entrusting toddlers and older children to the care of slaves and about white youngsters playing with slave children. Because Southern plantation homes were not private places to the degree that Northern single-family urban and suburban homes were, Southern white mothers could not protect their children from contact with the so-called lower orders. Instead, white mothers on plantations instilled in their children a haughty attitude toward slaves, a sense of slaves' inferiority and of whites' power to control slaves. "Warned from an early age about their contact with slaves, white children were indoctrinated with a sense of suspicion toward blacks and a demeanor of superiority."[50] This attitude is a distinctive result of Southern child-rearing practices.

Also unique to the antebellum South was a higher birthrate than in the urban North. Southern plantation mistresses did not curtail their fertility as much as did Northern middle-class women. In 1850, the average woman in the United States had 5.4 children, but among planter families in North Carolina, the average was six children. Larger families in the South may have in part been the result of pressure on mothers to preserve the family line by bearing enough children to ensure, even if several died in infancy, that an heir would survive.

More so than Northern fathers, Southern planter fathers were patriarchs, powerful heads of families, and they too did not play a major role in child rearing. Planters were often away from their homes for extended periods of time and counted on mothers to provide most child care. In some families, fathers offered their wives moral support, but in other families fathers were largely figureheads. Most fathers paid more attention to their children once they reached adolescence, when the time came to provide children a formal education, to prepare sons for careers, and to secure husbands for daughters.

Like Northern middle-class mothers, Southern mothers took on most of the responsibility for disciplining children. Southern mothers too avoided trying to break their children's wills and did not demand "complete submissiveness."

Mothers used physical punishment rarely, though if it became absolutely necessary, they would spank their children.[51]

Although in Southern planter families nurturing and disciplining children was primarily the responsibility of mothers, other kinfolk also took an active interest in child rearing. In the urban North, middle-class parents raised their children in nuclear households, but Joan Cashin's study of planter families in Virginia, North Carolina, and South Carolina between 1810 and 1860 reveals that only 35 percent of such families were strictly nuclear. Instead, she found that the custom of visiting brought planter families together with a variety of relatives for weeks and months at a time. Kin ties were very strong among such families, and children built powerful emotional relationships with distant relatives. Youngsters often participated in child exchange for extended periods of time when they resided with relatives in order to acquire an education or because their own parents were ill or traveling. Thus "raising children was often a collective activity in the planter family." Southern planter parents taught their children to rely on and value kin in part because of the high death rate in the South. In North Carolina, "almost two-thirds of the planter households lost at least one parent before the youngest child reached age twenty-one." It was almost a necessity for children to know and love their relatives, for they might very well be parented by them at some point. "Planters customarily adopted the orphaned offspring of brothers or sisters, while grandparents might supervise the rearing of motherless grandchildren." Childless aunts sometimes adopted favorite nieces.[52]

Partly because of the importance of kinfolk, Southern plantation mistresses early on inculcated in their children the value of politeness, especially to older relatives. "Jane Hamilton illustrated such concerns when she wrote about her four-year-old son: 'I try to make him behave himself at the table, and be polite to every body, but particularly his Grandfather.' " Politeness was a sign of obedience that, along with hard work, was as important to Southern white planter families as to Northern urban middle-class parents. Jane Censer observed that "Wealthy North Carolinians especially desired industrious children. Like middle-class American and English parents, [North Carolina] planters lauded the value of hard work; and none defended idleness as their class's prerogative."[53]

Although white Southern and Northern children learned many of the same values, Southern planters often had different reasons for teaching them than did Northern parents.[54] For example, Southern white children raised on plantations were trained in self-control, but not because this was an important virtue in a democracy or necessary for self-advancement in business. Instead, "by college age, sons were exhorted to provide their own discipline—a self-control that would bar such expensive and dangerous pastimes as gambling, heavy drinking, and the frequenting of prostitutes." In other words, self-control preserved children's safety and their parents' fortunes. Southern planters also urged their children to practice thrift, but not as in the North because it was necessary to advance their future in the professions or in business. In fact, the sons of Southern planters moved easily into professions such as the law at a younger age than could most Northern urban youth. Part of the reason for this difference "probably lies in the survival of so many elements of prescriptive status and hierarchy in the antebellum South at a time of their erosion in the North. Among southern aristocrats, family name acted as a guarantor of maturity and responsibility almost without regard to chronological age." Thus, Southern parents cautioned their sons to practice thrift, not for reasons of personal advancement, but in order to preserve the family fortune. Sons should not squander their money on foolish extravagances. Southern planter parents advised girls to practice thrift somewhat differently: by careful shopping. They were to avoid purchasing lavish clothing and should get good value for their money. Again the concern was with preserving wealth rather than acquiring it. In addition, elegance in dress was a sign that young women had "internalized self-control." Proper dress confirmed young Southern white women as morally proper. "Extravagance lay in an excess of display that exposed a young woman to the appearance of looseness, self-promotion, and limitless appetite. Fashion articulated class position; extravagance defied it."[55]

Child rearing was also gendered in the South, but in a different fashion than in the North. Because of the dynastic tradition, Southern parents especially welcomed the birth of sons. Mothers raised children of both genders to believe in the superiority of boys over girls. Southern boys began training in patriarchal roles with their sisters, of whom brothers were very protective. As in the North, brothers in white Southern planter families were expected to escort and watch out for their sisters. Southern parents also expected boys to compete in sports and in school. Boys had to be strong and athletic, in the South as in the North, but white Southern planter sons, who were trained to manage slaves, also had to be prepared to use violence if necessary. Young Southern men, who were free to indulge in sexual liaisons with slave women, also took advantage of the double standard perhaps more than did Northern young men.

Young white Southern women, like their Northern counterparts, learned their roles from their mothers, who trained daughters in how to manage households. As in the North, Southern white mothers and their daughters were often close friends and companions. Planters were just as protective of their daughters' moral purity before marriage as were Northern middle-class parents. Southern planter parents took care that their daughters met and chose mates only from among young men of their social status. The freedoms enjoyed by Southern white boys grew as they matured, but girls found their lives more constricted the older they became. In this, their experience was probably not too different from that of Northern urban middle-class girls. The words of a 15-year-old daughter of a North Carolina planter capture well the frustrations of young women growing up in prosperous white families in both the North and South in the mid-nineteenth century: "Oh do you not regret that as you grow up into womanhood, the world expects more from you and you have to renounce your childish pleasures, and amusements, and finally settle down into a sedate old maid, or else have a lord to rule over you and whose will you are obliged to obey, sometimes to receive his smiles, and then again when something provokes him bear his frown. Oh that I could be a girl forever."[56]

After the Civil War, child rearing in Southern planter families changed somewhat. The biggest difference was in the role of fathers. They spent more time at home engaging in hands-on farm management, and so they took a more active role in child rearing than they had previously. The terrible deprivation suffered by many Southern white planter families during the Civil War made fathers who had fought in the war and been separated from their suffering families more appreciative of the importance of a loving family life.[57]

Between 1850 and 1890, white urban working-class families developed a second style of child rearing. Because of both their cultural traditions and their position within the United States economy, working-class Americans living in cities, mill towns, and barrios raised their sons and daughters in a distinct fashion.

In the United States in the late nineteenth century, the majority of the working class were foreign born. The United States attracted thousands of migrants from northern and western Europe, and, after 1880, from southern and eastern Europe as well. The working class not only was ethnically diverse but also comprised individuals laboring in a variety of skilled and unskilled jobs in thousands of factories in hundreds of towns and cities.

Regardless of their jobs and their ethnic background, members of working-class families depended on one another. Most working-class fathers labored outside their homes, usually in factories, but their families could not survive on the fathers' paychecks alone. Many working-class women contributed to their family's support by keeping house for boarders, taking in sewing work, or doing "outwork" for manufacturers. Children often helped their mothers with these tasks. Whereas home and work were separate for urban middle-class families, the line between workplace and domestic space was not so clearly drawn in working-class homes. All members of the working-class family depended on those who were able to contribute somehow to their mutual support.

Like middle-class fathers, working-class fathers were family providers; they worked hard and were not home much. "Long working hours, cramped quarters in the home, and the masculine environment of saloons took many working-class men away from their families for most of every day." Italian fathers in East Harlem demanded public shows of respect from their children in city streets but at home "remained aloof and formal, insisting not on love but on deference and respect."[58] Much of working-class fathers' involvement with children came when sons and daughters were beyond infancy and childhood. Fathers found employment for children of working age—"preferably in rooms with kin who acquainted the greenhorns with workroom gossip, shop rituals, and labor shortcuts. This responsibility became quite important as the children, especially sons, reached marriage age; whereas daughters were expected to leave the work force upon marriage and pregnancy, sons would soon become breadwinners and fathers in their own right." In Italian and Jewish families, fathers sought out appropriate suitors for their daughters. Working-class fathers were also child disciplinarians, although most fathers did not share the middle-class desire to be companionate and gradually win youngsters over to appropriate behavior. In working-class families, "the father . . . was a vivid authority figure. He might use violence against his children, particularly his sons, to substitute for other patriarchal controls that were beyond his reach. More commonly he simply came home tired and, without intending to, lashed out against an unruly boy with words or fists."[59] Working-class fathers were also more likely than middle-class fathers to be unemployed some time during any given year. Unemployment or underemployment prevented fathers from fulfilling their roles as breadwinners. Working-class fathers expected children to work for family support, but fathers lost status and became resentful if youngsters' earnings completely replaced the fathers' during spells of unemployment. Such situations, common in working-class families but rare in middle-class ones, led to family conflict.

Working-class mothers were responsible for child rearing, but it was only one of the many tasks mothers performed. They were not full-time child nurturers as were most middle-class mothers. Working-class mothers could not be. In addition to earning money working within their homes, working-class mothers enabled their husbands and children to take jobs on the outside. Mothers shopped for food daily at a time when iceboxes and the ice to put in them were often prohibitive in cost for the working poor. Mothers often kept their own gardens and livestock and labored for hours hauling water by hand to launder the family's clothes.

Like middle-class mothers, working-class Jewish and Italian mothers breast-fed their babies. Some probably did so to avoid pregnancy. "In the Jewish tradition, intercourse with nursing women was forbidden by law and Jewish women often used nursing to avoid pregnancy." Many also probably breast-fed because breast feeding was traditional and was much easier and cheaper than hand feeding. Iceboxes and ice were costly, and therefore refrigerating milk with which to bottle-feed babies was virtually impossible for working-class mothers.[60] Moreover, few could afford a wet nurse. Of course, middle-class mothers may also have breast-fed to avoid having more children, although there is little evidence in mothers' letters and diaries of this intent.

Regardless of their reasons for breast feeding, working-class mothers were less successful in limiting fertility than were middle-class mothers. Late in the century, at a time when the typical Northern urban middle-class family had about three children, the typical French-Canadian, English, Scottish, Jewish, or Italian-American working-class family had about five. Immigrant women may well have wanted to control the number of children they bore, but they were at a disadvantage. Middle-class mothers enjoyed greater access to published information about birth control and could better pay for costly methods of controlling fertility such as abortions than could working-class women. In addition, white native-born middle-class women probably had more cooperation from their husbands in their efforts to limit childbearing. "Jewish and Italian culture stressed procreation. Adriana Valenti, for instance, recalled that large numbers of children were a point of pride with Italian men: 'When my father's friends would come to visit us, you know, the *paisanos*, they would say, "How many children you have?" and if one had six, my father would say I have eight. Another would say ten. The larger the family, the better; they were so proud of big families.' "[61] Immigrant women themselves may have been ambivalent about limiting childbearing. Although to do so was advantageous to them physically, many may have seen children as a reason for family creation and as an economic asset, because youngsters could first help out around the house and later earn wages to help support the family. (See chapter 5.)

Working-class immigrant mothers treated their infants differently than did middle-class mothers. Because immigrant women were too busy to attend to an infant's every cry, they typically used pacifiers to keep babies quiet, a practice of which middle-class mothers disapproved. Working-class mothers also did not dress babies in loose garments because mothers were not concerned with providing free movement for their infants. In crowded apartments up several flights of stairs, a baby who could crawl about could easily come to harm. Infants were swaddled both for their own safety and because wrapping babies tightly was traditional in many European cultures.

Both the material circumstances and ethnic preferences of working-class families also militated against their providing youngsters as much privacy as did middle-class parents. Few working-class parents could afford apartments or homes large enough to permit each child his or her own bedroom. Italian families disapproved of child privacy and interpreted it as "hostility and rejection" of the family itself. Most working-class parents did not keep their sons and daughters in the home, apart from the larger urban world. Instead, when mothers shopped or socialized, they took their children with them into the streets. Youngsters often played outside their stuffy, crowded apartments until midnight. Most of the year, families ate and slept inside only; but in the summer, on hot nights, whole families moved outside to sleep in the streets.[62]

Childhood and children had a very different meaning for working-class parents than for middle-class parents. "The working poor did not think of childhood as a separate stage of life in which boys and girls were free from adult burdens. . . ." Instead, working-class mothers and fathers expected children to do their fair share of work inside and outside the home as soon as they were able. Jewish and Italian children thought that American boys and girls stayed young too long. "Yetta Adelman, a Polish Jewish garment worker who had come to the United States when she was twelve years old and saved money to bring her family over, put it this way: 'When I was here I knew I had to go to work. I didn't come here for pleasure, you know. I was twelve years old but I wasn't. Compared to a child here in the United States I was twenty.' " Although Yetta was twelve when she began working in the United States, she had probably begun working in her family home when she was much younger.[63] By the age of seven or eight, most Jewish, Italian, and Mexican-American children began tending babies, running errands, or scavenging in the city streets for useful items such as coal. "Children were little adults, unable as yet to take up all the duties of their elders, but nonetheless bound to do as much as they could."[64]

Because of the poverty of working-class households, mothers had no choice but to encourage their children to go out into the streets to search for useful items or to find employment as soon as they were physically able. Parents "emphasized early independence contingent on early responsibility." Of necessity, mothers exposed their children to the physical dangers of the streets, including carts, carriages, and streetcars as well as the moral dangers posed by pimps, prostitutes, and gamblers. Some mothers so needed the money their children could earn that they literally forced children to learn a trade. One girl remembered, "When I wouldn't want to sew, my mother would stick me with a needle. You had to learn. First she taught me to baste, then how to make the back stitch and so on."[65]

Children employed outside the home labored not for themselves but for their families. Mothers and fathers expected children to sacrifice schooling and leisure time for the sake of the family. Family members pooled their wages so as to have enough money to support the needs of all. As a sign of respect, young people turned their unopened paychecks over to their mothers, who usually gave children 25 cents to a dollar a week for their own uses.

Because existence was so precarious for working-class families, it was essential that they remain in close contact with relatives, friends, and neighbors who could help out in time of need. Relying solely on the nuclear family unit was impractical and dangerous for working-class families. Relatives and friends helped fathers find jobs when they became unemployed and they took in children and parents when impoverishment forced their eviction from apartments or their removal to another city or section of a city. Mothers learned from neighbors where the best places to purchase cheap goods were;

neighbors watched children when mothers went shopping or when they were ill; friends and relatives took in children when a mother had to enter a hospital. Working-class mothers trained children to honor interdependency.[66]

Because working-class families required and relied on help from relatives and friends, child rearing was more communal than in the urban middle class. In Southern cotton-mill towns, "female relatives and close neighbors cared for infants and toddlers while their mothers worked in the mill. When children were old enough to venture away from home and play with friends, more distant neighbors joined in the responsibilities of discipline."[67] In Mexican-American communities in the West, families often took in the children of relatives who lived some distance away and kept the children for extended periods of time. In the Southwest, parents, aunts, uncles, grandparents, and godparents all participated in raising children of both genders. Early on, youngsters learned to address their elders properly, to ask permission of them, and to respect rank in the family.

Being polite and obedient to parents and other older family members and friends was expected of working-class children. Many immigrant parents were Roman Catholic and did not share the belief of Protestant American-born middle-class parents that children were innocent and loving. Rather, Roman Catholic parents believed that children were lazy and disobedient and should be sharply disciplined. Children were human beings and, like adults, possessed of a bad nature. "In California, [Mexican-American] parents took their children to public executions (until the 1870s, when they were banned) to teach the fatal consequences of evil acts. Rafael Prieto, in Monterey, California, remembered being whipped after one such execution so that he would always remember its moral lessons."[68] In sharp contrast to native-born white middle-class families, Italians disciplined their children by instilling in them fear, "especially with tales of evil spirits," and sometimes by pronouncing a parental curse on them. Many immigrants were not concerned, as were middle-class parents, with modeling within the family the democratic pattern of voluntary obedience to authority. Most immigrant parents came from countries where obedience was enforced from above by authoritarian governments, and those parents replicated the authoritarian pattern in their families. There were also practical reasons for working-class parents to be controlling. As one mother told settlement-house worker Jane Addams, "If you don't keep control over them from the time they are little, you would never get their wages when they are grown up."

Working-class mothers and fathers both worked long hours to earn enough to support their families; unlike middle-class parents, working-class parents did not have time to persuade their youngsters to obey. Parents required prompt obedience to their commands and had no compunction about relying on corporal punishment. Spanking was usually sufficient, although working-class parents sometimes disciplined youngsters more brutally.[69]

Working-class parents expected boys and girls to be obedient and respect the authority of adult relatives, neighbors, and friends, but they had more gendered expectations of adolescents. Mothers and fathers valued sexual purity in daughters and considered it a dishonor to the family if girls had sex before marriage. Italian-Americans were most strict in this regard. "While flirting and sexual banter were allowed within the [Italian-American] family, such behavior outside the family was seen as potentially destructive to the family itself, as well as to its honor." Italian-American parents expected their daughters to come home directly from work, to spend all their leisure time with their families, and to be chaperoned whenever they were in the company of young men. One Italian man remembered how he courted his wife: "I used to go to her house. She sat on one side of the table, and I on the other. They afraid I touch." When he was alone with his fiancée a short time prior to their marriage, he tried to kiss her. She promptly warded him off, saying, "No, not yet!"[70]

Regardless, most working-class parents were unable to restrict their daughters as much as they would have liked. The very nature of working-class life precluded parents from doing so. Young girls could not be sheltered as middle-class adolescents were in private homes in suburban communities. Instead, working-class girls dwelt in crowded tenement buildings, ran errands for their parents in busy city streets, and held wage-labor jobs to help support their families. Working-class parents desperately needed the money their daughters (and sons) earned, yet as the girls matured, they wanted to retain some of their earnings for their own pleasures. Parents who refused a daughter money of her own risked losing her entire income if she rebelled and left home. Most working-class girls struck a bargain with their parents and gave them most of their earnings in return for some freedom from parental oversight.

That freedom took many forms. It often began with girls simply walking the city streets in the evenings in the company of friends, male and female. Girls also went to dances in rented halls sponsored by community organizations such as lodges and fraternal organizations. Families monitored such affairs fairly closely, but dances or "rackets" held by youthful neighborhood social or pleasure clubs were much more open. Often the club charged admission, and all young men and women were welcome. "Extensive advertising and indiscriminate sale of tickets often brought crowds of seven hundred to eight hundred dancers to a single event." At such affairs, familial supervision and protection of young women was absent.

Many young working-class women did not attend such dances or enjoy other urban amusements alone. Because most girls earned little and turned over much of what they earned to their parents, girls counted on young working-class men to "treat" them to food and drinks at dances, ferry-boat rides to picnic sites, and admission to music halls and theaters. "Treating" could become courtship. In the crowded homes of working-class girls, it was difficult to find the privacy necessary for courting. Instead girls found it with the young men who treated them in more public places such as streets, dance halls, and theaters. However, treating also raised the issue of what young women would provide in return; would they extend sexual favors in exchange for the cost of dinner, drinks, or other entertainment?

> Caroline Wood, who charged a suitor with rape in 1858, seemed to have drifted—perhaps knowingly, perhaps unwittingly—into widening circles of erotic commitment. She had met the young man at a "place of amusement" and agreed to a rendezvous late one afternoon. As the pleasures he provided expanded from ice cream to an omnibus ride up Broadway to a boat trip to Newark to an excursion to the Jersey countryside, so did his sense of his sexual rights. By the time they left Newark, he had raped her, and by the time they returned to New York, he was introducing her as his wife.[71]

Some young women made a deliberate choice to provide sex in return for treating, but many young women "carefully guarded their reputations." Women who had steady boyfriends whom they intended to marry "might justify premarital sexual activity." But such a choice might be dangerous, for what if the relationship did not endure? For young working-class women, negotiating between the restrictions placed on them by their parents and church, their own desires for urban pleasures and relief from monotonous work, and the demands placed on them by young men was tricky. Many young women called upon female friends for help. Working-class young women often formed close friendships with girls their age with whom they shared confidences. Pairs of female friends provided protection for each other from unwanted male advances at dances and in other public places. Young middle-class women also made enduring same-sex friends, but as historian Kathy Peiss points out, those friendships existed in a privatized female world; in contrast, working-class girls relied on female friends in the public world of urban leisure amusements. Christine Stansell has shown how adult working-class women depended on female neighbors to provide them some degree of protection from abusive husbands.[72] Their daughters may have learned from them the value of friends in potentially dangerous encounters with men.

Working-class parents tried, not always successfully, to protect their daughters from early sexual activity, but parents did not do the same for their sons. Parents granted young men considerable freedom once they began working. Because working-class sons earned more than daughters, boys' earnings were especially important for family survival. Boys rarely had to negotiate for spending money as did girls. Instead, parents customarily permitted boys to contribute half the amount of their paychecks to the family for board and pocket the remainder for their own use. Working-class families needed boys' earnings too much to risk losing boys' support by restricting their activities. Moreover, parents knew that boys would spend most of their lives in the public world—in city streets, factories, and places of amusement—so why not let them become accustomed to that world early on? There had long been a double standard that permitted working-class men opportunities for sex outside of marriage but proscribed the same for their wives. Working-class men often spent evenings in saloons frequented by prostitutes, and this sexual freedom extended to their sons. Young men themselves cast about for ways to prove their manhood at a time when they still lived at home, not independently, and when most worked in subservient roles. "Youthful sexuality was the clearest addition to the roster of manly attributes. There is no question that heterosexual activity among young working-class men increased from the late eighteenth century. . . ." Parents felt differently about daughters, who had to be virginal to secure a husband, would live only temporarily in the public work world, and, after marriage, retreat to the more private world of family. Working-class parents' differential expectations of their adolescent daughters and sons are reflected in parents' reasons for sending their children to juvenile reformatories: parents sent girls because of fears about their sexual purity, and boys because they refused to contribute to familial support. (See chapter 7.)

Working-class boys who worked and dutifully contributed to their family's income usually still had enough money to enjoy many pleasures in Victorian-era cities. Some boys joined urban gangs, but "by the late nineteenth century, street gangs were increasingly being transformed into social or pleasure clubs throughout the working-class neighborhoods" of cities like New York. Clubs usually had fewer than 50 youthful members, who "met once a week in a rented hall, saloon, or tenement basement to discuss business and organize dances and entertainments. Other nights club members might gather in a cigar store or cafe to drink, smoke, play cards, and gamble." Young men spent much of their time in their own male subculture, "designed to prove masculinity through fighting, wenching, and sometimes drinking." Working-class young men frequented penny arcades "crammed with slot machines, phonographs, muscle-testing apparatus, automatic scales, and fortune-telling machines" or patronized music halls "where crude jokes, bawdy comedy sketches, and scantily clad singers entertained the drinkers." However, by the end of the century, working-class young men enjoyed more heterosexual leisure-time activities and accompanied working-class girls to dances, picnics, and summer outings to amusement parks.[73] For young working-class men, premarital sexual activity was probably even more common than it was for middle-class young men. Working-class men had easy access to prostitutes in urban areas, and the ability to "treat" young working-class women to urban amusements might secure young men sexual favors.

Most families who lived in the rural North and Midwest as well as those who moved west to the frontier developed the third mode of child rearing characteristic of Victorian America. Their methods of raising boys and girls were shaped by inclination and circumstance. Children raised in the rural North and Midwest and on the frontier experienced infancy much as did urban middle-class children elsewhere in the country. However, as they matured, many aspects of their childhood experiences resembled those of the urban working class, and some aspects—such as the role of fathers in farm children's upbringing—were unique. Child-rearing practices of well-off Midwesterners who mechanized their farms reveal that when farm families had the wherewithal to do so, they preferred to follow the urban middle-class style of raising children, not only in infancy, but throughout their youngsters' youth.

In the second half of the nineteenth century, the middle-class method of child rearing, which emphasized the uniqueness of childhood and the seclusion of youngsters within nuclear families controlled by mothers who provided loving training in obedience and self-control, spread beyond the northeastern cities in which this method had originated. Maternal associations disseminated the new ideas on child rearing. Beginning in New England in the 1820s, hundreds of these organizations formed in small towns and rural communities. The mothers who joined such organizations met to talk about how best to raise children and to discuss the latest literature on Christian motherhood. Women learned about this literature by either borrowing books from libraries established by maternal associations or reading articles in magazines published by the associations. "Like thousands of other women, Sarah Ayer joined a maternal society 'soon after the birth of my little sarah,' and recorded in her diary her hope that 'the metings have been profitable.' At stake, she considered, was the welfare, not only of little Sarah, but of 'generations yet unborn.' "[74]

Mothers on farms in the Northeast and Midwest considered child rearing to be their foremost obligation. Most families that migrated westward had also been exposed to the new view that babies needed to be lovingly nurtured and protected. As elsewhere in the country, mothers on the frontier assumed primary responsibility for child rearing. They worked hard to keep their infants and toddlers within their protective care. "An Arizona ranch wife insisted on taking her seven-month-old on a three-day mule trip, nestling the girl in a box set behind the saddle horn, and when a Texas sheepherder's wife lost her way looking for a stray cow, she wandered the entire night with an infant strapped to her chest and toddlers clinging to her skirts." This is not to say that mothers on either established farms or the frontier could devote all their time to child rearing. Mothers also hauled wood for fires, processed food, milked cows, "baked bread daily, kept a kitchen garden, and preserved vegetables and fruit." Mothers did not have as much time to devote to child rearing as did urban middle-class women, yet farm women considered child rearing their paramount duty.[75]

Like urban working-class women, farm women had large families. However, first in the Northeast and later on the frontier, farm mothers came to follow the pattern established by urban middle-class women and curtailed the number of children they bore. In 1860, on average, a farm woman in the Northeast bore 4.54 children, and in the Midwest or on the frontier, 6.66 babies.[76] However, as frontier farms gave way to more settled communities, fertility declined. In Sugar Creek, Illinois, the first generation of settlers averaged 8.2 children per family, and the second generation averaged 5.9. Historians have surmised that this change occurred when the amount of available farmland in rural communities diminished, and so it became more difficult to pass on land to large numbers of children.[77] The change may also have occurred because farm families, like prosperous families in cities, sought to invest more time and effort in raising fewer children.

Farm families were unique in that fathers on small farms probably devoted more time to their children than did either urban middle-class or working-class men. Farm fathers were chiefly responsible for raising crops and livestock and not for child rearing, yet they worked close to home, their children often worked with them, and during the winter months, after crops had been harvested and before spring planting, fathers spent considerable time inside with their families. Because men were with their children so much, men who operated small family farms had the opportunity to participate more actively in children's upbringing, at least until youngsters were old enough to hire out for wage labor on larger farms (see chapter 5). This pattern was less characteristic of fathers on the frontier. They helped out with child care when they could, but most were too busy building farms or working at wage-labor jobs to support their families to participate actively in raising small children. Frontier mothers, like middle-class mothers, raised boys and girls almost single-handedly.

Regardless of the section of the country, farms were comparatively isolated. This isolation meant that there were few distractions (such as the youth culture of street life in cities) to pull children away from their families. The influence of both mothers and fathers was strong in the lives of farm youngsters.[78] Individual responsibility was a value farm and frontier parents, like middle-class parents living elsewhere in the country, taught their youngsters. Inevitably, on isolated farms, children gained "an independence and self-reliance through the daily practicalities of coping with new situations. . . . One of Wallace Wood's earliest memories of his new Kansas home was of the 'long and solitary journey' across unfamiliar plains to take food to his father, who was breaking sod and building a house miles from their home camp."

Whereas teaching children independence was a goal of middle-class child rearing, few middle-class parents did so by sending their children on long and difficult errands. Such journeys left children unprotected—a practice that urban middle-class parents deplored but one that farm parents could hardly avoid. Even as frontier families sought to follow the middle-class model of child rearing, circumstances often prevented them from doing so. On farms and on the frontier, it proved impossible to protect the innocence of young-sters. Wherever there were livestock, boys and girls were often responsible for caring for them. Farm youngsters could hardly have avoided becoming aware of the methods of procreation. On the overland trail westward, in min-ing towns and on ranches close to army outposts, children might well come in frequent contact with heavy drinkers, gamblers, and prostitutes. "As a girl, Lizzie Moore gawked through knot holes in a friend's fence at the action in a saloon and in the shacks of the hurdy gurdy girls behind it." And although "Jessie Newton carefully investigated part of the Texas frontier before mov-ing his wife and children there, he found his neighbors 'as wicked a family as I ever seen. Thay follow swearing, drinking, fiting, fiddleing, dancing, and hors. . . .' " These physical circumstances of frontier children's lives approxi-mated those of the urban working class more than those of the middle class.

Certain qualities of the homes of farm and frontier families also resem-bled those of the urban working class. For example, there was little privacy in the first homes families built on the farming frontier. Most homes were one-room structures with beds on one side and a kitchen on the other. "One boy described his mother and sister dressing each morning in bed, then springing from their blankets so their dresses would quickly cover them." These first homes were often flimsy and not altogether safe for children. "Mice, cen-tipedes, and spiders seemed everywhere; snakes came out of the walls, dropped from ceilings into beds." As soon as they could, farmers tried to introduce some privacy and safety for children. "A first step typically was to add sleeping space, sometimes a small side room but more often a loft or half story for the children. When confined indoors, youngsters could play there out of the parents' way, and during cold stretches the rising heat would keep them warmer." Ultimately, most farmers sought for their children living quar-ters that were somewhat secluded and protected.

While such a goal brought farmers closer to a middle-class ideal of child rearing, there was one aspect of childhood on farms that was almost identical to urban working-class childhood. Parents expected farm children to help out in any way they could as soon as they were past toddlerhood, much as urban working-class parents counted on their children to work as soon as they were able.[79] By the age of seven, and sometimes before, farm children were assigned regular chores to do around the barnyard, and children also helped their mothers in the garden and in the house. "Since there was no certain sup-ply of labor outside the family, wrote one Midwesterner, 'the rule was, that whoever had the strength to work, took hold and helped.' " During lulls in farm work, there was always something more to do. One woman said of her father, "When the farm work was a little slack, we pulled stumps."[80]

Boys and girls experienced gender segregation in their work roles on farms. When farm children were small, their parents treated them similarly. Boys and girls performed more or less the same chores around the home and, on isolated farms, were more likely to play together than they were in cities and towns, where it was easier to find many same-sex companions. However, when children reached their teen years, parents expected girls to begin working almost exclusively with their mothers at domestic tasks inside the home, while boys worked in the fields and barns with their fathers. (See chapter 5.)

Regardless of where they worked on farms, youngsters inevitably encountered dangers that middle-class youngsters in more secluded and safe environments did not. The physical circumstances of farm life, while unlike those of urban working-class life, were still dangerous. Children fell down uncovered wells, stumbled into fireplaces and were burned, and fell from and were kicked by horses. In their inability to protect youngsters from such dangers, farm parents resembled working-class families.

Early on, working-class and farm children also learned the value of interdependence. Although farms might be far apart, farm families built a rich communal life through their churches and sometimes their schools. Families helped one another during illnesses and at harvest time. Children learned to respect and count on other adults in the community and other young people as well.

Parents on the frontier, like parents of all social classes in the United States, expected obedience from their children. Because many frontier families lived under economic stress, some parents took their anger out on youngsters by harshly punishing those they deemed disobedient. In small homes, on isolated farms, family members could get on one another's nerves, and "some adults responded by lashing out at those close at hand, and the smallest and youngest were the easiest targets." The strong presence of fathers in farm families was not always benevolent. Men who felt their children were not performing as they should might very well beat them. As among the urban working class, hardworking frontier parents expected children to obey promptly. Even the most benevolent of frontier families spanked children for threatening the family's livelihood by such actions as "letting cows into the cornfield."[81]

The child-rearing practices of farm families mirrored the practices of the urban middle class in some ways and the practices of the urban working class in other ways. Like middle-class parents, farm families believed in the uniqueness of early childhood, the singular responsibility of mothers for the nurture and training of youth, the importance of inculcating independence and self-reliance in young people, and the value of directing teenage boys and girls toward diverse roles: boys to breadwinning and girls to homemaking. Conversely, farm and frontier families also had much in common with

nineteenth-century urban working-class families. In both, parents could neither protect their many children from unsafe environments nor provide
them much privacy within the home. Interdependence, or learning to value a
network of friends and family, was a key value shared by working-class and
farm parents, and both also harshly disciplined youngsters who failed to
obey parental commands promptly.

This unique blend of child-rearing practices characterized most farm and
frontier families between 1850 and 1890. During and after the Civil War,
however, the child-rearing practices of one group of Midwestern farmers
became more like those of the urban middle class. By the 1860s, because of
the mechanization of farming, larger farms became more common in the
Midwest, and fathers on such farms spent more time away from home operating machines or supervising hired hands. As fathers spent less time with their
children, mothers devoted more time to child rearing even as they continued
to keep gardens, milk cows, and do housekeeping. Homes became more child
centered. Playrooms appeared in many farmhouses, indicating the importance of infancy and early childhood, and parents gave older children more
privacy than was usual on farms. By the 1870s and 1880s, well-off farm parents provided adolescent girls and boys with their own bedrooms—thereby
allowing them more freedom from the family, more independence. Girls did
less domestic work, and boys did less farmwork on progressive farms. Both
girls and boys devoted more of their time to education than did urban middle-class youths (see chapters 4 and 5). Yet even the children of the most
prosperous Midwestern farmers were rarely spared some farm chores. Girls
helped their mothers, and boys sometimes kept their own gardens. In this
way, their lives remained similar to those of other farm youths.[82] Nonetheless, the experience of prosperous farm families reveals that, when farmers
had the economic ability to do so, they replicated the child-rearing practices
of the urban middle class to a very large degree.

Whereas child rearing among whites on Northern, Midwestern, and frontier
farms was both like and unlike child rearing in the white urban middle and
working classes, the child-rearing practices of African-Americans were distinctive. The harsh conditions under which African-Americans lived, both in
slavery and freedom, markedly affected their methods of child rearing. Even
when there were similarities between the values taught by African-Americans
and white urban working-class parents, such as interdependence, respect for
elders, and quick obedience, African-Americans, of necessity, had a unique
rationale for inculcating these principles.

Between 1850 and the end of the Civil War in 1865, most African-
American children were slaves and lived in the South. Legally, slave children
took the status of their mothers. Owners acknowledged the mothers of children born in slavery but rarely recorded the names of their fathers. Among

former slaves, 18 percent to 20 percent recalled that they had grown up in female-headed families. However, most former slaves from various parts of the South remembered that they had grown up in two-parent households; they knew both of their parents and remembered their marriages to be long lasting.[83]

Whether they lived in families headed by women or by women and men, former slaves remembered their mothers as being primarily responsible for child rearing. Owners encouraged mother-child bonding, but so did the "slave community [where] motherhood ranked above marriage." Fathers were less important in child rearing. An analysis of narratives of former Virginia slaves reveals that 82 percent remembered their mothers to be physically present through "most of their childhood years, while only 42 percent recalled continuous contact with their fathers." Slave fathers often did not live on the same plantations as mothers, so youngsters saw their fathers only on their days off. Fathers were also more likely to be sold and separated from their families than were mothers—especially if the women were prolific and well-behaved.[84] In slavery, such conditions produced the female-headed household, which "while different from the matricentric cell of the polygynous African family, was sufficiently similar in physical structure—a woman and her children living together in a separate residence—that this phenomenon would not have appeared altogether alien to slave society." If fathers were present, their roles in child rearing grew as their sons and daughters matured. Fathers hunted and fished to provide their youngsters with extra food. If fathers had a skill, they passed it on to their offspring, teaching "their sons and daughters how to read and write, how to doctor and conjure, how to dance, sing, tell stories and make and play a variety of musical instruments."[85]

The centrality of mothers in the lives of slave children began in the children's infancy, when most mothers breast-fed their babies. However, unlike free white women of all social classes, slave mothers did not have exclusive care of their babies. Only a few weeks or a month after slave mothers gave birth, owners sent slave mothers back to the fields to work. Mothers had to leave their infants in the care of others during their work days. Most owners permitted mothers to take time off from work to nurse their babies three times a day, but slave mothers wanted to nurse more frequently. In a recent study of the growth patterns of slave children, Richard Steckel has shown that slave mothers were probably forced to give up breast feeding before their babies were six months old. Slave nurses then fed infants "pap and gruel," often from unclean bottles and spoons. Such a diet was deficient in protein, iron, and calcium. Not surprisingly, the death rate among slave infants was exceedingly high: in the antebellum era, among infants one month to four months old, 201 per thousand born to slave mothers died compared to 93 per thousand born to all other women.[86]

While slave mothers were working, either older children or elderly female slaves cared for their infants and toddlers. On large plantations, there were "chillun's houses" or "nurse houses" where one slave woman cared for many babies. She might or might not be able to provide them all attentive and nurturing care. One former slave remembered how slave children ate communally:

> Dere was a great long trough what went plum across de yard, and dat was where us et. For dinner us had peas or some other sort of vegetables and corn bread. Aunt Viney crumbled up dat bread in de trough and poured de vegetables and pot likker over it. Den she blowed de horn and chillen comes-a-runnin' from every which way. . . . Sometimes dat trough would be a sight, 'cause us never stopped to wash our hands, and before us had been eatin' more dan a minute or two what was in de trough would look like real mud what had come off our hands. . . .

Children had to fight one another to get enough to eat, and there were no second helpings of what was a meatless diet. Owners fed meat only to working slaves, thereby depriving slave children of protein necessary for proper mental and physical growth.[87]

At the end of each day, slave children returned to their cabins and the care of their mothers. Such cabins were small, usually fourteen feet by eighteen feet, and afforded little privacy. In them, slave mothers taught their children basic cooking and cleaning skills. Mothers also modeled religion, often through personal prayer. As one ex-slave recalled of his mother, "Me and my sister used to lazy around in the bed at night and listen to her and my aunt talk about what God had done for them. From this I began to pray like I heard them pray. . . ." Slave mothers also instilled in their children a love for learning and a longing for freedom. Mothers taught all these values to youngsters before they were between six and ten years old. At that time, childhood ended for slaves and they began to work full-time.[88] Like white working-class boys and girls, slave children had short childhoods.

However, unlike white children, slaves belonged to two family networks, one white and one black. White owners, and not just black mothers and fathers, had considerable power over slave children. Whites could sell children or their parents, thereby breaking up family units. Whites also undermined the authority of black parents in various ways. Some used cruelty to confirm the primacy of white power. Former Virginia slave Caroline Hunter remembered, "During slavery it seemed lak you' chillun b'long to ev'ybody but you. Many a day my ole mama has stood by an' watched massa beat her chillun 'till dey bled an' she couldn' open her mouf. Dey didn' only beat us, but dey useta strap my mama to a bench or box an' beat her wid a wooden paddle while she was naked." Such treatment may have led slave mothers to try to protect their youngsters by teaching them to keep away from whites. White travelers in the slave South often noted how African-American children fled from them. Other owners secured their power not with harshness but with generosity. Some gave children toys or treats their parents could not afford. Many assisted ailing slave children. "As R.R. Gibbes of Columbia, South Carolina, wrote in 1858: 'The kindness in sickness in seeing after the comforts of these dependent beings causes a strong attachment from early childhood towards their masters and mistresses; and this grows with their growth and strengthens with their strength.' " Yet even as slave children recognized the power of their white "families," slave children clearly understood that the black family network was of most importance to them. The enormous efforts made by former slaves to reunite their families when slavery ended indicates just how crucial to African-Americans were their parents and other relations.[89]

Out of choice and necessity, slave parents socialized their children to respect and depend on slaves other than just the children's natural parents. In western Africa, where most slaves or their parents or grandparents were born, lineage was of central importance, and families of "same-sex adult siblings with their spouses and children" lived together in compounds. The "parenting role was exercised by all adults." In the American South, slaves sought to re-create west-African patterns of lineage. Parents often named youngsters after grandparents, aunts, and uncles, thereby ensuring that members of the extended family would have a stake in the child's upbringing. Parents also taught youngsters to call older slaves "aunts and uncles" whether or not they were blood relatives. Because families could so easily be separated by sale and death, not only tradition but also practical considerations motivated parents to extend the network of kin, real and symbolic, that might be called upon to raise youngsters should their natural parents be unable to do so. In addition, in a society in which older slaves passed down family history, folklore, and proverbs orally, it was essential that youngsters learn to respect and rely upon the knowledge of their elders. Children themselves learned to be reliable when they took responsibility for caring for younger children while their parents worked. Parents also taught interdependence when they cautioned youngsters not to speak unless spoken to and not to repeat what they heard said inside their homes, "for a careless slip could bring down the wrath of masters on all."[90]

The most critical value slave parents taught their children was obedience—to their parents, to their real and "fictive" black kinfolk, and to their white owners. For no other group of children but slave children was learning to be obedient a matter of life and death. If a child did not obey an owner promptly, with a respectful and deferential attitude, the youngster could be killed. Parents taught obedience in several ways. They modeled it in their own behavior toward whites, and by insisting on unquestioned, swift obedience to themselves and other black kinfolk, they prepared children to obey whites similarly. As part of this process, slave parents often ordered their children around in the same manner as did whites, using loud voices. A white Southern woman observed: "[Slave parents] have a rough way of ordering [their children] around that sounds savage. 'Talk, talk. Why you not talk?'—in the most ordersome tone to the silent one." Slaves lived under authoritarian rule, and they taught their children the kind of unquestioning obedience such a system demanded.

To secure obedience, slave mothers and fathers did not hesitate to whip their children. From white owners, slaves learned that whipping was an effective way of establishing power, and by similarly chastising their children, slave parents not only taught their children to obey but also established their own power over their offspring. Corporal punishment was also a necessity for slave parents, who "had to teach their children how to survive in an extraordinarily dangerous world. They had little margin for error and could not permit their children to learn from their mistakes." Mothers also scared youngsters into obedience by telling them the slave bogey man, "Raw-Head-and-Bloody-Bones," would get children who misbehaved.[91]

Slave parents taught their sons and daughters the same values and raised them together, rarely separating work or play into masculine and feminine. Both boys and girls helped their mothers with household chores. As with white children, androgyny among slave children was reflected in their dress, although it was much simpler than that of whites. Throughout childhood, all slave children wore only "smocklike shirts or slips," sometimes made from large sacks with one hole cut in the bottom for the child's head and two others in the corners for his or her arms. Each youngster had one such garment, which was expected to last a year. At about the same age as white boys and girls gave up similar attire, so did slave children. Between the ages of six and ten, when slave children were old enough to work, boys donned shirts and pants, and girls received their first dresses. Yet boys and girls still worked together, first in "trash gangs" (see chapter 5) and later in the fields. Unlike most white girls in the nineteenth century, African-American girls in slavery were socialized to more than purely domestic roles.

However, many slave mothers, in common with white mothers of all social classes, were particularly concerned about protecting their adolescent daughters from early sexual activity. Some slave mothers insisted that their daughters wear very long skirts and meet men only in the mother's presence. Yet most slave parents, following the pattern of many African peoples, probably accepted early courtship and prenuptial intercourse. Herbert Gutman has found that many young slave women bore a child before settling into a permanent relationship with a slave man. Because slave owners highly valued women who were fecund, young slave women and their parents may well have realized that their families were less likely to be broken up if a young woman bore a child early. In addition, "two people contemplating marriage surely knew that they might be sold from one another. Doubtless they realized that if they had children early, their owners would have both economic and ethical reasons to allow them to remain together." If most slave mothers did not object to consensual unions between their daughters and men in the slave-quarter community, mothers greatly feared sexual exploitation of their daughters by whites. In a society where white masters had absolute control over all slaves, female and male, slave mothers were at a unique disadvantage. They could not prevent whites from sexually abusing their daughters.[92]

The problems of rearing children in slavery were serious and led to unique styles of parenting. The dilemmas faced by free African-Americans inevitably differed, but they were similar enough to produce considerable continuity in parenting methods. Before 1865 there were some blacks, mostly living in cities in the South, who had been freed by Southern whites, and some blacks who had been freed by Northern states in the aftermath of the American Revolution, but the vast majority of African-Americans became free only after the Civil War. At that time, most newly free persons took up share-cropping or rented land from whites in the South. Free black families deliberately chose to live together on farms apart from whites. After freedom, as before, most African-American children in the rural South grew up in two-parent households. Such families were large, often including six or seven children, who could, of course, soon make themselves useful as farmworkers.[93] Free blacks lived crowded into small homes usually no larger than those of slaves. Living close by were other kinfolk and friends. "Large extended families were dominant, anchored by married couples at the center, other relatives in close proximity, with augmented family members (those not related by blood or marriage) playing important roles in the family system." As share-croppers and tenants, blacks remained very poor. They relied on one another for help in hard times.[94] Thus, after slavery, African-American children in the rural South continued to learn the value of interdependency—to count on nearby kin and friends to help out in times of need, and to help out their families by themselves tending younger children and working on the farm as soon as they were physically able. As in slavery, their childhoods were short.

African-American children who lived in Northern and Southern cities before and after the Civil War also typically lived in two-parent families, although they were smaller than Southern rural black families. Fertility declined among urban African-American families for many reasons, one of which may have been the desire to provide for their children better. In cities, African-American men could usually obtain only low-wage jobs as unskilled laborers. Such employment was precarious. Steady work for black husbands was a rarity. To make up the shortfall in family income, many African-American wives also went to work, usually as domestic servants. Their jobs were low paying but much steadier than those of their husbands because cooks, laundresses, and maids were in high demand among the white urban middle-class. In impoverished African-American urban families, as in rural ones, parents expected children to help with child care and household chores—to learn interdependence. However, in cities, there were few paying jobs open to

African-American children, and their parents often preferred that children stay in school rather than seek full-time employment (see chapter 4). Impoverished urban African-American families may have had fewer children so that they could better support those few they had and invest in their future education. Black children raised in cities consequently may have had longer childhoods than African-American boys and girls living in slavery or on postbellum sharecropping farms. Urban black children also dwelt in slightly larger homes, usually including two rooms, one for sleeping and the other for cooking, washing, and entertaining.[95] Although these were an improvement over the one-room slave and sharecropping cabins, such homes still afforded children minimal privacy.

After emancipation, as before, while most African-American children lived with their mothers and fathers, a minority lived in female-headed households. Families headed by women were rare among white middle- and working-class women, but between 1865 and 1900, 25 percent of black households in Northern cities and 34 percent in Southern cities were headed by women. Of course, not all these families included young children. Elizabeth Pleck found that in Boston in 1870 and 1880, 12 percent to 14 percent of black youngsters under the age of six lived in fatherless families. This number is not too different from the number of former slaves who remembered living in families headed by women. Pleck believes this family pattern persisted because of the poverty of blacks and the anonymity of city life. High rates of unemployment among African-American men led many to desert their families. Conversely, employed black women were often willing to set up on their own rather than depend on jobless men. Among blacks who had lived in Northern cities for some time, the absence of community social controls that kept marriages together and punished adulterers also contributed to the formation of female-headed homes.[96]

The poverty of urban African-American families of all types and the unwillingness of whites to provide blacks access to many social welfare programs (see chapter 7) led urban blacks to rely, as did Southern blacks in slavery and freedom, on networks of kin and friends. Black urban families often included unmarried daughters and their babies. Premarital intercourse continued to be acceptable among African-Americans after slavery, and whereas in the rural South premarital intercourse was usually followed by marriage, the same was not always true in cities. Young women might reject marriage with unemployed young men, or the men might well refuse to form families with the young women they impregnated. Regardless, most children of such unions still lived within families where kinfolk helped raise them. Moreover, children who lived in female-headed households typically had grandparents, aunts, and uncles living nearby to help in rearing them. Black urban families also took in boarders, whom the families assisted in hard times, who in turn helped out as needed with child care. In addition, siblings and their families often resided near one another, baby-sat each other's children, and took in nieces and nephews when their parents were ill or unemployed.[97]

In city and country, in the North and South, in all types of free African-American families, child rearing was principally the responsibility of women, just as it had been in slavery. Yet free African-American fathers, unlike slave fathers, were clearly heads of their families. Fathers resided with their wives and children—not on adjacent plantations. On behalf of their families, fathers signed the annual labor contracts required of sharecroppers. Nonetheless, certain features of black life in post–Civil War America kept African-American fathers secondary to mothers in child-rearing responsibilities. Sharecropping and tenant fathers often had to work wage-labor jobs away from their families in order to earn enough to make ends meet. Urban fathers who lost their jobs often had to leave their families temporarily to find work. Unemployment and the consequent inability to support children put strains on black family life. Frequently, African-American mothers also found it difficult to devote as much time as they would like to child rearing. Immediately after the Civil War in the rural South, African-American mothers retired altogether from field work in order to devote more time to their families. As a married mother of 11 reported, under slavery she had "to nus my chil'n four times a day and pick two hundred pounds of cotton besides." She liked it better as the wife of a sharecropper. "I've a heap better time now'n I had when I was in bondage."[98] However, to survive, most black sharecroppers soon found it necessary to require all family members, including mothers, to work in the fields. Field labor was not compatible with child care. Mothers often took their infants with them to the fields and put them to sleep. One woman who did this found "a great snake crawling over the child." Others somehow had to persuade toddlers to play beside them in the fields, for unattended youngsters could fall and injure themselves or even drown in streams. African-American mothers who lived in cities preferred to work as laundresses in their own homes so that they could care for their children. However, many mothers had to take jobs as cooks or nurses for white families and leave their children at home because "white folks don't like to see their servants' children hanging around their premises." Black servants often did not finish work until 8 P.M., when they would return home and "have to scour the community for little ones who had gotten lost or fallen asleep in some tucked-away nook or cranny."[99] Many white middle-class children enjoyed the full-time care of their mothers at the expense of African-American youngsters. The sons and daughters of black domestics often saw their mothers only at night or on their days off because they were tending house for white middle-class mothers, thereby enabling white women to devote most of their time to child rearing.

Free African-American mothers certainly coped with difficult child-care problems, but the abolition of slavery also improved the lot of mothers and children. Free mothers, unlike those held in bondage, could choose to breast-feed their youngsters as long as they were physically able. Mothers were no longer forced to wean their infants early nor to put them in large nurse houses during workdays. Yet because of the problems posed by the need to labor both on farms and in cities, African-American mothers continued as freedwomen to rely on their older children to help care for the young. Mothers also had to call upon their female kin, neighbors, and friends for assistance in rearing children. Moreover, because of their poverty, free African-American mothers were not always able to provide their youngsters with a healthy diet. After slavery, many black children continued to suffer from nutritional deficiencies.[100]

The abolition of slavery did put African-American mothers (and fathers) solely in control of their own youngsters. No longer could white masters interfere with black parental authority. Nonetheless, the economic and political weakness of African-Americans vis-à-vis whites still made it necessary for black parents to teach their children deference and obedience to white authority. Youngsters had to learn how to react to racial slurs and how to cope with racial discrimination. In addition, the perennial need to rely on black kin and friends for economic aid meant that African-American children still had to be taught to respect and obey older black persons. Given the pressures of work and familial obligations, free African-American parents, like slaves and white working-class mothers and fathers, expected quick obedience from their children and enforced such obedience with corporal punishment.

Although parents of different social classes and ethnic and racial backgrounds raised their children in varying ways, all parents shared a common goal: to preserve the health of their youngsters. Parents faced almost insurmountable obstacles in doing so. In the second half of the nineteenth century, even children of "upper white-collar groups" did not have a much better chance of living through infancy than poorer boys and girls. "Thus richer and poorer children sometimes played apart, often were schooled differently, and usually looked ahead to different economic opportunities, but death took them democratically."[101]

According to the most detailed recent estimate of the death rate of children, 18 percent of the youngsters in the United States in 1895 died before they reached the age of five. The leading causes of child death were gastrointestinal diseases, respiratory diseases, and infectious diseases. Perhaps the most frightening was a gastrointestinal disorder named cholera infantum. Once a child contracted this "summer complaint," he or she had diarrhea for eight to twelve days. The youngster would vomit, become thirsty, but be unable to retain fluids. The child's body would grow thin, its belly large, its eyes sunken, and its skin white and cold. The child would cry continuously and eventually go into a coma and die. Today medical experts are still unsure about what caused cholera infantum (it may have been bacteria or a virus), but they do know the bacteria that caused most of the other diseases that claimed the lives of children in the past. However, the germ theory was new in the late nineteenth century, and Americans were slow to accept it. In 1900 there were only two effective drugs to prevent childhood diseases: smallpox vaccine and diphtheria antitoxin.

Although children everywhere were at risk, the death rate among children living in cities was higher than among children living in rural areas. Conditions on farms were not especially healthy; more children died in cities because they were crowded and contagion spread rapidly within them. The poorest children in cities were the most likely to die young. Death rates among African-American children were the highest: 25 percent of them died before the age of five. Children of the foreign born also suffered greatly: they died in larger numbers than did American-born white children.[102]

By the 1850s, Americans understood that cities were particularly unhealthy places, especially for children in the summer months. White middle-class Americans, who by this time viewed children as innocent and loving and undeserving of harm, especially lamented infant deaths. According to the medical theory of the day, a person's health depended on the interaction between physical constitution and environment. Ill health resulted from the failure of one's body to adjust to one's environment. Infants died in larger numbers presumably because their bodies were weak and unable to adapt to their surroundings.

Between 1850 and 1880, Americans tried to solve the infant-death problem by bettering the environment. Cities cleaned and paved their streets, improved garbage removal, constructed better water and sewer systems, rehabilitated poor neighborhoods, and regulated housing. When by 1880 none of these measures had substantially reduced infant mortality, reformers and doctors turned to a second solution; they would improve the diet of infants, for poor diet surely weakened infants' bodies and made them less likely to withstand harsh environmental conditions.

Improving infant diets was of special interest to doctors in the new field of pediatrics. The first course in pediatrics was taught in medical schools in 1860 by Abraham Jacobi, a German émigré who became America's leading pediatrician. The specialty was slow to develop; few doctors were interested in treating children because so many died inexplicably. Doctors found it troublesome to diagnose illness in patients who could not explain their symptoms well, and the treatments of the day did not help ailing youngsters much anyhow. However, by the 1880s, specialization in medicine was proceeding apace, professionalism was well accepted among the middle class, and children appeared especially deserving of treatment by select medical professionals. Most major cities had children's hospitals where doctors could, for the first time, obtain clinical experience with children. Pediatricians specialized in the whole child, not in just one part of the body or illness as did most doctors. Because there were few therapies for child illness, prevention seemed best. To gain the confidence of parents, pediatricians sought to prove the value of medicine to child rearing by arguing that illness could be prevented by proper infant feeding—supervised by doctors, of course. Few mothers could afford such close medical supervision, which entailed having a pediatrician discover the right infant formula for a baby; but concern about diet, particularly about the milk children drank, did bring about improvements in the milk supply in cities.[103]

In the mid-nineteenth century, commercial dairies supplied milk to cities, but it was often contaminated by the time it reached consumers. "Many rural cows were sick with tuberculosis or other communicable diseases that ultimately were transmitted to consumers, especially since rural dairymen took few sanitary precautions. They commonly milked cows whose flanks and udders were caked with mud and excrement that often fell into the milk. If they washed milk pails and cans at all, they more often than not used dirty or contaminated water. They also allowed the cans to stand uncooled in barns or at roadside pickup points." In cities, grocers often tried to mask contaminated milk by diluting it with water or by adding adulterants. In the 1880s, states began to pass laws to curb watering and adulterating milk, but such laws did not prevent "bacterial contamination." By this time, in Germany, physician Robert Koch had isolated and cultivated bacteria. From 1877 to 1890, researchers identified the bacteria that caused "malignant edema, typhoid, cholera, pneumonia, tuberculosis, diphtheria," but researchers did not know how bacteria were transmitted or how to prevent their transmission. In 1887, a researcher in Massachusetts began to monitor water for bacteria, and soon milk was identified as a carrier of germs as well. Yet it seemed impossible to regulate the thousands of dairies that supplied milk. In the 1890s, in several cities, philanthropists and governments set up milk stations that gave out pure milk to impoverished mothers. These stations did not solve the health problems of infants, because mothers who were employed or who had many children could not pick up milk as required—on a daily basis. Mothers used milk stations only when their children were already sick. It was not until the early part of the twentieth century that pasteurization (heating milk to kill germs and then cooling it rapidly) substantially diminished the bacterial content of milk. Pasteurization may have been one factor that led to the dramatic drop in the infant death rate after 1910.[104]

Between 1850 and 1890, given both the poor quality of milk and doctors' lack of knowledge about how to treat childhood diseases, mothers agonized over how to raise healthy children. Fortunately, most mothers breast-fed their infants, and we now know that breast milk provides babies with natural immunities to disease. Those mothers unable to breast-feed could purchase nursing bottles in pharmacies: "in 1845 Elijah Platt of New York patented a rubber nipple that eventually replaced the ones made of pewter, ivory, or silver. And by the 1860s a commercial baby formula was available." However, feeding infants by hand and not by breast was a viable alternative only for middle-class mothers. Milk that had been certified by doctors as pure cost twenty-five cents a quart in an era when laborers earned a dollar a day. Refrigeration was also expensive: immigrants had to pay five cents to ten cents a day to fill their iceboxes with ice. In the summer, if bottled milk was not refrigerated, it went bad by midmorning.[105]

Most mothers and doctors believed that children began to experience serious health problems only when dentition began. This belief was probably right, because when teething started, breast-feeding usually ended and so too did the health protection breast milk provided. Teething children were also old enough to walk and might pick up "unhealthful bacteria both indoors and out."

Medical remedies for infant disorders were few. "The most common employed treatment for [teething] was to lance the gums and give the child something hard to chew on." For intestinal disorders such as cholera infantum, doctors recommended "a dose of rhubarb and magnesia, and if that failed, purging with calomel." With good reason, some mothers distrusted doctors and hospitals as well. Ailing children who entered such institutions often contracted additional infections. In 1894, a mother objected to doctors taking her child, sick with smallpox, to a Milwaukee hospital. A sympathetic crowd of persons who knew that another of the woman's children had died in the hospital prevented a second from being carried to the same institution. Most middle-class mothers appreciated the value of smallpox vaccinations, but many foreign-born mothers did not understand their purpose. Foreign-born mothers often feared that vaccinations were poison and refused to allow their children to have them. The high death rate among immigrant children may have been in part due to the fact that few were vaccinated.[106]

Mothers were chiefly responsible for the health of their children, and most mothers spent long hours tending sick youngsters. Despite mothers' best efforts, their babies often died, and mothers and fathers mourned their infants' passing. Parents of different social classes and religious, racial, and ethnic backgrounds dealt with child death in various ways. Middle-class parents adopted elaborate funeral rituals when their youngsters died. They wrapped their babies' bodies and kept strands of their hair and pictures of them as well. Such rites helped parents work through their grief, but many people also sought an explanation for such meaningless suffering. Protestant authors "assured bereaved parents that children who died in infancy were preparing a place in heaven for family members who had been receptive to their purifying influence and that in death they would once more be reunited as a family." These reassuring ideas first became popular in the North before the Civil War, and families who moved to the frontier in this era shared such beliefs. Nonetheless, parents of children who died in the West often blamed themselves for endangering their child's health and lamented the child's death in a strange place, far from home and friends. In contrast, many working-class parents were fatalistic about the deaths of their infants; parents expected some children would die.[107] By 1875, insurance companies were selling large numbers of working-class parents policies that protected the lives of children under 10 years of age. Middle-class persons complained that this was insurance against the loss of child labor, but in fact, working-class parents used the insurance money to provide their youngsters proper burials. A nice burial was a sign of affection for the child. Sociologist Viviana Zelizer believes the popularity of insuring children "suggests that working-class parents adopted the middle-class cult of child mourning. The sentimentalization of childhood cut across social class distinctions; the sacred child was mourned with new intensity even in the poorest homes."[108] Such mourning was not common to all ethnic and racial groups, however. Among Mexican-American Catholics, a child's death was often a time of celebration rather than sorrow, for they believed a baptized baby went directly to heaven. Slaves coped with infant death by relying on the west-African belief that a baby born after the previous one had died was the first infant returned to life. Thus slaves often named a new baby for one that had previously died, although they waited a while to do so in order that "the spirit should have a chance to familiarize itself with . . . [the] locality before it is pegged down."[109]

Between 1850 and 1890, middle-class city dwellers, commercial farmers, and Southern plantation families redefined childhood as a separate, extended, precious time of life—a time to shelter and protect youngsters and provide them loving nurture. Material prosperity allowed such parents to assuage their concern for their youngsters' future by keeping them in school throughout their youth. However, most American families, including African-Americans living in slavery and on Southern sharecropping and tenant farms, white working-class parents in cities, and white farmers and frontiersmen, out of both choice and necessity treated childhood as a relatively short period when youngsters were in training for adult chores.

Although the mothers of poor urban- and rural-born children were as central to their lives as mothers from more wealthy backgrounds were to their youngsters' lives, lower-income mothers had huge familial and work obligations and could not devote all their time to child care. Lower-income mothers also did not have the economic wherewithal to shield their youngsters as fully from physical or moral dangers in the larger world outside the home. Slave mothers operated at the greatest disadvantage—they had the least time to spend with their babies and the greatest difficulty in safeguarding children from abuse.

Virtually all fathers, regardless of economic status or ethnic or racial background, spent less time with their children, especially during infancy, than did mothers. However, the experience of urban middle-class children and white farm youths (except those living on the frontier) was somewhat unique, for their fathers often tried to be companionate. For white middle-class boys preparing to enter the working world and their sisters seeking prosperous mates, the considerable economic resources of their fathers could be especially helpful. Of course, middle-class fathers sometimes wielded such economic power to keep their children dependent, and forced dependency made some boys and girls rebellious. Conversely, working-class fathers were often dependent on the earnings of their children. Parental economic need gave employed children more power and often afforded working-class sons and daughters the freedom to participate in urban youth culture. Among all nineteenth-century fathers, slaves faced the greatest limitations. Many slave fathers were unable to participate actively in rearing their children because male slaves lived on neighboring plantations apart from their families. Other male slaves sold by their owners lived far from their families and were unable to function as fathers. However, freedmen quickly established family homes and exerted more patriarchal control over children.

Using census records, historians have proved that virtually all nineteenth-century American children lived in nuclear, rather than extended, families. Nonetheless most youngsters, including those in slave, white and African-American working-class, and Southern planter families, learned to rely upon and respect other kin, neighbors, and friends of their families. Even middle-class girls who grew up in nuclear families learned to value interdependency through their female friends and relatives of their mothers. Only middle-class urban boys in their late youth learned to value individualism above interdependency. Thus, the inner-directed individual of the nineteenth century described by David Riesman was probably atypical. Most youngsters were raised not to think first of themselves, but to be respectful of and responsive to the needs of family, neighbors, and friends.[110]

As most parents trained youngsters to interdependency, so did they also expect obedience. All families employed corporal punishment to enforce obedience, but parents who had the least time to teach their children and the most dangers from which to protect them regularly resorted to spanking and whipping. African-American parents in the South instructed their children rapidly and harshly in order to protect their lives. Urban working-class parents required prompt obedience in order to safeguard their children from the omnipresent dangers in city streets. Although it might seem more appropriate for all parents living in a democratic society to educate their youngsters to obey voluntarily, many parents in nineteenth-century America had not themselves been raised in democracies. Immigrant parents who had previously lived in authoritarian states or African-Americans who lived or had lived under authoritarian rule as slaves were most accustomed to and most willing to use corporal punishment.

The majority of American children learned interdependency and obedience and also gender-appropriate behavior. When children were very young, parents raised boys and girls together, but by late childhood parents treated their sons and daughters differently. Virtually all parents accorded sons but not daughters occupational choice and sexual freedom. African-Americans were the exception: in slavery white owners and in freedom economic necessity required African-American girls to work outside the home and to continue to do so throughout their lives. All parents sought to shield their daughters from sexual experience prior to marriage, although urban immigrant parents and slave parents, who had minimal control over their environment, were least able to do so.

Finally, all parents struggled to raise healthy children. Urban-born babies, especially those who were African-American, died in the greatest numbers, but no child was truly safe from disease. The state of medical knowledge at the time and the unhealthy conditions in which most people lived meant that all parents faced the very real possibility that one or more of their children would die before reaching maturity.

Even as parents faced this unpleasant prospect, most remained optimistic and sought to provide their children with not only the basic necessities of life but also an appropriate education. In child rearing, class, race, and occupation had the most impact on how any particular family raised its children. In the next chapter, we shall see that the section of the country in which a family lived was the most decisive, though not the only, factor in determining the amount and type of schooling a child received.

4

Education for All?
Schooling in an Expanding Nation

Access to free, tax-supported public schooling was a privilege enjoyed by a majority of youngsters in the United States between 1850 and 1890, thanks to the efforts of a dedicated group of reformers. After midcentury, these reformers succeeded in disseminating their philosophy of universal schooling beyond the Northeast to the Midwest, West, and South by calculatedly appealing both to common religious, economic and political beliefs, and to fears many parents shared about the future. The new public schools created by reformers and parents differed considerably, but by the end of the century, teachers, texts, and educational methods were remarkably similar everywhere in the country. Most youngsters studied under the tutelage of female instructors. In virtually all schools, youngsters learned their lessons by memorizing textbooks. Teachers, textbook authors, and parents expected youngsters to learn obedience, punctuality, self-reliance, and competitiveness, while at the same time they acquired the ability to read, write, and do basic math. Beyond these commonalities, educational experience diverged considerably. The amount and nature of education any particular child received varied by geographical location. A child growing up in the urban North, Midwest, or West typically spent more months and years in primary, grammar, or high school than did a child coming of age in the rural North, Midwest, or West, and a youngster who lived in the South had the least opportunity for an extended public education. Moreover, within each of these three locales, class, ethnicity, race, and gender also affected the amount and quality of education children received.

In the eighteenth century, there were a variety of schools in the United States, including charity schools for the poor, subscription schools run on a

Rural school class in Richfield, Pennsylvania (1888-1900). As in most nine-teenth-century rural communities, this school class is small (27 students) and includes youngsters of varying ages. Since there are more boys than girls in the picture, it was probably taken in the winter when boys had little farm work and more time to attend school. One of the two young women in the back row is probably the teacher. Like most nineteenth-century rural school teachers, she is not much older than her pupils. (U.S. View Company, Library Company of Philadelphia)

fee basis by individuals, private academies, and some district schools funded by taxation.[1] In the North, enrollment in such schools before 1840 was siz-able.[2] However, with some exceptions, most schools were neither free nor open to all children. In the 1830s, 1840s, and 1850s, public school reformers such as Horace Mann, Henry Barnard, Catharine Beecher, Emma Willard, and Mary Lyon sought to convince states and localities to create free public schools, supported by local taxation and administered by local lay boards of education, for children of all social classes. Common-school reformers were Americans of British descent, Protestant, white, and middle class. They spread their ideas by traveling, speaking, and writing on the value of the common school and by corresponding with and quoting one another. Newspapers, which depended for their survival on a literate citizenry, published reformers' speeches and reported on common-school proposals presented to state legislatures.[3]

Advocates sold citizens on the worth of the common school by appealing to accepted religious, political, and economic beliefs. In the mid-nineteenth century, most Americans were Protestants, and many had been touched by religious revivals that encouraged individuals to work together to bring about the millennium, or the thousand-year rule of Jesus Christ on earth. In the 1820s and 1830s, evangelical Christians established Sunday schools in many parts of the country to provide instruction in moral values to children of various social classes. Sunday schools helped convince Americans that school reformers were right: if the United States was to prepare for Christ's second coming, then all Americans had to learn similar moral values, not just on Sundays, but five days a week in common schools. As Sunday schools had shown, these values could best be communicated through biblical teaching.

Politically, school reformers reminded Americans that a republic such as theirs depended on each individual's behaving in a moral, upright manner. There was no king nor any other external power to force citizens to behave in certain ways. Moreover, no republic could survive unless its citizens were literate enough to read about and elect good leaders. Common schools would educate Americans to be moral and literate.[4]

Last, reformers geared their arguments to a capitalist economy. They appealed to Northern industrialists and Midwestern farmers who depended on a mobile wage-labor force that arrived at work on time, in a sober condition. Both industrial and agricultural capitalists understood that owners and workers and their children must recognize the sanctity of property, value competition, and endorse promotion based on merit rather than social connections. Common-school reformers made a powerful argument when they contended that only if children of all social classes learned such principles when young, in school, would the capitalist economy survive.[5]

Even as they appealed to shared beliefs, common-school reformers also touched on the fears of many Americans about their country's future. Reformers warned that the Republic was new and fragile, that it might not survive unless schools trained children to sacrifice for the good of the whole. Common-school reformers appealed to American-born whites' fears of Irish and German immigrants, who flocked to the United States in the 1840s. Many people believed that immigrants were lazy, drunk, and immoral, and worried that their offspring would undermine the Protestant, capitalist republic by following in the footsteps of their parents. In addition, prosperous Americans worried that the poor, who had become more numerous in economic recessions in the 1820s, 1840s, and 1850s, might fail to raise their children to be moral, industrious citizens. Common-school reformers responded to such fears by arguing that public schools would educate immigrant and poor youngsters to common values and regular habits of work.

Between 1840 and 1860, common-school reformers won approval of the public school because their religious, political, and economic arguments made sense to most Americans. Protestant farmers throughout the North and West endorsed the religious goals of common schooling. Many farmers also agreed with reformers that the agricultural republic could be kept intact only by individuals trained to common values. Farmers in the Northeast who had switched from subsistence to dairy farming and farmers in the Midwest who had switched to commercial grain production were acutely aware that their children required language and mathematical skills to survive as agricultural capitalists or, if need be, to make the transition to industrial, urban employment.[6]

As for city dwellers, by the 1840s and 1850s, industrialists in the North and Midwest, concerned about urban crime, poverty, and disorder, agreed that schools could provide them with an obedient, law-abiding, and literate labor force. In urban or suburban areas, white native-born middle-class parents, who kept their children at home through their teens, hoped that public schools would keep children safe and appropriately occupied for much of each day, teach youngsters the same moral principles parents valued, and equip their sons with skills necessary for middle-class employment and their daughters with the ability to rear the next generation properly. White urban working-class men also endorsed public schools. By the 1830s, workingmen had gained the right to vote without a struggle with government. Most viewed institutions, such as schools, sponsored by government as beneficial and willingly used them to prepare their children for citizenship. Artisans recognized that industrialization was making many skilled jobs obsolete, and they hoped that schools would train their children for alternate forms of employment.[7] Immigrants hoped common schools would prepare their children for citizenship and employment. Most foreign-born parents recognized that common schools would not prevent them from passing their own culture and values along to their sons and daughters in their homes and churches. Yet because public schools were so relentlessly Protestant in their teachings and relied on English as the only language of instruction, some immigrants dissented from the common school. Beginning in the 1840s, first Irish and German Catholics and later Catholics of other nationalities, often at great personal sacrifice, built an alternate, parochial system of schools in Northern and Midwestern cities.[8]

With the exception of these Catholics, in the rural and urban North, Midwest, and West, common-school reform appealed to most white men regardless of class. However, because the common-school argument sought to preserve a republican government and a capitalist economic system, we may wonder why the idea of the common school appealed to white women,

who could neither run for government office, nor vote, nor to any significant degree participate in the paid labor force. Middle- and working-class white women living in the North, Midwest, and West endorsed public schools because they provided girls with the same education offered young men. Schools also opened new careers to women—first in teaching and later in clerical work. Educators granted white women equal education partly for religious reasons (women's souls were equal to those of men in the eyes of God) and partly for practical reasons: administrators found it too costly to build separate schools for boys and girls. Educators also discovered that youngsters behaved better and acquired greater respect for members of the opposite gender when they studied together in coeducational classrooms.[9] Moreover, by midcentury, women were the principal child rearers, and as such, they required education to be able properly to train future citizens to morality.

African-American men and women also endorsed public education, although the common-school ideology was seemingly not applicable to them any more than it was to white women. The political and economic arguments for common schools popularized by reformers before the Civil War in the North, Midwest, and West did not apply to blacks, who could not vote in most Northern states and held the lowest-wage jobs in the economy. Common-school reformers gained white females' support of schools by awarding women egalitarian education, but reformers treated blacks as inferior and either denied them access to or segregated them in public schools. Nonetheless, African-Americans believed that only through education would their children achieve social advancement, and hence blacks pressed for equal access to public schools. In the antebellum South, where common-school reform was not especially successful, slaveholders denied blacks any education, and blacks began to identify the ability to read and write with freedom and opportunity.[10] Consequently, in the post–Civil War era, Southern blacks joined Northern blacks in support of common schooling for all.

Besides immigrant Catholics, many antebellum Southern whites found common-school reform unappealing. Although most were Protestant, they were not particularly interested, as were Northern and Midwestern Evangelicals, in working together through schools to achieve religious goals. Southern whites did not agree that public schools were necessary to sustain the republican form of government, but preferred to rely on families and private schools to instill the moral values that Northerners and Westerners hoped public schools would teach. Like the North, the South was capitalist, but Southern white planters relied on slaves, not on free wage labor. Unlike Northern businessmen, Southerners did not feel education would make their workforce more productive.[11] Enjoying virtually absolute control over slave workers, Southern planters did not require schools to teach the next generation of workers values that promoted voluntary submission to their economic superiors.

Although white Southerners and some Northern immigrant workers opposed common-school reform, its supporters far outnumbered its detractors. By 1850, among all ethnic and occupational groups, enrollment of children between five and nineteen years of age in public schools stood at 50 percent. By 1870 enrollment had risen to 60 percent in the Northeast and to 61 percent in the Northwest (Ohio and west). The South was exceptional and the only part of the United States where "judging from enrollment figures in 1860 and 1870, the average southern child was more likely not to attend a school in any given year than to attend one."[12]

In the late nineteenth century, the experiences of the thousands of children who attended public schools were remarkably alike. Nearly all children learned their lessons from female teachers. Before the Civil War, when school sessions in rural and many urban areas were short, young men often taught temporarily between terms in college or while seeking more permanent employment. However, after the war, when urban educators lengthened the school year and when more lucrative employment opened to young, educated men, women increasingly replaced men in the classroom, first in cities and later in rural schools. At a time when child-rearing literature exalted women as morally superior and best able to develop good habits in young children in the home, it seemed appropriate for women to do the same in school. As disciplining children more by moral suasion and less by corporal punishment became the rule in middle-class families, so too did mild discipline, such as that administered by women, seem appropriate in school. Of course, there was another, practical reason for employing female teachers: in both rural and urban schools, women were paid considerably less than were men. As demand for public schools spread, taxpayers who supported costly school-building and expansion programs economized by staffing classrooms with women.[13]

Teaching attracted women, even if it was low paying, because it was a professional occupation in an era when few such jobs were open to women. Teaching required an education that was readily available to females in public schools. Training was minimal. Some teachers attended training institutes in cities for a few weeks in August, and others enrolled for a year or two of normal school, which was the equivalent of the first two years of high school.[14] Yet because there were few normal schools (not until 1900 did every Western state and territory except Wyoming have one), many teachers had little education beyond grammar school. Most women began teaching after they left school, in their teens or early twenties, and remained in the job until they married, or about 18 months to three years. Women had no incentive to prolong their careers in education to achieve promotion to administrative jobs. School boards reserved such posts for men, because members shared the social belief that women were secondary to men and should always remain under male supervision.[15]

Children raised almost exclusively by their mothers probably found the transition to school easier in a classroom monitored by a woman. Youthful teachers, not far removed from school themselves, probably related well to youngsters. However, teachers' lack of experience and short tenure in the classroom meant that few had prepared lesson plans or become skillful in explicating difficult concepts. Partly because of their youth, inexperience, and lack of training, nineteenth-century teachers created their lessons almost exclusively from textbooks. Teachers expected students to memorize letters, words, paragraphs, and rules and recite these back exactly as written. Teachers rarely explained ideas but instead acted as "drillmasters."[16]

In all schools, the main subjects taught were spelling, reading, writing, and math; math was the last subject taught, usually only to students nine years old and above. Youngsters also studied some geography, literature, and history. The method by which students learned to read depended on the textbook used in their classroom. If it was Noah Webster's *American Spelling Book,* students memorized each letter of the alphabet first, then began to spell words of varying lengths. There were no passages to read in the first one hundred pages of the book. A woman who attended school in Illinois in the 1850s and 1860s remembered, "If one were a good speller, he was noted throughout the community much as a strong man was noted. He was pointed to with pride." However, if the text of choice was by William Holmes McGuffey, children learned to pronounce syllables first and, after each pronouncing lesson, completed a short reading exercise. In either case, teachers drilled students in letter recognition or pronunciation. Older students read passages aloud, and the teacher simply corrected their pronunciation. Rarely did she discuss the meaning of a passage or ask students to do so.[17]

As for writing, teachers emphasized the graphic rather than the creative. Rarely did they assign compositions. Instead teachers usually instructed pupils how to use a pen and copy words and then corrected the students' mistakes. In rural schools without pens, ink, or copybooks, teachers made pens and concocted ink for their students and then wrote passages that the youngsters copied on paper or slates. In better-equipped urban classrooms, teachers "sometimes explained how to hold a pen, how to sit, how to place the paper, and how to hold the arms in order to produce a perfect copy."

Math was also taught by drill and, as with reading, the way a student learned depended on the choice of text. In books by Nicholas Pike and Thomas Dilworth, math lessons began with rules that students memorized and then applied in doing problems. Teachers assigned and corrected problems; they rarely explained the rules. In contrast, authors Warren Colburn and Joseph Ray emphasized not rules but object lessons to prepare students to perform mental arithmetic. A lesson from an elementary Colburn text reads, "If you have two nuts in one hand and one in the other, how many have you in both?" Teachers using Colburn or Ray organized exercises for their classes in the manner of a New Jersey instructor of the 1860s. "She stood facing the class . . . and began an exercise in mental arithmetic, the plain purpose of which was to train us to fix our attention and to follow with concentration . . . 3 plus 2 minus 1 divided by 2 multiplied by 4 plus 1 divided by 3 plus 2 divided by 5 is how many?"

With this form of education, most children probably acquired basic language and math skills in four to six years of regular school attendance. Most children did not learn to think for themselves. Classrooms were not very intellectually stimulating places. Youngsters probably acquired good handwriting, which was a prerequisite for almost any professional job; they acquired math skills useful to accountants and bookkeepers; or they developed the mental arithmetic ability of cashiers and salespersons.[18] But schools did not stimulate creativity. For many young people, employment was probably a more attractive and certainly more profitable way of spending time than in the rigid, unappealing learning environment of primary and grammar schools.

In reading, math, and all other subjects taught, textbooks were essential, and their content changed very little during the nineteenth century. In many rural classrooms, students simply used the texts their parents had retained from their youth. When and if a school district adopted a new textbook, publishers helped schools continue to use the old textbook by keeping the page numbers the same as in previous editions and adding new material at the end. Between 1850 and 1890, the ideas texts purveyed to students changed little. Virtually all readers included passages exalting the rural life of independent farmers (not of Southern planters) and contrasting such virtuous, moral living to life in the city. "Innocence and virtue prevail in the country, artificiality and vice in the city: 'The town for manners, the country for morals.' " While these sentiments may have been "natural in a society in transition from a rural to an urban life,"[19] they may also have reflected the late-nineteenth-century market for textbooks: most students who required them attended rural schools. Certainly, students who lived in farming areas found more to identify with in texts, more to support their rural way of life, than did urban youngsters.

Textbook authors also identified virtue exclusively with Christianity. Like the common-school reformers, textbook authors were staunchly Protestant and committed to the idea that Americans were the chosen people of God. Before 1870, texts directly condemned Catholicism, labeled the Pope a "hoax and conspiracy," and called the Catholic Church greedy for money. After 1870, textbooks still exalted Protestantism but less frequently condemned Catholicism. Perhaps, as disaffected Catholics founded parochial schools, schoolmen realized the danger of driving Catholics from public schools and pressed for moderation on religious matters in texts.

Throughout the century, textbooks were explicitly racist. They categorized all peoples of the world by their color, ranking whites at the top and African-Americans, "the least civilized of all the races," at the bottom. Several books depicted God creating blacks first, realizing his mistake, and then creating whiter persons. Both before and after the Civil War, textbooks condemned slavery, but they were not optimistic about the political and economic future of freed persons. Textbooks negatively depicted not only African-Americans but also Irish and Italians. Textbook authors labeled the Irish lazy, poor, evil, and too fond of drink. Italians were described as "artistic but degenerate" and identified with crime and immorality. Among all nationalities, only the Swiss and the Scots garnered totally complimentary descriptions, perhaps because their Calvinistic faith was so close to that of New England, home to most textbook authors. They made fewer comments about Germans and generally viewed them favorably because of their thrift, industry, inventive ability, and faith in a common-school system.[20]

Textbooks most confirmed the identity of native-born white Protestant children, who were in the majority in many parts of the country. Youngsters from Swiss, Scots, and German backgrounds also found much to flatter them in texts. Conversely, Catholics, African-Americans, and children of Irish and Italian extraction must have been shamed and humiliated to repeat textbook passages that denigrated them and others like them before teachers and classes. Anti-Catholic and racist material in texts also encouraged the white majority to belittle members of the Church of Rome, African-Americans, Irish, and Italians. The racism and xenophobia that characterized so much of white America in the late nineteenth and early twentieth centuries was a direct product of teaching in the country's public school system.

Through their use of textbooks, teachers conveyed skills and social beliefs to youngsters, but teachers taught values even more explicitly in the ways they arranged and managed their classes and rewarded and punished students. After 1850, in most urban and many rural classrooms, students sat at individual desks facing the teacher. Often a teacher expected youngsters to look only at their books and speak only to her. Students were not to look at or talk with one another. Teachers also expected students to learn their lessons independently and not to help one another. In these ways, schools encouraged students to think of themselves as individuals and to become self-reliant by learning on their own without help from friends.

Individual competition was also a constant in nineteenth-century schools. In rural areas, teachers held weekly spelling bees in which youngsters stood in a line before the teacher (toed the line) and vied to be at the head of the line rather than at the foot. Teachers also held speaking contests in which students competed to recite material they had memorized. There was even competition to enter local high schools, for students had to pass exams to gain admission.

Respect for private property was another value emphasized in school. Teachers expected students to treat classrooms and books with appropriate care. Stealing or defacing books and writing on school desks or walls were offenses that teachers punished harshly.

Obedience to the teacher's authority was of prime importance because it served to preserve social order. As a national commission of school administrators observed in 1874: "The student has an obligation to his teacher . . . in order that he may be prepared for a life wherein there is little police-restraint on the part of constituted authorities." Demanding conformity to authority in the classroom (and in the home) was a way of preparing youngsters to support "the legal order of things" without compulsion once they were adults. There were often physical rituals associated with obedience and conformity. A visitor to a New York school in the 1860s said: "Down would go all the slates and the work of ciphering would proceed . . . as the work was completed . . . the slates would pop up against the breast, one after another; and when a boy was called upon to explain, up he would jump, rattle off his explanation, and then thump down again amongst the perfect stillness of the rest. . . ."

By the 1850s, teachers in rural and urban classrooms meted out somewhat different punishments for misbehaving. In rural classrooms, especially when men were in charge, punishment was often physical, and teachers sometimes prominently displayed switches. Female instructors relied more on humiliation by using "lazy boy's corners, [and] dunce or wisdom stools." In urban classrooms, female teachers rarely punished physically but instead elicited appropriate behavior by using status, recognition, rewards, and fear of humiliation. Urban female teachers ranked students daily or monthly, and those with the highest marks had the honor of sitting farthest from the instructor. Report cards, which appeared in many cities by the 1850s, 1860s, and 1870s, were another way of recognizing students' successes and failures. Teachers rewarded students with prizes. Some boys and girls, however, suffered humiliation by being held back a grade or by being sent to "ungraded classrooms, usually in basements, or in separate schools to house the academically incompetent and indolent."[21]

The rigid order and strict discipline of nineteenth-century schools were partly a function of the fact that neither teachers nor students remained in school for long. Most students attended only for about five years, between the ages of 10 and 14, and most teachers served no more than three years. Often, when values and principles must be communicated quickly, as in the military, they are drilled into recruits by regular discipline. Military discipline is justified on the grounds that soldiers need to learn quickly how to defend their own and their fellow soldiers' lives. There was a similar sense of urgency about schooling in the nineteenth century. At a time when the United States was barely one hundred years old, when it had experienced a bloody and divisive Civil War, vast economic expansion accompanied by unemployment, depressions, violent labor disputes, and large-scale immigration of persons from dramatically different cultures, there appeared good reason to quickly train all American children to self-discipline and restraint. Ironically, the very methods used to instruct may well have encouraged students to leave school early to seek employment, thereby reinforcing the necessity for continued education by drill.

While much that went on in the classroom was the same throughout the United States, the opportunity to enroll in or attend school regularly, for how long and in what type of classroom, varied considerably in different sections of the country. So too did the degree of control that parents exerted over education. Within each part of the United States, the class, race, ethnicity, and gender of youngsters also affected their schooling. Among the regions, however, there was little unity based on any of these variables. In other words, a white boy from a prosperous farm family living in the North or West had quite a different experience of schooling than did a white middle-class boy living in a city in the same regions, or than did the son of a Southern white planter. Because most Americans in the nineteenth century resided on farms and, as late as 1890, 70 percent of all children enrolled in rural schools, it is appropriate to begin discussion with such schools, first in the North, Midwest, and West and second in the South.[22] In the South, because of the structure of class and race relations, rural and urban education developed differently than elsewhere in the country. The last topic discussed will be urban schools in the North, Midwest, and West.

By 1850, public schoolhouses were common in the rural Northeast, but not until after 1860 did farmers in the Midwest and Far West create tax-supported schools. Many of these new settlers had themselves been born in the Northeast and received a common-school education there. Some settlers used that education to tutor their own children at home. Others enrolled their sons and daughters in subscription schools. Not all settlers were immediately willing to create universal, tax-supported education because of the uncertainty of farming in newly settled regions, where the population was transient and few people had yet accumulated savings from a succession of profitable harvests. By 1860, most Midwesterners put aside their worries, convinced by common-school reformers in their region that publicly supported schools were necessary to preserve a Protestant, republican, capitalist country. By 1880, settlers in the Far West had established schools equally accessible to youngsters.

In the North, Midwest, and West, it was local residents, parents of potential students, who created and administered rural schools. Parents designed the school year to suit farm-labor needs. In rural areas, the winter term did not begin until after the harvest was in, some time between September and November, and ended when it was time for children to help plant the next year's crop. The spring or summer term commenced between March and May, once fields were plowed and new crops planted, and ended when harvesting began. The length of each term was about three to four months, but farmers adjusted terms yearly depending on the vagaries of local agriculture.[23]

Because parents controlled rural schools and made certain that schools accommodated farm-labor needs, large numbers of children entered schools every year. In 1860, throughout the North and West, more children (aged five to nineteen) of farmers than of nonfarmers enrolled in school.[24] Between 1860 and 1880, more children in Massachusetts were enrolled in rural than in urban areas, and in 1890, there were more youngsters enrolled in the largely rural Midwest than in the more urbanized Northeast. Schools in rural areas were in session only when children had little work to do on farms. At such times, parents were probably pleased to have youngsters out of the home and in school, and children themselves were probably glad to escape from their isolated farms and join their friends in the sociable atmosphere of the country school.

Although yearly enrollment totals were high in the rural North and West, attendance of children was irregular—more so than in cities.[25] There are several reasons for this disparity between enrollment and attendance. Because farm children usually had to walk a considerable distance to their schools, children frequently did not attend in bad weather. Moreover, because farm families were highly interdependent, whenever a youngster was needed to help out at home, as when a parent or sibling was ill, then the schoolchild missed school. Transience was also high in many farm communities and may have contributed to irregular attendance. However, the chief reason why enrollment was higher than attendance in rural schools was that teenage boys who enrolled for the winter term often did not return at all for the summer term because they had to help plow, plant, and harvest crops.[26]

On Northern and Western farms, seasonal demands for the labor of boys age 15 to 19 help to explain the large number of them still in school when most urban-born boys of the same age were employed full-time. Of course, in the rural North and West, as elsewhere in the country, the typical student was not a teenager. In 1860, 75 percent of children attended school between the ages of 10 and 14, but over 50 percent of farmers' older teens and only about 40 percent of nonfarm teens were still in school. Because so many farm boys missed school terms for work, boys continued to enroll for more years than did girls, who customarily did not do field work and so attended both summer and winter sessions. Because farm girls were in school more months every year than were farm boys, many girls dropped out by the age of 14, when they had acquired basic language and math skills.[27] Moreover, most 14-year-old farm girls were fully employed year-round at domestic labor, while farm boys of the same age had little to do in the winter months after the harvest and before the spring planting. In the winter, when there was little else to do, teenage farm boys continued to attend school to acquire a basic education and to meet their friends.

In 1860, in Northern farming areas even more than in cities, the wealthier the parents, the more likely their teenage child was to be in school. Wealth and class impacted on rural schooling in the North and West largely among teens; poor and rich parents were equally likely to send young children under the age of nine to school. Poor parents required the labor of their teenage sons and daughters on farms and withdrew them from school. Conversely, the most prosperous farmers were more likely than well-to-do parents in cities to keep their children in school. On farms, wealthy fathers could hire poorer boys and girls to replace the labor of their natural children. In parts of the Midwest where agricultural modernization had advanced the farthest, parents may have felt especially anxious that their older sons obtain an education to equip them with the language and math skills they needed to manage mechanized farms or to find employment in cities.[28] There were certainly a greater variety of good urban than rural jobs available to sons of prosperous parents, which also helps explain why boys from affluent urban families were less likely than their rural counterparts to remain in school into their late teens.

In the rural North and West, children of prosperous parents were especially likely to attend school, and so too were children of the native born. Just as wealth affected children's school attendance, so did ethnicity: there was a greater disparity between the attendance of immigrant and native-born children in cities than on farms. In the North, more children of Irish-, Scots-, and Canadian-born farmers attended school in 1870 than did children of the same nationalities whose parents had nonfarm occupations.[29] Of course, it was difficult for foreign-born children who did not speak English to fit into public schools anywhere in the country, but at least in rural sections of the North and West, where parents exerted so much control over schools, immigrant parents might influence public-school education:

De facto if not de jure, immigrants dominated public schools where they constituted sizable enclaves in Wisconsin. There were 15,000 Belgians across three Wisconsin counties who effectively controlled their own rural schools with French-speaking teachers only. In many German settlements only German was used in the classroom, in school board meetings, and in keeping records—a practice that persisted in some places down to World War I.[30]

Even in rural areas where immigrants were not in the majority, they may have been more willing than urban immigrant parents to send their children to public schools. Owing to the short terms of farm schools, immigrant farmers knew their children would spend more time at home learning their language and culture than they ever would in school. Immigrant parents in cities, where public-school terms were much longer, could not be so assured.

Rural parents assumed responsibility for building and furnishing schools and hiring and housing teachers. There was little bureaucracy in rural education. Of course, some farm families had more power than did others. Those who owned land made decisions; before the 1870s and 1880s, tenants in some parts of the Midwest could not vote on school matters. The number of tenants in rural areas varied considerably, but in 1860, 80 percent of families in the Northeast, Midwest, and on the frontier owned the land they farmed. Those families built the schools their children attended. In Iowa, Kansas, and Nebraska, early schools convened in parents' homes or in "an abandoned soddy or dugout."[31] When enough taxes had been collected, rural parents constructed rectangular, frame school buildings and painted them white like the parents' own homes. Most Midwestern schools did not have privies until the 1890s, and then, like most farms, they had only one. In schools without privies, boys and girls went out the school door in opposite directions and relieved themselves in fields or woods. A typical rural school consisted of one large room in which children sat on backless benches. When taxpayers could afford to pay for improvements, teachers installed individual desks. Younger children often sat in the front of the classroom; older children sat in back. Youngsters helped teachers stoke the stove and clean the classroom, much as they helped their parents at home by performing similar chores.

Rural schools often doubled as community centers or as churches on Sundays. Parents who built schools had a real stake in them and watched over them closely. On Fridays, parents and other members of the community often came to school to observe children reciting or participating in spelling bees. Teachers also organized annual programs or picnics where children demonstrated what they had learned to parents.[32]

Rural teachers were often young people from the community who shared the values of parents who hired them and knew the local children.[33] Teachers boarded with families of schoolchildren and thus could be closely monitored by parents. During the winter terms, when so many teenage boys attended, parents often preferred to employ male teachers, who, though more costly than women, were physically better able to discipline youths. In the 1850s and 1860s, parents hired females only to teach summer sessions. However, after the Civil War, young men proved as disinclined to teach in rural schools as elsewhere, and women took men's place. In the 1870s, 56 percent (and by 1900, 73 percent) of public teachers in the 10 North Central states were women.[34]

The children who filled rural classrooms varied in age from two or three to twenty years of age. When school was in session, parents preferred to send all their children who were old enough to walk the necessary distance and not needed at home for farmwork or housework. Whole families of children attended and studied together in ungraded rural schools. Boys and girls occasionally sat apart, but they learned the same subjects and recited together before the teacher. Early in each session, the teacher examined youngsters and placed them in groups based on ability rather than age. Because most rural school districts could not afford to purchase textbooks for all children until the 1880s or 1890s, teachers made assignments for individual children in whatever textbooks boys and girls could collect from their families and bring to class. Once youngsters finished a book, they went on to another. They proceeded at their own pace and received considerable individual instruction from the teacher, who customarily examined each student in several 10-minute recitation periods during each school day. When not reciting, youngsters studied on their own and listened to their sisters, brothers, cousins, and friends recite.[35] Rural schools were sociable places. However, for the youngster who did not speak English, school could be a frightening, confusing place. Older, foreign-born children might be assigned to lessons with very young, native-born boys and girls. This experience could be embarrassing in formal recitations before the teacher.

Children who attended rural schools learned basic skills and moral values as did children in elementary schools elsewhere in the country. Rural children acquired vocational skills not in school but in the fields with their fathers or in the farmhouse with their mothers. Parents prized obedience above all other values. Parents taught obedience at home, and they expected it to be taught in school. In rural areas where, inevitably, children roamed about fairly freely, parents worried that such freedom made their youngsters too wild and uncontrollable unless they were sharply restrained both in school and at home. An unruly youngster thrashed by a teacher at school was likely to be punished for the same offense at home by parents.[36]

Rural schools were communal institutions that reinforced communal values. Parents controlled these schools: parents built and equipped school buildings and employed teachers known and liked in the community. As for the children themselves, for most, the rural schoolhouse was not a threatening place but almost an extension of home. The teacher was a young person with whom many of the students had grown up; she played with them at recess and lived in one of their family homes.

In the late nineteenth century there was also a downside to rural education in the North, Midwest, and West. Local control meant that poor communities had poor schools. In fact, facilities were primitive in most rural schools. "In a decade of teaching in several districts of three Kansas counties, Martha Byrne knew only three schools with anything but dirt floors. . . . As for educational tools, a blackboard typically consisted of two or three painted planks; chalk often was picked up from nearby streambeds." Teachers were young and often did not know too much more than many of their pupils. Teachers taught from textbooks that varied depending on what their students happened to bring in to school. Children whose parents were poor and uneducated and lacked schoolbooks to pass down to their offspring probably did not attend school at all. In ungraded rural schools, youngsters obtained only an elementary education. There were very few high schools in rural areas. Children who were small in stature or not too bright might be ridiculed by others when they recited. Those who did not catch on to their lessons quickly, for whatever reason, had to keep repeating these lessons in the same texts—a discouraging prospect.[37] And for those children who did not have siblings of school age or lived in isolated areas and were unaccustomed to interacting with others of their age, rural schools could be lonely and frightening places.

In the North, Midwest, and West, rural common schools were far from perfect, but by the 1860s, they did at least exist throughout the region. In the predominantly rural South, public schools were a rarity before the Civil War, and even afterward, they were not as universal as elsewhere in the nation. Between 1850 and 1890, public schooling was both less accessible to and less accepted by children and their parents in the South than in any other part of the United States.

This is not to say that the South was without schools. Even before the Civil War, in the South as in the North and the West, there were a variety of schools, including academies maintained by religious groups, subscription schools (some in log cabins known as "old field schools"), and charity schools. Yet all these schools served only a fraction of the white children in the region and virtually none of the black youth. Before the Civil War, the only group of Southern youngsters who had certain access to education were the sons and daughters of white planters. These children began their education at home studying with mothers and tutors, attended local subscription schools for their elementary schooling, and enrolled in private boarding schools when they were between 10 and 14 years of age. Southern white planters sought to raise their sons and daughters in a protected environment (see chapter 3), but on plantations parents could not fully prevent contact between their children and slaves. Sending youngsters away to private, white, same-sex boarding schools in the South or Northeast was part of a protective child-rearing strategy. Boys and girls studied many of the same subjects, but only in boys' schools were Latin and Greek offered, and only in girls' schools could students learn needlework.[38] By 1850, a tradition of inequality in the education of white boys and girls in the South had been established that would persist throughout the remainder of the century.

Before the Civil War, the common-school reform movement that resulted in the creation of tax-supported public schools throughout the North, Midwest, and West did not have much impact on the South. In the antebellum years, North Carolina, Alabama, Kentucky, and Louisiana were the only Southern states to establish schools supported by public taxation. Common schools proved unpopular in the South for several reasons, the most important of which was race.

Southern whites believed that in a slave society education could not be universal; it had to be denied to blacks. By the 1830s, Southern states passed laws forbidding any person from teaching blacks—and forbidding blacks from learning—to read and write. Those few slaves who did manage to learn in secret were often whipped. The official punishment for learning to write was to cut off the forefinger of the slave's right hand. Powerful white Southern planters who controlled state legislatures feared educating slaves, who might then become dissatisfied with their lot and rebel. Such planters also saw no economic or other advantage to themselves in educating slaves. Most slaves were field hands, and they would not become much more productive by learning to read and write. Unlike Northern children, who might profit themselves and others when they went to work either on mechanized farms or in factories if they knew how to read directions or calculate how much seed or fuel to order, slaves had to perform only physical labor.

Slavery also influenced the attitude of white Southern planters toward universal common schooling for whites. Planters depended for their very existence on slaves and cotton or some other cash crop, and not much on the skills of Southern white workers. Planters had little incentive to tax themselves to create common schools for all whites.[39] Naturally, planters did not require public schooling for their own children because they could afford to send them to private schools.

Before the Civil War, there were a few Southerners, especially "among the white yeomen of the Piedmont—people whose economic circumstances and religious world views were more similar to those of northern rural populations than they were to those of prosperous slaveholders," who supported common-school reformers such as Calvin Wiley in North Carolina and Robert Breckinridge in Kentucky. But by and large most Southern white farmers did not feel public education was worth the cost: they did not want to pay school taxes. Many distrusted the idea of government providing education for their children and preferred to educate their sons and daughters on their own or in schools of their choice. By the 1850s, when the South and North grew increasingly at odds, white Southerners came to identify common schools with Northern abolitionism and industrial capitalism. It then became virtually impossible for Southerners to support public schooling.[40]

Before the Civil War, the one group of persons in the South who developed a strong desire for free public education were slaves. When the war began, only 2 percent to 5 percent of adolescent and adult slaves were literate. Those few who learned to read and write did so in secret, and for them the experience of becoming literate was unique. Slaves "viewed reading and writing as a contradiction of oppression" and "literacy and formal education as means to liberation and freedom." When the war ended, slaves regarded education as a sign of freedom from slavery, as a chance to take their destiny into their own hands, and "as a safeguard against fraud and manipulation" by whites.[41]

During Reconstruction, Southern freed persons, Northern white religious groups, and the federal government (operating through the Freedmen's

Bureau) worked to provide free education for blacks (see chapter 2). These groups were somewhat successful: in Southern public schools, enrollment of blacks between five and nineteen years of age rose from virtually zero before the war to 20 percent by 1880. Uncounted others were enrolled in Sunday schools operated by black churches, where children also learned to read and write. Blacks were determined that the universal free public education they had long sought would endure after Reconstruction. With the help of white Republicans, blacks wrote into the new state constitutions created during Reconstruction that states would provide all citizens a free public education. By 1872, all Southern states had statewide, tax-supported systems of public education.[42]

However, between the 1870s, when Reconstruction ended, and 1890, Southern public schools never came to equal rural or urban schools in the North and West in quality or popularity. "In 1890, per pupil expenditures in southern public schools equalled only 43 percent of the average outside the region. The average length of the school year was ninety-two days, two months shorter than the average elsewhere." Southern children studied in poorly equipped classrooms and spent less time in school than did children who lived elsewhere in the country. In 1870 the proportion of all children aged five to nineteen in school was 60 percent in the North and 35 percent in the South. By 1890, the total public-school enrollment rate was over 61 percent in the Northeast, Midwest, and West, but just 53 percent in the South.[43]

Compared to schools elsewhere in the country, public schools in the South remained underfunded and underenrolled because they were not as heartily endorsed by parents of all social classes and races. Unlike in the rest of the country, common-school reform came to the South as a consequence of war. Liberating the slaves permitted them to press for free public schooling and to obtain it with the assistance of Northern white Republicans. It is no wonder that once elite whites resumed control of Southern state governments at the end of Reconstruction, they were unwilling to improve and expand schools, especially for blacks. Middle- and lower-class whites used the schools, but at least by 1890 neither ardently supported them nor tried to alter them much. Freed persons continued to use the schools, but they too became discouraged by the schools' poor quality and their failure to enhance opportunity for most children who attended them.

From the time the Civil War ended until 1890, Southern white planters did not enthusiastically endorse free public education for all Southern children—black and white. Southern planters continued to believe, as they had before the war, that blacks who were agricultural laborers did not need to know how to read and write. Planters felt, as Carl Schurz noted in 1865, that "learning will spoil the nigger for work." However, once public schools were established during Reconstruction in the 1860s and 1870s, Southern elite whites, who resumed control of Southern state governments between 1869 and 1877, found it impolitic to abolish the schools. Because many blacks had challenged the myth of their inferiority by becoming literate, to maintain faith in white superiority, all whites needed the opportunity to become educated as well. Thus the Southern planter elite did not abolish public schools, but neither did they appropriate much money for them.[44] Not many Southern planters were interested in taxing themselves for a public educational system to which they sent few of their own children. The white Southern elite still enrolled their sons and daughters in sex-segregated private schools, as they had before the Civil War. These schools continued to offer girls a less demanding curriculum: unlike boys, girls in private schools rarely studied Latin, algebra, geometry, or Greek. The tradition of sex-segregated private schools in the South carried over into the public arena, so when public high schools opened in this region, they were not only reserved for whites but also segregated by sex. Officials appropriated less money for the girls' than for the boys' divisions. In the South, unlike in the rest of the country in the late nineteenth century, most young white women from prosperous families did not receive an education equal to that of young men. Southern white women's experience, as well as that of blacks, confirms that segregated schools are rarely equal.[45]

Although initially skeptical about the value of common schools, the majority of Southern whites, most of whom were farmers, came to accept free public schools—as long as farmers controlled the schools. The development of such schools in Virginia after the Civil War closely parallels the evolution of public education in the rural North and West before the war. One difference is that rural white Virginians did not seek to create public schools; they came as a consequence of Reconstruction. But once state officials announced that free schools were a privilege that local farmers could choose to use or not, farmers endorsed common schools. The schools Virginia farmers constructed were small and blended into the landscape. They were furnished simply, as were rural schools elsewhere in the country. Based on labor needs, farmers chose when it was convenient to open and close school sessions. As in the rural North, attendance was irregular, and older boys customarily came only during the winter. Virginia farmers also chose their own teachers, most of whom had been born and lived in the community where they taught. By the 1880s, most of the teachers were women. Such teachers, like others in the country, relied heavily on textbooks for instruction. Because most texts were written by New Englanders and contained unflattering statements about the South, Southern teachers coped by pinning together the pages they disapproved of and forbidding children to read them.[46]

Southern rural whites controlled their local schools in much the same way rural parents did in the North, Midwest, and West, yet Southerners proved less willing to send their youngsters to these schools. In 1890, 67 percent of Midwestern children of school age (five to nineteen years) were enrolled in public schools, but only 48 percent of Southern white children attended school. Youngsters in the South also spent fewer days in school each year than did children living in other sections of the country. There are several reasons for these differences. In all agricultural regions, child labor came before education, but in the South, most white farmers were poorer than their counterparts elsewhere and may have depended more on the year-round labor of their children. According to William A. Link, historian of Virginia education: "For the average rural Virginian school took second priority." Moreover, farming in the South was less mechanized than in the Midwest, so fewer Southern farmers had the financial ability to send their children to school for extended periods or felt that their children required education to become successful agricultural capitalists. Most Southern farmers, white and black, were tenants or sharecroppers who stood little chance of improving their lot and had to perform hard physical labor simply to remain solvent. "Agriculture in the South generated no demand for skilled or literate workers of any color. Once established, such an agricultural system also left little room for educated whites. As a result, the poor white's incentive to educate himself was suppressed nearly as effectively as the black's."[47]

Poverty and pragmatism also influenced the attitude of low-income Southern whites about schooling provided to their children by Southern textile mills. Mill owners in various parts of the South built their own schools as a way of attracting responsible workers from the countryside. Mill owners employed children as well as adults and kept the schools open only when the mills did not require much child labor (see chapter 5). Yet even when mill schools were open, parents often did not take advantage of them. In parts of North and South Carolina, attendance in mill schools was lower than in other public schools in the area. Poverty is part of the answer: mill workers required the income of their children to survive. Mill owners who supplied families with housing expected them to furnish a worker for every room they occupied. Practicality was also an issue. Mill schools were not vocational. For their children's sake, parents often felt it better to take the youngsters out of school and bring them to help parents on the job, thereby preparing boys and girls for future employment.[48]

After the Civil War, African-Americans had the greatest faith of all Southerners in the value of public schools. Once Reconstruction ended, however, a series of events undermined some of that faith. From the time public schools were founded during the Civil War, they were segregated by race. For African-Americans, segregation was not necessarily objectionable. Black parents could and did choose the location of their own rural schools, build and supply them, and select the teachers to staff them. African-Americans also exercised considerable control over the day-to-day operation of their schools. Blacks did not segregate by sex as did Southern whites, partly because this practice was costly, and partly because they saw no necessity for it; black boys and girls who had been raised together and labored together in slavery might as well attend school together. Unfortunately, once Reconstruction ended, segregated black schools—although they were coeducational—were at a disadvantage. White landowners and urban business leaders now took control of education, and they had little interest in spending much on black schools. Black parents still had the same powers over their schools, but whites now allocated less money to the construction of black schools than white schools and less money to pay the salaries of black teachers than white teachers. Black schools rapidly became overcrowded. In 1900 the average black school in Virginia held 37 percent more pupils than did the average white school. In some parts of the South, such as Atlanta, blacks fought the cuts in financial support to their schools.[49] However, once African-Americans lost the right to vote, as they did in most parts of the South in the 1890s, they had little power to prevent white politicians from slashing their schools' budgets.

> In Alabama, for example, the annual reports of the state superintendent ceased reporting expenditures by race at just about the time when whites were pressing to deny blacks the vote, in 1891–92. Before then the per capita expenditures per year for teachers' salaries had been roughly equal—and low, ranging from $.82 to $1.20—blacks typically receiving a dime to a quarter less. When the superintendent resumed reporting by race, in 1907, whites were receiving $5.05 per capita and blacks $.89.[50]

African-Americans not only lost financial support for elementary schools but also had little opportunity for public secondary-school education. Between 1880 and 1920, no public high schools were built in the South for black students, except in a few Southern cities where blacks had the support of whites who believed in separate-but-equal education to preserve racial harmony. There were a few private secondary schools, maintained by religious groups and missionary societies, for African-Americans, and such schools offered education comparable to that in Northern secondary schools. However, many poor African-Americans who sought to teach school or obtain an education in a trade turned to Hampton Institute in Virginia or Tuskegee Institute in Alabama. Both schools claimed to offer inexpensive but useful education to black students; actually, they offered something rather different.[51]

Samuel Chapman Armstrong founded Hampton Institute in 1868 and was its principal until his death in 1893. He and other Southern whites who hoped to promote industrialization in the South did not reject education of blacks as many Southern planters did but instead "viewed mass schooling as a means to produce efficient and contented labor and as a socialization process to instill in black and white children an acceptance of the southern racial hierarchy." Armstrong and other proponents of the New South hoped that if they trained black teachers to respect manual labor, such teachers would do the same with black children in public schools throughout the

South. In this fashion, blacks could be socialized to accept their status as agricultural laborers; education would promote acceptance rather than rejection of their lowly station in life. To accomplish his goals, Armstrong and his disciple Booker T. Washington, who later founded Tuskegee Institute, admitted students who had less than an elementary education. Pupils performed manual labor around the school so that they could appreciate the value of such work and "so that they would have no problems in teaching the 'dignity of labor' ethic to children of farm laborers and servants." In Hampton classrooms, black students also learned that they were 2,000 years behind whites in terms of culture, hence the discrimination they faced was not unjust but appropriate. After graduating with the equivalent of a 10th-grade education, Hampton students dispersed throughout the South to teach black children this philosophy of hard work and cultural inferiority. Writers for black newspapers criticized Hampton, as did black educators. Nonetheless, between 1880 and 1900, schools such as Hampton Institute, known both as "industrial schools" because they prepared pupils for manual vocations and as "normal schools" because they prepared young people to teach, proliferated in the South.[52]

African-Americans reacted negatively to the many setbacks to their educational advancement in the South from the 1870s to the 1890s. Although enrollment of blacks in Southern schools grew from 10 percent in 1870 to 20 percent in 1880 to between 30 percent and 34 percent in 1890, only in Mississippi did approximately half of black children between ages five and seventeen enroll in 1875 and 1880. Elsewhere, the proportion of black students in most Southern public schools did not match that of whites. The reasons for this disparity in black and white enrollments are many. Blacks attended schools that were grievously overcrowded. In 1873, white schools in Georgia held an average of 164 students, and black schools held an average of 575 students. In overcrowded classrooms, black children probably received little of the personal attention they needed to help them learn to read and write. Because most came from families where parents were former slaves and hence illiterate, students could receive little help with their lessons at home. Such children needed more attention at school but might instead have a teacher who had graduated from an industrial normal school and emphasized the importance of doing the laundry or chopping wood rather than of spelling and reading. Of course, the families of most black Southern children were wretchedly poor and often in need of their help in the home or fields, so children probably could not attend school very regularly—thus adding to the frustration of their learning experience. At home their parents taught interdependence, and black youngsters probably appreciated that if it was necessary to work to help the family, then they would have to sacrifice their education. Perhaps it did not seem that much of a sacrifice in an agricultural society where to become a tenant farmer or sharecropper, the chief prerequisite was physical strength, not an educated mind. Moreover, when Southern blacks observed the few educated black men they knew, they did not see persons who had become independent landowners or artisans because such jobs were closed to blacks, regardless of their education.[53]

Before we conclude that most African-Americans gave up on education in the South by the 1880s and 1890s, we need to examine one anomaly: black parents sent more of their daughters to school than their sons. The difference was largest among children over 11 years old. Had black parents concluded that schools were inadequate and literacy difficult and perhaps useless to attain, they surely would have kept all their children out of school. Parents may have enrolled more of their older daughters than sons because boys' labor in the fields was so necessary to black family survival and because, for girls, school was an alternative to domestic service, an occupation in which girls were subject to sexual abuse by whites. Another, positive reason for keeping older girls in school was that education prepared them to become teachers, and by 1890, 52 percent of black teachers in the South were female. Teaching was a respectable job for black women and virtually the only occupation open to them besides domestic service and field labor. During Reconstruction, most teachers in black schools were men, because teaching was the one professional job open to them other than the ministry. However, when whites took over Southern school systems, they replaced black men first with white females and later, when blacks objected, with black women, who were "less threatening to the racial caste system" than were black men. Thus black parents may well have kept daughters in school to help them avoid domestic service and prepare for something better: teaching. Still, only a fraction of black parents made this choice. In 1890, in all age-groups, more white girls and boys attended school than did black girls.[54] Yet the fact that Southern black parents enrolled more girls than boys in school indicates that when schools proved useful, a substantial minority of African-Americans in the South would make the economic sacrifice necessary to send their children to school.

Public schools in the urban North were not fashioned by parents of various backgrounds working together in localities, as in the rural North, Midwest, and West, nor by African-Americans in cooperation with the federal government and Northern missionary groups, as in the South, but rather by one group of city dwellers: members of the white, native-born middle class. They conceived of public schools as a method to control and socialize children of the poor and immigrants and as a way both to protect their own children and to prepare them for the future. Urban schools developed in a distinctive fashion, and city dwellers, middle class and working class, black and white, native born and immigrant, responded to them variously.

Bostonians had already developed their public school system by the late eighteenth century, but other northeastern and Midwestern cities did not

Room 5, Lincoln School, Pittsburgh, Pennsylvania (1896). As in most cities by the late nineteenth century, this school class is large (46 children), age-graded, and coeducational. Northern urban schools were segregated until after the Civil War, when most, like this one, integrated black children into formerly all-white classrooms. The teacher is a young white woman, as were most nineteenth-century urban educators. (Library Company of Philadelphia)

form common schools until the nineteenth century. In the 1830s, 1840s, and 1850s, when common-school reformers launched their campaign for public schools, huge numbers of immigrants from Ireland and Germany arrived and settled chiefly in large northeastern cities. Some arrived with a nest egg and a skill they could develop, but many others were wretchedly poor and unskilled. After the Civil War, the same was true of immigrants who flocked to American cities from southern and eastern Europe. At about the same time that immigration increased, American businessmen began to streamline production of many products. In factories, businessmen expected workers to be punctual, industrious, and obedient to authority. To prosperous native-born urban whites, poor immigrant children were both a present and future menace. The urban middle class worried that such children grew up in dirty, overcrowded neighborhoods, spent too much of their time in city streets, and might well turn into criminals rather than into hardworking, industrious citizens. To prevent these eventualities, urban white middle-class businessmen supported the creation of public schools to socialize and Americanize poor and immigrant children.[55]

Middle-class parents were also acutely aware that the new industrial economy was quite volatile. It was certainly possible for them and their children to move up the social scale, but it was also possible for them to lose their savings and even to go bankrupt in a depression. Thus middle-class parents were anxious to prepare their sons to earn a living in more than one way and daughters to rear children regardless of their family's circumstances. Youngsters who attended public schools acquired good language and calculating skills, which might prepare them for many contingencies. Public schools were advantageous to middle-class parents in another way as well. At a time when they sought to keep their children protected from infancy and childhood through to adulthood, the common school could be the parents' ally. It offered a sheltered, structured environment in which children could be safely deposited for a portion of each school day.[56]

Urban school systems had longer terms than did country schools. In 1880, in most states, urban schools were in session for an average of 9 months per year, whereas rural schools were in session for an average of 6.5 months. Farmers designed short terms to enable children both to work and go to school; urban schoolmen expected long school terms to keep children out of the workforce and in school virtually all year. Their intent was to keep middle-class children in school when they were not being cared for in their own homes, and to keep poor and working-class children off the streets, out of the workforce, and in a protected and appropriately uplifting environment.

Long school terms did not necessarily accomplish this purpose. Enrollment in urban schools, as a percentage of all school-age children, was lower than in rural schools partly because school-building programs could not keep pace with urban growth. In the 1880s, thousands of youngsters in Philadelphia and New York were unable to enroll because classroom space was so limited.[57] In addition, in these and other cities, many parents, who desperately needed the labor of their children for family survival, chose not to enroll them in school at all. Conversely, attendance levels were higher in cities than in rural areas, perhaps because limited classroom space was so valued and because parents who enrolled their youngsters planned for them to work at the most part-time while they were getting an education. Because well-paying, full-time employment was rarely available to urban youngsters under the age of 13 and part-time city jobs were less seasonal than agricultural labor, urban children, once enrolled in school, had little reason to drop out for a term (unless their parents were ill or unemployed) as farm boys often did. In addition, there were few physical barriers to regular attendance, because schools in cities were closer to pupils' homes than were country schools. Youngsters between the ages of 10 and 14 who attended urban schools regularly for nine months a year probably learned the basic skills and values nineteenth-century educators emphasized. Most students dropped out by the age of 15 to take jobs; therefore fewer older teens were in school in cities than on farms. In 1870, in the urbanized Northeast, just 36 percent of young men between the ages 15 to 19 were in school, whereas in the more rural Northwest, 51 percent were.[58]

Northern and Midwestern urban schools typically admitted children of both genders and, by the end of the Civil War, children of both races as well. The chief argument for admitting white girls was that they needed to be educated to the same degree as white boys if, as women, they were to raise their children to become responsible citizens. Common-school reformers talked of public schools that would prepare youngsters for citizenship and voting: either directly, as with white boys, or indirectly, as with white girls who would train their sons for citizenship. Because only in New England and New York could black men vote before the Civil War, reformers also implied that public schools should not admit blacks, and most schools did not. Free African-Americans in Northern cities refused to accept denial of educational opportunity. Instead they founded schools of their own or sent their children to special schools, founded by philanthropists, for blacks. By the 1840s and 1850s, Northerners who sought to abolish slavery urged an end to other forms of unequal treatment of blacks, including separate schools. Consequently, states and cities where abolitionism was strongest, such as Massachusetts and Cleveland, Ohio, integrated their public schools.[59] Before the Civil War, racism impacted education in both the North and South: there were few schools open to black children because most whites assumed blacks were inferior and destined for low-level jobs that did not require an education. In the South, blacks learned to read and write only in secret; in the North, they learned only if they lived in abolitionist strongholds or had access to a few specialized schools.

After the Civil War, with the addition of the Fourteenth Amendment to the U.S. Constitution, Northerners could no longer refuse blacks access to public schools. In cities such as Chicago and San Francisco, where there were few African-Americans, integrating them into public schools was not much of an issue. In cities that had larger black populations, integration proved more controversial, and African-Americans "became involved in political activities to end or limit the practice of segregation. . . ." Black parents, who typically held the lowest-wage jobs in nineteenth-century cities, were determined to educate their children for "social advancement." Although blacks gained admission to Northern urban schools, it was not always on an integrated basis. Philadelphia public schools remained segregated until the 1930s.[60] Yet blacks expressed mixed feelings about integration. It might provide their children an education more comparable to that of whites, but it also meant that their sons and daughters would be taught by whites, because only a few urban public schools employed blacks to teach integrated classes.[61] After the Civil War, African-Americans probably received a more equal (to whites) education in the North than in the South, yet racism did not disappear from Northern public schools.

Even before urban schools integrated, they became bureaucratic organizations. Unpaid laymen administered the first urban schools, but they soon found the tasks of school inspection and teacher training too burdensome and turned these and other tasks over to school superintendents. In an era when specialists assumed control of other urban services such as fire fighting and policing, and when bureaucracy characterized business organization, it seemed sensible for school organization as well to become hierarchic and be placed in the charge of experts.[62]

With specialization came age grading. As in rural areas, urban schools began as large, ungraded classrooms, but when the school population burgeoned, teachers had difficulty managing large numbers of children of diverse ages in one room. In the 1850s, schoolmen began to divide urban schoolchildren by age and assign each age-group a teacher; by the 1880s, the practice became standard in cities. With age grading came standardization of the curriculum: if children were to proceed in an orderly way through the schools, they all had to learn the same thing at the same ages from different teachers.[63]

New age-graded urban schools were located in neighborhoods and served homogeneous groups of children. In cities, children could easily walk with their brothers, sisters, and friends to their local elementary or primary school. Such schools typically resembled "large private residences, complete with friendly entrance porches." Once inside, youngsters could not remain with siblings as they did in rural, ungraded schools but instead entered the appropriate classroom for their age-group. For middle-class children, urban schools probably resembled their own homes at least from the outside, but for working-class youngsters, who lived in small apartments or homes, a large urban school might be intimidating. Inside, urban schools, with their many graded classrooms and their large auditoriums, were nothing like city homes of any sort.[64] Urban classrooms probably did not feel as comfortable and familiar to their students as did rural schools to their pupils.

Although located in neighborhoods, urban primary schools were arms of the centralized public school system. They were not directly under the control of pupils' parents as were rural schools. Administrators, not parents, appointed teachers, sometimes on the basis of their political connections. In cities, parents did not see their children's teachers much, nor did they come to school often to observe their youngsters perform. Most parents' contact with the local school was indirect—through their children's homework and report cards and occasionally through formal meetings with a teacher. Of course, age grading allowed parents to determine if their youngsters were performing adequately and hence moving upward through the grades yearly.

Although urban parents did not have the kind of direct control over schools that rural parents did, both groups strongly supported the common school's effort to make children obedient. For middle- and working-class Americans, obedience to parental authority was a goal of child rearing. Outside the home, parents expected children to learn obedience from teachers, or "parent-surrogates." Working-class mothers and fathers especially feared the dangerous freedom of city streets and worried that without the steadying influence of school, their children might mature into uncontrollable, rebellious youths. "Recalling a school in Chicago which catered to the children of the working poor, the Superintendent of Instruction described . . . an emaciated woman with tears in her eyes, who directed the teacher in this manner: 'There, Mister, I have brought him. He won't mind me. What shall I do? He won't go to school. Can't you whip him and make a good boy of him?' "[65]

Unlike the teacher in this example, the typical urban teacher of the late nineteenth century was female. In 1890, 92 percent of teachers in cities that had over 10,000 inhabitants were women. Age grading made the introduction of female teachers easier. Because women were presumably best able to handle young children, in age-graded schools, women could be assigned to teach the lower grades. Men could be designated to teach high school, where older boys might require harsher discipline and, perhaps, a manly role model. Of course, as elsewhere, women were paid less to teach than were men, but at least the long terms in urban schools allowed women (and men) to make teaching a full-time career rather than part-time as in rural areas.[66]

Age grading produced other changes in urban schools, including the exclusion of young children under the age of six from the classroom and, with the development of high schools, the inclusion of older youths. Educators found children between the ages of two and five difficult to instruct. Given the thrust of child-rearing advice to the middle class, it seemed more appropriate that very young children remain at home in the care of their mothers. In 1832, Amariah Brigham published an influential book in which he threatened that early education led to insanity. Gradually, beginning in the 1830s and continuing through the 1850s, urban public-school administrators excluded children younger than six from schools. Most middle-class mothers then kept their toddlers at home, but poor mothers who had to work outside the home turned to relatives, friends, or private charities for day care. Philanthropic groups founded day nurseries in many Northern cities; there were 90 by 1892. However, most day nurseries provided minimal care for white youngsters only; one woman often cared for 30 to 50 toddlers.[67]

In 1860, in Boston, reformer Elizabeth Palmer Peabody introduced the kindergarten: a new type of schooling, imported from Germany, for very young children. Its object was not to train youngsters intellectually but to instruct them through play; therefore, the kindergarten seemed acceptable to middle-class mothers. Charitable volunteers also found the kindergarten appropriate for working-class children. In 1889, when Jane Addams opened Hull House in Chicago to serve the poor, the first activity of her settlement-house workers was to found a kindergarten to train children from working-class immigrant families in the neighborhood "in elementary principles of hygiene and manners and the development of social instincts and inclinations through cooperative play and group activity." In Chicago, public schools later assumed control of kindergartens after the 1894 Pullman strike that awakened businessmen to the dangers of immigrants who had not learned "self discipline" and "good citizenship."[68] Schoolmen discovered that the kindergarten could prepare five-year-olds for the discipline of the school; the kindergarten could teach the same values that common schools had long espoused. "The child could be taught self-control, discipline, and good manners without repressive means, without resort to heavy-handed authority. . . . The kindergarten children in their daily games would march—and learn that their marching was part of an allegiance to country. They would set out to make a clock . . . and learn that 'the clock helps us to be good.' "

Thus, urban public education for very young children first disappeared because it presumably failed to serve the interests of children and of schools and later reappeared because, in the form of the kindergarten, it accomplished both. Its reappearance was very gradual, however, and even by 1920, just 10 percent of youngsters attended kindergartens.[69]

So too did the public high school serve very few children. In 1890 just 6.7 percent of youths aged 14 to 17 enrolled in high school, and only 3.5 percent of 17-year-olds actually graduated. Many cities added such schools to fill out age-graded systems in an orderly fashion and to keep children of the powerful white urban middle class in school. Public high schools functioned as capstones to age-graded schools: to be admitted, youngsters had to take an entrance exam on what they had learned in the lower grades. Thus, high schools both stimulated students to excel and went hand in hand with standardization of course work in the lower grades.[70] Although high schools were presumably open to all children with the proper academic qualifications, in reality, most high school students were sons and daughters of middle-class parents, who, unlike many working-class families, could afford to forgo their children's earnings and send them to school in their teen years. In very large cities, public-high school buildings were "stately" in appearance and intended to impress affluent parents of potential students. As the superintendent of St. Louis said of its new high school in 1855: "It is an expression of the refinement, public spirit, and taste of that community." In smaller cities, high schools were less grand; they were frequently attached to grammar schools and, in 1890, housed an average number of only 80 students.[71]

As for the student body, high schools in most cities were coeducational, as were most elementary and grammar schools. In the lower grades, girls excelled academically, so more of them entered high schools than did boys. Schoolmen did not deny girls admission because to do so would not only remove the very population that made the high school viable but also undermine the egalitarian ideology of the public schools. Moreover, in most cities, it proved too costly to erect separate high schools for girls and boys. In coeducational public high schools, girls and boys studied the same subjects, including Latin, Greek, algebra, geometry, physics, chemistry, history, and literature. Girls generally performed as well or better than boys in all academic courses, and more girls graduated. In 1890, girls constituted 57 percent of high school students and 65 percent of high school graduates. In the late nineteenth century, coeducation meant equal academic opportunity for women. Such education may have given women confidence so that in later years they could engage in social reform and the campaign for women's suffrage. Certainly, coeducation prepared many women for careers in teaching at the same time as it created a reading public for much of the literature published in this era.

In 1882, separate high schools for boys and girls existed in just 19 of 196 cities in the United States, most in the South or Northeast. Separate schools were not equal, for educators spent less on girls' than on boys' high schools and offered girls a less academically demanding curriculum. Southern girls suffered disproportionately from this disparity because most public high schools in the South were same-sex schools. In the North, although high schools were sex segregated in cities such as Philadelphia and New York, in moderate-sized cities, where most girls enrolled, high schools were coeducational.[72]

The academic curriculum of public high schools prepared some female students to become teachers, and some male students for college, seminary, the ministry, or one of the other professions. High schools were not originally intended, however, to prepare youths for other forms of employment except in the loosest sense: high schools taught values employers might find useful in potential employees.[73] Late in the century, some high schools began to take on a more direct vocational role—a role that became more prominent in the twentieth century. The new vocational education took two forms: manual training of boys and clerical (commercial) training of girls and boys.

Beginning in the 1880s, some city high schools offered manual training for manufacturing work to boys. In Philadelphia, the program began when the president of the board of education worried that labor protests in the depression of the 1870s had revealed that young people needed to learn more respect for labor and more discipline. He believed public schools should provide both. Although two public manual-arts schools opened in Philadelphia in the 1890s with the clear intent of better socializing working-class boys for employment, the program fizzled when working-class parents and trade unionists objected to schools replacing union men as the educators of young workers. Neither were manufacturing firms very enthusiastic: they preferred to train their own employees or draw students from one of the many private trade schools in Philadelphia. In contrast, in Chicago, businessmen believed the public schools could provide them with a "steady supply of manual workers with appropriate industrial skills and habits." In the 1880s and 1890s, in Chicago and San Francisco, businessmen founded their own trade schools. Educators in both cities, fearful of private competition for students, responded by creating public manual-training schools. In this decision, educators were supported by labor unions, which preferred "publicly controlled vocational education" to "the formation of 'scab factories' controlled directly by businessmen." Manual training in public schools was controversial. To many it seemed to subvert the idea of the common school, which was to train all children equally. To others it appeared democratic to train working-class children for the kind of employment they would eventually pursue. Manual training programs were designed more to retain boys in high school than girls; such programs, however, were not very successful, at least in the nineteenth century. "By and large, young men did not go to high school to learn a trade; it was much easier and faster to acquire job-related skills from employers or craft unions or through specialized schools."[74]

More popular and successful than manual training was commercial education. In 1869, enrollments increased when Pittsburgh added both a Normal School and a Commercial School to the academic department of the high school. In 1870, in Somerville, Massachusetts, the introduction of the English or "mercantile" program "preceded a climb in enrollment at Somerville High School" and a rise in graduation rates as well.[75] Although commercial programs varied, they usually included training in clerical skills, typing, filing, and sometimes accounting and bookkeeping. In the late nineteenth century, the emergence of large corporations required more administrative coordination, more information, and more correspondence. Clerical work became the prerogative of women; by 1890, a majority of typists and stenographers were women. Women liked clerical work for the same reason they liked teaching: it was one of the few good, respectable jobs then available to them. Businesses preferred to hire a female clerical staff because women worked for less than did men, and women did not demand promotion because most worked only briefly before marrying.[76] When high schools offered commercial courses, girls, who already constituted the majority of the high school population, willingly signed up for them. "Companies hiring clerical help, on the other hand, found the schools a vital agency in labor recruitment and training." Because commercial education appealed to both high school students and employers, and because it was not designed to lock students into working-class jobs (as manual training appeared to do), commercial education was the more popular form of vocational education in the 1890s.[77]

Once urban public-school systems were fully articulated, from elementary school through high school, parents of all classes, races, and nationalities responded by enrolling their children in public school. Young children between the ages of five and nine of both genders from all social, racial, and ethnic backgrounds were equally likely to attend urban schools. Some poor parents began to withdraw their youngsters at the age of ten so that they could work, but even so, most youngsters of all backgrounds remained in urban schools until age thirteen.[78] In 1880, in Providence, Rhode Island, "At age eleven, for example, 89 percent of the children of laborers were still in school, as were 88 percent of blacks and 91 percent of the Irish. Dropout rates increased very rapidly with each succeeding age, so that by age thirteen 73 percent of Providence children were still enrolled, by age fifteen only 42 percent, and by age seventeen a mere 19 percent." Because children in nine-teenth-century schools customarily became literate by age eleven or twelve, apparently the majority of children who enrolled in urban schools remained long enough to learn to read and write.[79]

Because prosperous white businessmen developed urban public-school systems, it is not surprising that such schools appealed especially to white middle-class families. Their youngsters enrolled in them for the most years, often from ages seven to seventeen.[80] Extended schooling fit with middle-class child-rearing practices. Youngsters remained in their homes in the care of their mothers until the children entered school. They then passed into the care of female teachers who, like mothers, emphasized obedience as a prelude to self-control and preferred to punish by inducing guilt rather than by spanking. Attending local public schools also allowed middle-class boys and girls to live at home until well into their teen years. Public schools provided boys with some preparation for employment, and girls with some preparation for marriage, child rearing, and possibly employment.

Because they remained in school the longest, middle-class children were more likely than any other group to be enrolled in urban public high schools. There were more jobs open to middle-class boys than to their sisters, so boys usually quit high school as soon as they obtained a white-collar job. Attending high school, whether they graduated or not, substantially improved the likelihood that middle-class boys would obtain white-collar employment.[81]

Middle-class girls formed the majority of public high school students. Of the girls whose careers could be traced after they graduated from Somerville High School in the late nineteenth century, most married men with white-collar jobs, while a minority went into teaching or clerical work. Middle-class parents typically sent their daughters to high school not to prepare them for employment, but to provide them with something productive and interesting to do in their teen years before they married. Because urban public high schools enrolled largely middle-class young people, such schools appeared to be safe and protected places for girls. Girls themselves probably enjoyed staying in school because it allowed them to leave home—and the domestic chores associated with home—and spend much of their time with young women and men like themselves. At a time when same-sex friendships were so important and enduring for women, many of these friendships were formed in secondary school. In public school, girls could also relate well to the teachers, most of whom were female. Young women performed well academically in high school because parents and teachers expected them to do so. "For many middle-class girls in this period, it may not have been acceptable to perform inadequately at anything they were expected to do."[82]

Nonetheless, the late nineteenth century was a time when there was considerable medical concern about young women at puberty and about the dangers school might pose to their health. In 1873, Edward Clarke, a Boston doctor, published a book entitled *Sex in Education* in which he argued that prolonged schooling at a time when girls' reproductive organs were developing was detrimental to girls' health. Although the book was aimed at women in college, it applied as well to girls in high school. Frailty was assumed to be characteristic of middle-class teenage girls, and indeed, in the 1850s and 1860s, one-third of girls who left high school in Somerville, Massachusetts, before graduation did so because of ill health. Yet most middle-class girls did not quit school. Because they lived at home, their parents could monitor their health, and educators responded to medical and parental concerns by providing girls with some physical education.[83] (See chapter 6.)

Although working-class parents withdrew their children from urban public schools before middle-class parents did, working-class parents too were active supporters of education, at least when their youngsters were young and not yet able to find full-time employment. The strict discipline characteristic of public schools may well have appealed to working-class parents, who typically demanded instant obedience from their children and willingly employed corporal punishment. Working-class parents probably liked the fact that, in public schools, their children could become literate by their early teens or before and could obtain a basic education before they were eligible for most full-time, blue-collar jobs. Yet working-class parents were fully aware that their children benefited most from primary and grammar schools and rarely from high schools. In several cities, when public high schools were first built, working-class parents demonstrated their opposition to paying taxes to support them. Not until the 1870s and 1880s, when high schools in some cities introduced some "practically oriented coursework," did high schools become more acceptable to working-class families.[84]

As for the children themselves, working-class youngsters trained to respect their elders at home may well have been willing to extend that respect to teachers in schools. For working-class girls, schooling freed them from a dulling round of domestic chores at home. However, for working-class boys, the strictness of schools contrasted sharply with the freedom of the streets so many boys enjoyed. They may have been fairly willing to comply when their parents required them to withdraw from school and go to work, often between the ages of 10 and 14 and almost certainly before their late teens. Interdependence was a key value taught in working-class homes; therefore children certainly understood that they had an obligation to quit school and work at a time when most working-class fathers could not earn enough to support their families (see chapter 5). When boys left school, they typically took blue-collar jobs, and girls either worked at home or entered domestic service.[85]

Some working-class families were not as enthusiastic about public schools. Occupation, race, ethnicity, and religion divided working-class parents and caused them to differ in their attitudes toward schooling and their inclination to prolong their children's education in urban public schools. Skilled workers usually sent their children to school for more years than did unskilled workers. Artisans earned enough to be able to prolong the education of their children more easily than could lower-paid, unskilled workers. In addition, by the 1880s and 1890s, in cities such as Pittsburgh, larger companies (in iron and steel, glassblowing, and clothing manufacture) adopted new technologies that made some types of skilled work obsolete. Employers also sought to undermine the power of craft unions. In such an atmosphere, skilled workers kept their children in public school to prepare them for alternate careers, especially in clerical work. As did middle-class parents, artisans often sent their daughters to school longer than their sons. Among skilled workers, keeping a girl in school was a sign of social prestige, an indication that the worker could, for some years, afford to forgo a daughter's help at home or in the working world.[86]

Another group of working-class Americans very likely to keep their children in school into their teens were African-Americans. Blacks in Northern cities lobbied for equal access to education for their children, and by the time they obtained it, after the Civil War, they took advantage of it. Between 1890 and 1940, "despite the position of blacks at the bottom of the economic ladder, older black children were more likely to be in school than foreign-born children." Urban African-American families had fewer children than native-born or foreign-born families partly because of the later age of marriage of blacks, high death rate among African-American men, and the decision of African-American families to invest their meager resources in just a few children. Black mothers, more than white women, worked outside the home, thereby enabling their children to remain in school into their teen years. Had children been withdrawn earlier, they would probably not have found work, because many urban employers refused to hire African-American children. Therefore, black children stayed on in school, although there is evidence from Providence, Rhode Island; Boston; New York; Philadelphia; and Chicago that few black teens entered public high schools—most remained in the lower grades. Apparently, African-American children did not excel in nineteenth-century urban schools for several reasons. Many had parents who were themselves illiterate or simply worked too-long hours to have much time to assist boys and girls with their schoolwork. Racist texts employed in schools certainly did not build the confidence of blacks to achieve and probably inclined their teachers as well to doubt blacks' abilities. Finally, those black teens who spent long years in public schools, even those who attended high schools, obtained only low-paying manual jobs once they entered the workforce, which was a disincentive to achievement for all Northern urban African-American youth.[87]

African-Americans in both the South and the urban North strongly supported public education, but only in the North did a high proportion of school-age black children actually enroll in and attend school. In the South, large black families dependent on the labor of all family members in a sharecropping economy had little incentive to send many of their children to low-quality, overcrowded, segregated public schools. In contrast, small black families in the North supported by the income of working mothers and fathers willingly enrolled their children, for whom employment was unavailable anyway, in public schools that offered black children virtually the same education afforded whites. Of course, in neither section of the country did education lead to better jobs for black youths. However, at least in the North, the black community may have found other advantages to educating their youth. Even if school textbooks were demeaning to blacks, becoming literate permitted them access to other reading materials of their choice. Literacy among blacks probably contributed to the growth of newspapers in black urban communities. Literacy also enabled blacks to cooperate to achieve common goals and may have enabled them to form black women's clubs and organizations seeking racial equality such as the National Association for the Advancement of Colored People.[88]

Among the working class, ethnic groups differed in their willingness to support public schools. Families from two particular nationalities were especially likely to endorse public schools. First were the Scots, whose children enjoyed the advantages of speaking the same language and sharing the same Protestant faith as the founders of public schools. In 1870, 66 percent of children of Scots fathers attended school—equaling the percentage of children from native-born families in school and exceeding the percentage of any other nationality. The other ethnic group that heartily supported public schools were neither Protestant nor English-speaking—they were eastern European Jews. After 1880, they migrated to the United States and settled largely in cities. Jews came from a tradition that valued learning and honored the scholar and the student. Mothers and fathers praised children for their knowledge and pressed them to do better: " 'What do you mean you only got ninety-eight on that science test? Who got the hundred?' many a Jewish child was asked." Though poor when they arrived, Jewish men avoided factory work and other manual labor in favor of commercial occupations. They often began work as peddlers. Partly as a result of their employment, Jewish parents appreciated the value of math and language skills, which could be acquired through public education. In Providence, Rhode Island, Jewish youngsters averaged one or two more years of high school education than did children of other ethnic backgrounds, and such education probably helped Jews succeed in the business-related fields most entered.[89]

Of course, children from other ethnic backgrounds who remained in school into their teen years also benefited by improving their job opportunities. In Providence, in 1880, Joel Perlmann discovered that Irish boys who graduated from high school obtained better jobs than their fathers; in Somerville, Massachusetts, Reed Ueda found that "for all ethnic groups, secondary schooling led to outstanding chances for white-collar work."[90] Nonetheless, unlike the Jews, most immigrants perceived little economic value in keeping their children in school for so long; too often, poor, foreign-born families required the earnings of teenage children to survive.

To many immigrant youngsters, public schools appeared to be hostile environments, places youngsters willingly left when it was time for them to work full-time. In immigrant neighborhoods, schools were often over-crowded. "Sadie R. recalled that on her first day of school she had to sit in a seat with another girl 'and put an arm around her waist so I wouldn't fall off.' " Non-English-speaking children who were turned away from overcrowded schools might go to work instead and never enter them at all. Youngsters whose families did not speak English often became terrified when they entered public school. "Isidor B., escorted by a neighbor to kindergarten in the Bronx, recalled his terror when she left and he realized that he could not understand what anyone around him, including the teacher, was saying." When older, foreign-language-speaking children enrolled, they often became discouraged, because due to their limited knowledge of English, they ended up in classes with native-born children three or four years their junior. Their parents could not help them learn the new language. Some foreign-born parents even resented their children speaking anything but their native tongue at home. Teachers were often unsympathetic to immigrant children. Many teachers consistently mispronounced youngsters' names or called them by more "American" names. "One memoirist said that when her school friends called at her home and asked for her under her American name, her parents told them no one by that name lived there." Instructors also assumed that immigrant children were dirty and inspected them for cleanliness in front of the whole class.[91] The teachers' attitudes reflected that of the textbooks used in schools, and native-born children certainly picked up the same views from about the schools. Officials did not care whether Catholics attended public schools. Irish and German Catholics were the first to respond by creating parochial schools, but by the end of the century, other national groups also built parish schools to teach their languages and cultures in ethnically similar neighborhoods. Poles not only did not want their children to attend public schools but also did not want their children to enroll in German Catholic schools; the same was true of Slovaks and Lithuanians. Both the hostility of the public schools to Catholics of various nationalities and the determination of Irish, German, Polish, and other national groups to build their own schools meant that "by 1880, 94 percent of the Catholic parishes in Chicago had schools. . . ." Moreover, "of the combined public-Catholic school population in Chicago, 22 percent attended parochial schools. . . ."[94]

Boston is a third example. Here public schools compromised and the Irish Catholic minority was less inclined to build a separate system than in Chicago. Boston had a long tradition of support for public schools, and school officials were determined to use the schools to Americanize Irish immigrants. Yet too heavy-handed a program might alienate Irish Catholics and drive them from the schools. In 1860, public officials chose to compromise when they allowed that no Catholic schoolchild had to read the Protestant Bible or version of the Lord's Prayer. In turn, Boston's Irish, impressed by Yankee tradition, "psychologically compelled to absorb the dominant culture," accepted the compromise and sent most of their children to public schools. Boston's Irish were also less interested in building parish schools than they were in building parish churches. As a consequence, in 1880, only 37 percent of Boston's parishes had schools, and just 10 percent of the public-Catholic-school population attended parochial schools.[95]

Locally administered parochial schools were in many ways advantageous to students and parents alike, yet even in cities such as Chicago where such schools were most popular, a majority of Catholic children still avoided them and enrolled in public schools. For all the benefits of parochial schools, they also had disadvantages that alienated some of their potential constituents.

Immigrant Catholics endorsed parochial schools both for religious and ethnic reasons. In such schools, catechisms were the most popular text; youngsters learned the same catechism that their parents had memorized when they were of school age in Europe. "Each catechism generally included prayers and devotions, and children learned the same prayers at home and at school that their parents cherished." Rather than contradicting the religion of immigrant parents, as did public schools, parochial schools confirmed children in the faith practiced in their homes and churches. Parochial schools also taught children in the language that they spoke at home—thereby making the transition to school easier than it was if they attended most public schools. Because parish schools were located in ethnically homogeneous neighborhoods, children could walk to school with their siblings and friends.

both teachers and books. Thus, in public schools, immigrant children
be humiliated by both teachers and fellow students—all the more rea
quit school as soon as their parents required them to do so.

To avoid such humiliation, as well as better to preserve their lan
and culture, some immigrant groups demanded that public schools intrc
foreign-language teaching. Germans were especially successful in wir
concessions to permit bilingualism in Cincinnati, Cleveland, Baltimore
Louis, and Chicago schools. Because Germans were "prosperous, politi
self-conscious, and educationally advanced," school boards more willi
accorded Germans the right to learn their lessons in their own language t
they did other less powerful and respected immigrant groups.[92]

Immigrants who dissented most strongly from public schools w
Roman Catholic in faith and Irish or German in nationality. These imn
grants were offended by public schools that often taught children values fro
the Protestant version of the Bible and required youngsters to read textbool
that denigrated Catholics and reviled the Irish. Yet parochial schools did n
develop in a uniform fashion throughout the United States because publi
schools were not hostile everywhere. In some cities, school officials wer
more flexible and accommodating to Catholic concerns than in others. The
key variables that determined whether a separate parochial-school system
developed in a given city were the willingness of public officials to compromise with Catholic ethnic groups, the strength of the ethnic group's commitment to separate education for their children, and possibly (historians are still
divided on this factor) the willingness of Catholic church leaders to establish
parochial schools.

In New York City, Catholic bishop John Hughes protested against the
Protestant orientation of the public schools and demanded that Catholics be
given a share of school moneys. In 1842, New York denied Hughes' request
for money, but offered a compromise: the Protestant-dominated Public
School Society lost its monopoly of school funds, and city schools were
decentralized to the ward level. Immigrant Catholics thus had the opportunity to control their neighborhood schools. Although Hughes persisted in his
effort to create a parochial-school system in New York City, only a small proportion of Catholic children enrolled in it: 20 percent in 1840 and 16 percent
in 1865. Catholic parents who lived in wards "where they chose the teachers
and the textbooks, inspected the schools, and set the general tone" may well
have been disinclined to invest in parochial schools. Conversely, Catholics
living in city wards where they were in the minority were probably those who
sent their children to the separate school system created by Hughes and his
successors.[93]

In contrast, in Chicago, where public-school officials refused to compromise with Catholic critics, a strong parochial-school system evolved. In this
city, Yankee, Protestant school officials ignored Roman Catholic concerns

Parochial-school children learned their lessons from teachers who were usually of their same ethnicity and often from similar humble origins. There was less likelihood of a cultural clash between teachers and pupils in parochial schools than there was in public schools. Because Catholic schools were often sex segregated, they pleased immigrant parents concerned about protecting the morals of their daughters. Parochial schools also eschewed biased public-school texts and instead used books authored by Europeans. Such texts did not attack Protestantism but rather held up Catholic saints as heroes for children to emulate. Some Catholic writers also portrayed the Irish in a much more favorable light than did the authors of public-school texts. A reader that included a chapter on "Character of the Irish Peasantry," described the Irish as "sharp of wit, shrewd, hospitable, heroic, just, and cheerful." Such descriptions built confidence rather than denigrated the self-worth of Irish children.[96]

The principal disadvantages to a parochial-school education were cost and quality. In Providence, Rhode Island, Catholics paid tuition of 50 cents to $1 a month per child. For the average worker with an annual wage of $400 to $600, such tuition amounted to one percent to two percent of his income—for one child only. Catholics tried to hold down school costs by employing few teachers and economizing on facilities. In consequence, Catholic class sizes were large and some schools met in church basements—not much of an improvement, if any, over public schools. The quality of teaching in Catholic schools was also an issue. As in public schools, most parochial-school teachers were women. Parochial schools preferred to employ orders of nuns because it cost less to pay their expenses (the nuns received no salary) than it did to pay men's orders. There were also more nuns available to teach because fewer male than female religious orders established branches in the United States, and convents attracted more novices than did male religious communities. Nuns were younger than public school-teachers and less likely to have completed a normal school education. Most nuns trained for teaching by apprenticeship only. Due to the minimal education nuns received, church officials deemed them qualified only to teach young children. Nuns preferred female students, and some refused to teach boys at all. As a consequence, most parochial schools provided only an elementary education, principally in "moral development and manners," to young girls. Because of the cost of building and staffing schools, there were few Catholic secondary schools before 1900.[97]

Regardless of the advantages and disadvantages of a parochial-school education, one group of immigrant Catholics rarely enrolled their children in either parochial schools or public schools: Southern Italians. Like eastern European Jews, most Italians entered the United States after 1880. Many were teenage boys who spoke only Italian and could not easily make the transition to English-language public schools or to English (Irish) or German-language Catholic schools. Because about one-half of Italian immigrants returned to Italy, many had no interest in educating their children in the United States. Italian immigrants, most of whom were poor and unskilled, also distrusted schools, because in southern Italy schools were of low quality and largely the prerogative of the elite. In this country, Italians had reason to be suspicious of public schools in which their youngsters studied texts that denigrated Italians. As Leonard Covello said of his education: "We soon got the idea that 'Italian' meant something inferior, and a barrier was erected between children of Italian origin and their parents. This was the accepted learning process of Americanization. We were becoming Americans by learning how to be ashamed of our parents."[98] Italians, who valued manual labor, also feared that education might incline Italian boys to nonmanual jobs, of which parents had a low opinion. Parents were especially protective of their daughters, whom they typically withdrew from school before age 15. Parents preferred to keep their girls at home or working with other family members in places such as textile factories or canneries. Parents believed that schools might be dangerous places filled with evil persons. Italians in the Bunker Hill section of Paterson, New Jersey, referred to the local public school as "Bunker's College of Criminal Knowledge." In general, Italians valued the family before the individual and feared that schooling might teach the opposite—as indeed was the purpose, at least of public schools.[99]

Between 1850 and 1890, the most powerful predictor of how much education a child received, in what type of school, was the part of the country in which that child lived. The dimensions of regional difference in education are obvious if we use as our example the most favored of children in this era, the white native-born Protestant middle-class boy. In the rural North, Midwest, or West, such a boy, from the time he was a toddler through his late teens, would probably have attended a one-room school for no more than six and perhaps as few as three months each year. If the same white boy lived in the South, his prosperous parents would probably have enrolled him not in a public school but in a same-sex private school. Finally, if our white, middle-class boy grew up in a city in the North, Midwest, or West, he probably began his education at about the age of seven, when he enrolled in an age-graded elementary school for nine months a year, and ended his education after completing one or two years of high school.

Yet there was variety within regions, and not all children in rural and urban parts of the North, Midwest, and West or in the South received the same type of education as did our native-born white Protestant middle-class boy. Yet if we return to the question that forms the title of this chapter, we can answer it with a qualified positive. Yes, the majority of children between the ages of seven and fourteen obtained schooling that included a basic education in moral values and in reading, writing, and arithmetic. Most children attended public schools, but some enrolled in parochial schools. Unfortunately, a minority of children rarely obtained even the bare minimum of education. Most of these children lived in the South, where the public education system was least developed. African-American children were the most deprived.

With this important exception, youngsters growing up between 1850 and 1890 typically spent six to eight years in school. When those years passed, and sometimes even while they were still attending school, most youngsters worked. Their experience of labor in fields, homes, and factories forms the subject of the next chapter.

5

Farm, Factory, and Home: Children at Work

When they were five and six years old, sisters Blanche and Kathryn weeded the ground between rows of cotton and corn under the supervision of their older siblings on the family farm in the Carolina Piedmont. When the girls were a few years older, and "could distinguish between blades of grass and corn or between weeds and cotton," they began "hoeing entire rows."[1] Another young girl overcast "the long seams of garments made by her mother" in their Boston flat. By her fourth birthday, the child could overcast "from three to four pants every day." A visitor noted: "There, on a little stool she sat, her fingers moving rapidly and in as unerring a manner as an old experienced needle-woman."[2]

There was nothing unusual about the labor of these three young girls in the nineteenth century. Both in the United States and Europe, children labored on farms, in homes, and in artisans' shops. Until the end of the century, few Americans or Europeans doubted that such labor was beneficial to youngsters: it taught them industry and thrift and prepared them for future employment. Before 1850, only the most well-to-do families could afford to exempt their children from labor in field, home, or factory. However, in the second half of the century, a division developed among American families. A growing number of affluent middle-class city dwellers and some prosperous farmers were able to delay employment of their children and instead prolonged their education. Conversely, many more parents, including those who owned, rented, or sharecropped small farms, as well as parents who worked at unskilled or semiskilled jobs in cities, were so poor that they had to put their children to work at a young age. Such children labored to ensure family survival and sometimes to help purchase a family home, which provided a measure of security against poverty and homelessness. Several interrelated factors determined the likelihood of any particular child's working, including the financial situation of her or his family, ethnicity, race, gender, family size, and the youngster's position (oldest, youngest) within the family. The sharp

"Watering the Horse" by George Bacon Wood (circa 1887). As soon as farm children were physically able, they were expected to work at tasks assigned them by their parents. This young boy and girl have been collecting wood in a cart. (Library Company of Philadelphia)

division that developed between parents who could afford to keep their children out of the labor market and parents so poor that child labor was essential to family survival culminated in the anti-child labor movement of the late nineteenth century. The movement proved marginally effective in limiting child employment in factories in the North but not in the South.

After 1850, as before, most working children labored on farms. In 1900, 60 percent of employed children between the ages of ten and fifteen performed farm labor.[3] Most labored on family-owned farms. In 1860, 80 percent of farmers in the Northeast, Midwest, and on the frontier owned their own farms. Less than 10 percent were renters, and the remainder were part-owners.[4] On most farms, parents expected children to help out as soon as they were physically able. A Kansas farmer said of his son: "Little Baz can run all over, fetch up cows out of the stock fields, or oxen, carry in stove wood and climb in the corn crib and feed the hogs and go on errands down to his grand ma's." The child was then just over two years old. Little Baz was remarkable.

Most youngsters were unable to be of much real help until they were between the ages of seven and twelve. Before puberty, farm boys and girls performed similar tasks; they helped out wherever they were needed.

When families first established farms on the agricultural frontier, which between 1850 and 1890 encompassed the Great Plains, the Rocky Mountains, and the Pacific Coast, children helped feed their families by gathering edible wild plants, which they labeled "vegetables out of place." Older boys and girls hunted wild animals. "Fresh to Kansas in 1871, Luna Warner soon was boasting to her diary of bringing home rabbits, ducks, turkeys, and even a stray steer she found mired beside a river." On the Great Plains, fuel for cooking meat and heating homes was scarce. Children proved especially useful when they collected the "dried dung of bison and cattle" to use for fuel.[5]

As frontier families began to farm, they found that preparing the sod of the Western plains for planting was tough work. Because such labor was so physically demanding, especially for young children, farmers with a little extra cash probably preferred to hire teams of men who "specialized in breaking ground for new settlers at fees of $1.50–$5.00 an acre." However, after this first plowing, children helped their parents further prepare the soil. As Linnaeus Rauck remembered, his "parents each took up an axe and gave each child a knife, then all set upon the land, hacking and chewing their way through several acres to make a seed bed for a garden and the first crop of kaffir corn" on their Oklahoma homestead. Children and adults next planted crops, but caring for them was child's labor. Boys and girls pulled weeds and acted as scarecrows to chase birds and cattle away. Tending livestock became a task of boys and girls age eight and older. They kept cattle and horses out of fields and herded them while they grazed on grasslands. "At ten, Helen Brock was riding the range, and by fifteen she was branding calves and building fences. She and her sister were nine when they broke their first horses." When it came time to slaughter animals, fathers "killed and butchered the stock, while . . . [mothers] processed it in the kitchen, and the children acted as carriers and helpers." On sheep farms, "children helped with cleaning the sheep before shearing and cleaning the wool afterwards," and in the Northeast, children "helped empty the sap buckets during the production of maple syrup."[6]

Farm children also helped their mothers around the house, where the youngest children tended infants, and older boys and girls helped with milking cows, churning butter, feeding chickens, collecting eggs, cooking, and canning vegetables. Children also hauled the water, built the fires, and scrubbed on laundry days. In general, boys and girls under age 12 did not work in the fields or participate in harvesting crops, although they did help their mothers prepare, cook, serve, and clean up the three hearty meals a day typically served to men and youths who performed the heavy field labor. However, if crops had to be harvested quickly and there were not enough men available to get the job done, everyone on the farm, including young children and their mothers, turned out to help. In other words, while young farm children routinely performed certain tasks, they also helped out with other, more physically demanding labor whenever needed.

Gender segregation of labor among farm children began when they reached puberty. Boys began to work in the fields with their fathers, and girls labored in the home and garden beside their mothers. Such gender segregation appears to have been most pronounced on farms in the Northeast, where sons typically worked in dairying for "market production" while their sisters "specialized in household production."[7] In the Midwest, teenage girls were somewhat more likely to work with their fathers, especially if there were no boys in the family, or none old enough to perform field work. Marie Dageforde Monthey of Block, Kansas, noted: "I was the oldest and a lot of times Mama would have liked to have had me in the house, but if Daddy needed me, then I would have to help him chase the horses or cows or take care of the sow with the little pigs or something like that." Conversely, teenage farm boys almost never helped their mothers around the house. On frontier farms, girls who had enjoyed considerable freedom before puberty often resented the change in their lifestyles and that although they often crossed the gender line in work, the same was not true of their brothers. Susie Crocket, who helped plant the fields and trap animals on her Oklahoma farm, remembered: "I hated to see Ma come in with a big batch of sewing, for I knew it meant many long hours sitting by her side sewing seams." Susie believed she was treated unfairly. "I could help the boys with the plowing or trapping, but they would never help me with the sewing."[8]

The labor that children performed on their parents' farms was entirely compatible with school attendance. Farm boys usually attended school only three to four months a year, in the winter, when there was little outdoor labor for them. Girls attended six to seven months a year, so when most girls quit school at age 14, they had probably obtained the equivalent of a sixth-grade education. Because of the labor boys performed, it took them longer, until they were 17 or 18, to obtain a comparable amount of schooling. (See chapter 4.)

Farm children typically attended school while living and working at home. But some worked elsewhere. Teenage sons and daughters of tenant farmers or of farm owners who had not been too successful or had families too large to support typically left home to work for wages on neighboring farms. Nora Ohlmeir Prothe of Block, Kansas, "was the oldest of three girls in a family of eight. When asked why she worked out, she answered, 'if you had a couple of girls at home why you couldn't all stay at home.' "

Hired boys and girls were sometimes paid in cash and sometimes with credit at local stores, from which they and their families purchased clothing as well as staples such as coffee, salt, and sugar. The experience of Minnesota farm boy Frank G. O'Brien, who in 1858, at age 14, was hired out by his father, is probably fairly typical: "The boy was given pocket money for the tramp to the place of employment. Upon arrival Frank was extended the courtesy of the rain barrel, given a tin wash basin, and provided with home-made soap. He then received dinner . . . The house had one story and a small attic; Frank's quarters there were reached by climbing boards nailed to the studding. This attic room . . . was jointly occupied by Frank and several mice. . . ." Hired boys rose at about 4 A.M. and worked until dusk. They did "all kinds of work, including planting, hoeing, harvesting, haying, and husking." Hired girls rose at the same hour but might work well into the evening. They usually cooked three or more meals a day for the family and the hired hands. Girls also washed dishes, ironed, baked, swept, made beds, and helped with the laundry.[9]

White hired girls and boys were "helps" or "hands," not servants; they worked alongside their employers and customarily lived and ate with the family that employed them. Young hired hands labored not far from their family homes and could visit parents and friends weekly.[10] Depending on the arrangement they made with their employers, hired girls and boys might be able to combine work and school. In many ways, the experience of white farm children who hired out did not diverge much from that of other farm children of middling rank. The main difference was that hired boys and girls did not have the option to remain at home with their families through child-hood. Wage work outside the home made their childhoods briefer than those of more fortunate farm children. Moreover, if they labored for a fairly well-off farmer and his wife who had children of their own, hired boys' and girls' labor substantially supplemented or replaced that of their employers' children. Young hired hands were probably well aware that these more privileged children had a greater opportunity for schooling and for leisure.

African-American children living in slavery also toiled on farms, doing many of the same chores that free white farm children did, but under much harsher conditions. Slave children customarily started to work year-round between the ages of six and ten, when they began "cleaning yards, gathering brush, carrying water and supplies to field hands, chasing birds from newly seeded fields, shelling corn, assisting in the gardening in the slave quarters, and helping in meal preparation." Young slave boys and girls also tended babies. Sometimes youngsters helped adult slaves by doing simpler tasks such as carding wool while their mothers spun. Between the ages of 12 and 16, slave boys and girls on large plantations entered the work gang, or "trash gang," where youths labored alongside pregnant, nursing, and aged female slaves at "such tasks as raking stubble, pulling weeds, or doing light hoeing. At harvest time on cotton plantations they usually picked cotton." In general, young slaves of both genders did similar tasks as children, just as when they were grown most female and male slaves would perform similar work in the fields. Nonetheless, there was some sexual division of labor, for girls usually worked more with children than did boys, and boys helped out more with blacksmithing and tending livestock than did girls.[11]

For African-American boys and girls, there was no time out from work for schooling because, by the 1830s, education was forbidden to slaves in the South (see chapter 4). On plantations, slave children who spent time with their white owners' children were quite aware when their young masters became students and slave children remained laborers or servants. Henry Johnson, who grew up a slave in Georgia, explained: "When my young master went three miles to school, he rode on a horse. I had to walk alongside de horse to carry his books, den go home and fetch him a hot dinner for noon and go back at night to carry dem books."[12] Slave children's labor privileged white planters' children, providing them freedom from farm labor and the time to go to school.

Slave children customarily labored with and under the supervision of family members or other adult slaves who taught the young useful skills as well as how to behave around whites. Yet slave children also worked *for* whites, in plantation homes and sometimes in the fields, where youngsters learned to carry water and dinner to the white foremen before serving the slaves. As most slave children grew older and stronger, their work roles gradually became more demanding. By their teens, all young slaves left the trash gang and entered field labor, although some began field work earlier depending on the size of the farm, local custom, and the type of crop. As a child, Andrew Moss began working very young. He noted: "I weren't nothin' but a child endurin' slavery, but I had to work de same as any man. I went to de field and hoed cotton, pulled fodder and picked cotton with de rest of de hands. I kept up too, to keep from gettin' any lashes dat night when us got home."[13]

For some young slaves, the transition from part-time labor as a child to full-time labor as an adolescent in the fields or elsewhere was traumatic. When the owner of a South Carolina slave boy named Jacob assigned him to work for the plantation horse trainer, "the trainer fell into the habit of beating Jacob on a regular basis, for no reason the child or his parents could understand." When Jacob appealed to his family for help, his father "coolly advised him to try harder." Jacob soon learned that even though his parents cared deeply for him, they could do little to save him from harsh and capricious treatment by whites. Historians disagree about how many slave children experienced such crises in their work lives.[14] Yet all would agree that among nineteenth-century child laborers, slaves were peculiarly subject to a harsh transition from labor as a child to labor as a youth.

Whereas the differences between the labor of slave children and of free white children on farms are great, there are some obvious similarities. All did about the same chores at about the same ages. There was some gender segregation in labor among both slave children and free white farm children, although this segregation was probably more pronounced among free whites.

To some degree, both groups of children, but especially slave children, worked so that other youngsters did not have to do so. The major difference between these two groups is the degree of parental control over the children's labor. White farm children usually worked only for their parents and were subject only to their authority, although in the children's teen years they might be hired out to work for other farmers and housewives. In contrast, slave children of all ages always worked under two authorities: that of their parents and that of their white masters. If a white farm parent objected to the treatment of a son or daughter by a neighboring farm family that had hired the youngster, the parent could decide, albeit at some economic sacrifice, to end the child's labor. No slave parent could make such a decision. Neither could any slave parent choose, as could free white farmers, to apportion their children's time between work and school. And whereas both white and slave parents could complain to employers or masters about their treatment of working children, only slave parents made such complaints at very grave personal, physical risk to themselves and to their children. Any slave parent or child could be whipped, or worse yet, the objecting family could be broken by the sale of one or more of its members.

When slavery was abolished after the Civil War, sharecropping and tenantry replaced plantation labor in many parts of the South. White plantation owners divided their land and apportioned it to black families who lived on and worked their individual plots in return for a portion of the harvest. There were few machines on sharecropping farms, so everyone, mothers, fathers, and children, performed a lot of hand labor. African-American sharecropping families were large. Although in the short term the birth of a child might prove burdensome for family members, especially the mother, in the long run, parents believed that "children were a distinct economic asset." By the age of five or six, youngsters could help around the house, tend younger brothers and sisters, carry water from wells or streams to house and field, drop seeds in fields, or worm tobacco plants (check the underside of leaves for worms and twist off the heads of any found there). White landowners actually encouraged child labor among African-American sharecroppers by advancing "food to a household in proportion to its 'working hands' and not its actual members." However, blacks often had difficulty earning enough to support their families by sharecropping alone. "Parents at times hired out children to white employers in order to lessen crowding at home and bring in extra money." Boys could be hired out to work at younger ages and for longer hours than could girls. In addition, during slack seasons on farms, black families often split up. Fathers and sons left to seek day-labor jobs wherever they could find them, and mothers and daughters stayed behind and worked for whites as laundresses and domestics.[15]

The poverty of black sharecroppers in the South necessitated their dependence on the labor of their children and often precluded the youngsters from going to school (see chapter 4).[16] Black boys were less likely than girls to attend school, in part because more boys were hired out or away from home with their fathers trying to earn enough to support their families. Rural schools in the South, as elsewhere in the country, were open during slack seasons on farms, which was just the time when black boys and girls sought wage work to supplement their family's meager incomes. Because girls earned less as domestics than boys did as field hands and were more subject to sexual abuse by their employers, black parents were somewhat more likely to send girls to school with the hope of preparing them for future employment as teachers.

The tasks performed by free black children on farms after the Civil War were much like those performed by slave children on plantations earlier. The major difference was that after freedom, African-American parents managed the labor of their sons and daughters. Whites could command that labor, but they had to pay wages for it. If black parents were willing to make economic sacrifices, they could now keep their children out of white employ and allot their children's time more to school than to work. After the Civil War, the options of poor free black farm families became very similar to those of poor white farm families. As for the children themselves, both black and white farm children who were hired out to whites experienced family separation and observed that their labor privileged the children of their employers. Yet race also led to differences in farm children's work experience. Although farmers and their wives treated young white hired hands to some degree as their equals, white Southern farmers treated black children exclusively as servants.[17]

Wherever parents owned, rented, or sharecropped farms, children, with the exception of those who were hired out, customarily labored together with other family members as a productive unit for at least part of the year. However, when families lost their farms, as many Mexican-Americans in California did in the 1880s, youngsters performed farm labor in quite another context. In 1848, at the end of the war between the United States and Mexico, most Mexican-Americans living near Santa Barbara owned family farms where they raised cattle and sheep. In the 1850s and 1860s, declining prices for their livestock, a flood, and a subsequent drought so hurt farmers that many mortgaged their land. When they could not keep up payments on these mortgages, many Mexican-Americans lost their farms to more affluent Anglos who moved into the state after the war. Consequently, Chicano men took up migratory farm labor, but they rarely earned enough to support their families. Economic necessity forced their wives and children, who had previously worked only on family farms and ranches, to seek jobs in local fruit-canning factories, to shell almonds, or to harvest olives.[18] Although African-American sharecropping families in the South also split up, with fathers and sons working in different areas and for different employers than mothers and daughters, this employment pattern was a temporary, part-year experience for sharecroppers. In contrast, many young California Chicanos worked and lived apart from their fathers indefinitely.

Children who worked on farms between 1850 and 1890 reacted variously to their jobs. Some Midwesterners who wrote of their childhood experiences in this era recalled their youth fondly, but the details of their lives belie this conscious optimism. They remembered their farm chores as both numerous and monotonous. Inside farm homes, where women and girls did most of the work, there were "clothes to be sewn, mended, laundered, ironed, folded, and sorted; dishes to be scraped, stacked, washed, dried, and polished; ashes to be drained, boiled, poured, and leached for soft soap; fabric to be spun, carded, loomed, and dyed; candles to be molded, rugs to be woven . . ." Boys' work in the fields was also routine and boring, "terracing, furrowing, and plowing the soil, planting, seeding, cradling, tasseling, threshing, pitching, raking, tramping out, cleaning, separating, binding, stacking, storing, and selling the grain. . . ." Authors perceived work to be endless and leisure time nonexistent. Mildred Renaud recalled how her grandmother insisted that no one should ever be idle. The girl had little time for doing anything but "drying dishes, peeling potatoes, and shaving off the calluses and corns that grew on the older woman's overtaxed feet. . . ."[19]

Farmwork could also be discouraging. Children might work hard to plant a crop and then see it eaten by locusts or ruined by drought. Farmwork could also be dangerous: "A California mother wrote relatives that her son had survived a difficult week. First a friend with a shotgun accidentally had peppered him with birdshot, then a hay-cutter had taken off the first joint of the boy's right index finger—'his most important finger!' "

Yet children did not altogether resent farm labor on family farms. Most children knew that their work, even when it was most discouraging, was essential to their family's survival. Edna Matthews Clifton recalled how much she hated picking cotton on her family's Texas farm. " 'Sometimes I would lie down on my sack and want to die,' she wrote. 'Sometimes they would pour water over my head to relieve me.' Still, Edna understood why she was there: 'It was instilled in us that *work was necessary*. Everybody worked; it was a part of life, for there was no life without it.' " Farm children also appreciated the camaraderie of working with their parents, brothers, and sisters. All shared the joy of planting and harvesting crops successfully. Conversely, when crops failed, all shared in the sorrow. In California, Mexican-American children who helped harvest or process fruits and nuts at least worked alongside their mothers for a good part of every year. On the frontier, children who worked by themselves herding animals learned how to manage on their own and gained a sense of self-reliance.[20] So too did older boys and girls hired out to work for other farm families. While these children did indeed live apart from their natural families, most worked fairly close to home, and all understood that such work was temporary.

Between 1850 and 1890, while the majority of children living on farms in the United States labored for long hours starting at a young age, one group of farm children labored somewhat less than their peers. This privileged group were the sons and daughters of farmers who were able to purchase new machinery.

In the 1850s, Midwestern and Northeastern farmers began to purchase new horse-powered machinery. "By 1864, three-quarters of farmers owning over 100 acres possessed a reaper or mower." Astute, affluent farmers who utilized the new machinery produced more using fewer workers and used some of the increased profits to acquire additional land. The wives of such progressive farmers, however, did not enjoy the benefits of labor-saving machinery. These farm women continued to labor intensively at household tasks such as hauling wood to build fires, baking bread, preserving vegetables and fruit, sewing clothes, and cleaning.[21] Although their daughters helped them some, by the 1870s, well-off farm wives and their husbands preferred their girls to attend school, learn to play the piano, and sew. Wives of progressive farmers relied on hired girls to help with heavy household chores, thereby permitting their daughters to attend school into their late teens and prepare themselves for middle-class careers in teaching and for marriage to similarly well-educated young men.

In the Northeast, where dairying was the most important source of farm income, teenage boys who helped with milking and making butter and cheese were of considerable economic value to their families. However, by the 1870s, there was less for boys to do on other types of progressive farms. Fathers sent boys to school throughout the year and replaced their labor with that of machines and hired hands. In the rural North and West, the wealthier the parents, the more likely their teenage child was to attend school.[22] Yet even as well-off farmers hoped that extended schooling might prove useful to sons in managing large farms and producing for profit, farmers also worried that boys who performed little agricultural labor in their youth might lack an attachment to farming and ultimately abandon it. Urged on by the farm press, many progressive farmers gave sons and sometimes daughters their own gardens and livestock, thereby providing youngsters a new kind of employment. Boys who had previously worked with their fathers in fields or with mothers and sisters in kitchen gardens now farmed their own garden plots alone for profit. The children liked such work because they were able to keep the proceeds of what they sold and spend the money as they chose. For example, 10-year-old Arthur C. Hackley of upstate New York spaded the plot of ground his father gave him, planted strawberries there, and later sold them for twelve and one-half cents per quart.[23]

Between 1850 and 1890, whereas the sons and daughters of prosperous farmers who introduced new, labor-saving machinery onto their farms did not stop working altogether, these boys and girls certainly labored less and attended school for more years than did most other farm children. As early as the 1830s and 1840s, a similar division developed between children in urban America. Industrialization both permitted a large number of children to avoid work through their youth and necessitated the labor of countless other youngsters in factories, mills, mines, homes, and city streets.

With industrialization came new high-paying white-collar employment for middle-class men, who, unlike farmers and artisans, left their homes each day to work elsewhere. At the same time, commercial production and sale in cities of items such as cloth, soap, and candles obviated home production of such items by women. As work and home came to be separated, there developed a doctrine of separate spheres. Men's sphere of activity was in the larger world of work and government, and women's sphere of activity was in the home, managing the household and caring for children.[24] It became economically possible and culturally acceptable for children of the middle class to remain under the care of their mothers within their family homes throughout infancy and youth.

In addition, after 1850, middle-class urban parents, anxious to provide for the future of their children, found early employment less appropriate. The best new jobs for boys were in the professions and business, and the best jobs for girls were in teaching and clerical work. Such jobs required that boys and girls remain in school to 16, 17, or even 18 years of age; few children who quit school before that age secured jobs that ensured middle-class status. In 1880, in Providence, Rhode Island, among a sample of 14- and 15-year-olds who had quit school and were fully employed, "less than one in twelve . . . had a real clerical [white-collar] job." Among the girls, "93.5 percent . . . who worked at age fourteen or fifteen—were employed in semiskilled or unskilled manual occupations." This lesson was not lost on middle-class parents: among 14- and 15-year-olds in Providence, "fewer than one in ten of the boys [and none of the girls] from the high white collar stratum were at work in 1880."[25] Most prosperous middle-class urban parents who expected to prepare their sons and daughters for white-collar jobs kept children in school until their middle to late teens.

While the industrial revolution enabled many middle-class children to remain at home and in school until well beyond puberty, it had a different effect on working-class children. After midcentury, although decent-paying jobs in skilled trades did not altogether disappear, many jobs were eliminated. Parents who earlier might have apprenticed their sons between the ages of 12 and 14 to master craftsmen to learn a skilled trade could no longer do so.[26] Apprenticeship itself did not totally disappear; it persisted well into the twentieth century in cities such as Philadelphia. Both businessmen in companies that needed an adequate supply of skilled workers loyal to their firms and organized working people in trade unions seeking to protect "the status of their jobs and the jobs themselves" kept apprenticeship alive. Yet companies and unions offered such apprenticeships only to youths age 16 and older.[27] Working-class parents who earned low wages or lost their jobs in depressions could not afford to wait until children were in their late teens to put them to work as apprentices. Out-of-work fathers needed immediate help. In Chicago, in 1890, among working-class heads of household who were out of work eight or more weeks, 45.6 percent relied on the income of their children to survive.[28]

Even in good times, when fathers were employed, just to get by, many working-class families required the wages of more than one worker. In Newburyport, Massachusetts, in the 1850s, children under the age of 15 contributed 20 percent of the family income of workers.[29] Among Massachusetts working-class families in the 1870s, children between the ages of 10 and 19 provided an average of one-quarter of the family income, and among the families of the unskilled, children supplied more than one-third of the family income. In 1882, 20 percent of all Chicago working-class families depended on the earnings of wives and children, and the children provided an average of 36 percent of family income.[30] Using a federal government study of workers in nine major industries between 1888 and 1890, two sociologists have found that the lower the income of the father in families with school-age children, the more likely one or more of the children were to work.[31] As historian Linda Gordon has observed: "Parents who overworked their children were not lazy—most often they were mothers already exhausted and fearful for the family's survival."[32]

It should come as no surprise that family poverty, more than any other factor, occasioned children to seek employment. In the late nineteenth century, because women earned so little in comparison to men, children of widowed mothers were especially likely to leave school and go to work. So too were children of the lowest-paid male laborers—unskilled and semiskilled workers. In 1880, in Providence, Rhode Island, among 14- and 15-year-olds from all occupational groups, roughly six out of every ten of the sons and daughters of unskilled and semiskilled workers were employed.[33]

Foreign-born children were more likely to be employed than native-born children. In the 1870 census, the first in which children's occupations were recorded, more foreign-born children than native-born children ages 10–14 and 15–19 had jobs. It is probable, however, that foreign-born children were especially likely to work outside the home because immigrant families were so frequently impoverished. Native-born white youngsters were just as apt to perform wage work as were immigrant children if their families were equally poor.[34]

Yet ethnic culture also affected child employment. Most immigrants were from European farming communities and were accustomed to children performing productive labor with other family members on farms. In the industrial city, where all worked for wages, the family as a productive unit no longer existed. If parents were to profit from their children's labor, they had to secure wage work outside the home. Few parents hesitated to send their children to work, because most came from traditional societies where parenthood meant controlling a child's labor and life choices. Such control was a benefit of parenthood.[35]

There is some evidence that Irish and Italian parents exercised that benefit regardless of their income. In Providence, Rhode Island, in 1880, 17 percent of the children of native-born men in low-paying, low-manual occupations avoided work and entered the high school, but only 8.8 percent of Irish youngsters did the same, even though one-third of their parents held comparatively well-paying skilled or white-collar jobs.[36] Among Italians in Buffalo in the late nineteenth century, boys with fathers from all occupational groups were likely to be employed. There was a popular Italian expression that the "door [of a house] is open to he who contributes—otherwise you stay outside." Italians believed that youngsters old enough to work should do so to repay the cost of their upbringing and to demonstrate their loyalty to family.[37] It was not exclusively family economic circumstances but also ethnic cultural values that resulted in high levels of employment among Irish and Italian children. Neither group regarded extended education as very useful for children.

On the other hand, in the 1880s and 1890s, eastern European Jews, though just as poor as other immigrant groups, were especially willing to make sacrifices to keep their children out of the full-time labor force and in school through their teen years. The respect for learning that was a part of their ethnic tradition outweighed other considerations and disposed Jewish parents to put their children's education before more immediate family economic needs.[38]

Immigrant Irish, Italian, German, and Jewish families, as well as poor native-born whites, agreed on one issue: children, rather than mothers, should supplement parental income by working outside the home. Before 1850, white American-born and immigrant married women rarely took up wage work, and few did so thereafter. Most felt it appropriate for single women but not for married women to labor for wages. If their family situation required it, married white and immigrant women preferred to earn extra money by taking in boarders or manufacturing items in the home—work they could do while still fulfilling their other obligations as housewives and mothers.[39]

Whether poverty or ethnic cultural heritage or some combination of the two influenced parents to send their children into the labor force, most parents could not do so with any prospect of real financial advantage until the youngsters were between the ages of 10 and 15. Younger children were an economic drain on poor families. In 1875, in Lowell, Massachusetts, one immigrant father earned $510 working on the wharf and an additional $80 at a second job. However, with a wife and four children under the age of 10 to support, his wages were insufficient. By the end of the year, the family was $45 in debt. They lived in a three-room apartment that officials noted was "out of repair." All were attired "miserably" and their faces were "haggard." They had very little to eat beyond bread, coffee, tea, potatoes, and occasionally meat and fish. Even when children could enter the labor market, they did not command very good wages until the age of 15. Thus, in Lowell, another family barely managed to get by in 1875 with the earnings of a mill laborer and his 10-year-old son. Together, father and son earned $572, but that was not enough to support them, the boy's mother, and three other small children. The family was not in debt, but officials described their apartment "as dirty as the surroundings and very poorly furnished."[40]

The low wages children commanded until their teen years help to explain why even the poorest parents were willing to send their youngsters to public schools between the ages of seven and fourteen (see chapter 4). Moreover, even before children took full-time wage work and while they were attending school, urban working-class children could still contribute to the economic well-being of their families. For example, children as young as five years old could root out junk in the streets, vacant lots, and back alleys of their neighborhoods or in the local dumps, where dry garbage accumulated. In every working-class neighborhood, junk men, ragpickers, and pawnbrokers willingly purchased items scavenged by youngsters. At local railway yards, children also collected stray pieces of coal and wood, which they hauled home to burn in their family stoves. In the open-air food markets in cities, youngsters ferreted out overripe and discarded fruits and vegetables to share with their families. Little girls often helped out at home. Most commonly, they tended babies while their mothers did more strenuous household chores. However, in the absence of refrigerators, shopping was a daily activity, and mothers often sent their daughters out to buy small amounts of food. Girls helped out with the laundry, all of which, from sorting, soaking, washing, rinsing, starching, drying, to ironing, had to be done by hand. Children hauled wood up several flights of stairs to cooking stoves in apartments and later toted ashes downstairs when cooking was done.[41]

Once working-class children reached their teens, white families typically sent boys to work before girls. There were good economic reasons for this choice. Because boys commanded higher wages than girls, it made sense to put boys to work first. In Philadelphia, in 1880, girls age 15 and older earned 70 percent of what boys earned.

The composition of families also helped determine whether a white teenage working-class child would enter the labor force. In large families, if most youngsters were over the age of 14, more were likely to be employed. However, if there was an age range within a white family, if there were very young children present, older boys and girls generally stayed at home to help their mothers. Once infants and toddlers reached school age, their older brothers and sisters usually left home to find wage work. In a large white family where several older youths were employed, younger children might well avoid wage work and remain in school into their late teens.[42] Thus large family size among the white working class resulted both in more older children working and also in younger ones remaining in school. Among families of unskilled workers who enrolled a child in Pittsburgh's Commercial High School in 1900, virtually all families had older children who were working in manual jobs and hence helping to finance the younger child's education. Parents often used the extra income that teenage children generated to purchase a home. Home ownership provided protection—a secure place to live in good times and bad—not only for the parents but also for the children: a home was a financial asset that parents could pass on to their children. Because in large white working-class families so many older children worked, these families were often able both to purchase a home and to send younger family members to secondary school. In 1865, at the age of 16, James Kenney came to the United States. He married a young Irish woman who bore him seven children. Their oldest son became a bookbinder, their eldest daughter helped her mother at home, the youngest daughter became a saleslady, and two younger sons also worked, one as a salesman and the other as a machinist's apprentice. Together, family members saved to purchase a home in Somerville, Massachusetts. Moreover, because of the labor within and outside of the home provided by their five oldest children, the Kenneys were able to keep up their mortgage payments and to send their two youngest boys to the Somerville High School.[43]

Whereas white urban working-class children were very likely to be employed by the time they entered their teens, the same was not true of all urban African-American children. In Northern cities, the experience of white and black working-class children diverged considerably. In 1880, in both Philadelphia and in Providence, Rhode Island, black children worked less than did immigrant children and about the same as did native-born youngsters, even though blacks were poorer. Black women worked more than did either white native-born or foreign-born women. African-Americans elected to keep their children in school longer and to put mothers to work instead of children—a choice few white families made. There are several reasons why black families may have made this decision. First, unlike whites, many black women took for granted that they would work for wages both before and after marriage. Women's wages and those of their husbands were usually sufficient to support their families, which were smaller than urban white working-class families. Second, many black families apparently moved to Northern cities in order to secure a better education for their children rather than to find them jobs. In fact, there were many fewer jobs open to black children in Northern cities than there were to white children. Textile mills and other factories rarely hired African-American children.[44] Accustomed to married women working, anxious to have their children educated, and aware that wage work was difficult for them to find, many Northern urban black families determined that mothers, but not children, should seek wage labor.

The experience of black children in Southern cities was somewhat different. In 1870 and 1880, in seven Southern cities, more black children than white children in every age group were employed. Urban African-American children in the South worked because their parents had difficulty supporting their children and because they could find employment. In Southern cities, black men worked more than did white men, but blacks earned less than whites and were more often unemployed. Black women also labored at wage work (usually as servants and laundresses) more than did white women and were more steadily employed than were black men. Yet despite urban black parents' willingness to work and to limit the number of their children, because wage rates were lower in the South, urban black parents probably could not support their children as easily in the South as in the North. Schooling for blacks in the South was of poorer quality than in the North and was not so attractive an option, especially because young Southern blacks had an easier time than Northern black youths finding jobs. In the South, African-American girls readily found employment in domestic service, and boys and girls worked in tobacco factories, which hired only blacks. In such factories, pay was extremely low, and working conditions were poor. Laborers stood up all day in hot rooms with inadequate lighting. Such labor did have the advantage of allowing mothers and children to work together as they "stripped individual leaves off their central stem and hung them up to dry."[45]

Unfortunately, no matter what choices African-American families made in regard to child labor, neither parents nor their children derived much economic benefit from sending children to work. Southern rural African-Americans who had large families and put all of their children to work as soon as possible rarely improved their economic lot. Urban black families in the North and South limited their fertility, but both parents and children earned such low wages that neither moved up the economic scale. Even when African-American youngsters remained in school and out of wage work until their late teens, as was true in Northern cities, racist employment practices prevented blacks from securing the higher-paying jobs that working-class white children obtained if they deferred employment in favor of extended schooling. (See chapter 4.)

Once working-class children were ready to enter the labor force, the particular job they took depended both on employer preferences and practices and on parental needs and inclinations. Gender and racial preferences influenced employers' choices of whom to hire, and parents were willing to let their sons and daughters work for certain employers but not for others. How employer and parental concerns interacted to influence child labor is illustrated by examining the employment of children in textile mills, mining towns, urban homes, and street trades.

Both in the Northeast and in the South, cotton textile mills welcomed child laborers. Between 1889 and 1890, a government study of 6,800 industrial families revealed that more children were employed in the textile industry than in any other industry. Mill owners prized youngsters for their "speed and agility."[46] Machines were simple enough for children to operate, and boys and girls provided a reserve of cheap labor that could be called out of school in good times but easily laid off during depressions.

Southern cotton mills, which grew in number after the Civil War as part of the effort to build a more industrialized New South, deliberately recruited whole families of workers—but only white families. At a time when segregation characterized many aspects of Southern life, when whites replaced blacks in many skilled and semiskilled jobs, and when there was a strong "taboo against bringing black men into association with white women," most mill owners sought an all-white labor force.[47]

To attract that labor force to Southern cotton-mill towns, mill owners had to persuade white families to leave their farms. To accomplish this task, cotton mills advertised. One such advertisement, distributed by a North Carolina mill, purported to be advice from a former farmer turned cotton-mill worker:

> Three years ago I owned a little mountain farm of two hundred acres. I had two good horses, two good cows, plenty of hogs, sheep and several calves. I had three girls and two boys; ages 11 to 21. . . . After I clothed my family, fed all my stock during the winter, I had only enough provisions and feed to carry me through making another crop, and no profit left. I sold my farm and stock, paid up all my debts and moved my family to a cotton mill. . . . Now my youngest daughter, only 14 years old, is making $6 per week, my other two are making $7.50 each per week and my two boys are making $8 per week and I am making $4.50 per week; a total of $166 per month. My provisions average $30, house rent $2, coal and wood, $4, total $36; leaving a balance of $130, to buy clothes and deposit in the bank.[48]

The first parents willing to respond to the entreaties of cotton-mill owners were single mothers. Because most women who headed families were poor, they were particularly attracted by employers who promised their oldest children employment and themselves an opportunity either to work or to keep house. Cotton mills offered poor mothers the chance to hold their families together. In 1880, in Cohoes, New York, one out of every four families of cotton textile workers was headed by one parent, usually a woman.[49] In the same year, in Augusta, Georgia, women headed 45 percent of all mill homes. One woman who moved her family to be near the cotton mills in Atlanta illustrates both the special problems of rural widowed women in the post–Civil War South and the particular attraction of cotton mills. She reported: "I lost my husband in the War. We lived on a rented farm. I tried to work the farm with three small children. I couldn't make bread, and pay the rent. I came here eight years ago. My son works in the city, at the carpenters trade, gets three dollars a day. My two daughters earn eighty and ninety cents each at the loom. I keep house and milk the cow. . . . We bless God every day for this shelter—good food and good clothes."[50]

Eventually, not only families headed by women but also families headed by impoverished men migrated to cotton-mill towns. Drawn by the promise of work for both parents and children, poor immigrant families from Canada and Ireland settled in Northern mill towns such as Manchester, New Hampshire, and Lowell, Massachusetts. In the South, after the Civil War, many black families, but also numerous white farm families, became deeply in debt to white landowners and merchants. When low prices for cotton in the 1880s and 1890s made that debt more burdensome, many white farmers realized that their capital was in their children and moved to mill towns where they could make use of that capital.[51]

Once settled in a mill town, however, parents almost inevitably lost the opportunity to choose whether their children should work. Because mill owners paid adult men such low wages (about one-third less than men earned in other industries), sending children into the mills became an economic necessity for most workers. After Marie Proulx and her family migrated from Canada to the mill town of Manchester, New Hampshire, she said, "My father was never able to support a family of eight children on $1.10 per day. It was miserable at first. Oh, were we miserable! . . . So I had to go work somewhere, and all there was were the mills, there was only Amoskeag. We had to help our father; I was the oldest one."[52] Children began working in cotton mills on a regular, wage basis when they were between 10 and 14 years old. Younger boys and girls played around the mills after classes or during summer vacations. Younger children helped their parents and their older brothers and sisters in what became "an informal family apprenticeship system." "Ethel Faucette carried lunch to her sister. 'While she was eating,' Faucette explained, 'I learned how to work her job. I was already learned when I went to work.' " Children's help also enabled parents and siblings to work more themselves. Once youngsters began full-time employment in cotton mills, youngsters labored 12 hours a day, six days a week.

Boys and girls worked at different tasks. Girls did spooling, winding, and spinning and earned better wages than did young boys, who were initially assigned to doffing or sweeping and cleaning around machines in the carding room. However, once boys reached their late teens, they had usually learned how to tend machines and work in the carding room, and these jobs paid more than the tasks assigned to girls. Boys in their late teens could also become supervisors, but girls could not. The few black children employed in cotton mills had the least attractive jobs of waste gatherers and sweepers.

In the parts of the mill where white youngsters labored, there was often an atmosphere of play. "One observer noted that 'as their chief indoor sport [children] claimed the privilege of hanging onto the shafting belts as the machinery slowly started and riding towards the twenty-foot ceiling. . . . A game of catch, with a ball improvised from yarn was [also] a very natural way in which to wish to spend one's time while waiting for the machines to fill. . . .' "[53]

It is not surprising that supervisors disliked such child's play and some-times harshly disciplined children. Former mill worker Paul Cline remem-bered: "Some second hands in the mills, back years ago, used to take little old kids by their heels and stick them out the window and say, 'I'm going to drop you if you don't behave yourself.' That's the way they done." There was dan-ger from more than supervisors. Children who worked for long hours often grew tired or inattentive. At such times, accidents were common. One girl explained how both she and her sister lost fingers while twisting flax: "You couldn't talk or look off a minute. My sister was just like me. She forgot and talked and just that minute her finger was off, and she didn't even cry till she picked it up." Children who were fearful of tough discipline or of accidents did not have the option to quit and leave the mill. They had to work.[54]

Yet when they labored, no matter how harsh the conditions, child labor-ers in cotton mills toiled within a family context. Children lived with their parents and siblings; they learned their jobs from family members and worked in the mills alongside them. This is probably one of the reasons why parents approved of such child labor, and why parents willingly removed their children from school so that they could work in the mills. In both the North and South, textile-workers' children between the ages of 10 and 14 were more likely than other children to leave school for work. Young mill laborers understood why they had to work. Said Yvonne Dionne about her labor as a child at a New Hampshire cotton mill:

> I always enjoyed the work at the Amoskeag when I was there, though if I could have done without, I would have stayed home. But when everything is hard to get, and you want to have a few extra things, you have to help out the family. We were brought up in a large family—my father was a weaver and a loomfixer—and as soon as one girl was old enough, she went to work. That was the way. The oldest one started, and the rest of the family had to follow suit. We didn't feel bad about not going to school because nobody could afford to. Our parents were too poor.[55]

Not only Northern and Southern textile factories but also anthracite coal mines in Western Pennsylvania were particularly receptive to child laborers. Mine owners began to rely increasingly on child labor as owners engaged in deep mining, which necessitated employing more cheap child laborers to process coal above ground. Typically, owners hired boys of eight or nine to work in coal-processing plants called breakers. Breakers were buildings of four or more stories. At the top, heavy machinery broke the coal into smaller pieces, which then flowed through various chutes until the coal ended up in freight cars lined up at the bottom. Along planks nailed to the chutes sat the breaker boys, who picked through the coal as it passed by and removed from it pieces of slate. "The rooms in which they worked were noisy and filled with coal dust. In the summer the breakers were stiflingly hot and in the winter bitter cold. The youngsters were subject to a variety of minor and major injuries. It was not uncommon to see them leaving the breakers with fingers cut and bleeding from picking through the coal." Supervisors were quick to use a stick on the heads and shoulders of boys who betrayed "lack of zeal." Once boys reached the age of 12 or 13, they left the breakers to go underground. By the age of 17 or 18, boys could become miners' helpers. "The risks of serious injury and death were much higher in the mines than in the breakers. The adolescents were confined underground, sometimes spending their entire shift partially submerged in water, where they were exposed to mine dust, mine gas, and injury and death from explosions and rock falls."[56]

Parents responded to employers' preference for child laborers for several reasons. First, miners had become dependent on the family-wage economy. Between 1875 and 1899, mine owners broke the mining union, cut wages, and, on the average, employed miners for 189 out of a possible 312 working days a year. To survive, miners needed their children's wages to supplement their own. Second, in mining towns, there were many silk mills, which, like other textile mills, willingly employed young girls. Miners could put their sons to work in the breakers and their daughters to work at the looms.

Third, many parents attracted to mining towns were Welsh immigrants who were accustomed to putting their children to work in mines. In a sample of Welsh and Irish working-class families in Scranton, Pennsylvania, between 1880 and 1890, 100 percent of Welsh immigrant sons aged 11 to 15 were employed compared to 67 percent of Irish sons of the same age. Fewer daughters worked, but even so, 30 percent of Welsh girls aged 11 to 15 were working compared to 14 percent of Irish girls. Welsh families were accustomed to child labor in the mining towns from which they had migrated and simply continued that tradition in the United States. Conversely, in Ireland, fewer children worked outside the home, especially in mining, though many labored on family farms.[57] Of course, the Irish were not unwilling to put their children to work; they were just a little less enthusiastic about mining-town labor than were the Welsh, who were so long acclimated to it.

As in cotton-mill and coal-mining towns, in commercial and industrial cities, employer and parental preferences determined in what context children worked. Clothing manufacturers and cigar makers in cities such as New York provided materials to workers who assembled ready-to-wear clothing or cigars in their tenement apartments. As long as the product was properly made, employers were willing for workers of all ages to participate in its manufacture. Jewish and Italian families were particularly attracted to such employment. In their homelands, some Jews had worked as tailors, so their experience inclined them to continue this trade. Jews and Italians also found the idea of working in a family context very attractive. In home manufacture, their young children worked beside them; boys and girls sewed, pulled bastings, and carried completed garments to contractors. Italians and Jews, who were very protective of their daughters, also preferred them to work in the safety of their homes.[58]

Perhaps the most common employment of children in cities was working in a street trade. Parents supported such employment because it was part-time, it could be combined with going to school and helping out at home, and it was often done in conjunction with fathers, mothers, or other family members, who also peddled items in city streets. Boys and girls occasionally sang, danced, or acted for pennies, but most children were hucksters. As they shopped with their mothers, young people learned how to sell by observing older peddlers. Children sold items such as gum, peanuts, and crackers, which were small enough for children to carry on their persons and cheap enough to market for a profit. In some Western mining towns, children kept their own vegetable gardens and marketed the produce in city streets. Other children peddled pies baked by their mothers. "Their youth was their greatest selling point. There was something irresistible about innocent-looking children trying so hard to earn money."

For young boys, the most popular and profitable street trade was selling newspapers. Through most of the nineteenth century, boys sold papers all day long, but by 1890, when two-thirds of dailies were published in the afternoon, boys sold papers part-time after school. Newspapers welcomed children because they were the papers' sales force—they were the method by which papers got to their reading public. Newsboys were the children of skilled and unskilled workers and came from every ethnic group, "in numbers roughly proportional to the adult working-class population." Newsboys were independent businesspersons. They decided how many papers to purchase depending on how exciting were the headlines and how important were the sports scores. The young salesmen then stationed themselves wherever there were a lot of commuters, at trolley lines, subways, and department stores. Papers sold for one cent, and if a boy received a nickel and was slow to make change, he might earn additional money from a tip.

Although a few girls sold newspapers, this was largely a male street trade. Parents endorsed the trade for boys because it was profitable and acquainted them with the city in which they would work as adults, but parents felt that

Atlantis (daily Greek newspaper) newsboys, New York City (c. 1890–1900). In the late nineteenth century, a common job for urban working-class boys was to sell newspapers in city streets. The faces of the boys in this photograph reflect the pride they felt in their work. (Balch Institute for Ethnic Studies Library, Philadelphia, Pennsylvania)

selling newspapers or anything else in city streets was dangerous for girls. Parents feared that girls were more subject to sexual exploitation than were boys. Such activity was also unladylike. "Young girls were not supposed to be brash, aggressive and loud."[59] City-labor jobs for children were segregated by gender. Whereas boys and girls both worked in home manufacture, boys toiled more in street trades, and girls worked more in domestic service.

As middle-class families became more affluent in the late nineteenth century, they sought domestic servants to replace the labor of mothers and daughters. Middle-class women engaged more in church and charity work outside the home and their daughters continued their education through high school and some few through college. Most working-class parents preferred to have their teenage daughters help out at home, but if families required the girls' income, parents chose to place the young women in domestic situations. Presumably, girls working as servants were somewhat protected and acquired useful homemaking skills. African-American, Irish, and Scandinavian parents were especially likely to send their daughters to work in homes as maids, cooks, or nannies. Service was about the only job open to African-American girls. Some also became laundresses. They began by helping their mothers at home do laundry for white families. In Irish and Scandinavian families, working as a servant in someone else's home was a traditional occupation for young girls before they married. However, white native-born, Italian, and Jewish young women usually avoided domestic service if they could. Italian and Jewish parents particularly worried about placing their daughters in homes where the young women might be the objects of sexual advances by their employers' husbands and sons.

Young girls who entered domestic service enjoyed some advantages, such as full room and board, in addition to their wages. However, these girls had to labor for long hours, from 4:30 A.M. until 10 P.M. at night. Servants performed a variety of tasks; they tended children, cooked, sewed, and washed in homes with few utilities. Employers rarely permitted their servants to have visitors. Each week, a maid enjoyed only one half-day and one evening out on her own. Finally, there was the disadvantage of working in close family quarters where the potential for sexual harassment was very real.

Unlike hired farm girls, domestic servants were not treated as members of the family. Servants lived in, but they did not work alongside their mistresses and ate separately from the family in which they were employed. Servants also lived entirely apart from their own families and had very little free time to visit parents and siblings. However, in one important way, the labor of young urban domestic servants resembled that of hired farm girls: servants' work freed more affluent young women from household chores and permitted them an extended education.[60]

The forms of employment of working-class children advantaged some youngsters more than others. Native-born white and foreign-born boys had the largest range of jobs open to them. Many of these jobs offered a degree of independence and sometimes opportunity for advancement. In street trades, young white native and immigrant boys labored most autonomously. In cotton mills, boys who learned to operate machines increased their wages and responsibilities, and in mining, boys who began in the breakers could advance to higher-paying jobs underground. The job outlook for native-born white and foreign-born girls was limited to factories, mills, and domestic service, but job opportunities were most limited for African-American children. They might work as servants or in some few factories. The jobs available to all African-Americans and to most white and foreign-born girls encouraged subservience rather than autonomy and offered little chance for promotion. In private homes, employers supervised young African-American, native white, and immigrant female domestics closely. Gender-segregated jobs in cotton mills taught native white and immigrant girls that no matter how well paid they were as children, there was little hope for advancement. African-American children who worked in tobacco factories earned low wages and had little prospect of upward mobility.

Urban industrial labor kept some families close. Children who engaged in home manufacture as well as children who worked in cotton mills and mines learned their jobs and labored in a family context. Many urban children took advantage of the proximity of factory and street labor to their homes and elected to live with their natural families throughout their youth.[61] Still, because of the jobs open to them, it was native-born white and foreign-born boys who most often lived at home. Adolescent working-class girls, especially those who were Irish, Scandinavian, or African-American, could not elect to remain in their family homes but typically lived as servants in the homes of others. How ironic that girls, who needed to learn homemaking skills and presumably required special protection when young, were the most likely of working-class children to take jobs that required them to live away from their own homes. This irony was not lost on their parents, for by the end of the century, mothers who had themselves once been servants proved particularly unwilling to place out their daughters. There were few second-generation domestic servants. Yet not all children who could live in their own homes chose to do so. Some children preferred to leave home as soon as they were able; African-American boys in Southern cities were especially likely to live apart from their families as soon as they could earn a decent wage on their own.[62] It is possible that the greater poverty and consequent smaller living quarters of African-American families made remaining at home less attractive to their teenage children. Or, given the strong kin networks among African-Americans, living apart from their natural families may have meant nothing more than living next door or down the street. Children, parents, and other kin may have continued to help one another financially and otherwise.

Nonetheless, most urban families probably preferred their children to live at home, partly in order to collect their wages. Young people understood this, but once they reached their teen years, many wanted to retain some, if not all, of their earnings to spend for their own pleasure. On family farms, parents and children pooled their labor for a common goal, but in cities and towns, each family member became an individual wage earner. In the urban context, children often began to believe that what they earned belonged at least in part to them and not exclusively to their families. Many African-American children apparently acted on that belief, for as soon as they could earn good wages, young blacks left home and set up separate households of their own.[63] Still, we cannot be sure if they kept all their wages or returned a portion to their families. Native-born white boys and foreign-born boys also challenged the family-wage economy, customarily by trying to retain some of their earnings, not by setting up on their own. Native-born white girls and foreign-born girls were more likely to pool their earnings with those of other family workers. Data from a 1889–90 study of 6,800 industrial families reveal that by the time young women reached 21 years of age, only 15 percent of daughters kept any of their own earnings. Of course, children could find ways to retain some of their wages without directly challenging parents. A New York working girl explained "how most of the girls she worked with got the money they needed. 'Oh sure, there's a lot of girls that "knock down." You take this week in our place,—we all made good overtime. I know I got two forty-nine. Well, I guess there wasn't a single girl but me that didn't change her [pay] envelope, on our floor. Whatever you make is written outside in pencil, you know. That's easy to fix—you have only to rub it out, put on whatever it usually is, and pocket the change.' " Even when parents suspected children of withholding some of their earnings, parents were often reluctant to say anything. Most desperately needed whatever boys and girls earned and hence feared challenging children, alienating them, and consequently losing their income.[64]

Although throughout the eighteenth and nineteenth centuries, many children began their work careers very young, the United States government took no official notice of children's employment until 1870. In that year, the U.S. census documented for the first time that over one out of every eight children between the ages of 10 and 15 was employed. By 1900, about one in six—or roughly 1.75 million—children earned wages. Both figures were underestimates, because many children who labored as domestics, in home manufacturing, in street trades, or for their parents were not counted. Studies of particular cities reveal a much higher proportion of child laborers. In Providence, Rhode Island, almost one in three children between the ages of 10 and 15 was at work in 1880, and the same was true of Chicago in 1888 and of Philadelphia in 1900. In the South, among black children between the ages of 10 and 15, half of all boys and one in three girls held "gainful occupations" in 1900.[65]

By the late nineteenth century, the relative ability of parents living in urban America to support their families diverged to such a degree that neither could sympathize with the position of the other. Working-class parents earned so little that they could neither put food on the table nor pay the rent without the help of their working-age children. Working-class parents did not appreciate criticism of their choice to withdraw children from school and put them to work to ensure family survival. Conversely, middle-class parents, who could easily afford to keep their own children in school and out of the workforce until their mid to late teens, became so alarmed by the census figures and by exposés of the terrible conditions under which some children labored that they began to lobby for laws to limit child labor.[66] Yet none sought to abolish it entirely. Most people continued to believe that in some cases child labor was acceptable and even valuable to the child. Between 1870 and 1890, because of the ambivalent attitudes of many reformers toward child labor, the opposition of working-class parents to any restrictions on their ability to elicit financial support from their children, and the determination of the largest of child employers, textile-mill owners, to keep children on the job, the anti-child labor movement proved only modestly successful.

Although by 1890 prosperous farmers and middle-class urban families largely withdrew their own children from the labor force, they nonetheless recognized the value of child labor under certain conditions. For example, middle-class reformers did not challenge the employment of children on farms. Reformers believed that working in the out-of-doors alongside family members was wholesome and beneficial for the young. Reformers also accepted the labor of girls in home manufacturing and in domestic service because such labor presumably fitted girls for their future roles as homemakers and mothers. Reformers were somewhat more concerned about children involved in street trades. While the reformers worried that such work exposed youngsters to moral danger, they also admired the entrepreneurship of newsboys. Generally, middle-class reformers blamed working-class parents, especially mothers, who were supposed to protect children, for requiring youngsters to work in dangerous streets and factories. Middle-class parents, who themselves could afford extended schooling for their children, objected to working-class parents who withdrew their children from school so that they could earn money for family support.[67]

The child-labor laws passed by 28 states before 1900 reflect these biases. The legislation applied mainly to children working in mining and manufacturing and not to youngsters working on farms, in domestic service, or in street trades. Most laws set a minimum working age of 10 or 12 years and a maximum working day of 10 hours. The laws also required all employed children to attend school for a certain number of years. Nonetheless, the legislation was not very effective. Working-class parents, dependent on the earnings of their children, objected to and circumvented the laws. B. B. Snow, superintendent of the Auburn, New York, schools, expressed the views of many working-class Americans in 1884 when he said: "while every community would approve the compulsory attendance, in a suitable school, of idle and vagrant boys, there would be little sympathy in the project of taking children from work when the proceeds of their labor are needed for the support of indigent and infirm parents." Because the laws provided simply that a child's age be attested by her or his parents, they often asserted that their sons and daughters were of working age when they were in fact younger. Organizations of working-class Americans such as trade unions did not consistently support child-labor laws. "Some trade unionists believed that child labor regulation was an interference with family rights; indeed, some of their own children worked." The ambivalence about child-labor laws is also reflected in states' unwillingness to enforce these laws. Few states hired an adequate force of factory inspectors to check on the employment of children. As Jeremy Felt said of New York, "Fully aware of the small number of inspectors, manufacturers unlucky enough to be inspected and found violating the law simply bided their time." Sometimes employers hid children when the inspectors came or fired the children and hired them back once inspectors left.[68]

All the child-labor laws enacted before 1900, imperfect as they were, regulated employment of children in the North, Midwest, and Far West. In the South, where cotton mills employed so many child workers, there were no laws regulating such employment. By 1900, 90 percent of the children employed in the South labored in the leading textile states of North Carolina, South Carolina, Georgia, and Alabama, yet none of these states had laws restricting child labor or mandating education. In the South, textile-mill owners strongly opposed state laws restricting the employment practices of textile mills in any way. The mill owners, who were respected members of their communities, argued that by giving employment to children they were helping poor families. Moreover, in the South, it was difficult to argue that mill employment denied children an education, for in the rural communities from which mill workers came, there was little schooling available. Finally, many Southerners viewed child-labor laws as a Northern invention that was not appropriate for the South.[69]

In the second half of the nineteenth century, despite the efforts of reformers, child labor remained characteristic on farms, in factories, and in homes. If so many children worked, does that mean child labor advantaged the farm and urban families that relied upon it? For farm families, the most definitive answer to the question has been made by Lee A. Craig in a careful study of farming in the North and Midwest in the antebellum years. He argues that the value of a farm child at birth was between negative $100 and $200, regardless of whether the cost of bequests to children and the financial aid they provided parents in old age are included or excluded. "If children represented purely investment goods, then these figures would indicate that on average they were not very financially rewarding investments—a result that should not surprise today's parents. In the South at the same time, the net present value at birth of a slave child was close to zero but positive." No comparable study has been made of urban working-class children and their value to parents. However, historians and economists have closely studied the value provided by young cotton textile workers—a sizable group of child laborers in the nineteenth century. Donald Parsons and Claudia Goldin found that even though children earned one-quarter of the income in textile families, "total family income in textiles was . . . 5 percent less than in other industries."[70] Industries that employed many child laborers paid low wages to all—including the parents of child workers. Thus, for families engaged in textile work, children provided essential financial aid, but they still could not bring their family income up to that of other working-class families. Because farm and later urban working-class families began to control their fertility in the late nineteenth century, historians have generally concluded that youngsters were not that economically valuable to their families.

But what of children themselves? What advantages, if any, did child labor bring them? For youngsters who worked, labor at a young age probably brought them the satisfaction of knowing they were helping their families to get by and perhaps improve their situation. Children may also have gained some skills they might find useful in their later working lives, but given the types of work that most children performed as farm laborers, domestics, textile workers, miners, and street sellers, working when young did not prepare children for high-paying or even decent-paying employment as adults. Most youngsters derived little direct economic benefit from their labor. They turned their wages over to their parents, and at least in the case of children engaged in industrial labor, their parents rarely compensated children in the form of a transfer of assets, such as property or income. Of course, some children did benefit from child labor, but not necessarily the ones who performed it. Younger children in large working-class families were often exempt from labor and able to attend school because their older siblings worked. Middle-class urban youngsters and the sons and daughters of prosperous farmers in the North and South had more leisure time and more opportunity to go to school thanks to the labor performed by young domestics, slaves, and hired boys and girls.

Whether they worked or attended school, young people of the nineteenth century, like children everywhere in all time periods, sought to find their own enjoyment in play. Few would challenge the aphorism, "All work and no play makes Jack a dull boy." The next chapter will examine the toys, games, books, sports, and other amusements that became the pleasures of youth in the late nineteenth century.

6

The Pleasures of Youth

Between 1850 and 1890, American children's experience of play—the games they enjoyed, the toys they played with, the sports they engaged in, and the books and stories they read or listened to—differed considerably. Whereas there were some similarities between the ways children played, there was no common culture of play in this era, just as there was no common pattern of child rearing, schooling, or work. The settings in which children played, from large nurseries in middle-class suburban homes to busy city streets to the hard-packed earth of farmyards, varied enormously. So too did the number of years children could be exempted from labor and allowed hours of free play. Throughout the country, although boys and girls played many of the same games, there were gender-specific toys, sports, and books. The pleasures of youth varied most markedly between three groups of children. The first comprised the majority of white youngsters growing up on farms and in more prosperous middle-class homes. The second group comprised white working-class youngsters, both native and foreign born, raised in cities. The final group comprised African-American children, most in the South, growing up in slavery and freedom.

By 1850, urban and suburban middle-class whites, as well as Midwestern and Western farm families and most prosperous Southern white families, believed that childhood was a special time in life when youngsters should be nurtured by their mothers. Because they so valued childhood, such families also believed that youngsters should be allowed to enjoy themselves—to play freely inside and outside the home.

Frontier and poor rural families could not afford to set aside much play space within their homes for youngsters, but more prosperous farm families did just that. Before 1860, in large farm homes, young children played in special nurseries adjacent to kitchens where their mothers worked. Later,

Playing "horse and wagon" by Robert Redfield (circa 1890). In the late nineteenth century, middle-class children enjoyed long childhoods during which they were free to engage in fantasy play as these suburban youngsters are doing. Preadolescent boys and girls were equally free to play outdoors away from direct parental supervision. (Library Company of Philadelphia)

between 1860 and 1880, playrooms for older youngsters also appeared in prosperous farm homes. These playrooms were usually on the second floor, out of range of direct maternal supervision, and afforded older boys and girls the chance to play alone or with a few others in a space they decorated themselves.[1] Middle-class families living in large suburban homes also provided their sons and daughters with special rooms in which to play. Such homes typically included nurseries with high chairs, cribs, child-sized dishes, and special toys and games for girls and boys. In these homes, each youngster had her or his own bedroom as well as family play space elsewhere in the home.[2] Autobiographies of middle-class Americans born between 1822 and 1913 reveal that most remembered with especial fondness attics and basements where they could play alone well outside their mother's field of vision.[3]

As white boys and girls living in rural and suburban homes matured, they left those homes to play in farmyards, local fields, and streams. Outside the home, children could easily avoid adult supervision, while younger boys and girls enjoyed the protection of older siblings. Lucy Larcom remembered that as youngsters growing up at midcentury in a small town in Massachusetts, she and her brothers and sisters roamed across fields near their home down to an ocean inlet where they played about old wharves and occasionally embarked on a boat rowed by a neighbor boy.[4]

Both white boys and girls enjoyed considerable freedom of movement. Types of play varied with the seasons. Autobiographies of women who recalled their youth in the years before 1875 mention how "they dammed streams, fished and trapped, swam in ponds and rivers in summer, sledded and skated in winter." Boys were even more active year-round at out-of-doors play, building and flying kites and balloons; fishing and boating in summer; and sledding, skating, and engaging in snowball fights in winter. Many forms of play were equally appealing to boys and girls. In 1896, T. R. Crosswell studied 1,929 children, most between the ages of nine and fifteen, in Worcester, Massachusetts, and discovered that five of the top ten play preferences of both boys and girls were ball, sled, tag, skates, and hide-and-seek. Children of both genders enjoyed physical activity, which sometimes became violent in the absence of much adult supervision. Sixty-two percent of male and female middle-class authors of autobiographies describing their youth between 1850 and 1880 mentioned rough play. Boys more than girls raided one another's toys and territory and joined in ritualized fighting games such as lickety-cut or rap jacket where "two boys stand face to face and hit each other with beech poles or switches until one gives up."[5]

In rural areas, where there were few choices of playmates, boys and girls played together most frequently. As one rural Midwestern boy remarked, "How could we do without girls when numbers were so few that we could not make up two baseball teams without them?" In larger families, among children living in small towns and suburban areas, very young brothers and sisters may have played together, but older boys and girls commonly played separately. Lucy Larcom remembered being forbidden to play with any boys but her brothers, and she did not enjoy their rough play as much as she did playing ring and singing games with other girls. Among the top ten play preferences of boys and girls in the Crosswell study of 1896, half were different: more boys than girls preferred football, relievo (hide-and-seek played in teams), hockey (shinney, polo), and checkers; and more girls than boys favored dolls, playing house, playing school, or playing with a tea set or jacks. All but one of the ten favorite activities of boys involved physical skill, and about half of the girls' preferences were for quieter games of make-believe most associated with the homemaking role girls would eventually assume. Much of girls' play also modeled their experience with their mothers, with whom girls spent so much time. Accustomed to being directed by their mothers around the home, girls preferred to play games in which a leader moved players around. Conversely, because many white urban middle-class and farm parents expected boys to play fairly independently, boys were more willing to participate in games (such as football and hockey) as individual players rather than to seek games where they could act as controllers.[6]

Until the 1870s and 1880s, most white boys and girls in farm and suburban areas played with other children; more rarely did they play with toys. Until the 1870s, the few toys sold in the United States were manufactured in Germany and were quite costly. Not many families could afford them. Before the Civil War, when parents gave toys to their children (customarily at Christmas), these gifts were handmade items. Fathers made wooden toys, and mothers sewed dolls. Sometimes children made their own toys. Farm kids made jacks from corn they soaked and strung together with needles and thread, balls "from tight, raveled old wool socks," and bats "from boards with whittled-down handholds."[7] Autobiographies of middle-class men and women who grew up between 1850 and 1880 reveal their fondness for self-created toys. Sometimes called "playthings" or "play pritties," handmade toys could be sticks that served as horses, writing tools, boats, and guns; or planks and cigar boxes that became toy trains. Meta Stern Lilienthal turned a rocking chair upside down in her large New York home, and "the crossbars of wood that held the rockers together served admirably as a coachman's seat. Then it became a wagon, a carriage, a sleigh, and later a Roman chariot."[8]

After 1865, American manufacturers began to produce more toys. For most, toy production was a sideline. Publishers turned out paper dolls and games, and kitchen and laundry-machine manufacturers brought out toy versions of their products. About the same time, new methods of mass marketing made manufactured toys more available to urban consumers in department stores (Macy's opened the first toy department in 1875) and to rural families through mail-order catalogues (Montgomery Ward advertised toys beginning in 1885). Such toys were sold only at Christmas until after 1900, for that was the only time parents customarily purchased gifts for their youngsters. In the nineteenth century, children themselves rarely bought toys.[9]

Middle-class parents were the first to give up handmade toys and instead purchase manufactured ones for Christmas giving. Prosperous parents could afford the new toys, and they fit with the middle-class style of child rearing, which isolated small groups of siblings in large homes apart from the work world. Parents reasoned that such boys and girls needed toys to reduce their loneliness, to entertain them, and to educate them for the roles they would play in later life. Nonetheless, middle-class parents felt somewhat guilty about giving up handmade toys, which were traditional, individualized gifts of the parents' precious time more than money. For these middle-class parents, Santa Claus served as a way to reduce their guilt; he became the mediator of gifts. Before Thomas Nast's drawings of Santa Claus in the 1860s and Clement Moore's 1822 poem about his "broad face and little round belly," the American Santa Claus, part of an earlier European tradition, was both generous and punishing. He gave toys to good children and coal and switches to bad ones. By the late nineteenth century, however, he was portrayed only as happy and rewarding. He was generous to children, as were middle-class parents. By giving gifts through Santa Claus, who, according to tradition, hand made his gifts at the North Pole, parents continued the old tradition of Christmas giving while still being able to take advantage of the new toys that new technologies produced.[10]

Toys manufactured by and sold to adults reflect values they want to impress upon the young. Some toys made after the Civil War were frankly racist. At a time when white Southerners were determined to prove that blacks were inferior, that they not only required proper control by whites but were happiest serving whites, and when many Northerners agreed with such ideas because they too were unsure how to treat blacks after slavery, many manufactured toys demeaned blacks. Most such toys portrayed blacks as foolish, greedy, or servile and easily controlled. The Jolly Nigger bank was a molded-metal bust of a black with a huge, smiling red mouth and white teeth, one hand extended to take the child's coin and feed it into the mouth. There were also black dolls whose body parts could be easily manipulated by even a small child.[11] Such toys reinforced the negative view of blacks that white youngsters learned in school through their textbooks.

Like toy banks and dolls, board games reflected the principles that some adults hoped children would learn. This is certainly true of "The Mansion of Happiness." Manufactured about 1850, it "was a board game in which players moved toward the mansion by way of squares marked with traits of character." Players spun to determine how many numbers to move. If they landed on positive traits of character such as piety, honesty, temperance, truth, and chastity, players moved ahead six spaces toward the Mansion of Happiness, but if they landed on bad traits such as audacity, cruelty, immodesty, and ingratitude, players had to return to their former space and wait to spin again. Here was a game that reinforced the same values that most parents and public schools sought to teach the young. However, later in the century, new board games appeared that reflected not qualities of character but the growing materialism in American culture. In 1883 George S. Parker invented his first game—of banking—and by the 1890s, The Monopolist, in which Capital and Labor battled it out, the Game of Moneta: or Money Makes Money, and the Game of Business were also on the market.

Among children, games were less popular than toys. In Crosswell's 1896 study of children's play preferences, the most popular board game, checkers, although mentioned by over 400 children out of 1,000, was the favorite game of only about 100.[12] Conversely, four of boys' and four of girls' top ten play preferences involved toys including balls, sleds, skates, marbles, dolls, and tea sets.

Toys were gendered to a degree: both boys and girls played with many of the same toys, but in 1896, only girls placed dolls at the top of their play list, and only boys put marbles in their top ten. Of course, boys and girls did not consistently stick to gender-specific toys. Marbles were 19th among girls' favorite toys in 1896, and although dolls were 51st among boys' preferences, that placement may simply reflect the age of the boys in the Crosswell survey. In another 1896 study, psychologist "G. Stanley Hall found that 76 percent of the boys he studied played with dolls to age 12."[13] Because middle-class boys and girls under the age of seven dressed alike and often played together, young boys' interest in dolls is not surprising. Still, few boys chose dolls as their favorite toys, probably because they knew dolls were not "masculine" toys.

White farm and frontier families and prosperous urban and suburban white parents made gender distinctions in toys by giving their boys rocking horses, other riding toys, and whips.[14] In Karen Calvert's analysis of 325 paintings of boys under the age of seven painted between 1830 and 1870, two-thirds of the boys held toys of 55 different types—most commonly a pony whip or other military-type toy. After 1870, prosperous parents were likely to give their boys toy trains and miniature steam engines, which encouraged boys to think about the larger world in which they would work, to participate in new technologies, and to dream about having power over them.

Conversely, well-off white parents gave their daughters fewer toys, and when they did give a toy, it was usually a doll. In Calvert's study of 309 portraits of girls under the age of seven, she found only 20 percent held a toy at all, and 80 percent of those toys were dolls. Before the modern toy market of the 1870s, most girls sewed their own dolls—in the process learning housewifely skills. Well into the twentieth century, many parents continued to encourage sewing skills in their daughters by giving them dolls for which clothes had to be hand made.[15] However, between the 1860s and the 1890s, prosperous parents also encouraged other skills in their daughters by giving them lady dolls, with which the girls could imitate adult activities such as tea parties, housewarmings, the paying of social visits or even attending funerals, which, by that era, had become very elaborate. In contrast to the toys given boys, the dolls given girls by their middle-class parents taught girls the proper way to dress and behave in social settings. After the Civil War, there were even books about dolls and books for dolls, which encouraged girls to learn the appropriate way to play with them. Such books reveal parental fears that girls in the late nineteenth century were not as interested in or as able successfully to perform traditional female duties as girls had been previously. To some degree, parents were right. The play choices of girls indicate as much interest in active, outside play as with doll play. Yet parental fears were exaggerated, for girls in this era did play with dolls, although they preferred not

Hazel Rich by James Bartlett Rich (circa 1890s). Late in the century, girls from prosperous families, like Hazel, often possessed many store-bought (as opposed to handmade) dolls and used them, as Hazel is doing, to practice middle-class rituals such as the tea party. (Library Company of Philadelphia)

the fancy dolls of rubber, kid, wood, tin, or celluloid often given them by their parents, but simpler dolls—those made out of wax, paper, rags, and china. Some white girls even preferred black dolls. Miriam Formanek-Brunell, historian of dolls, attributes this preference to the affection many white girls felt for their African-American nurses. However, given the racism of the era manifested in textbooks and toys, white girls may have preferred black dolls because they accepted the prevalent stereotype that blacks were childlike and easily dominated, even by a young white person. Girls played with dolls in a nurturing and caring manner, although they also used their dolls to express anger and aggression.[16] In this era, middle-class parents strongly proscribed such emotions in their daughters, so girls may have taken out their animosity on their dolls, rather than on their siblings or their parents.

In the 1870s, most white parents, whether farmers or middle-class professionals, provided their children with manufactured toys. However, by the

1880s, two books written about the play of boys and girls reveal some growing concerns about children and their toys. The first, written in 1882 by
Daniel Carter Beard, who grew up in rural Ohio in the 1850s the son of a
successful artist, was entitled *What to Do and How to Do It; The American
Boys Handy Book*. Beard, later a founder of the Boy Scouts, explained how to
build kites, aquariums, boats, balloons, blowguns, snow houses, sleds, pup-
pets, magic lanterns and numerous other play objects. As he said in the pref-
ace, "The author would also suggest to parents and guardians that money
spent on fancy sporting apparatus, toys, etc., would be better spent upon
tools and appliances. Let boys *make their own kites and bows and arrows.*"
Beard was not so much concerned about poor farm boys or boys living on the
frontier as he was about white boys growing up in comfortable family homes
in the late nineteenth century. Beard believed such boys were becoming too
soft, too lazy, too dependent on material objects, and unable to take on tough
physical tasks or to build things on their own. This same fear leads to the
expansion of sports programs for such boys. Beard's two sisters, Lina and
Adelia, subsequently published a similar book for girls, entitled *How to
Amuse Yourself and Others, The American Girls Handy Book*. They too aimed
their book not at girls growing up on small farms or on the frontier but at the
daughters of prosperous farmers and professionals. The Beard sisters' book
describes how to preserve wildflowers, celebrate various holidays, decorate
rooms, draw, paint, and make fans, tennis nets, hammocks, and dolls. The
emphasis in their book is different from that in their brother's advice manual
for boys and reflects the fact that girls were more involved in social activities
associated with the home. Yet the Beard sisters too were worried that girls
were losing the ability to make things on their own. As they said in the pref-
ace, "We desire also to help awaken the inventive faculty, usually unculti-
vated in girls . . ." and "one of our objects is to impress upon the minds of the
girls the fact that they all possess talent and ability to achieve more than they
suppose possible. . . ."[17] While readily available manufactured toys were presumably undermining the ability of white boys from prosperous homes to be
strong and tough and to manage alone in the outdoors, store-bought toys and
other household items reduced their sisters' confidence and limited their
capability to fashion the items and plan the activities that would make a house
a home.

   The number of years that white children living on farms or in suburban
homes were free to play games or with toys varied depending on the economic status of their parents. Rural, small-town children from families that
were not especially prosperous were at work inside and outside the home by
the age of 10. Employment limited their play time, even though some could
combine work and play, as when boys pretended that plows were cannons
and girls knitted while they read.[18] By their teen years, many rural boys and
girls had left their homes to work for more prosperous farm families. Their

leisure time and recreational opportunities were then markedly limited. Among middle-class youth, time to play lasted longer. Boys and girls did not go to work or marry until their late teens or early 20s. When not in school, boys were free to play and engage in organized sports throughout their teen years. However, girls from middle-class families usually ended active out-of-doors play at puberty, between the ages of 13 and 15, when concern about preserving their purity led parents to keep girls protected within their homes. Not all girls welcomed this change. Said Lucy Larcom: "I clung to the child's inalienable privilege of running half wild; and when I found that I really was growing up, I felt quite rebellious."[19]

Once parents restricted girls' outdoor play, the opportunities of white middle-class girls to socialize with other young women and men became limited. Girls might accompany their mothers on social calls to other families; invite friends to their own homes to play cards, dance, and eat; or themselves attend local church socials, musical events, parties, and dances. In small towns and suburban communities, girls always socialized under the watchful eye of adults. It was only in cities, with the rise of commercialized leisure activities late in the century, that prosperous parents felt it necessary to provide chaperones for their daughters.[20]

Whereas teenage farm girls had to be physically strong to perform the tasks required of them by their parents or the families for whom they worked, white middle-class parents of girls growing up in towns or near cities did not expect their daughters to be physically active. In fact, the ideal Victorian middle-class female was rather fragile and certainly not an athlete. At midcentury, the two physical activities approved for such girls were walking and croquet. As it happened, both activities became more available to middle-class teenage girls because of the construction of rural parks throughout the urban Northeast. As urban planners in New York, Worcester, Boston, and Philadelphia began to worry about congestion and the decreasing amount of open space in cities, they built large parks on the outskirts of these cities. Designers planned parks to be restful, scenic places where persons of all social classes could walk and enjoy the natural environment. Because these parks were constructed closest to the large homes of middle-class families, who lived well away from industrial centers inhabited by the working class, middle-class families were the first to use the parks. Park designers such as Frederick Law Olmsted (who planned Central Park in New York City, as well as many other large city parks) disapproved of any sports being played in these parks except those that left the natural environment undisturbed. Two such sports were croquet and ice skating—both activities akin to walking and engaged in enthusiastically by middle-class young women. When English players introduced tennis to the United States in the 1880s, young women from well-off families took up the game most enthusiastically. Shortly thereafter, urban park officials began to respond to their prosperous clientele by allowing some sports facilities in the parks—among the first were tennis courts.[21] Although the parks were not constructed with the needs of white middle-class girls in mind, the parks certainly benefited such girls by allowing them to engage in the few physical activities approved for them in a pleasant, safe environment.

By the 1880s, young white middle-class women had taken up another sport: roller skating. It became enormously popular throughout the country, and rinks appeared under tents or on stages of old theaters. Perhaps because it was a new activity, made possible by the invention of metal wheels with pin bearings, and was so like ice skating, a sport long enjoyed by girls, middle-class parents approved of roller skating for their daughters. White, well-off teenage girls and boys enjoyed roller skating (not until late in the century was it considered a children's activity), for it was more exciting than their alternative social activities: "the opera house, the public dance, or the party at home."[22]

As sport activities in the community for young white women from prosperous families expanded, so did sports programs in the public schools. In 1889, in Boston, Mrs. Mary Hemenway, who had opened the Boston Normal School of Gymnastics to train teachers in this form of exercise, convinced members of the Boston School Committee to introduce gymnastics in all the city's public schools. Subsequently, other school systems also introduced gymnastics. It was a cheap physical-education program that took little time, developed the whole body, and fit into the schools' structured curriculum. Physical-education programs also served as a corrective to the theory proposed by Dr. Edward H. Clarke in 1873 that academic education for young women in schools was physically debilitating.[23]

For teenage white middle-class urban and suburban girls, the most exciting new physical activity of the late nineteenth century was bicycling. From the beginning, cycling was a middle-class sport because the cost of even a cheap or medium-grade bicycle, between $50 and $100, was well beyond the budget of most working-class Americans. Bicycling was also a sport of adults and youths, and not of children, until after 1900. From the 1860s to the 1880s, there were many styles of bicycles, including tricycles that allowed modest females to sit sedately between large wheels and keep their ankles covered. However, after 1887, when the safety bicycle, with its two wheels of similar size connected by a triangular frame, "propelled by an endless chain," became the bicycle of choice, female bike riding became controversial. Doctors spoke both for and against it, and parents worried about compromising the purity of their daughters by allowing them to sit—with exposed ankles and legs—astride bicycles. New cycle costumes with divided skirts promptly appeared, for women and girls proved determined to continue cycling.[24] By the end of the century, whether young women traveled alone or in the company of friends, cycling, more than gymnastics, walking, or skating, allowed young women a measure of independence from parental control.

Just as there was a limited range of social and sport activities available to teenage white middle-class women, there were also few organized youth programs for them. The few that existed promoted religion and morality, principles that middle-class females were expected to uphold within both their families and communities. By far the most popular were Sunday schools, first opened in cities in the 1820s and 1830s to provide religious education for the children of the poor. The Sunday-school program expanded by leaps and bounds, and by the 1870s, virtually all churches throughout the country operated Sunday schools for the children of their members. In 1880 Sunday schools enrolled about seven million children and, by 1890, enrolled almost twelve million. Because most church members were women, so were most Sunday-school teachers. Before the age of 12, boys and girls attended in roughly equal numbers, but after that boys dropped out and girls stayed on because the female teachers provided them with role models, "Bible classes offered the kind of friendship and intimacy that appealed especially to girls," and there were few sport or other activities to compete for girls' time and interest. By the 1870s, 1880s, and 1890s, other national religious and temperance organizations, including the Methodist-sponsored Epworth League and the Juvenile Templars of the International Order of Good Templars, which promoted temperance, also recruited teenage girls (and boys). Both organizations attracted young members with special rituals, songs, and badges.[25]

There were comparatively few organized sports or other activities for white middle-class teen girls, but the opposite was true for their brothers. Prosperous white parents were fairly confident that they could control the moral development of their adolescent daughters at home, but they were much more worried about their sons. Parents believed that boys who lived at home and attended school through their teen years needed healthy outlets for their energies. Too-little physical activity might lead to masturbation in boys—a practice much frowned upon by white middle-class parents and medical professionals. Boys who lived in the country were less a worry than those who lived in or near cities. Farm boys kept busy working except in the winter months, when they attended school and there played sports with other boys, hunted rattlesnakes, and copied adult farm chores by branding gophers with little irons "made from a length of hay wire." However, any youth that lived near a city could, with time on his hands after school, easily find his way into saloons, dance halls, theaters, and pool rooms. He might very well be enticed into gambling on sporting activities such as boxing and cockfighting, both part of the social life in taverns. After the Civil War, white middle-class parents also feared that their sons were becoming too weak, too sedentary in their habits, and too under the control of women at home and in school.[26] One important corrective for all these impending dangers was organized sports activities for boys.

White middle-class boys and youths took up sports enthusiastically. Most boys lived near the edge of towns and close to empty fields available for play. Some boys played cricket, but by the 1850s, the most popular sport among young white men was baseball. In the 1840s, Alexander Cartwright of the New York sports club, the Knickerbockers, drafted the rules of modern base-ball, and by the 1860s, the game was popular from the East Coast to the West. In the 1880s, middle-class patrons of the large rural parks in New York, Boston, Philadelphia, and other cities convinced park officials to open baseball fields on park land. Baseball remained extremely popular because it seemed to keep young people in touch with their rural heritage and promoted individualism, fair play, team spirit, honesty, and respect for authority.[27]

In rural America, especially on the frontier, organized sports such as baseball were less popular among boys than intensive achievement-oriented games that rewarded individual aggression. Such games included shinny, which is played with leather-covered balls and golflike sticks and is akin to hockey; and prisoner's base, black Tom, and pom pom pullaway, which are all variations on tag and base games. Ante over was especially popular in rural areas. In this game, two teams of boys array themselves on each side of a building; a player from one team calls "Ante over" and throws a ball over the building. If the ball is caught, all the players from the second team run around the building and try to hit one of the players from the first team, who are run-ning around the building themselves. Any player hit joins the opposing team. When play ends, the team with the most players wins. Such tag games "favored in the West trained children for a society that applauded individual aggressiveness kept within broad rules that were loosely enforced." Con-versely, baseball "embodied a cooperative individualism that mirrored the increasingly urban, interdependent, industrialized culture of the East."[28]

Sports played in towns and cities differed somewhat from sports pursued by boys in rural frontier areas, but in both places, boys organized their own games. On farms and in country school yards, boys played with little adult supervision or sporting equipment, chose their own teams, and planned what games to play. In the 1860s, in urban and suburban high schools, male stu-dents, most from prosperous white families, also organized their own sports programs. Boys formed clubs to compete against other schools in baseball, football, track, and ice hockey. Boys' athletic teams encouraged school and community spirit and probably pleased middle-class white parents, who were so anxious to keep their sons physically active and content with school during their teen years. Not until after 1906, when student-run athletic programs drew criticism for cheating and for using ringers (athletic nonstudents) in competition, did adult educators take over the sports programs.[29]

Virtually all white boys played team sports that put a premium on com-petition and aggression. They were the opposite of the individual, fairly nonaggressive activities, such as walking, croquet, and skating, pursued by girls. Sport activities for white youths in urban and rural areas prepared boys to enter a work world full of conflict, where they had to adapt to the demands of coworkers and competitors. Meanwhile their teenage sisters learned values appropriate to homemaking from their outdoor recreation: the importance of quiet, peaceful activities pursued in the company of friends.

White, middle-class parents encouraged their sons to participate in organized sports and also in character-building organizations such as the YMCA, Sunday schools, the Epworth League, or the Juvenile Templars. For prosperous parents of small families who could afford to forgo their children's labor to prepare them for future success by means of an extended education, building a child's character was a way of protecting the youngster and the family's investment in him. Middle-class white parents relied on organizations to build character in both their sons and their daughters, but parents were most concerned about their sons. Because boys had more freedom than girls, parents worried that young men could well make "inappropriate friends" who might subvert some of the values parents had carefully tried to instill in their sons.

One well-known nineteenth-century character-building agency for middle-class youth was the YMCA. London clerks founded the organization in 1844, and supporters opened YMCAs in the United States in the 1850s to help white middle-class rural youths between the ages of 18 and 30 adjust to living and working in cities. In the 1870s, physical-education programs developed by YMCAs to make youths physically strong and keep them from temptation in saloons proved especially attractive to young men and boys. At first, the YMCA attempted to appeal to young men, but the organization's athletic programs attracted middle-class white boys between the ages of 10 and 16, who asked to join. In the 1890s, when many YMCAs built gymnasiums, boys wanted to play basketball, a new game invented in 1891 by James Naismith, a young instructor at the YMCA's Springfield College. YMCAs accepted middle-class white boys partly because they could use the facilities in the afternoons after school when older members were at work. Only middle-class parents could afford the fees charged by YMCAs, and these parents willingly paid them to keep their sons in protected places, apart from lower-class youth, yet under the supervision of responsible adults.[30]

White middle-class boys in small towns, and to a lesser extent in cities, were best served by YMCAs. Before the Civil War, YMCAs made little effort to attract black members of any age, and only after the war did some blacks begin to form Ys in various Northern and Southern cities with the purpose of promoting racial solidarity and education. Most of these early efforts folded because of lack of money, and only late in the century did Northern YMCA leaders make a more serious effort to recruit young black men to form segregated YMCAs in the South. Moreover, the few YWCAs formed in the nineteenth century, like the YMCAs of the 1850s, served young women moving from farms to cities and not younger girls.[31]

YMCAs enrolled about 30,000 boy members by 1900, but other youth organizations attracted even more. Like teen girls, many teen boys joined the Juvenile Templars and took temperance pledges or continued to attend Sunday schools. However, other religious organizations made more direct appeals to boys. Christian Endeavor had 660,000 members by 1890, and the Epworth League had one million youths on its rolls by 1895. In the 1890s, to attract boys, these organizations and the United Boys Brigades, which sought to prevent boys from dropping out of Sunday schools, emphasized military drill. In this era when "Onward Christian Soldiers" was composed, there was a military rhetoric to Protestantism. Drill also fit with the militia tradition that antedated the Civil War, and might also prepare middle-class youths to deal aggressively with laborers in the many strikes of the 1870s and 1880s. Many boys liked the activity and the competitions with other boys' groups, but some found drill boring.[32] Marching in tight order in youth groups was a far cry from free out-of-doors play and permitted less individualism than did playing on sports teams.

While middle-class white boys joined organizations founded by adults for youths' benefit, boys also formed a few organizations themselves. Most of these organizations, such as debate societies, were purely local, but budding young journalists built a broader, national network of middle-class teens "who shared the experience of reading the same stories and debating the same issues." In the 1850s, young editors built their own presses, but by 1867, the Novelty Press Co. manufactured and sold presses to middle-class youths, the only ones who could afford the $15 to $50 price tag. Youths who printed their own newspapers circulated them among subscribers, exchanged newspapers with editors across the country, and formed a National Amateur Press Association (NAPA). Debates among these amateur teen journalists allow us a glimpse of how middle-class youth viewed gender and race issues of their day. White boy journalists sometimes wrote stories about adventuresome girls, but boys were very unwilling to accord real girls editorial status or equality within NAPA. The few teen female editors ably articulated their case for equality, but it took 10 years for them to become "full, dues-paying members" of NAPA. There were no stories in the amateur press about African-Americans, but a few black male teens in Northern cities became editors, and although they were very eloquent and enjoyed the support of Northern white adolescent editors, these blacks faced enormous opposition from white Southern male amateur journalists.[33]

The example of the organization of amateur pressmen indicates that white middle-class boys, although able to conceive of fictional independent women, generally accepted what most of their parents taught—that teenage boys deserved more freedom than girls, who should play a somewhat subsidiary role to males. Even as white teen female editors disagreed with this proposition, the fact that there were so few of them confirms the success of most middle-class parents in keeping their girls confined to domestic roles. The few black boys and total absence of black girls among amateur pressmen reveal both the constricted economic circumstances of most black families and their concern about rejection in largely white youth organizations. And black editors did face blatant racism, especially from Southern whites, not surprising in a culture full of racist textbooks, toys, and literature. Yet the fact that there were any articulate black youths in teen journalism at all demonstrates that the investment black parents made in educating their children after the Civil War did pay off for some and provided them access to forums open only to the literate.

The popularity of amateur journalism among middle-class white youths is only one sign of their fondness for reading. Because most white children, except those living in the South, became literate at an early age thanks to ready access to public schooling, it is not surprising that reading was one of their favorite recreations. Children and their parents read together in the nineteenth century; there was as yet no separate category of children's literature and "adults and children alike took pleasure in strong narratives, romantic characters, high adventure, and an idealized picture of the world, both contemporary and historical." Youngsters read almost anything they could get their hands on, from seed catalogues, to newspapers, to Shakespeare, but by the middle of the century, special fictional stories written especially for white middle-class American boys and girls appeared for the first time.

The purpose of this fiction was to teach children moral values through example, with just enough entertainment to keep children reading. Each story had a child in it who needed "moral correction," and who typically learned from experience. In one story, "a girl whose fondness for sweets took her into the pantry by night to lick the honey jar managed to burn down the house with the candle she left there."[34] The plots and characterization were simple enough for young children to understand and often required them to choose between a hardworking, often poor youngster and a lazy, richer, vice-ridden child. Children also learned from parents in these stories—especially in the well-liked Rollo books, written between 1835 and 1840 by Jacob Abbott, a Congregationalist minister from Maine, and in the stories by Maria Edgeworth, an English writer popular in the United States from the 1790s to the 1890s. This early fiction for children assumed, as did middle-class parents of the day, that children were both good and bad, but that the good had to be encouraged early in childhood. Also, like middle-class parents, authors of children's stories expected obedience but hoped that children would learn from experience to become independent moral agents in a rapidly changing world. The values taught children by middle-class parents and by teachers in public schools were lauded in this early children's fiction as well.[35]

After 1860, fiction for middle-class children changed. Didactic moral formulas disappeared, replaced by a greater variety of children's books and popular magazines such as *St. Nicholas, The Youth's Companion,* and *Wide Awake.* Many books and stories portrayed children as fully realized human beings and not as simply a compendium of good and bad qualities. Much of the new children's literature was also romantic and sentimental. Authors now portrayed children as naturally good, so there was no need to restrain them but rather to encourage their moral energies. Children had some bad qualities, but authors assumed that the good would inevitably triumph. A new concept emerged: children did not so much need the example of adults, but instead "their God-given moral purity could redeem fallen or strayed adults." Thus, in *Elsie Dinsmore* (1868), Martha Finley [Farquharson] described a child who, at the age of eight, already knew about Christ; she did not need adults to teach her. Moreover, Elsie often disputed with her father and always won their arguments. In 1890 Laura Richards wrote *Captain January,* in which 10-year-old Star Bright was rescued by Captain January after a shipwreck, stayed to live with him in a lighthouse, and became the inspiration and moral center of his life.[36]

The new children's literature of the late nineteenth century appeared at a time when middle-class children spent longer childhoods in their protected family homes. Authors and parents agreed that it seemed appropriate to let these children enjoy their youth by allowing their imaginations free rein. Parents themselves liked this romantic literature because it contrasted so sharply with the gritty, industrial side of late-nineteenth-century America and harked back to an earlier, more appealing, agricultural small-town America.[37]

After the Civil War, fiction became more gendered. The best was very down-to-earth, and portrayed girls and boys in realistic situations. Much of the new fiction for girls centered on families, because that was the arena in which female life was played out. Novels such as those written by Louisa May Alcott depicted not only the advantages but also many of the disadvantages—such as the constraints put on creativity and female independence—of family life for middle-class women.[38] New fiction by Alcott and others continued to propound moral values even as writers of fiction for boys abandoned such teaching. Alcott's *Little Women* is about girls trying to control feelings, such as anger, envy, and shyness, that at the time were thought inappropriate for middle-class white females. The novel is realistic in portraying how tough it was for girls to be self-sacrificing, as when Jo cuts her hair and sells it in order to raise money for the family but bitterly regrets doing so afterwards. Moreover, in this novel, as in previous children's fiction, when someone violates a moral rule, she or he must pay for doing so. Jo must acknowledge that when she gives in to anger at Amy while ice-skating, she almost causes her sister's death. *Little Women* and virtually all of the new fiction for girls centered on the time in life, between ages 12 and 16, when white females from comfortable families moved from the freedom of girlhood to the constraints of adolescence and young womanhood. In Alcott's *Jack and Jill* (1880), a boy and girl who are close friends accept dares to sled down a dangerous hill. On the third run, both are seriously injured, Jill in her back. Alcott accepts girlhood freedoms, but she also shows how Jill at age 15, as she recovers from her injury, must change from being "headstrong, proud, willful, dominant, competitive" to becoming "nearly as meek as a dove." Similarly, in *What Katy Did* (1872), Susan Coolidge (Sarah C. Woolsey) describes how a wild young girl, who spends most of her time outside leading a pack of neighborhood kids, has an accident due to her own negligence. Thereafter, in four years of invalidism, Katy learns to be an appropriately demure nineteenth-century woman.[39]

Like fiction for girls, the best of the new post–Civil War books for boys were true to life: they were stories of boys realistically portrayed. However, unlike fiction for girls, fiction for boys left behind the overt moral lesson. Thomas Bailey Aldrich's *Story of a Bad Boy* (1870) and later Mark Twain's *Adventures of Tom Sawyer* and *Adventures of Huckleberry Finn* are all good examples of this new fiction. All make clear—Twain in *Huckleberry* Finn is most explicit—that no moral lesson is to be drawn from their stories, and their boy characters are far from moral paragons. Tom Bailey gets into many scrapes but never has "a moral balance to pay" as Jo does in *Little Women*. Tom Sawyer is also far from perfect: "he steals, lies, threatens his brother, fights, shows off outrageously in Sunday School" and never seems to feel any guilt for his transgressions. Neither does Tom seem to learn from his experiences. All three books proclaim that boyhood is a separate time when the rules are different than they are in grown-up life. This notion fits well with the experiences of rural, small-town, and suburban white boys, who enjoyed years of youthful freedom of play with few adults imposing rules on them. All three books also imply that this freedom is permissible because boys are inherently good; they may get into minor scrapes, but their hearts are in the right place, and they are not truly bad or evil. Sometimes the boys do have to make moral choices, as when Tom Sawyer has to choose whether to testify against Injun Joe, and Huck Finn has to choose whether to turn in Jim, a runaway slave. Certainly the contention that boys are basically good must have pleased white, comfortably well-off parents and justified their willingness to permit their sons so much unfettered and unregulated free play. Finally, much of this new literature for boys centered on the problems of growing up and separating from families and parents. Thus, in Twain's novel, Huck Finn breaks with his own, abusive father and goes on through a succession of other families.[40] Such a story fit with the experiences of white middle-class boys who spent long years at home and struggled with how to move on and live independently of their parents.

All the new books for white middle-class boys were exciting, and this seems to be what boys liked best about them—the adventure. When boy journalists wrote stories for their papers, they copied the works of writers such as

Oliver Optic, whose books were one long series of exciting scrapes. Mark Twain wrote boy adventure books that were also profound commentaries on human beings and American social mores, but later nineteenth-century writers for boys, including Optic and Horatio Alger, wrote much less memorable stories. Optic was the pen name for William T. Adams, a school principal and Sunday-school superintendent who began writing full-time in the 1860s. After his first book, parents and other role models disappeared from his stories, and all featured heroes who were poor boys, orphans or sons of widows, who went through a series of adventures trying to make it on their own in the world. Whereas the good hero always triumphed, he did so thanks to impulsivity and daring; there were few moral choices embedded in the stories. Excitement was all that mattered. Optic wrote not only for middle-class boys but also for working-class readers, and so too did Horatio Alger. He wrote orphan boy adventure stories, beginning with *Ragged Dick* (1868), in which a poor but hardworking city bootblack, after being befriended by a Christian businessman, improves himself by learning to read, saving his money, and altering his dress. Thanks to an act of heroism on the boy's part, a rich merchant sets him on the road to middle-class success with a job as a clerk. In *Ragged Dick* and other Alger stories, his heroes succeed not so much because of hard work but because of luck. This plot device did not undercut middle-class nineteenth-century values, for good Protestants believed that luck and good fortune came to the deserving.[41] Alger used other formulas besides the "poor boy makes good" one, but in all, he emphasized adventure. His middle-class boy audience found such values familiar, but they especially liked the romance and excitement of Alger's and Optic's plots.

The pleasures of white middle-class youth were comparatively safe and quiet compared to those of urban working-class boys and girls. Working-class youngsters grew up in crowded tenement apartments, where there was little privacy for anyone and no special play space reserved for children. Parents often kept infants and toddlers confined to the corner of the kitchen or tied them in a chair unless there was an older child to tend them and take them outside. When mothers shopped, as they did almost daily, they took young children with them into the busy streets. As soon as youngsters were physically able, parents encouraged them to stop getting underfoot and play in the street or alley close to their family apartment.

In the street, children shared their play space with shopkeepers, pushcart vendors, adults socializing in front of saloons, prostitutes, policemen, horses and wagons, and streetcars. All this adult activity provided children with some degree of safety, for if they ever got into trouble, there was someone nearby to call to for help. Yet city streets were dangerous, and working-class children were often injured and sometimes killed by horse-drawn wagons, trucks, and streetcars. Parents expected youngsters to stay within a block or two of home to ensure some maternal oversight. Children who ranged farther afield were in danger of being assaulted by youthful gangs protecting their turf. It was almost a necessity that children learn to play amicably with others of their age who lived nearby. Just as they had to learn to accommodate family members and other adults in the interdependent urban working-class world, youngsters had to learn to get along with older and younger kids on their block. Unlike white children from more affluent families or children who lived on farms and on the frontier, working-class boys and girls rarely played alone.

The games of urban working-class youngsters were much like those of other white children living in rural or suburban areas, although city youngsters often had to improvise and incorporate into their play items they found in the streets. Trucks parked outside saloons "became the home run fence for the ballplayers" and manhole covers and fire hydrants served as bases.[42] Generally, urban boys and girls played games, such as marbles, hopscotch, and leapfrog, that were best suited to constricted play spaces, but children also found ways to use "blocks, curbs, walls, and pavement squares as bases and boundaries" for games of tag and chase. In addition, they played some games unique to urban youths. For example, boys collected small picture cards from cigarette packs and pitched the cards against a wall or stoop. The boy who pitched his cards the closest to the wall got all the cards. He then twirled them into the air, and those that fell face up became his. All other cards went to the player who came in second, who twirled them in turn, and so on.[43]

Girls' activities in the streets were somewhat different from boys' activities. Girls usually gathered on the stoops of their apartment buildings to talk with other girls, tend babies and toddlers, play hopscotch, and jump rope. Sometimes they gathered around an organ grinder or other street musician and danced. Like white girls raised on farms and in middle-class homes, urban working-class girls preferred quiet forms of play. In contrast, working-class boys in cities played chasing, tag, and ball games in the centers of streets. They also built bonfires, stole items from pushcart vendors, hitched on to the back of delivery wagons, and, in summer, stripped off their clothes to swim nude in city rivers. Boys engaged in more violent activities when they formed gangs to defend the block on which they lived and fought off other gangs with "paving stones, bottles, bricks, and garbage can lids as shields."[44] Like their male counterparts living on farms and in urban and suburban middle-class homes, working-class boys engaged in rougher play than did girls, but poor city boys' play was also more violent and dangerous than that of boys from more well-off families.

By the 1870s, cities were so crowded that children playing in the streets often interfered with commercial transactions, as when boy sports impeded wagons making deliveries or when errant balls shattered shop windows. Storekeepers joined with working-class parents worried about the physical dangers to children in city streets to press urban officials in cities such as Boston and Worcester to provide special play areas for children. Now that cities had built parks much enjoyed by middle-class children, it seemed only fair that cities should also provide working-class boys and girls with safe play spaces. By the 1880s and 1890s, middle-class reformers, anxious to protect urban youth from the immoral influence of pool halls, saloons, and brothels in working-class neighborhoods, as well as to Americanize immigrant youngsters, also urged city officials to build playgrounds.[45]

The first playgrounds constructed in northeastern cities were simply open spaces where children could create their own types of play. These playgrounds contained no play apparatuses, and there were few adults employed to supervise youngsters until after 1900. In Worcester, city officials appropriated little money to maintain playgrounds, and working-class youths soon made use of the playgrounds in unanticipated ways. Here and in other cities, ethnic groups who lived closest to playgrounds appropriated portions of them for their exclusive use—thus dividing play space into ethnic enclaves. Sometimes gangs of boys fought over playground space; the winners controlled access. It is not surprising that fewer than 10 percent of urban children made use of these playgrounds. Not only were they often under the control of hostile immigrant groups or gangs, but they were often more than onequarter of a mile from a child's home—the farthest distance most working-class parents would allow their youngsters to travel.[46] Because playgrounds in some cities were attached to urban schools, and working-class children often found such schools forbidding, they may not have been much attracted to the new play areas.

Working-class parents could not afford to purchase toys for their children, so youngsters, in the process of scavenging their neighborhoods for junk to sell to earn money for themselves and their families, found their own toys. Youngsters converted garbage-pail lids into sleds, bicycle wheels into hoops, broom handles into bats, and tied rags together for footballs. Inventiveness was a necessity for working-class youngsters. Boys and girls also used the pennies they earned in the streets to purchase inexpensive toys such as marbles, play guns, and trumpets for themselves. Or they spent their pennies on candy purchased from one of the many shops in their neighborhoods. In New York, these stores became after-school hangouts for children. Those without money stood outside and chatted, but children with pennies in hand agonized over their purchases inside. There were also "kiddie slot machines," where for a penny, youngsters got "a tiny piece of gum *and* a chance at the jackpot: five, ten, or twenty more tiny pieces of gum."[47]

By the time urban working-class boys and girls reached their teens, most were out of school and working. Unlike middle-class girls and boys, working-class adolescents were not much affected by social or athletic programs attached to high schools. Instead they participated in the rapidly growing commercial leisure culture of cities. Teenage working-class youths turned much of the money they earned over to their parents, but youths kept some money for themselves to spend on urban entertainments.

Working-class adolescent girls were more protected by their parents than were their brothers, but because they earned money and spent much of their time in public places, such teen girls had access to many more social activities than did farm or suburban girls. Young girls, who began dancing to the music of organ grinders in city streets, moved on in their teens to lodge dances, church socials, and weddings held in neighborhood halls. Late in the century, many girls also went in groups to commercial dance halls, of which there were hundreds in New York City. Girls who worked for long hours in factories and lived in small apartments welcomed the "bright lights, blaring music, and festive atmosphere" of dance halls, which were especially popular in the bleak winter months. Girls usually entered dance palaces not with male dates but with female friends, with whom they danced until young men "broke in" and took them as dance partners. In the summers, teen girls accompanied their families on outings to New York's Central Park and to the beaches of Staten Island, but by the 1890s, they could take boats or trolleys to Coney Island on their own. Coney Island was New York's largest amusement resort, and on the island, West Brighton most attracted working-class youth. There teen girls and boys attended variety shows, penny arcades, and open-air dances. Urban working-class adolescent girls enjoyed much more freedom from parental control and more access to new and exciting leisure activities than did farm girls or those from middle-class families, but "the custom of treating, which enabled many women to participate in the life of the dance hall, undercut their social freedom. Women might pay trolley fare out to a dance palace [or to Coney Island] . . . , but they often relied on men's treats to see them through the evening's entertainment." With little money at their disposal, working-class teenage girls had to rely on more well-paid young men, to treat them to drinks and food.[48] Treating compromised the independence of working-class young women and sometimes put them under pressure to provide sexual favors to the young men who paid their way.

Perhaps the challenge of coping with the demands of young men helped to make another form of entertainment popular with working-class young women—the theater. Before 1900, in New York's Bowery, melodramas were the most popular plays, and they were attended by working-class women and men of all ages. In melodramas, male villains sought to undermine the virtue of young women yet were always defeated in the end.[49] The message of such plays was what working-class parents and their daughters, living at a time when the sexual purity of young women was so lauded yet so precariously maintained by those with little money, wanted to hear: that female virtue would not be compromised, even by evil men.

Young working-class women had little time for or interest in participating in sports. They were busy enough with their wage-labor jobs and household chores and preferred to spend the little leisure they had in the evenings in social activities. Young women sometimes joined mutual-benefit groups associated with their work or their ethnic group, but they more commonly formed social or pleasure clubs that held dances and sponsored picnics. Such clubs served to introduce young working-class women and men to one another; the clubs were "mediators of urban courtship."

The social and athletic interests of young working-class men differed from those of females of their age and class. Among the urban working class, as among the white middle class, teenage boys enjoyed much more freedom than did teenage girls. Working-class boys earned more money than did girls of their same age and class and gave less of it to their parents. Families who depended on boys' earnings feared to compromise boys' goodwill by limiting their social activities. After work, with money in their pockets, working-class boys entered an urban male subculture of pool parlors, saloons, sporting events, and music halls. Candy stores, barbershops, coffeehouses, and saloons usually had pool tables; the cost of a game was five cents per player, but the loser usually paid the winner's fee. Saloons sponsored boxing matches, which were quite popular with young working-class men, many of whom had grown up in the streets fighting to defend their city blocks from interlopers. Until the end of the century, most dance and music halls were associated with saloons and were places where young men could pick up prostitutes.[50] At the end of the century, when more entertainments in dance halls and on Coney Island attracted young, respectable women, working-class youths attended these establishments as well as their old male haunts.

Many working-class boys also enjoyed athletic contests, although in a different context than did white farm- or suburban-born young men. In their late teens, some boys converted their childhood gangs into social and athletic clubs that met in rooms behind stores or saloons. These clubs sponsored dances and formed athletic teams to compete with other local clubs in football and baseball. Like white middle-class youths who formed their own high school sports teams, some working-class youths took the initiative and formed teams of their own, although not in association with school. Some youths also participated in ethnic sporting clubs. Boys of German extraction often joined in turnvereins, gymnastics clubs formed by immigrant Germans in many American cities. Young male Bohemians enjoyed sokol halls, which promoted both Czech culture and American baseball. However, athletics were not as universally popular among working-class youths as among middle-class boys. Laboring for long hours, Monday through Saturday, boys from poor families had less time to play sports than did more affluent youngsters. In addition, some parents born in southern and eastern Europe thought that sports were childish and discouraged their sons from participating. Italians especially rejected team sports. Italians believed in loyalty to one's boss and to one's family but saw no point in loyalty to a sports team of one's peers—persons of the same social class who could not improve "the individual's and hence the family's social standing."[51]

As they did with middle-class youth, some concerned parents and reformers attempted to organize the leisure-time activities of working-class youth. While YMCAs, Sunday schools, and temperance organizations worked to manage the free time of boys from prosperous families, by the 1870s and 1880s, city missions, working-class churches, and settlement houses formed clubs for working-class boys. Protestant middle-class club founders wanted to protect boys from the dangers of city streets and provide boys with some innocent fun, while working-class volunteers thought the boys needed order and discipline in their lives. Clubs for working-class boys did not seek to build character as did clubs for more prosperous youths but rather sought to save working-class boys from delinquency. In missions and churches, reformers created club rooms open largely in the evenings when working boys were free. Boys soon added the clubs to their other urban haunts and dropped in occasionally to socialize with one another, play games, and read books and newspapers. Boys brought the ways of the streets with them, and petty theft and boisterous play were as characteristic of these clubs as of other working-class boy activities.[52]

The books that working-class boys found in such clubs were different from the books boys chose to buy for themselves. Their literature of choice, and that of their parents and sisters, was exciting reading. Between 1850 and 1890, the literature favored by working-class youths came in three inexpensive formats: the story paper, dime novel, and cheap library. By the 1850s, eight-page weekly newspapers known as story papers (because they carried five to eight stories in serial form) were widely distributed by newsstands and dry-goods stores in American cities. In the 1860s, the dime or pamphlet novel, containing a single story of about 100 pages, appeared. Beadle's dime novels, issued monthly, were the most successful. By 1875 the cheap library, issued by Beadle and other publishers, attracted urban readers. Cheap libraries serialized stories in a progression of pamphlets, each 16 to 32 pages long, that cost five to ten cents apiece. "Many stories were first serialized in the story papers, then printed as dime novels, and eventually reprinted in the libraries." Some of these stories probably originated as stage melodramas, popular among the urban working class, and were then retold in dime novels. Nineteenth-century budgets of working-class families indicate that almost 90 percent "had significant expenditures for newspapers and books." School-age children often read the stories aloud to their families, while older youths read during their lunch hours or while traveling on public transport to and from work.[53] Irish, German, and white native-born working-class men, women, and children read this popular fiction, just as middle-class adults in this era joined their children in reading moralistic and imaginative stories about children. All the stories were sentimental or melodramatic and emphasized emotion before character and plot. The stories contained a moral message: the good triumphed in the end. But authors and publishers designed the contexts of the stories to appeal to working-class lifestyles, interests, and values.

Like fiction directed at white middle-class young persons, the popular dime-novel stories were gendered. Stories for working-class girls depicted love and danger as faced by young women employed outside the home, as were most teenage working-class women in cities. Popular dime-novel fiction, like fiction directed at middle-class girls, featured the problems of adolescent females. In popular fiction, however, authors portrayed adolescence not as a time of constraint but as a time of romance, excitement, and danger. The most popular author of such fiction was Laura Jean Libbey, the college-educated daughter of a physician, who wrote 52 serials for two story papers. A typical title was *Leonie Locke; Or the Romance of a Beautiful New York Working-Girl*. Such stories revolved around the seduction-rape of a poor working girl by a wealthy man. At the end of each story, the girl is not raped but escapes. She is a hero, who faces real threats, is cheated in some way, yet still defies the wealthy. Throughout, there is lots of physical action including "assaults, abductions and imprisonments," much of the action taking place in the streets and in public places, but not in homes. Such stories reflected the real sexual dangers faced by young working-class women both on the job and in public dance halls and amusement parks. As in melodramas, so in this popular fiction derived from it: the fact that young female heroines are not victims, confirmed what working-class girls and their families wanted to hear and to believe: it was possible for young female workers to maintain their virtue outside the protection of the home. This concept also ran counter to the view of many middle-class men and women of the day who believed that wage-earning women were far from virtuous. Historian Michael Denning argues that by making heroines orphans without siblings, this popular fiction also dodged one of the real problems faced by working girls: how to make their own romantic choices without offending their parents. However, working-class girls probably preferred the orphan heroine because she was independent and did not need parental counsel in order to make appropriate decisions about young men.

Popular dime-novel fiction directed at working-class boys and men was also often set in working environments, such as factories, familiar to readers and made villains of characters whom readers distrusted: wealthy mine owners, railroads, or banks. In all cases, the stories were full of exciting adventure and often violent confrontations. In the 1870s and 1880s, authors such as Frederick Whittaker wrote dime novels with titles such as *John Armstrong, Mechanic*. Such books, set in factories, detail the rise to success of a country boy or orphan, who learns a skill, gains an education, and earns the respect of his fellow workers. Along the way, he fights, participates in strikes, and woos and wins the love of a good woman. The factory settings, the ability of the hero to use his fists, and his solidarity with fellow workers all fit with the experience and the values of working-class youths. Horatio Alger, who published in story papers and dime novels, may also have appealed to working-class boys, although he intended to convince them of the possibility of mobility and success. Alger did not describe the real-life experiences of most working-class boys: his novels did not take place in factories, success came from a stroke of luck rather than hard work, and his heroes were individualists who did not rely on mutual support as did most members of the working class. Those working-class boys who purchased Alger novels may have read them as did white middle-class boys—principally for excitement and adventure.

Other dime novels differed considerably from stories for middle-class boys. These stories were about contemporary events and villainized persons who were enemies of workers. In the 1870s, there were many stories about the Molly Maguires, 20 Irish coal miners hanged in the 1870s for presumably committing murders as members of a secret society. One such story aimed at boys was *Coal-Mine Tom; Or, Fighting the Molly Maguires* (1884). It is the tale of the son of a mine foreman who is shot by the Molly Maguires; the boy and others seek through many plot twists to find the villain—who turns out to be the son of the wealthy mine owner. The well-to-do boy, and not an ordinary miner, is the real Molly Maguire. After the national railroad strikes of 1877, which pitted laborers against the big railroad companies, a new hero for working-class boys appeared: Deadwood Dick. Altogether, over one hundred stories were written about this Western hero who defies the law and robs stages and banks. Whereas Dick was a fictional character, other outlaw heroes featured in dime novels were drawn from real life, such as Joaquin Murieta and the Jesse James gang that robbed trains and banks. All these stories are unusual in dime novels or other fiction because in them "outlaws defied the law and got away with it." Middle-class cultural arbiters deplored these stories, which seemingly exalted illegal acts, but the stories appealed to working-class boys because they were exciting and featured appropriate villains: rich men, banks, and railroads, the traditional adversaries of workers.[54] Overall, dime-novel fiction for working-class boys was like other fiction for middle-class boys in that it was full of thrilling escapades, but the similarity ended there. In fiction directed at the working class, the rules were no different for boys than for anyone else—there was no concept of childhood as a time in life when inherently good boys could do almost anything they liked. These books were about boys functioning as most working-class youth did— in an adult world of work. Dime novels also did not deal much with the problems of boys breaking with families, because that was an issue only for boys who experienced extended childhoods in families protective of their few sons. Working-class boys from large families who entered the workforce early usually had parents grateful for the boys' financial support and willing to accord them considerable freedom.

Most African-American youngsters, whether they were slaves or freed persons, had the shortest childhoods and consequently the least time to play. As slaves, black children lived in small, one-room cabins that afforded youngsters neither privacy nor play space. Because both slave mothers and fathers worked for long days, either in the fields or in the master's home, from infancy onward, their children played six days a week in the care of older siblings or older slaves. Slave parents were less able than were white parents to supervise their children's play. Most youngsters under the age of 10 spent their time playing around the slave cabins. Historians disagree to what degree black children roamed through the countryside playing in fields and streams. Although Eugene Genovese and David Wiggins feel that free play in pastures and along local creeks was commonplace for slave children, Bernard Mergen points out that when the New Deal Federal Writers' Project interviewed three thousand ex-slaves, only 20 percent of the men and 8 percent of the women recalled this type of play.[55]

Historians agree that slave boys and girls played together, usually in large groups. Because slave parents socialized sons and daughters similarly and because there was little opportunity to be alone in the slave quarters, youngsters of both genders joined in group play of ring, chase, and acting games. Ring games involved drawing a ring from 15 feet to 30 feet in diameter on the ground. Youngsters all entered the ring, clapped their hands in rhythm with one another, and sang songs. The regular clapping of the group required collaboration. It reflected the importance of cooperation and community that slave parents taught their children. Although ring games were not unique to slave children, the songs they sang to accompany such games were. For example:

> My old mistress promised me,
> Before she dies she would set me free.
> Now she's dead and gone to hell
> I hope the devil will burn her well.[56]

Slave children enjoyed tag games such as ante over, also popular on the frontier, where any youngster tagged moved from one team to the other. Slave children preferred games that did not require a child to be eliminated from play. When excluding players was an integral part of a game, slave youngsters figured out ways to avoid such exclusion. Because families were so often broken up in slavery, African-American children were loath to emulate such tragedies in their play. Children also played tag games of concealment, which taught them useful skills as slaves.[57]

Some games of slave children involved violence, just as did games played by free white children. Whipping games such as rap jacket and hide the switch (where the child who finds the hidden switch uses it to beat the other youngsters) were exciting games played everywhere in the country, although they may have taken on different meanings among different groups of youngsters. In the North and West, white boys played whipping games, which presumably prepared them to be tough competitors as adults. Among slave children, such play may have prepared boys and girls for the beatings they would receive from both white masters and the children's own parents. Said ex-slave Julia Banks of Texas of a whipping game: "You know after you was hit several times it didn't hurt much."[58]

When they engaged in large group acting games, slave boys and girls often reenacted events such as church meetings, funerals, and auctions that the children had seen played out in the slave community. Slave children did not imitate the social events of whites. Eugene Genovese and David Wiggins believe that slave children may have used role-playing games, such as staging mock auctions, to neutralize some of their fears of sale and family separation, but Bernard Mergen disagrees. He argues that playing auction was not really a form of fantasy play at all for slave children. In fantasy games, children pretend to be something they are not. In auction games, slave children could pretend to be whites, but they could not pretend to be slaves.[59]

Some games were played more by one gender than the other. Slave girls jumped rope and played with dolls more than did boys; boys played marbles more than girls. All three forms of play were gendered among whites as well. And whereas marbles was a game of skill everywhere, slave boys often bet on it, making marbles "a way for boys to gamble and acquire property, however meager, within the system of slavery." Gambling games are often associated with cultures (such as the culture of American slaves) dependent on chance and luck rather than on individual initiative for survival.[60]

On plantations, slave and white children inevitably sometimes played together, at least until white youngsters entered school. Sometimes they became friends, but rarely did children of different races play equally. Slave boys and girls "normally thought of themselves not only as morally superior to white children but as superior on a physical level as well." Conversely, white children raised by their mothers to have a sense of superiority over blacks sometimes tormented black playmates by assuming the role of overseer—complete with pony and whip. The sons and daughters of plantation owners had ready access to manufactured toys, but slaves had only the toys they or their parents could make, or toys handed down by older white or black children. Slave children molded marbles from clay and dried them in the sun, fashioned whistles from cane, and used acorns as teacups. One acting game that white and black boys played together during the Civil War was "Yankees and Confederates." The whites always played the Confederates, and as one Virginia ex-slave remembered: "Take us black boys prisoners an' make b'lieve dey was gonna cut our necks off. Guess dey got dat idea from dere fathers."[61]

Whether they played with whites or with other blacks, slave children enjoyed only a few years of free play until they started work, normally between the ages of six and ten. After that, what pleasures they enjoyed were often associated with labor, and one of the most important was singing. Slaves created their own music, and improvisation was central to it.[62]

Verbal facility was much admired among blacks. When youths were old enough to seek a mate, they had to "know how to talk," a skill they learned from older men in the slave quarters. "The courtship ritual consisted of riddles, poetic boasting, innuendos, put downs, figurative speech, repartee, circumlocution, and a test of wit." As for young women, former slave Frank D. Banks reported that the ability of a woman to answer back cleverly was "the test of wit and culture by which the slave girl was judged in the society of the quarters."[63]

The importance of clever speech is also reflected in nineteenth-century African-American games of ritual insult. Games such as the dozens were probably played in slavery by both young people and adults, although the first recorded evidence of such verbal games is in a Texas song of 1891. Playing the dozens involved a joking relationship in which two or more people freely insulted one another and their ancestors and relatives. The insults could be direct or indirect. Direct insults were referred to as "sounding," and indirect insults were called "signifying." Other people usually observed the game and commented on the quality of the insults, often egging the players on. The dozens is based on exaggeration, which was very common in nineteenth-century folklore. Black children learned riddles such as: "What is the tallest man you ever see? De tallest man ah ever seen was gittin' a hair cut in Heaven and a shoe shine in Hell." From such riddles, older youths, especially boys, moved on to playing the dozens with exchanges such as: "Your mother so old she fart dust. At least my mother ain't no cake—everybody get a piece." There was no expectation that the contest would end in violence—in fact, a player lost if he used his fists instead of his voice. Playing the dozens was a way for young black men to assert their ability to speak cleverly and to defend themselves verbally. It also trained them in self-discipline. Through it, young blacks learned how to take insults and how to control their anger—skills that were essential both to slaves and to free blacks living in a country that continued to be quite racist after the Civil War. Boys may have played the dozens more than girls because males were especially likely to be the targets of verbal and physical abuse from whites, who feared the physical power of black men more than women. As black youngsters began to "signify," they learned how to say something that on the surface seemed innocent enough, but was in fact highly critical. Such verbal techniques could be used not only in playing the dozens, but also to put down whites without physical risk.[64]

Play among black children did not change much after they were freed from slavery. Those who grew up on sharecropping farms in the South did not have much play space within their homes, although children enjoyed more attention from their mothers, who could now take youngsters along to the fields in which parents labored.[65] Boys and girls continued to play together as they attended schools together, without much sex segregation. Poverty still precluded most African-American boys and girls from owning many toys, except those they made themselves—such as wagons and scooters. Black children who lived in Northern and Southern cities usually occupied small homes that had little space in which children could play. Like other working-class children, black children played in the streets, although they had to be especially careful not to trespass on blocks controlled by whites, who might viciously attack them. When Northern cities built playgrounds, blacks had so little political clout that few playgrounds were constructed near African-Americans' homes. As late as 1920, "black children were permitted into only 3 percent of all American playgrounds and had few alternatives to the streets." In the South, few municipal parks were built until the 1880s, and then they were segregated. Parks set aside for blacks had the fewest amenities. When African-American youths, like whites of the same age, formed baseball clubs, to play the game, they had to seek out fairgrounds or sections of municipal parks set aside for blacks to use.[66]

One of the pleasures of white children was reading, but few slave children knew how to read. By the 1870s and 1880s, more black children were literate; those in the North attended public schools, and so, to a lesser extent, did those in the South (see chapter 4). African-American boys and girls who could read discovered that most stories about children were about whites. Blacks in such fiction often appeared as contented slaves. Thus, in Thomas Nelson Page's *Two Little Confederates* (1888), young blacks hide their youthful Confederate masters from the Union army because the slaves have no desire to be free.[67]

Mark Twain's *Huckleberry Finn* is one important children's book in which a black character is central. Twain's treatment of blacks in this novel remains a source of controversy among literary scholars. Twain (Samuel Clemens) grew up in a Southern state, Missouri, and was himself fairly racist until after his marriage to Olivia Langdon. She was from an abolitionist family, and the couple made their home in Hartford, Connecticut, where one of their neighbors and friends was Harriet Beecher Stowe, author of *Uncle Tom's Cabin*. Thereafter, in both speech and print, Twain was much less racist.[68] Nonetheless, in *Huckleberry Finn,* he used the term "nigger," which had unflattering connotations in the nineteenth century as it does today. Some critics believe Twain's use of the word was racist, but others argue that he employed it as a synonym for slave, a common nineteenth-century usage, or in a context where its use reflected poorly on the speaker.[69]

In *Huckleberry Finn,* Twain told the story of a white boy trying to free a black man, Jim, from slavery. The novel took place in the 1830s or 1840s, though it was written in the 1870s at the end of Reconstruction. Although Jim is a sympathetic character who is kind and generous both to Huck and to Tom Sawyer, some critics argue that Jim is portrayed as having weaknesses that white nineteenth-century Americans viewed as typical of blacks: he acts foolishly, is superstitious, and exaggerates stories. Some of these critics contend that Twain depicted Jim as a minstrel-show black. Minstrel shows, in which white actors dressed up as blacks and acted as clowns, were performed in circuses or between acts in better theaters and were very popular in nineteenth-century America. Twain was fond of them.[70] He may have drawn from the minstrel-show tradition in depicting Jim, but Shelley Fisher Fishkin has recently demonstrated that Twain drew on other, African-American traditions as well. In fact, she argues persuasively that Twain's Huck, a white boy, is in the way he speaks and in "character traits and topics of conversation" much like a young black boy named Jimmy, whom Twain had met and about whom he had written before creating Huck Finn. Moreover, Fishkin believes that throughout the novel, Twain is "signifying," or speaking indirectly, in order to lambaste the terrible state of race relations in the South at the end of Reconstruction. Yet Fisher Fishkin also says: "One cannot get around the fact that Jim's voice is, ultimately a diminished voice. . . . It is not a voice with which any student, black or white, whose self-esteem is intact would choose to identify for very long."[71] If this is true about young readers in the twentieth century, it was probably true about African-American children in the nineteenth century as well.

Fortunately, nineteenth-century black children were not entirely dependent on whites for storytelling and probably enjoyed most the folktales told by African-Americans in slavery and in freedom. In the 1880s, some of these stories were first published by a white Southern journalist named Joel Chandler Harris. The context created by Harris for the stories was that of a benevolent old black man, Uncle Remus, telling them to the son of white plantation owners.[72] Although Uncle Remus is a black character conceived by a white, the stories themselves are purely African-American. Thus, by 1890, black children could read their own literature, but most probably still heard these tales from black storytellers.

This oral culture took several forms: moral tales, stories of animal tricksters, and stories of human tricksters. Similar fables were told in Africa, but American blacks adapted these fables for their own purposes. Some of the stories that had moral messages taught a distinctly African-American view of history. According to one story, just before George Washington died, he begged those gathered around his bedside to "Forever keep the niggers down."[73] Such interpretations of American history differed from what black children in the South learned in public schools after the Civil War. This dissonance may have created in black children a distrust of written history because it was so different from what they and their parents had long believed. Such distrust may have been another reason why many black children did not attend Southern public schools regularly. (See chapter 4.)

Most moral tales were not about history but about how to get along in everyday human relationships. They explained the importance of friendship, of family ties, of fulfilling obligations, and of being obedient. For example, "in one tale a frog trapped in a deep well begs a rattlesnake to aid him and promises to reward him. When he is saved he refuses to fulfill his obligation. Shortly afterwards they meet in the woods and the rattlesnake grabs him." The frog than desperately promises to pay the rattlesnake, but the rattlesnake chews the frog up. Storytellers also warned children who disobeyed their mother that they would suffer, just as a chick that disregarded its mother's cry of warning might be devoured by a hawk. Moral tales were ways of reinforcing the values that African-American parents tried to instill in children.

Animal trickster tales had a different purpose. They taught children about authority relationships and were themselves indirect attacks on authority. Animal characters allowed for more freedom in telling and listening than would stories about humans. Both in slavery and in freedom, direct criticism of all-powerful whites was dangerous.[74] The animal trickster tales were ways of "signifying" whites. Of course, these tales were not exclusively stories for children; adults as well listened to them. In this practice, African-Americans were not exceptional, for in this era the stories that attracted white working-class or more prosperous child readers entertained their parents as well.

Animal trickster stories are about the weak surviving by using their wits, but the stories are also about being careful not to act too quickly. They illustrate that there is danger in believing the strong will triumph and how understanding the more powerful and knowing their weaknesses helps the weak survive. The slave is usually the rabbit, the weaker animal, the trickster. The well-known story about Rabbit, Wolf, and the tar baby is typical. Wolf builds a tar baby and leaves it beside the road. Rabbit comes along and addresses the tar baby. When it doesn't reply, Rabbit becomes furious and hits it with his hands, feet, and head until he is entirely entangled in the tar. Rabbit has acted too quickly. Wolf then prepares to kill Rabbit, but Rabbit understands that Wolf wants to kill him in the most painful way possible. Rabbit takes advantage of the stronger animal's desire, and begs Wolf to kill him in any way other than by throwing him into the briar patch. Of course, Wolf throws Rabbit in, and he escapes. Many of the stories are about food, because for slaves, who had a "minimal diet," food was a sign of "enhanced status and power" or about "sexual prowess," also a sign of prestige. In all cases, Rabbit outwits a stronger animal in order to get the food or the woman. "He convinces Wolf that they ought to sell their own grandparents for a tub of butter, arranges for his grandparents to escape so that only Wolf's remain to be sold, and once they are bartered for the butter he steals that as well." "When Brer Bear promises his daughter to the best whistler in the forest, Rabbit offers to help his only serious competitor, Brer Dog, whistle more sweetly by slitting the corners of his mouth, which in reality makes him incapable of whistling at all." A few animal tricksters were female, but most were male.[75] Boys may have particularly relished these stories of the triumph of the underdog, because males were so likely to feel the brunt of their white masters' anger and distrust.

Sometimes the moral conveyed in the animal trickster story is the opposite of the values taught in the slaves' moral folktales. Often, animals do not help one another when they are in trouble, or if they do assist one another, they are tricked out of food or something else. Rabbit frequently tricks other animals into taking his place when he is in trouble, but he never asks for their assistance. When an animal does ask for help, he suffers, as when Brer Rooster "unselfishly tries to help a starving Hawk and is rewarded by having Hawk devour all of his children." The stories also picture an irrational world, one in which the animals are friendly to one another one minute and at war the next. "In an extremely popular tale Alligator confesses to Rabbit that he doesn't know what trouble is. Rabbit offers to teach him and instructs him to lie down in the broom grass. While Alligator is sleeping in the dry grass, Rabbit sets it on fire all around him and calls out: 'Dat's trouble, Brer 'Gator, dat's trouble youse in.' "

In these stories, the animal trickster is a white person. Slaves remembered well how whites often deceived them. In some stories, the stronger animal is a trickster, as when Wolf constructs the tar baby, or when "Fox asks Jaybird to pick a bone out of his teeth, and once he is in his mouth, Fox devours him." Slave storytellers often warned their listeners to be careful not to be tricked as animals were in the stories. Moreover, when the animal trickster stories seemed to subvert the moral tales, the message was that if an animal did the wrong thing, he suffered. Thus Rabbit suffers because he is too quick to get angry at the tar baby, Wolf loses because of his cruelty in wanting to kill Rabbit in the most painful way possible, and Alligator suffers because he is too curious to know what trouble is.

Animal trickster tales did not always have a happy ending, and they were not always logical or reasonable. They reflected a world where justice did not always prevail and where suffering was inevitable.[76] In these ways, the animal trickster tales are remarkably different from the literature read by rural and suburban white children and the dime novels read by white working-class youngsters. White youngsters read tales in which the good, the just, always prevailed. The stories that provided pleasure for white and black children were very different and reflected the sharply divergent worlds in which they grew to maturity.

The third type of tale told by African-Americans in the nineteenth century was the human trickster story. These tales probably originated in a real event that was embroidered upon and told to others. In human trickster stories, the humans do not do as the animals do in other stories—such as dream of taking the master's place, or his woman, or destroying him. The stories are more realistic and tell of human trickery and of gaining a small advantage such as food. For example, at hog-killing time on a plantation where the master was very stingy and did not feed the slaves enough, the field hands told the master that all the hogs had died. When the master arrived at the hog pen, all the slaves were looking down sadly at the hogs and acting afraid to touch them because they had died of "malitis." The master acts as slaves expected whites to do— with cruelty and stupidity: he gives the presumably tainted meat to the slave families. The master does not know that "malitis" was caused by a slave who "tapped Mister Hog 'tween the eyes with that mallet."[77] In human trickster stories, the slave often triumphed by using his verbal facility—in this case by creating "malitis." Through African-American folktales, children learned the same lessons as they did by playing the dozens: if they were quick-witted, they could survive and covertly triumph over whites.

The pleasures of youth varied depending on class, race, gender, and to some extent, the place the youngster lived—whether on a farm or in a city. Youngsters from prosperous families living in rural, urban, and suburban areas had the most space within their homes to play in and the most privacy and opportunity for individual play. Play experiences reinforced what parents taught children: that they were precious, distinctive, and independent humans. Conversely, white and black working-class children in cities and slave children on plantations had virtually no private play space within their homes and instead played with others in the streets or in plantation farmyards. Their play experiences also bolstered what their parents taught them: that they had to adapt to and respect others. All children typically played with others like themselves. There were distinct childhoods, and youngsters knew little about any but their own.

As for games, everyone liked ring, tag, and chase games. Nonetheless, youngsters played these games differently depending on where they lived and their social condition. Farm children and children of middle-class families who lived on large lots near open fields engaged in these games with abandon, but working-class, city-bred children adapted them to a constricted environment. Slave children modified traditional games to exclude no one. Game play differed by race and gender. Only blacks played the dozens, and among both races and all social classes, more girls than boys engaged in doll play, and more boys than girls participated in games of skill such as marbles and, to some degree, in violent games. Through play, youngsters modeled nineteenth-century socially defined "feminine" and "masculine" activities.

All children enjoyed toys, most of which children fashioned themselves. Only middle-class parents could afford the new array of manufactured toys that appeared after 1870. But parents worried that if their youngsters possessed such objects, they would fail to acquire essential skills that poorer youngsters learned of necessity. The precariousness of social-class status in this era is evident in the fact that middle-class parents worried that purchasing toys to enhance the pleasure of their children might ultimately work to their social detriment.

Individual and team sports were most popular among middle-class youth. White working-class and African-American boys, although they had less time to play and less access to playing fields than more well-off boys, still participated in sports to some degree. Sports developed strong bodies and competitive spirits—approved masculine attributes among all boys. There was also a powerful gender division in sports. More boys than girls played team sports, but virtually all of the sports in which girls participated were individual and comparatively restful and noncompetitive. Girls' sports did not conflict with middle-class women's future roles as homemakers and child nurturers in individual-family homes. White working-class girls and African-American girls rarely participated in sports. These girls could not afford to purchase the equipment, such as skates, croquet sets, tennis racquets, and bicycles, required for all the sporting activities—except for walking—then deemed appropriate for girls. In addition, poor girls, who worked not only outside the home but in the home as well, had even less free time to enjoy sports than did their brothers.

The kind of stories children most liked reading or hearing depended on children's social class, race, and gender. For middle-class girls, the crucial time in their lives was their early teens, when parents required girls to give up free out-of-doors play and retreat to their family homes to prepare for marriage and motherhood. Girls favored novels about adolescence, family life, and the moral values young women learned and would pass on to their children. Middle-class boys, who throughout childhood and adolescence enjoyed considerable freedom to play as they chose, yet remained under the control of parents, preferred books about youthful adventure and freedom from moral constraints.

White working-class urban youths read dime-novel fiction that featured young people like themselves, who lived in fast-paced cities and labored in an adult world of work. For working-class girls, as for middle-class young women, adolescence was a turning point in their lives, but for different reasons. Rather than retreating to the home, urban working-class teenage girls left family homes to engage in wage work where sexual threats from men were real. Working-class girls preferred dime novels about employed young women who, through a series of exciting urban adventures, avoided the villain who sought to seduce them and found instead the love of a good man.

White working-class young men selected dime novels that supported their way of life and working-class cultural values. They read novels that either described the climb to success of physically tough, street-smart young factory workers, who remained supportive of their fellow workers in strikes, or described the adventures of tough male bandits who confounded rich men, banks, and railroads. The experiences of white middle- and working-class girls were so divergent that they rarely read the same fiction: many middle-class girls probably shared their parents' view that any wage-earning girl was immoral and thus not the appropriate subject of fiction, and working-class girls found stories about family life boring. However, middle- and working-class boys often read the same stories because both craved excitement and both liked orphan-boy heroes who could get along without parental help and achieve the American dream of success.

The fiction preferred by African-American children was unique. They favored folktales that lauded the ability of the underdog to survive and to triumph using little but his quick wits and his ability to talk fast and outsmart his opponent. Because black parents raised their sons and daughters similarly, and because both black boys and girls experienced many of the same problems with whites, youngsters of both genders enjoyed the same stories. Although African-American folktales featured male animals, the stories' appeal to children was less gender-specific than the appeal of stories read by whites of any class. Black folktales differed in almost every way from fiction enjoyed by white boys and girls. The folktales were not stories about families, children escaping from families to succeed on their own, wage work, seduction and rape, or economic success; rarely, in fact, were the folktales about humans at all. Impoverished, with little hope of social or monetary advancement, with their most pressing concern how to survive with whites in positions of power, blacks created folktales that focused on getting just a little bit more—of food, for example—and on how to outwit authority figures. Black folktales often taught a moral lesson as did stories for white children, but in African-American fiction, the moral was not necessarily that the good triumphed. Stories for black children taught them what they knew from real-life experience: that good persons often got beaten, and that the white masters who were their enemies usually triumphed.

By adolescence, the pleasures of young people diverged considerably. Adolescent white working-class children living in late-nineteenth-century cities had the greatest access and opportunity to enjoy a variety of amusements. Girls had slightly less freedom than boys, but both genders delighted in new commercial amusements such as dance halls, penny arcades, inexpensive theatrical shows, and amusement parks.

Middle-class reformers reacted with alarm to the new amusements that urban children enjoyed, and prosperous parents tried to protect their own sons and daughters from these forms of entertainment. Between 1850 and

1890, in part because of parents' fear for the morality of city youths, as well as their concern for the welfare of urban children whose parents were impoverished or dead, middle-class reformers created new child-welfare programs. The next chapter will examine such programs and how they affected needy children and their families.

7

When Families Fail:
Coping with Child Poverty and Delinquency

In cities, Americans discovered child poverty and delinquency among immigrants. Children of the foreign born, who lived in the poorest and most diseased sections of cities, frequently lost one or both parents. The Civil War also orphaned many youngsters, and the economic depressions of the 1870s and 1880s resulted in the separation of families as fathers moved about in search of work. As youngsters contributed to the family economy by hawking newspapers in the city streets, huckstering, and picking up stray bits of coal and wood, children's legal activities shaded into illegal ones. Scavenging could lead to stealing any unattended item. Impoverished parents were not inclined to question a child too closely about where he or she obtained a necessary item. However, children might also sell some of the items they scavenged to junk dealers and spend the profits on food or amusements of various sorts. Such behavior antagonized working-class parents, although they were not always capable of doing much about it. For girls, street life could lead to prostitution, something that both working-class parents and middle-class reformers greatly feared. In 1851, in New York, one young girl who scavenged around the docks got "in the habit of going aboard the Coal Boats in that vicinity and prostituting herself."[1]

By the 1820s, many Americans believed that the traditional welfare programs, including the almshouse and outdoor relief, that provided help to children and other poor were inadequate or even harmful to the young. Alarmed by child poverty and delinquency, middle-class women and men responded by founding new, specialized asylums and foster-care programs for urban immigrant children. These middle-class founders had one set of goals, but the impoverished parents who used asylums and placing-out programs had another, rather different agenda. In the end, the history of child-welfare pro-

General dining room, Southern Home for Destitute Children, Philadelphia (1895). Middle-class administrators of orphanages such as this one sought to teach poor children to value order and regularity by dressing them alike and seating them in neat rows in dining halls. Orphanages usually separated boys from girls (this is clearly the boys' dining hall). Like this one, most orphan asylums admitted only white children. (From the Forty-fifth Annual Report of the Southern Home for Destitute Children, Historical Society of Pennsylvania)

grams is the story of the interaction of the goals of their founders and of the families that used the programs. It is also the story of how children themselves affected the programs created for their benefit, and how the programs affected children's lives.

To middle-class Americans, accustomed to keeping their own children in the privacy of their homes, in the care of mothers whose chief task was to provide their children with a Christian, moral upbringing, the very public lives of working-class children in city streets was prima facie evidence of the inadequacy of their home lives. Middle-class Americans, who treated their children as precious and priceless, could not understand how working-class parents could treat their children as laborers and allow them out of the home to roam dangerous city streets without parental supervision.[2] This clash of values between urban middle-class Protestant Americans and urban working-class Roman Catholic and Jewish immigrant parents and their children led to the creation of a whole variety of child-saving programs between 1850 and 1890.

Child saving was not invented in the industrial age. Two types of public welfare for needy children had long been in existence: indoor relief in the almshouse and outdoor relief in children's own homes. However, early in the century, middle-class Americans grew skeptical of the value of both. Consequently, child savers campaigned to trim back these programs and replace them with institutionalization in specialized children's asylums and direct placement in family homes.

Almshouses were locally funded asylums that admitted poor of all ages. Children sometimes entered almshouses when one or both of their parents became ill and lost their jobs, for almshouses were among the few nineteenth-century institutions that provided free medical care. Mothers and their children often dwelled side by side in almshouse wards, although occasionally children lived apart from their families in nursery wards. When parents recovered their health, they and their children departed together. Other youngsters entered almshouses after the death or desertion of one or both parents. Sometimes youngsters in almshouses attended school in the institution or in a local public school, but in rural areas, they often did not go to school at all.[3] Almshouse practice was to indenture out children who did not have family in the institution to farmers or artisans until the child was 18, if female, or 21, if male. This practice relieved local governments of the cost of caring for the youngsters and presumably trained them for self-sufficiency.

Children were always in the minority in almshouses, but by the middle of the nineteenth century, eastern urban almshouses admitted fewer youngsters than previously. The flood of adult immigrants willing to work for low wages led local artisans to prefer hiring them rather than taking in an almshouse child who had to be fed, clothed, educated, and trained in a craft for years. As fewer artisans applied for almshouse children, officials elected to admit fewer children rather than retain youngsters at public expense in the asylum until maturity.[4]

Almshouses also attracted the attention of middle-class reformers who objected to children being cared for in such crowded and dirty public institutions alongside drunks, prostitutes, and insane persons. How could youngsters learn correct moral behavior in such an atmosphere? By 1866 states began to pass laws ordering the removal of children from almshouses. Some states, such as Ohio, Massachusetts, Michigan, Minnesota, Wisconsin, Rhode Island, and Connecticut, replaced almshouses with special public orphanages, while other states, such as New York, Pennsylvania, Maryland, and New Hampshire, paid for the care of young public wards in private orphanages or foster-care agencies. Nonetheless, not all states removed children from almshouses. By 1890, although most needy children received care in welfare programs designed for the young, almost five thousand children still lived in undifferentiated public poorhouses in the United States.[5]

Laws removing children from almshouses, while providing the young-sters with alternate care in specialized, cleaner institutions, might separate children permanently from their families. In states that passed laws excluding children from almshouses, when ailing mothers entered such institutions, their children could no longer remain with them until the women recovered. Instead, children entered public or private orphanages, from which children could be placed out with foster families without the consent of their parents. In this way, simply because of the illness and poverty of a mother, she and her children could be separated indefinitely.[6]

Because public almshouses were never very attractive places, and because a mother's entrance into one might, by the end of the nineteenth century, break up her family, most women tried to avoid such asylums. Homeless, elderly men constituted the largest group of almshouse inmates.[7] Impover-ished mothers preferred, if at all possible, to stay out of institutions and rely on public outdoor relief instead. For example, in Philadelphia, of all forms of relief granted to poor women throughout the nineteenth century, outdoor relief was most popular and placement of children in child-care programs of any kind was least popular.[8]

Outdoor relief came in several forms: in cash (weekly pensions), and in food, fuel, medicine, and free medical treatment. Mothers received outdoor relief for themselves and for their children. Although it cost localities less to dispense outdoor relief than to incarcerate the poor in almshouses, outdoor relief came under attack in city after city in the nineteenth century. Whereas almshouses were clearly so unattractive as to entice few to utilize them, tax-payers believed outdoor relief was more attractive; they argued that poor people preferred to live in their own homes, laze about in the streets, avoid employment, and get by on outdoor relief. Its very existence seemingly encouraged the poor to depend upon it instead of on their own labor. As early as 1835, Philadelphia abolished outdoor cash relief, and most other major cities eliminated it by 1900.[9] Mothers and their children could usually still obtain other forms of outdoor relief such as food, fuel, and medicine, but although such assistance was certainly useful, it was often not enough to allow a mother to keep her family together.

Needy mothers had other resources they could call upon: asylums and foster-care programs founded by middle-class child savers. By midcentury child saving was the special province of women. The industrial revolution opened well-paying jobs to middle-class men, who could afford to support their wives and children in single-family homes. New products made home production of many household items less necessary for middle-class women, whose chief preoccupations became managing their households and providing Christian moral guidance to their growing children.[10] Motivated by strong religious convictions about the importance of proper child nurture, Protestant middle-class women looked outside their own households and sought to assist the children of the urban Catholic immigrant poor. Founding orphanages was especially suited to middle-class women's talents, because such asylums were similar to the large households these women customarily managed and allowed them to use their well-honed child-rearing abilities. Even when men founded child-care asylums, they acknowledged that women were best suited to child care and household management by appointing women as matrons, nurses, and teachers. Orders of nuns commonly ran Roman Catholic orphan asylums.

Orphanages founded by middle-class women were usually small and admitted boys and girls between the ages of six and twelve. Few orphanages were well-funded. They survived with small monetary contributions from women (who did not usually have large amounts of discretionary income), donations of food, clothing, and household supplies, and sometimes board payments from the families of the children they admitted. The experiences of the women who ran the Bethesda Home in Philadelphia were typical. In August 1871, they noted: "Three ladies visited us today, who left seven dollars, this donation comes with peculiar acceptability, as in the heat of summer we have few gifts." And a few days later, "To human view all looks dark, our rent is due, and no visible means of help, but thine arm, O Lord, is not shortened."[11]

Middle-class men also founded child-saving asylums, although they differed from asylums founded by women in several ways. Because of men's public roles in government, roles denied to nineteenth-century women, men founded all public child-care asylums including the orphanages that replaced almshouses in several states, the public asylums for orphans of Civil War soldiers, and the juvenile reformatories that admitted impoverished and delinquent adolescents. Male Catholic and Jewish religious leaders also founded orphanages to protect youngsters from the aggressive proselytizing typical of all asylums run by Protestants—male and female. Affluent men opened a few orphanages such as Girard College in Philadelphia. Public asylums and large orphanages such as Girard College were better funded than orphanages founded by women, but most institutions founded by male religious leaders faced many of the same financial constraints as did female-run asylums. Nearly all orphanages counted on donations from religious groups, small contributions from many concerned persons, legacies, occasional grants from localities and states, and board payments made by parents and relatives of young inmates.[12]

Whether child savers were middle-class women or men, their goals were much alike. Most child savers established orphanages and reformatories that admitted only poor or delinquent white urban youngsters and deliberately excluded African-American children. Of course, between 1850 and 1865, the majority of African-American children were slaves and presumably were fully provided for by their masters. Although some free black families, most of whom were quite poor, lived in Northern cities, white reformers established only a few orphanages for blacks in the North before the Civil War. More were founded after the war, but as late as 1910, over half the benevolent institutions for children in the United States did not admit African-Americans.[13] After the Civil War, African-Americans in the South founded some orphanages for black youths, but not many, because asylums were costly to establish and maintain, and few former slaves were affluent enough to do so. African-Americans, out of necessity, practiced informal adoption methods carried over from Africa and from slavery. When slave parents and children were separated by sale, relatives or friends took the youngsters into their families. The same pattern prevailed in the North before and after the Civil War. In 1850, informal adoption clearly existed among African-Americans in Boston, where 12 percent of black youngsters "lived with a household head other than their natural parents."[14]

Juvenile reformatories in the North began to admit blacks in the 1850s but did not treat African-Americans the same as whites. Managers segregated blacks and paid white officials who supervised the reformatories' black divisions less than white officials assigned to the white divisions. In the South, most African-American boys and girls did not enjoy even the marginal benefit of admission to segregated reformatories. Before and after the Civil War, there were few juvenile reformatories in the South and, as of 1870, only one, the Baltimore reformatory, admitted blacks. Instead, African-American youths who violated the law were punished, just as were adults, through hard labor in the convict-lease system.[15]

While they clearly discriminated against African-Americans, child savers were equally interested in aiding white boys and girls. Some asylums admitted only males or females, but most took in children of both genders and kept them apart, usually in different wings of the institution. Such separation was intended to protect girls from the wildness and rowdiness that presumably characterized many young boys. Middle-class Americans of the nineteenth century believed that females were the guardians of religion and morality, and it was essential to keep young women pure and innocent if they were to find virtuous husbands and become proper moral mentors to their children.

Whether a child was male or female, most child savers expected that the asylum would replace the youngster's family. Orphanages and juvenile reformatories usually required parents to sign documents officially releasing children to the care of the asylums until the youngsters became adults, at 18 or 21 years of age. The child savers would provide young inmates with food, clothing, education, employment, and eventually new family caretakers. This was all part of the overall plan to save poor immigrant youth from city streets and reeducate them in secluded, private asylums for responsible adulthood.

Most of the asylums that replaced children's former homes were large, congregate buildings, often surrounded by walls. The walls kept indigent children out of dangerous city streets, protected and apart from the community in a private place, as were middle-class youngsters in their private homes. In congregate orphanages, youngsters slept in large dormitories. As a *New York Times* reporter observed in 1869: "In the dormitories are row after row of little beds, with uniform covers, and generally in the corner a large couch for an attendant, who puts the little urchins in bed and keeps all frightful things away by sleeping in the same room." He also noted that the dining rooms are "invariably large, cheerless apartments, furnished with rough tables and rude seats. Nothing is done to make this department attractive. . . ."[16] In smaller asylums, groups of children of the same age sometimes slept eight to a room. Orphan asylums diverged sharply from the homes of the working-class youngsters admitted to them. Although orphanages were much more isolated from the larger world than were working-class homes, they were also better appointed. Children's institutions usually had central heating and modern appliances, rare in late-nineteenth-century working-class neighborhoods, and institutions provided poor youngsters, most of whom were accustomed to sleeping with siblings two to four to a bed, with their own beds.[17] Orphan asylums may not have looked so bad to child inmates.

However, if asylums were intended to reeducate children in a homelike environment, congregate institutions were off the mark. In 1857 and 1859, two child-welfare conferences in New York introduced American child savers to European family reform schools, including Johann Wichern's Rauche Haus in Germany and Frederick DeMetz's Colonie Agricole in France. Some Americans became intrigued by the idea of replacing congregate asylums with cottage-style facilities. Groups of 12 to 36 children of the same sex and age would live and eat in homelike cottages presided over by officials who served as mother and father figures. The first cottage-style asylum in the United States was the Massachusetts State Industrial School for Girls at Lancaster, which opened in 1854, and the second was the Ohio Reform School, which opened in 1857.[18]

Whether children were in congregate or cottage-style asylums, child savers believed that children had to be reformed; their behavior and values had to be changed. Because reform could be thwarted by other children in the institution, some asylums required children to be silent, especially at mealtimes. In this way, youngsters who had learned proper moral standards and obedience in the asylum would not be adversely affected by new arrivals. Preventing children from learning one another's names was another way of protecting them and presumably preventing them from contacting other inmates once released. Thus, officials in some asylums assigned numbers to children upon entrance, stamped these numbers on all their belongings, and addressed boys and girls by their numbers rather than their given names.[19]

Reform could be undermined not only by other children in asylums but also by the families of youngsters. Therefore, asylum officials limited visits from parents and friends to one afternoon a month. Some asylum officials also examined mail that children received and both limited and censored letters that children wrote to their families. As Edward Dahlberg, a resident of the Cleveland Jewish Orphan Asylum, recalled: "Letter writing was once a week. . . . The letters received were opened by the Superintendent to see whether they contained a dime or a quarter—which was promptly confiscated. The contents of all epistles were read and censored; if an inmate said that the 'weisenhaus' was a reform school, the words were scratched out, and the turncoat who had reviled the Superintendent, the trustees or the meals was given fifty to a hundred demerits."[20]

A certain number of demerits resulted in punishment, and it was sometimes quite harsh. Child savers believed that orphans and delinquents whose parents allowed them the run of city streets lacked discipline and required sharp correction if they were to be reformed. Youngsters in juvenile reformatories received the most severe punishments. An investigation of the Philadelphia House of Refuge in 1876 "revealed that one youngster was beaten until he fainted and then placed in a solitary cell on bread and water only. A number of youngsters were confined in so-called 'iron fronts' where the doors were made of iron, there were no windows, and only a little light penetrated around the top and the bottom of the door. One boy was locked in such an iron front for several days with no clothes, no bed, and a chamber pot that was infrequently emptied." In the 1870s, at the Massachusetts State Reform School for Boys, officials confined boys for several hours in "a wooden box twenty-one inches by sixteen and a half inches, with a grate in the door and an opening in the top. . . . Inmate Frank Cunningham . . . admitted that, after six and a half hours in the sweatbox, he had trouble walking for two or three days." Nonetheless, an examination of the records of punishment of several reformatories in the 1850s and 1860s reveals that only a minority of children, between 10 percent and 18 percent of youngsters confined in a reformatory in any single year, were whipped or physically confined.[21]

Nonetheless, even if they were never actually whipped, all children in reformatories lived under the threat of harsh punishment, and so too did many youngsters in orphanages. Though rarely banished to cells or closets, boys and girls were regularly slapped, kicked, or hit across the palm with a rattan switch. One youngster, who lived in the Hebrew Orphan Asylum in New York in the 1860s and 1870s, recalled that a boy who wet his bed "was taken time and again from his bed in the early morning, placed in the bath and the cold shower turned on him, being threatened if he moved with a rawhide by the Warden, his screams could be heard all over the building and it was only when his cries became faint that he was released but not before he received a few welts from the rawhide."[22] Such punishment appears especially harsh, and it certainly reveals that middle-class asylum officials treated poor youngsters more harshly than was considered appropriate in middle-class families in this era. However, asylum children may not have been unused to physical reprimands. The working-class families from which most asylum children came demanded prompt obedience and often threatened disobedient youngsters with a whipping. (See chapter 3.)

Asylum officials believed that children had to learn not only to obey but also to cope with adversity. They could not be spoiled. They had to be trained to live in a hard world. For that reason, all asylums provided youngsters with minimal comforts. In some asylums, youngsters gave up their own clothes upon admittance and donned unattractive and often uncomfortable uniforms. Sarah Sander Wirpel described the uniform she wore in the 1890s at the Cleveland Jewish Orphan Asylum: "We put on a grey long-legged unionsuit of thick knitted material threaded with tiny black hairs which in the course of the day became a torture of itching; long black thick stockings, a red flannel 'underskirt' and a grey wool, ankle-length, long sleeved dress—severely plain, and a blue-striped apron over all. . . . The next day we were to lose our new shoes from home. My beloved patent-leather tipped, high buttoned shoes . . . were taken away and I was given instead a pair of thick leather, red-lined loose clodhoppers that fit nowhere and laced up high over my ankles. . . ." Daily bathing rituals were performed with cold water. Sarah Sander Wirpel noted that in her dormitory, "the faucets gave only cold water, very cold in winter."[23]

Most asylums had playrooms, and some had play areas outside. Cottage-style asylums had the most space for play. However, rarely were there any toys, musical instruments, or athletic equipment in play areas indoors or out. In 1868 the *New York Times* noted that most asylums had "A large room on each side of the building, vacant of anything in the shape of gymnastic apparatus or 'plaything,' . . . called the playroom, from the fact that the children are periodically turned loose therein to amuse themselves as best they can."[24] Middle-class asylum founders provided poor children with play space but not the range of toys middle-class parents gave their own youngsters. Play areas in orphanages were a lot like the early playgrounds provided poor working-class children in various cities—just large open spaces where poor youngsters were expected to entertain themselves. (See chapter 6.)

Asylum founders not only prepared their young charges for adversity but also sought to instill in them new, middle-class values. Officials rang bells to wake children in the morning and call them to meals, to work, and to school, thereby presumably teaching the youngsters to be attentive to time. The rigid daily schedules of asylums never changed, and thus the young learned the value of regularity. Boys and girls learned industriousness by being assigned chores. Girls made beds, cleaned, and mended clothes, while boys did yard work and heavy chores. Officials expected all children to become future oriented because they received points for good behavior and were promoted to higher grades and granted more privileges. Military-like drill, introduced in many asylums during and after the Civil War, would teach boys to be orderly and responsive to authority.[25]

Youngsters in asylums also learned values in more formal ways—through asylum education programs. Such programs were of three types: religious, academic, and practical. All nineteenth-century child-care asylums taught religion. None was truly nondenominational. Asylums founded by Protestants upheld the Protestant tradition and sought to convert Catholics and Jews. In 1853 a member of Boston's city government expressed the view of many child savers when he said: "the only way to elevate the foreign population was to make protestants of their *children.*" Catholics founded orphanages to prevent their children from being converted in Protestant asylums. Jews used asylums to protect their children from Protestantism and keep them within the Jewish cultural tradition. German Jews founded most child-care asylums, and by the end of the nineteenth century, owing to the huge influx of Russian Jews, asylum officials sought to acculturate this new population. Acculturation meant converting youngsters from Orthodox Judaism to Reform Judaism and educating children in German and English rather than in Yiddish.[26] Catholics, Protestants, and Jews all used asylums to reinforce religious and moral values in children, but Protestants and Jews also used child-care asylums as a method of changing the religious and cultural perspective of some youngsters.

In addition to religious instruction, orphanages and reformatories taught youngsters basic academic skills, including the ability to read, write, add, and subtract. Between 1850 and 1870, most children's institutions hired female teachers to educate youngsters in asylum classrooms. Later in the century, when public and parochial schools became more common, Protestant and Jewish orphanages often sent children to local public schools, and Catholic asylums sent children to local parochial schools. Such youngsters had the opportunity to make friends and contacts outside the asylum. Even children educated within asylums received an education comparable to noninstitutionalized youngsters: they were taught by female teachers who emphasized memorization and expected students to be silent unless called upon (see chapter 4). Asylum officials did not generally hold high academic expectations for most children but simply hoped that they would learn to write their names and to read and write letters to family and friends. However, very bright children who grew up in some orphanages received additional education in local high schools. The degree to which children benefited from asylum education depended on how much time they spent in institutions, and that varied considerably. Some children spent only a few months in asylums; others, many years. Those who remained in orphanages and reformatories for a year or more profited from attending school on a regular basis, unlike many working-class children who often had to miss school to help out their unemployed or ailing parents. Children in asylums were not excluded from schools as were many poor children in cities where schools were overcrowded. And orphans educated in asylums in the South, where school years were the most abbreviated and schools least accessible, received much more education than did other Southern children.[27]

Whereas asylum officials were perfectly willing to provide orphans with basic academic skills, officials felt that education in practical skills the children might ultimately use in the working world was much more important. Most middle-class child savers believed that orphans had to be properly trained for working-class occupations. In the late nineteenth century, when some public schools were just beginning to experiment with industrial education (see chapter 4), boys in orphan asylums learned how to work with their hands and sometimes acquired a skill such as shoe making. Industrial education gave boys mechanical skills they could use when trying to get jobs after they left orphanages or reformatories, and it kept them busy a good part of every day. Asylum managers believed that filling every day with activity kept youngsters occupied and less troublesome. Industrial education might also result in the production of items that could be sold for a profit.

In juvenile reformatories, industrial education first took the form of contract labor. Contractors paid asylum officials for the labor of boys in shops in asylums that contractors managed and equipped. "The youngsters did book-binding, basket-making, wicker work, umbrella making, and seat caning." Yet the work was irregular. During depressions, contractors shut down the shops entirely. Boys were bored by the labor, and endured harsh punishments for their lack of interest. By 1884 many states responded to the objections of adult free laborers, who decried the unfair competition of contract labor in asylums, and made it illegal. Subsequently, asylum managers themselves set up shops in reformatories and kept trying to teach boys mechanical skills.

For girls, practical education in orphanages and reformatories was always training in domestic tasks, for child savers believed the only appropriate training a young, working-class girl needed was in housewifely skills. She could use them first as a domestic servant and later as a wife. Of course, having girls make all the beds and do all the sewing, cleaning, and much of the cooking in asylums also proved economical.[28]

Practical education continued once youngsters departed asylums. Institutions typically released children within a year or two of their entrance to work in family homes. Child savers believed that boys and girls were malleable and reformable within a short period of time. In the tradition of public almshouses, private child-care institutions signed indenture contracts with farmers or artisans who promised to provide children with food, clothing, and education in return for the children's labor. Girls worked as domestic servants; boys usually worked as farm laborers. This system was economical and hopefully allowed youngsters to acquire practical training to enable them to be self-sufficient as adults. The system also allowed farmers who could not afford to pay wages to local farm children for their labor to obtain cheaper child laborers through child-welfare programs. Jewish orphanages were the exception. They had no trouble placing out girls as domestic servants, but it was harder to find Jewish families willing to take in boys. Most Jewish orphanages retained boys until the age of 13, when they took their bar mitzvahs. Boys then reentered the community on their own or returned to their families and friends.[29]

Between 1850 and 1890, as one group of child savers founded asylums to reform indigent, immigrant, urban youth, another group sharply criticized institutionalization and instead supported direct placing out in family homes. The leading proponent of placing out was Charles Loring Brace. Educated to the ministry, Brace decided, after graduation from seminary, to apply his training not as a church pastor but as a child saver. In 1850 and 1851, he traveled to England, where he saw how British officials transported needy children to Canada and other parts of the British empire. He also visited Germany and discovered how "Friends in Need" placed vagrant city children in rural families.[30] Once back in New York City, Brace noted with alarm how many young boys and girls worked and, in some cases, lived in city streets. To reform such youngsters, Brace and several fellow ministers began to hold "boys meetings" to teach Christian principles to youths. The boys proved quite a challenge; many threw stones at the ministers, yelled derogatory remarks, or ran and fought among the benches set up for the meetings. Brace quickly determined that preaching to such youngsters was not enough to reform them. In 1853, he and other child savers formed the New York Children's Aid Society to create a more comprehensive program to reform indigent youth. Brace was the organization's general secretary.[31]

Brace sharply criticized his fellow child savers and their reliance on asylums in reforming needy children. He believed asylums were overly costly and did not accomplish the reformation of the young. Instead, asylums turned boys and girls into either hypocrites who behaved sweetly in order to avoid punishment or automatons who knew only how to respond to bells and to march. Brace believed that children raised in asylums did not learn how to function normally in society.[32] He also objected strongly to the asylums' practice of signing indenture contracts with employers. Such contracts denied children the freedom to leave homes they disliked, and made it difficult for agencies to remove youngsters from poor homes. Moreover, Brace believed children could be reformed only by families that truly cared for them, whereas indenture contracts emphasized the labor relationship between families and children rather than the emotional ties between them.

Brace's Children's Aid Society sought to help poor urban children in various ways, but the method he is most known for was removing poor boys and girls from the city and placing them directly in farm families. Brace was not antiurban or even very critical of individual city-bred children. He called urban youth the "dangerous classes" only when they massed together in crowded city slums. Brace admired streetwise young children who worked hard making it on their own. He believed placing out in farm families was one method, but not the only one, of offering city youngsters the opportunity to advance themselves. Like many other middle-class Americans of his day, Brace believed living on a farm was healthier than living in a city; farm life offered children more opportunity to rise up the social scale because the country was less stratified by class than was the city. No indenture contracts impeded advancement of children placed out by the Children's Aid Society. Children could, on their own, leave families; families could dismiss children; and the agency, at its discretion, could remove youngsters from families.

Children's Aid Society agents canvassed New York looking for needy white children who might benefit from placing out. Just as child savers who directed asylums gave preference to whites, so did the CAS. The agency's justification for placing out few African-American children was that there were few Western farm families willing to take black children in.[33]

When a group of 20 to 30 white boys and girls had been recruited, and their families (if they had any) had agreed to their placement, an agent of the society shepherded the children by train to a rural area, usually in the Midwest.[34] The growth of the railroads in the 1850s, 1860s, and 1870s made it possible for youngsters to be transported to Western farms fairly quickly. Railroads often gave the CAS discounts.

Once the CAS agent and his band of city children arrived at a likely-looking country town, the agent enlisted the support of local officials, who called a meeting of the area's farmers for the purpose of inspecting the children. Farm families then chose the children they wanted. As one boy remembered, "We were taken from the train to the Methodist Church. Speeches were made and folks were asked to take an orphan home for dinner. Later that afternoon we were brought back for the selection process. . . ." In areas where the Children's Aid Society placed a lot of children, local officials formed committees that advertised the arrival of children and screened applicants for them. Such committees helped city children adjust to farm living. The committees may also have protected youngsters from ill treatment, because local officials would not want children to complain to the CAS for fear the agency might not send any more child laborers to the area.

The CAS's only criteria in choosing families for the children was that the parents should be Christian. Most were two-parent families, some with children of their own, some not. Nonetheless, families headed by single women and by single men also received children from the agency. For many years, the CAS did not check up on children placed out in a very organized way. At first the society simply relied on the children themselves to report any problems in letters they sent the agency. Later it hired agents to visit the children, but as agent A. Schlegel reported in 1885: "These children are often in homes ten or twenty miles from town or railroad, and can only be reached by long drives, and often a whole day will be consumed in visiting a single child. Sometimes changes are made without notifying the Society, or a child may leave the home provided for him, and seek another for himself, and much time and labor is thus expended in following him up." Schlegel and other CAS agents did not visit all children placed in families.[35]

From its beginnings in 1854 until 1884, the New York Children's Aid Society placed out 60,000 youngsters. Such a massive child relocation program was bound to draw criticism. Among the first to object to Brace's program were Roman Catholics, who complained that he sought to convert Catholic youngsters by placing them in Protestant family homes. For many Catholics, it was the threat of conversion that was most serious, not the actual practice of placing out. In fact, some Catholic child savers responded by forming programs of their own to place out Catholic youths in Catholic family homes in the West. More critical were managers of Protestant, Catholic, and Jewish asylums. They contended that it was dangerous to send wild youngsters straight from city streets into country homes. The youngsters first needed to acquire some discipline in orphanages. But again, it was not placing out that asylum officials objected to, but the bypassing of institutions to place children directly in family homes. Citizens in some Midwestern states also complained that the Children's Aid Society was sending west child vagrants and criminals who would eventually end up in reformatories and jails and cost taxpayers large sums of money. By the 1890s, several states passed laws restricting the placement within their borders of children from out of state. Ironically, many of these Midwestern states were then placing out children in states even farther west. The Children's Home Society of Chicago placed youngsters in several Western states, including Nebraska. "That Nebraska had by 1890 its own institutionalized population of about 1,000 in the state's industrial school and the Home for the Friendless did not dissuade the Children's Home Society from its attempts at western placements."[36]

Although placing out city children in Midwest farm families was an essential part of the Children's Aid Society program, the agency also sought to save city children in other ways. In December 1853, Brace opened his first industrial, or vocational, school for girls. His object was to have refined, middle-class women teach "vagrant little girls" to become moral, responsible, self-supporting individuals. "Most of the girls had no shoes, and they were dirty, ragged, and unkempt. Neither the ladies nor the girls knew quite what to do with each other, but the ladies persisted in their efforts to establish order and finally had the school operating." The women prepared the girls to become seamstresses, domestic servants, and eventually wives. Such women sought to make working-class families stronger and more like middle-class families by training indigent girls to become agents of reform in their neighborhoods and to their children.[37] Of course, training girls to domestic tasks was exactly what child savers in asylums did as well. Unlike girls in orphanages, girls who attended industrial schools chose to do so, but all they could choose was the kind of training middle-class child savers offered working-class girls everywhere—in and out of asylums.

For Brace, saving city children meant providing them with opportunities to improve their own lives—in Western farm families, in industrial schools, and also in urban lodging houses. In 1854 the New York Children's Aid Society opened its first Newsboys' Lodging House. Newsboys and bootblacks were among the poor children most admired by child savers such as Brace: they were needy youngsters trying on their own to make an honest living and improve their lot. To appeal to their sense of independence, the Newsboys' Lodging House charged the boys six cents for lodging and four cents for supper. Once the newsboys grew to rely on the Lodging House, it began programs of reformation including "a night school . . . a Sunday religious meeting and a savings bank." In 1862 Brace opened a Girls' Lodging House to allow virtuous young girls similar opportunities to the newsboys—to provide for themselves and avoid temptation. However, saving girls proved more difficult than saving boys—largely because of the perspective of middle-class child savers like Brace. While boys could swear, gamble, and fight, as did the newsboys, and still be admired for their independence and honesty, girls who did the same or who went out unchaperoned with young men were branded as immoral and a threat to the community. Thus, by 1892, the Children's Aid Society operated five lodging houses for boys but only one for girls.

Child savers admired all of the programs of New York's Children's Aid Society, and by 1867 there were 50 comparable agencies in U.S. cities.[38] Several of these agencies began to experiment with more careful oversight of children placed out. Professional social workers controlled Children's Aid Societies in Philadelphia and in Boston, and they began to experiment with paying families to care for children. Such programs had the advantage of making it clear that children placed in families were to be treated well and not retained purely because of their ability to work. On the other hand, as children came to be defined as more emotionally valuable than economically valuable, some child savers objected to this form of foster care. Certainly a foster mother took in a child for economic reasons; how different was this from a mother who sent her own child out to work?[39]

As Children's Aid Societies proliferated in urban industrial America, so too did another type of child-care agency: Societies for the Prevention of Cruelty to Children (SPCCs). In 1875, in New York, when members of the Society for the Prevention of Cruelty to Animals discovered that there were no laws protecting children from cruelty comparable to those protecting animals, they founded the first SPCC. By 1880 there were Societies for the Prevention of Cruelty to Children in 34 other cities.

Middle- and upper-class founders of SPCCs believed that children should be disciplined gently, not harshly, by responsible mothers in the privacy of their own homes. By the late nineteenth century, reformers grew alarmed to see corporal punishment dispensed in public, in city streets, by immigrant mothers and fathers. Child savers believed that drink and immigration caused child abuse. The two were connected: reformers argued that it was drunken immigrants who slapped and beat their children. Because most leaders of SPCCs did not themselves consume alcohol, they did not distinguish between levels of drinking. Any sign that there was alcohol in the home they took as proof that the mother was unfit. Founders of SPCCs blamed child abuse on the actions of inferior, alcoholic immigrants, who had to be taught that harsh corporal punishment was not the American way.

The SPCC was aggressive in seeking out cases. In the early years of the Boston SPCC, agents walked the streets checking for cases of child begging, child peddling, and children who were not warmly enough dressed. The agency viewed child labor in city streets and child poverty as parental abuse of children. The SPCC also responded to complaints of child mistreatment made by family members, friends, neighbors, and employers. In New York, the police enhanced the power of SPCC agents by deputizing them. In Boston, agents took referrals from the police and sometimes called on officers to help them out. When cases of child abuse came to court, SPCC agents advised magistrates. Judges usually accepted the advice of SPCC agents and often appointed the SPCC to be the guardian of an abused child. The agency would then place the youngster either in an orphanage or in a foster family.[40]

In addition to direct intervention in working-class urban family life and in the court system, Societies for the Prevention of Cruelty to Children also lobbied on behalf of laws to prevent certain forms of child abuse the societies particularly deplored. The New York SPCC successfully campaigned for the passage of a law against child begging, "which also prohibited children under fourteen from going into saloons or dance-halls. . . . Children found begging or in saloons, dance-halls, or houses of prostitution, or 'found wandering and not having any home or settled place of abode, or proper guardianship or visible means of subsistence,' could be arrested and sent by the court to various institutions such as the New York House of Refuge, the Juvenile Asylum, or the Catholic Protectory." Both the New York and Boston SPCCs cooperated with the Italian government to end the *padrone* system. *Padrones* (contractors) paid Italian parents to take their children to the United States, where the youngsters were crowded into cheap, uncomfortable apartments and employed at playing musical instruments in the streets and begging.

SPCCs in New York, Boston, and Philadelphia also worked to eliminate baby farming, a practice whereby mothers of infants paid other working-class women to board newborns.[41] The term also referred to the practice of murdering infants for a profit. Impoverished, unwed mothers were particularly likely to use baby farmers, but so too was any needy mother who had to work outside her home and required child care. Mothers who gave their infants to baby farmers sometimes defaulted on board payments, and at that point, the baby farmer might be unable and unwilling to feed and clothe the child—to keep the baby alive. Hence the charge that baby farmers killed infants after having taken money for their board from their mothers. Of course, some mothers may have used baby farmers as a way of getting rid of unwanted infants. Others may have simply fallen on hard times and been unable to keep making board payments. Regardless, the SPCC viewed baby farming as child abuse and in Pennsylvania succeeded in getting a law passed in 1885 to regulate baby farming by requiring women who boarded infants to be licensed.[42]

Concern about baby farming and about the poor care of infants in almshouses and on outdoor relief combined with fears that illegitimacy, abortion, and infanticide were becoming too common in the United States and resulted in the creation of a new type of child-care program exclusively for infants: foundling homes. Before the 1860s, the only asylums that took in infants were public almshouses. If youngsters were not nursed by their mothers in the almshouse, the youngsters were given to wet nurses in the community: poor women who received outdoor cash relief. In 1859, "the *New York Times* publicized a tour taken by seven persons representing the Almshouse and the press which described the actual circumstances of the foundlings in the homes of their city-paid nurses. They visited . . . little 'Walter Craig' in the 'dimly-lighted 8' × 10' ' upstairs apartment of his nurse, described as a 'dirty Irishwoman.' He was a sickly child, as was the nurse's other charge, Annie McGowan, who . . . was described as a 'puny baby, whose flesh marasmus had consumed until the bones were clothed only with skin, of a livid, death like hue.' " The *Times* called for the creation of foundling asylums to replace the almshouse and outdoor relief as methods of caring for infants. Those child savers who responded were largely women—Protestant, middle-class women and orders of Catholic nuns. In New York, the early Protestant foundling asylums required poor women to stay and nurse their youngsters for at least three months. Rarely did the foundling asylums admit women who had previously given birth to an illegitimate child. In contrast, the New York Foundling Hospital, established in 1869 by the Sisters of Charity, at first allowed any mother to deposit her baby at the asylum. However, by 1873, the Foundling Hospital forbade married women from leaving their children, for "the Sisters assumed that married mothers who abandoned their babies at the Foundling took wet-nursing positions for pay in private homes, and this, they felt, was intolerable." Both Protestant and Catholic foundling asylums in

New York judged the mothers of infants, albeit in different ways, and thereby refused care to certain children. The morality of mothers came before the needs of babies.

As for those babies who were admitted, even in the best of foundling homes, the death rate was very high: from 1870 to 1871, the death rate at the New York Foundling Hospital was 56 percent.[43] Of course, this was an improvement over the death rate of infants abandoned in almshouses, which sometimes approached 100 percent. In both types of institutions, babies were frequently in fragile health when admitted, and even when child savers worked hard to be attentive to infants' needs, there were rarely enough caretakers available to provide babies with much individual attention. In foundling homes, youngsters were wet-nursed or artificially fed cow or goat milk until the age of three, after which they either moved to orphanages or directly into foster families. The New York Foundling Hospital copied the Children's Aid Society and by the 1870s placed toddlers in the West. The hospital made contact with local priests, who in turn recruited Catholic families to take the youngsters. The Sisters sewed into the clothes of children the names of their foster families, then transported them west, and upon arrival, the priest matched the children's tags with the names of their families.[44]

Foundling homes, Societies for the Prevention of Cruelty to Children, Children's Aid Societies, orphanages, and reformatories were all the creations of middle-class child savers determined to save the offspring of white urban immigrant working-class parents from the moral and physical dangers of city streets, poverty, and parental ignorance and abuse. As creators and funders of child-care programs, middle-class child savers were very powerful. Yet without the willingness of working-class families to hand over their boys and girls, the child savers would have seen their programs quickly expire. The programs endured because they met the needs of many indigent families. Moreover, impoverished mothers, fathers, and other relatives of children were not passive: they sought to obtain from child-care programs what they wanted for themselves and their children. Although their power never matched that of the child savers, families of needy children did exert some influence, especially over the operation of asylums run by women and of Children's Aid Societies.

Impoverished women were those most likely to make use of child-saving programs. The majority were mothers who were widowed or deserted or living with husbands who were unemployed or in ill health. A small number were unwed mothers.[45] A few were the female relatives of impoverished mothers who had left their child in the care of a family member. Such was the case with the grandmother of W. Z., who brought the boy to the Northern Home for Friendless Children in Philadelphia in the 1850s. The father had deserted his family, and the mother was described by asylum officials as "negligent." Because the grandmother was old, crippled, impoverished, and barely able to support herself, she relinquished the child to the orphanage.[46]

The case of W. Z.'s grandmother casts light on the problems of mothers who did not have husbands to provide them financial support. In the nineteenth century, few jobs that were open to women paid adequate wages. W. Z.'s mother may have been "negligent" for many reasons, but the most likely one is that she could not earn enough to support her son. Domestic service was the job most readily available to women, but it was not an attractive alternative for mothers. Servants worked long hours, 10 to 12 a day, at least six days a week, and most employers preferred the women to live in. Some employers allowed women to keep one child, an infant or toddler, with them, but many did not.[47] Servants who were the mothers of older children or of several children had to rely on relatives or friends to care for their children or find and pay caretakers out of the low wages they earned—not an easy task. Factory work paid more than did working as a servant, but again mothers had to rely on relatives for child care or find and pay others to care for their sons and daughters. In order to meet their child-care obligations and still earn some money, needy mothers also took in outwork or piecework—simple items that could be made in whole or in part in women's homes. In nineteenth-century New York, female outworkers made paper boxes, hoopskirts, shirts and collars, hats, artificial flowers, and ladies' cloaks. Women usually picked up the materials and returned the finished products to their employers, who were small proprietors and subcontractors. "It was not uncommon for employers . . . to postpone paying a woman when she returned her work, to require alterations before they paid, to refuse to pay her at all and to hold back the deposits that they required for taking out work." Impoverished mothers worked for long hours to earn enough to support their families. ". . . In the 1850s, the sewing machine drove piece rates so low that fifteen to eighteen hour workdays were not uncommon."[48]

To impoverished women trying to support their families on low wages, children could be an important resource. Children old enough to watch their brothers and sisters, help with piecework, do errands, or even themselves get jobs could be a huge help. However, children too young to help their mothers could be a real drain on the family's limited resources. Most mothers probably kept infants at home because they would perish if not breast-fed.

However, for unwed mothers, an infant could be a real liability. A young woman who had a baby out of wedlock might very well be ostracized by her family and turned out of her home—all the more reason to give the child up to a baby farmer or, if the managers would accept the child, a foundling hospital. "For instance, Mary G. was admitted to the Sheltering Arms [a Philadelphia foundling asylum and hospital] in September 1884 with her two-week old infant because 'her mother was dreadful worried about her and don't allow her to come home on account of the disgrace.' Other parents were willing to shelter a wayward daughter only if she could arrange other accommodations for her child."[49]

Married women also used foundling asylums; in fact, the majority of the mothers who left children at New York's Infant Asylum between 1870 and 1872 and between 1891 and 1896 were married women. Some may have deposited infants in order to take jobs as wet nurses. Although most nineteenth-century mothers of all social classes nursed their own children, some were physically unable to do so. If they could afford it, such women employed wet nurses. Naturally, mothers preferred to hire wet nurses "of good physical health and the highest moral quality." Rarely was a wet nurse allowed to bring her own child along to the home of her employer. As we have seen, the nuns at New York's Foundling Hospital were so alarmed about married women leaving their babies to take jobs as wet nurses that the nuns refused to admit the babies of married women. Married women may also have given newborns to foundling asylums because the women and their families were too impoverished to support the children they already had. For example, "A twenty-eight year old Irishwoman, who had three other living children, brought her newborn to the Infant Asylum in September 1896. . . . She gave up her three month old baby because her Irish sailor husband had died. A twenty-nine year old American-born woman who had five other living children brought her two week old baby to the Infant Asylum on July 29, 1896, because she was homeless. Her thirty-four year old Italian laborer husband was out of work. She left the asylum on August 3rd, leaving the baby behind."[50]

Although some single and married mothers used foundling asylums, most impoverished parents who could not adequately support all their children relied on orphanages, reformatories, and Children's Aid Societies. Given the high death rate in foundling asylums and almshouses, mothers were probably aware at some level that the infants they gave to such institutions would probably die.[51] Most mothers were too emotionally attached to their children deliberately to allow them to perish. Many probably expected that after they had invested a good bit of time and money into the rearing of a child, the youngster would return the favor and help support his or her family. Yet there were occasions in the lives of poor women and their families when it was almost impossible to support all of their children adequately. Mothers and fathers became ill or unemployed; so might other children in the family. Relatives who had previously helped take care of young children died or moved away. Husbands or older children whose financial contributions were essential to the survival of mothers, toddlers, and infants moved away, died, or deserted the family. For a family living on the edge of poverty, any of these, as well as many other, contingencies might require sacrifices—such as giving young children who could not yet contribute to the family economy into the care of child savers. For example, 11-year-old James Peters entered the care of the New York Children's Aid Society when his Irish mother, who had borne twelve children, only three of whom were still living, was deserted by her husband. Mrs. Peters took a job as a housekeeper to a physician and, because she could not keep James with her, gave him to the CAS. Basically, putting a child into an orphanage or into direct family-farm placement with a Children's Aid Society was an economic strategy—a way of coping with short-term emergencies.[52] Few mothers or fathers wanted to be rid of their children permanently. Many parents struggled hard to pay the board of their youngsters in asylums. These parents hoped their children would get just what the child savers promised: safety in a structured, protected environment, adequate food and clothing, and a basic, useful education.

Indigent parents felt somewhat differently about older children who could not find a job or who worked but did not contribute to the family economy. Boys could usually obtain the highest-paying jobs, so parents tried to put boys to work as soon as they reached their teen years. The most common reason why parents placed their children in the care of the New York Children's Aid Society between 1853 and 1854 was for the children to get vocational training. Most of these children were young teens (their median age was 13 years), and most were boys. "Children were of an age to work, but the positions they had would never lead them to stable, adult occupations. One, the sixteen year old son of a mason, worked in an ice cream saloon; the son of a pianoforte maker 'was in a dry goods store but his health is too poor for such labor.' Fourteen year old William Taggart . . . was the son of an Irish Catholic tailor. . . . He worked hanging paper for a wall paper store and was kept up at night for the work."[53]

Teenage boys who had decent jobs but refused to contribute their share to the family economy were a liability to working-class families. Sons were especially a problem if they were not respectful of parental wishes and also engaged in petty crime:

> In 1881, Mrs. L. C., a single mother who was jobless and ill, wrote to the Superintendent of the Michigan Boys' Vocational School asking him to admit her son whom she could not support and who was . . . "pretty wild." She hoped that in one year she would be working again and that he would have learned a trade and be ready to return to her home. In the same year, Mrs. A. M. C. asked the superintendent to admit her son who was constantly truant. As she explained, "He has no father and I fear if left to himself much longer he will do something that he will be sent for crime . . . I feel that [sending him to the reformatory] is best for I feare if I delay it he will get into some mischeif that may be far worse."[54]

Working-class parents were more reluctant to place adolescent girls than boys in asylums or with the Children's Aid Society because the work of girls within the home, as baby-sitters and as housekeepers, was so essential to family survival. However, teenage girls who worked outside the home and refused to contribute all of their earnings to their families, spent that money on clothes or amusements for themselves, or went out too frequently with friends their parents disapproved of were a real worry to working-class families. Rebellious adolescent girls might engage in illicit sex, become pregnant, or even turn to prostitution. They might jeopardize their chances of ever marrying as well as bring scandal on their entire family. Irish Catholic parents were so alarmed about these potential threats that they willingly committed their adolescent daughters to Protestant juvenile reformatories. "To preserve a daughter from 'ruin' they were willing to forgo her earnings and risk the possibility of her religious conversion." No girls came into the care of the Children's Aid Society unless the agency or her parents or both had some fear about her sexuality. For example, the city missionary found 10-year-old Ellen Weller on the sidewalk on East Broadway in New York. When questioned, she said that her mother and father were drunkards and beat her, and that she was now living with an aunt. The CAS believed that the aunt's home was a brothel, and so the agency placed Ellen with a family in upstate New York.[55]

Parents were sometimes disappointed in how asylums and Children's Aid Societies treated their children, and a few parents took action to correct the inequities they perceived. For example, parents and children found the food provided in Jewish orphanages to be inadequate in amount and generally tasteless. As Edward Dahlberg, a former inmate at the Cleveland Jewish Orphan Asylum, explained:

> The children abhorred the breakfast gruel which was served without milk or sugar ... they called it mush. ... The coffee was a slop of stale ground beans and hot water ... Each child was given a slice or crust of dead rye bread which was thinly swabbed with oleomargarine. A tin cup of milk was served for boys who looked tubercular. It took the orphans about three minutes to finish their meal. ... [As for dinner] Monday was goulash day; for Tuesday there was stringy, tepid stew with a piece of fat as old as Methuselah's toe. Every other Wednesday they got biscuits with raisins in them. ... On Thursday they got green-pea hash. By Thursday everybody was starving.

Some parents acted to relieve their children's hunger. Rose Weiner Rosen remembered how her mother "used to pass hamburgers secretly to her through the fence at the rear of the [Cleveland Jewish Orphan] asylum grounds." Naturally, parents risked the anger of asylum officials when they violated the rules. In 1853 the superintendent of the Philadelphia House of Refuge was enraged to discover tobacco, a substance forbidden in the asylum, secreted in a cake a mother had made for her inmate son.[56] Parents not only responded to asylum practices they disliked by giving "extras" to their children, but also reacted by removing some of the items asylums gave their children. The Charleston Orphan Asylum required girls to wear a uniform that looked like a "sacque of homespun." Parents considered these clothes so degrading that some "hesitated to commit their children because of this mark." Others, when they took their girls home for visits, replaced the girls' uniforms with more attractive clothing. Eventually, asylum managers provided the girls with calico dresses they could wear on Sundays and when they left the asylum for visits.[57] Such incidents of parental objection to asylum practices were rare. Few parents registered complaints, and few asylums responded to parental objections. Child savers had the greatest power: they could refuse to return children to their families, and families knew this.

Needy parents who had the best chance of getting what they wanted from child-care agencies were those parents that child savers defined as worthy. Although officials rarely defined an entire group as worthy, they did look with special favor on the widows and orphans of Civil War veterans who had sacrificed their lives for their country.[58] In Pennsylvania, such widows hesitated to release their children to state care because they feared the youngsters would be placed in orphanages far from their homes and would be indentured without the women's consent, thereby permanently separating families. Catholic mothers also wanted their youngsters placed only in Catholic orphanages. When the Pennsylvania state superintendent in charge of the placement of Civil War orphans realized that few mothers were willing to place their children in state care, he actually met with the mothers to hear their concerns. In the end, the superintendent deferred to the wishes of mothers and carefully placed Catholics only in Catholic orphanages, placed all children in asylums as close to their homes as possible, and did not indenture children out of the asylums without their parents' consent.[59]

Child savers also defined as responsible those parents who contributed to the cost of their children's care in an orphanage. Such parents were more likely than those who did not pay board to get their children returned to them at their request. For example, of all the single mothers who placed children in the Church Home for Children (an Episcopal orphanage in Philadelphia) between 1878 and 1894, 44 percent paid their children's board. Of these, 85 percent got their children back at their request. In one case, when Mrs. M. paid for her daughter's care and the orphanage gave the girl to Mrs. M.'s relatives without consulting her first, Mrs. M. complained so much that the managers returned half her monthly board charge. Conversely, among mothers who were not able to pay anything for their child's care, roughly half got their children back, and the other half did not. Of course, those women who did not pay board and did not have their children returned to them may not have wanted the children. Such was probably the case with Mrs. H., who placed her five-year-old daughter Mary in the Church Home. Mrs. H. was a widow with five other children, two under the age of three. When Mary was 16, the Home found her a job as a domestic. Given Mrs. H.'s other obligations, she was not able to pay board, and she probably never requested Mary be returned to her.[60] Thus, the very payment of board may have been an indication not only of the mother's earning power, but also of her commitment to her child. Although child savers could be very judgmental of working-class parents, they apparently respected and honored the wishes of those who made a financial commitment, no matter how small, to their children.

Child savers also respected the wishes of intact families more than those headed by single women. For example, the parents of Harriet Griegg, aged ten, and her sister Katie, aged nine, were very poor. An agent of the New York Children's Aid Society found the two girls picking wood chips off the street and approached the parents about placing the girls out in the country. The mother refused the agent's offer. The family was poor, but it was able to get along and did not desperately need the help of the agency. Thus, the Grieggs were in a position to bargain. The mother eventually consented to the girls being placed out, but only within the city where she could get them back easily. Katie stayed only three days in her foster home before returning to her natural family. Harriet stayed somewhat longer in foster care.

Single parents had less leverage with the Children's Aid Society than did two-parent families. In all probability, most parents preferred their children to be placed close by, in New York City, as happened with the Griegg children. Yet the offspring of single mothers in particular, but also of widowed fathers, were most likely to be placed in Connecticut, New Jersey, New York state, or even farther away. Thus, "Theodore and William Hunter . . . were sent to Pike County, Illinois in September 1853. These American boys, aged ten and eight, were the children of [a] 'ladies nurse' who was 'a worthy Protestant woman too poor to keep her large family together.' The boys kept in touch with their mother with letters, but they had not returned to New York in 1867, fourteen years later, the date of the last report." This example shows how foster care could keep families apart for many years. However, it is not entirely representative of what happened to the children of single parents in the care of the Children's Aid Society. "By and large these troubled families were not permanently disrupted. In the end single parents did not lose their children much more often than the intact families, and single women did not lose theirs much more often than single men."[61]

Single mothers faced considerably more discrimination from the Boston Society for the Prevention of Cruelty to Children. When single mothers came to the attention of the agency, its agents evaluated the mothers quite harshly. The child savers judged any sexual immorality or intemperance by mothers to be an indication of child neglect. Yet child savers did not draw the same conclusions from the same evidence about fathers. Child savers saw mothers, not fathers, as essential to the moral upbringing of children, so any moral laxity on the part of mothers was particularly dangerous. As a result, "in cases of equal average severity . . . children were removed from 75 percent of single-mother homes and 54 percent of two-parent homes."[62]

In general, Children's Aid Societies and asylums managed by women were most willing to return children to working-class parents at their request. For example, between 1853 and 1854, the New York Children's Aid Society always informed families where their children were placed out, and children normally returned to their birth families. Sixty-nine percent of children in the care of the New York CAS lived with family at the time they entered the agency's care. Of this number, 63 percent returned to those families after living with foster parents for a while. The same pattern held true between 1884 and 1897 in Philadelphia, where the Children's Aid Society returned 55 percent of youngsters to their families within three years or less.[63] Apparently, if parents wanted children back and children wanted to return to their natural families, Children's Aid Societies did not prevent reunions.

Asylums managed by women were also responsive to the wishes of poor mothers who placed youngsters with them. The female managers of the Poydras Asylum in New Orleans said, "It is not in the heart of . . . [one] mother to deny the request" of another for her child. Often, when girls entered Poydras, parents stipulated to whom they wanted the youngsters released, and "the managers usually complied with their wishes." Catholic nuns in charge of orphanages were also quite willing to return youngsters to their natural families. In New Orleans, after the Sisters Marianite took over the management of St. Mary's Orphan Boys' Asylum from the Brothers of the Holy Cross in 1880, the Sisters reduced the time orphan boys stayed in the asylum and returned over two times more boys to their families than had their male predecessors. "When women managed orphan asylums in New Orleans, whether they were Protestants at Poydras or nuns at St. Mary's, they restored more boys and girls to their families than did male orphan asylum managers."[64]

Public asylums managed by men were most likely to be judgmental and cautious about returning children to their natural parents. The male managers of Charleston's public orphan asylum were often unwilling to return children to impoverished mothers, no matter how hard the mothers worked to support their youngsters. In 1877, Susan Glen, recently widowed and poor,

. . . put her three children in the Charleston asylum. Within months, she retrieved her daughter. The next year she began a series of eloquent appeals for the Commissioners to release her sons, since by then she had established herself as a seamstress. She could scarcely believe that they rejected all her petitions, and wrote them that "You have done me a great wrong, and have caused me unnecessary tears. . . . I beg of you to give me my boys, I long at the close of the day to gather them around my knee." With her rent of $5 paid by the Presbyterian Church and meat supplied through the benevolence of a friend, she went to exhausting lengths to assure security for her family. "As God is my witness," she implored the unmoved Commissioners, "I can support my children all comfortably, and I wish to raise them together. I make with my needle $2 a day, teaching sewing school at night for $2 a month for five scholars." Her dependence upon outside charity dissuaded the Commissioners from returning the two boys, aged five and six to their mother, and they remained institutionalized for ten more years until apprenticed to local merchants.[65]

Large public orphanages founded in the late nineteenth century and managed by men rarely released children to their parents. From 1887 to 1907, the State Public School at Owatonna, Minnesota, returned just 11 percent of all children it admitted to their natural parents before placing the children with foster families. Ultimately, 27 percent of the children returned to their families after spending some time in a foster home. Officials at Owatonna "were determined to rescue children by removing them once and for all from their impoverished natural families." School agents placed the children out with farm families as soon as possible, usually within a year, and parents who were not able to get their lives back in order within that time rarely got their children back. This practice upset many parents. As one mother wrote to the superintendent of Owatonna: "Let me know weather she is dedd or alive yet and how she is and if she is well . . . it brakes my hart when I think I may nevere see theme again on earth."[66]

Unlike Owatonna, some large juvenile reformatories managed by men found themselves forced to return more boys and girls to their natural families after the Civil War. There was an increase in juvenile crime during the war, and more adolescents entered reformatories. When the reformatories became overcrowded, officials also found it more difficult to indenture youths. As farmers and artisans prepared themselves to go to war, they were not willing to take on indentured workers to train. Hence, to avoid the expense of keeping youths in reformatories for long stays, reformatory officials somewhat unwillingly began to return more children to their families. In 1869, for the first time, the Philadelphia House of Refuge returned most of its wards to their natural families, and by the 1860s and 1870s, the reform school in Lancaster, Ohio, reunited 70 percent of youngsters with their families. As financial exigencies made reformatories more willing to return youngsters to their families, reformatories became more useful to these families. As a result, needy families more willingly committed their children. "The proportion of white boys committed to the Philadelphia House of Refuge by some family member rose from 34 percent in the 1850s to 62 percent in the 1890s. . . . As Mrs. L. C. told the Superintendent of the Michigan Boys' Vocational School in 1881, she preferred to send her son there rather than to a certain orphanage because the orphanage would indenture him 'to whoever wants a boy and perhaps I would never see him again and I could not do that for I will need him after a while.' "[67]

As this and other examples demonstrate, needy parents in late nineteenth-century America certainly tried to use child-care agencies to accomplish the parents' own purposes. Poor parents wanted for their sons and daughters what child savers promised: a protected environment that provided adequate food, clothing, and education for employment. However, few parents desired what child savers formally advocated: permanent separation of young paupers from their indigent families. Yet parents had limited control over when and if their children would be returned to their home. The willingness of the New York Children's Aid Society to return children to their families may in part account for the enormous number of children placed in its care by parents.

Like their parents, the poor and delinquent children themselves had limited impact on child-saving programs. The amount of influence a child had on an asylum, reformatory, or foster-care program depended on age and gender. Older boys had the most influence. For example, in juvenile reformatories that housed adolescent boys, there were frequent acts of rebellion. Joseph Flynt, onetime inmate of the Western House of Refuge in Pennsylvania, reported that he and other boys who worked in the shops once protested the beating of a boy who "had thrown a wrench at a brow-beating guard." The boys complained to the superintendent, who fired the guard but also ordered Flynt and the other protesters to be whipped. At the Philadelphia House of Refuge, boys hated work in the shops so much that the boys tried to burn the shops down and succeeded in so doing in 1854. In 1859, 15-year-old Danial Creadan stuffed straw from his mattress into the ventilation system at the Massachusetts State Reform School at Westborough, set the straw on fire, and burned down two-thirds of the building. Adolescent boys also rebelled against child savers by trying to escape from reformatories—often successfully. At the Philadelphia House of Refuge, boys regularly stole equipment from the shops where they worked and used it to make good their escape attempts. Joseph Flynt eventually fled from the Western House of Refuge with the help of a local farm family that fed, clothed, and provided him transport.[68]

Dissatisfied boys also absconded from foster families. In 1853 and 1854, 15 percent of the children, most of whom were boys, placed out by the New York Children's Aid Society quit their foster homes within a month of their placement. Most returned to their natural families. Despite their claims to the contrary, child savers were willing to allow the most troublesome boys to rejoin their families. Thus, 10-year-old William R., who entered the public orphanage at Owatonna, Minnesota, in 1891 and was soon placed out, ran off from his foster home several times. When he turned up at his mother's home, Owatonna officials let him stay there.[69]

Running away was the ultimate form of rebellion against the influence of child savers, but many boys controverted the goals of reformers in more subtle ways. Child-care agencies considered their choice of proper foster families for youngsters to be vital to reform. However, children could influence this choice. One boy sent to Arkansas by the New York Children's Aid Society reported: "I refused to go home with two different farmers . . . but I was fortunate I did not. The two boys the farmers adopted were hardly more than slaves to them. . . . Everyone seemed to think I was a very bad character and I was left alone on stage that day alone, with no place to go. . . . A 60 year old couple heard about me and . . . persuaded me to go home with them . . . as it turned out, I had the best home of all the orphans I had come with." Once in foster homes, children would reject another goal of child savers—separating children from their natural families. Thus Benjamin Moore, who was placed out in upstate New York by the Children's Aid Society in 1854, managed to bring his mother up to visit him at his new home. Similarly, Arthur Turner, placed out by the CAS in Vermont, both returned to New York City to visit his mother and also brought her to Vermont for visits with him.[70]

Boys in children's institutions also repudiated the values of child savers in a variety of ways. In reformatories and some orphanages, boys who obeyed the rules, worked hard, and tried to please child savers were scorned by their fellow inmates. At the Western House of Refuge in Pennsylvania, boys who reported others for infractions of the rules were ridiculed as "softies" or "lungers" because they would lunge for a favor. At the Massachusetts State Reform School at Westborough, "Officials noted in 1852 that a boy who tried to reform was ostracized," and by 1877, "boys placed in positions of trust by the administration were as likely to be assaulted as were officials themselves." Catholic boys rebelled against Protestant efforts to convert them by singing out of turn during religious services or by yelling obscenities. Boys also routinely violated child savers' moral strictures against stealing.[71] Edward Dahlberg reported that while he was at the Cleveland Jewish Orphan Asylum, older and tougher boys "would sneak out at night when the governors were at their meals, crawl over the transom of the bread-room and steal bread and apples. . . . The JOA boys often climbed over the eight-foot fence to go to Becker's Bakery. . . . Sometimes seven orphans would come into the bakeshop at a time and while two of them pretended that they were at a stationer's or a candy store, and asked for lead pencils, a copy book, ice-cream cones or jawbreakers, in order to exasperate old man Becker, the others would run out with a tray of cakes." As this example indicates, boys refused to remain protected behind asylum walls as child savers wanted them to. At the Cleveland Jewish Orphan Asylum, older boys sneaked out to the hill behind the asylum in the winter to ice-skate, sled, and throw snowballs. As Edward Dahlberg explained: "Every winter the Irish micks came from Kinsman Road and the slums of Superior Avenue to fight with the orphans. These January battles had been going on for years, and though an eighth-grader wasn't afraid of anybody, he was always on his guard with these brawlers who had knives and hid stones inside icy snowballs. . . ."[72]

To some extent, within orphanages and reformatories, boys created their own subculture. In both, older boys took advantage of younger ones. At the

Massachusetts State Reform School for Boys at Westborough, older boys sexually exploited younger ones, as the assistant superintendent indirectly explained in 1877: "the older boys took 'the smaller and more innocent boys, and [those] most free from vice,' and 'chummed' with them. The younger boys were 'very affectionate' and the older ones took advantage of it." At the Boys' Aid Society in San Francisco, "in 1885 a sixteen- or seventeen-year-old boy was discovered in the water closet committing sodomy on one of the smaller boys. . . ."[73] In orphanages, young boys were often bullied by older boys who served as monitors. Older boys sometimes offered protection "from the brutality of others. The price they extorted from the frightened youngsters was usually . . . coffeecake and other favorite desserts, although it also included the performance of servile duties. . . . It was important to have a protector . . . [one former orphan asylum inmate explained] so that you weren't dunked while taking a bath in the large pool or beaten up in the playroom."

Upon release from asylums, boys sometimes rebelled against the working-class occupations for which child savers trained them. In orphanages and reformatories, boys learned to work with tools, to become mechanics or shoemakers. However, at least among those who left the Cleveland Jewish Orphan Asylum by 1883, few practiced the trades they had learned inside but instead became clerks, bookkeepers, and stockboys.[74]

There is little evidence that girls in asylums violated the rules as consistently as did boys. Certainly there was less bullying of younger girls by older ones in orphanages. As one girl explained about her first night at the Cleveland Jewish Orphan Asylum: "The girls were more sympathetic, so when they heard Pauline and me crying in bed, they came over and sat on our beds and told us about 'first picnic' and about getting a present on Chanukah—anything to stop our crying. . . ." When girls took positions as monitors, to help oversee the activities of fellow orphans, they seem to have been more understanding and protective of their wards and more honored by their peers than were boys in similar roles.[75]

However, like boys, girls did not consistently adopt the roles that child savers envisioned for them. Girls raised by nuns in Catholic asylums rarely elected to become sisters themselves. As one girl who lived in St. Vincent's Female Orphan Asylum in Boston remarked, "After years of that life, none of us was ready for a religious vocation." By the end of the nineteenth century, many girls began to reject the job they were trained for in asylums: domestic service. The girls' objections were strong enough to influence some asylum officials to offer girls training for what many preferred—office work. As the Superintendent of the Cleveland Jewish Orphan Asylum explained: "There is among our girls a decided aversion to domestic work, in which they are especially strengthened by their own mothers and relatives. . . . Girls abhor the thought of being considered a servant or of being treated as such. . . . We have been compelled to yield, finding all our efforts unavailing, to the pressing desire of so many to become stenographers. We have classes in stenography and typewriting for pupils considered fitted for this work, but many more want access to this education."[76]

Although older boys exerted more power over asylums and foster-care programs than did younger boys or girls of any age, the influence of older boys did not in any way match that of child savers. Youngsters rebelled in various ways, but they influenced reformers to change programs only rarely, and then only in minor ways. Rather, influence flowed in the other direction, and children were themselves much affected by their experiences in the care of child savers. Some of those experiences were positive; many more were negative.

While in asylums or in foster-family homes, youngsters obtained the basic necessities of life, including food, clothing, and housing. This was no small advantage for children who came from homes where meals were not always served at regular intervals, where clothing was scant and often handed down from an older sibling, and where accommodations were overcrowded and often uncomfortable. In orphanages, boys and girls also received medical treatment, which they might have been denied otherwise. Of course, epidemics of childhood diseases within asylums could be very serious, and ophthalmia and dysentery—endemic in orphanages—were crippling. Conversely, children isolated in asylums did not contract diseases that raged through the poor neighborhoods from which the children came. Moreover, many orphanages provided isolation wards for youngsters who were ill and employed full-time doctors and nurses to attend to sick children.[77]

For a minority of children, orphanages and reformatories did become their substitute families, just as child savers hoped they would. Such youngsters returned to asylums to visit and sometimes to stay while in between jobs. In the 1850s, 87 children returned to the Philadelphia House of Refuge to seek various kinds of help from officials there. Throughout the year, alumni returned to Baltimore's Samuel Ready School for Orphan Girls and its Hebrew Orphan Asylum to visit with friends and former teachers. Groups of youths also formed alumni associations at reformatories and orphanages. At the House of the Angel Guardian in Boston, successful alumni "befriended recent graduates. [Their organization] became an extended family for many young men without families or relatives who were alone and friendless in the city. . . . The 'Hag boys' developed their own inmate subculture with strong loyalties to their home and to one another. One alumnus observed that 'many boys found the routine and regimented life comforting' after the poverty and disorganized family life they had known as children. . . ." An alumni association also formed at the Cleveland Jewish Orphan Asylum, and many of the men and women who joined it eventually married one another.[78]

Nonetheless, most children probably did not harbor fond memories of institutional life. It was, after all, very dehumanizing. As Sara Sander Wirpel said of her first day at the Cleveland Jewish Orphan Asylum: "We were taken to another room in the basement where a barber cut off our long hair and trimmed what was left like a boy's hair-cut. Looking at Charlotte and myself in the mirror, I felt we had lost our identity. We cried. . . . I felt that a great indignity had been done to us when the barber cut off our hair . . . our faces changed; no longer eager and expectant but sad-eyed and subdued. . . ."

The regimen of asylums was also destructive in many ways. Child savers' belief that children should not be pampered meant that many youngsters endured a spartan and hungry existence. At the New York Hebrew Orphan Asylum, one former inmate reported "that some of the weaklings, poor fellows, when the chance offered, sneaked in the dining room after meal time and on their hands and knees crawled under the tables picking up the stray crumbs, even from the cracks in the floor."[79] Having to resort to such actions certainly did not build self-esteem. Neither did the practice of shaming children for their failings publicly in front of their peers and asylum officials. As for those children who endured the harsh punishments meted out in asylums for the smallest infraction, they may have learned that disagreements and conflicts could be solved only by resorting to violence.

Perhaps the most damaging feature of asylum life was that it might estrange children from their families. Youngsters who had grown accustomed to the regularity of asylum life often found it difficult to adjust to the uncertainty of life in their working-class households. Many children had seen very little of their families for many years because asylum officials so restricted parental visits. After her release from an orphanage, one woman remembered: "I wasn't used to kissing and affection. I'd run away from my mother every time she'd try to kiss me. I wasn't accustomed to this kind of female contact." Some children resented their families for putting them in institutions, and upon release, they expressed their resentment. Said one orphan boy, "There were no bonds connecting us. I felt a sort of obligation to them (his parents), but really no feelings toward them . . . I felt my parents never did anything for me in any way. After all, I came to the institution when I was four years old."[80] Other boys and girls learned new religious practices in asylums and even a new language, which alienated them from their families. Orphanages run by German Jews, which, by the late nineteenth century, admitted many children of Russian-born Jews, tried to convert the children from Orthodox Judaism to Reform Judaism and to Americanize them by removing their prayer caps and discouraging them from speaking Yiddish and from observing dietary laws. As former Cleveland Jewish Orphan Asylum inmate Julia Herskowitz Emrich explained: "Naturally, this caused a great rift between children and parents, not only while the children were in the Home, but also afterward. . . . There was no semblance of Kosher in the Home—also we were sort of led to believe that we had the best education, etc., and this led to intolerance of parents with their old-fashioned ways. . . . The one thing

I regret is that living away from my family and being brought up in a truly Reform Jewish atmosphere alienated me from my family in many respects." Other youngsters complained of not being able to communicate with parents who spoke only Yiddish.[81]

Boys and girls who were placed out from asylums or who directly entered family homes experienced another set of problems. The Children's Aid Society and some asylums led children to believe that they would be treated as full members of their foster families, and indeed that is what child savers hoped would happen. Of course, foster children would be expected to work, but no more than the natural children of farmers, child savers hoped. Families that took in foster children older than infants and toddlers had a different agenda. Most of these families probably wanted the children for their ability to labor. Children who believed the child savers and expected to be treated as members of their foster families were often disillusioned. One boy recalled of his foster parents: "They never touched me or said they loved me, and they didn't want me to call them Mom and Dad. Think what that does to you. They weren't mean, they were cold. . . ." Girls were particularly disillusioned by foster families and probably less able than boys to avoid exploitation by foster families. On farms, boys customarily worked outdoors doing chores on their own, unsupervised by the farmer. In the winter, when farm chores were fewer, boys had time to attend the local school. They had plenty of opportunity to meet other boys in the area and to learn from them and others about farmers who might pay them for their labor. Because boys had considerable freedom of movement, they could leave foster families fairly easily. In contrast, orphan girls placed in foster families worked as domestic servants under the watchful eye of the farm wife. Because girls labored year-round, they often did not get the schooling that boys did. Unlike boys, girls did not always have the chance to learn from their peers about other job opportunities in the area. Moreover, like all domestic servants, girls placed in foster families were likely to be sexually exploited by male family members, including fathers and brothers. One young woman placed in Missouri by the Children's Aid Society "recalled that after her third year of school, she was kept home to spend her youth as the family's full-time cook and housekeeper: 'My foster mother was so cruel—oh, she was a crackerjack. They wanted one of the sons to get me pregnant so I'd stay home and work. How could they do that?' "[82]

Between 1850 and 1890, middle-class women and men, alarmed by what they perceived as dangerous and abusive child-rearing practices among poor white urban immigrant families, created a range of child-care programs to reform impoverished youths. At the same time, working-class parents looked to the new orphanages, reformatories, and foster-care and cruelty-prevention programs for temporary help in times of severe economic stress. The priorities of child savers and indigent parents diverged, but the child savers had the upper hand. They determined the strict regimen of asylums, chose foster families for needy children, advised judges on how to deal with abused youths, and lobbied legislatures for laws against certain types of child labor and baby farming. Impoverished parents who had to use child-saving programs were often afraid to object too strongly to any of their practices for fear of being permanently separated from sons and daughters.

Nonetheless, indigent parents and their children were not entirely powerless in dealing with child-saving programs. Those people whom the child savers judged to be worthy, including Civil War widows, parents who paid board for their youngsters, and intact families, seized what little advantage they had. Children too were not passive. Older boys especially challenged the goals of child savers, but both boys and girls sometimes rejected the occupations chosen for them by child savers and structured their careers in divergent ways. Impoverished youngsters certainly benefited from child-care programs but also found them dehumanizing, destructive of youngsters' self-esteem, and likely to estrange them from their families. Foster-family placement was not much better. While boys labored on farms and girls labored in farm homes as servants, few children obtained in exchange for their labor what they had been promised—loving acceptance as valued family members.

Conclusion:
Uncommon Childhoods

In the second half of the nineteenth century, American children experienced childhood in uncommon, diverse ways. One hundred years ago there was no common culture of youth formed through extended years of public schooling, movies, music, *Sesame Street,* and MTV. Between 1850 and 1890, in a nation divided by the consequences of industrialization, including widening disparities in wealth, greater population concentration in cities, and expanded immigration, as well as by the Civil War and Reconstruction, it is understandable that young people's lifestyles diverged considerably. Some disparities resulted chiefly from where a youngster grew up, but most came about because of dissimilarities in class, race, gender, and ethnicity.

Where youngsters were born and grew to maturity most directly impacted their experience of the Civil War and Reconstruction and the extent and quality of their schooling, although in both, race too played a part. During the war and its aftermath, Southern children experienced more poverty and homelessness, more parental separation and death, and more exposure to military invasion and battle than did Northern youngsters. African-American children in the South suffered from such hardships more acutely than did white boys and girls. During Reconstruction, blacks endured continuing harassment by former masters and other whites, who enforced apprenticeship laws and physically attacked black children, parents, schools, and churches. As for the impact of geography on education, boys and girls who grew up in the rural North, Midwest, and Far West typically attended one-room public schools, controlled by their parents, from three to six months a year from the time they were toddlers through their teens. In contrast, youngsters who lived in cities in the same regions commonly attended age-graded public schools (primary, grammar, and high schools), managed by professional educators, nine months a year from the age of seven through their teens. Finally, there were few public schools at all in the South until African-Americans and their Northern allies created public schools during Reconstruction. However, terms were short in Southern schools, and fewer youngsters attended than anywhere else in the country. Race impacted education, for black youngsters had no opportunity for schooling in the South and little in the North until after the Civil War. Even then, the majority of black youngsters who lived in the South had access only to poorly funded, segregated schools.

The geography of their birth influenced the lives of American children, but the combination of the social class, race, and occupation of their parents most determined children's lives in the years between 1850 and 1890. Although each youngster's passage to maturity was unique, the evidence of the preceding chapters confirms that the upbringing of most boys and girls fell into one of three broad categories based on children's familial backgrounds. Within each category, children's life patterns varied somewhat depending on gender and sometimes ethnicity.

The first modal childhood is that of boys and girls whose parents were white middle-class professionals, but it also includes many children from prosperous white Northern and Midwestern farm families and Southern white planter families. Such parents raised children with the help of advice manuals that cautioned them to inculcate values of obedience, self-control, thrift, punctuality, and individual responsibility in a loving, gentle manner. Parents tried to avoid corporal punishment and use guilt to build a child's conscience. Mothers devoted virtually all of their time to nurturing youngsters in large, comfortable single-family homes. Fathers were supportive but too occupied with their careers to play much of a role in the home life of their sons and daughters. Both parents tried to protect children from dangers in the wider world. Parents also provided youngsters with the material comforts of private bedrooms and family playrooms filled with store-bought toys, including dolls for girls and marbles, balls, and riding toys for boys. These youngsters enjoyed long childhoods that lasted until their late teens.

Most white girls and boys from prosperous families who lived in Northern and Midwestern cities or on farms enjoyed equal educational opportunities in public schools from the primary grades through high school. Southern white children from prosperous families more frequently attended sex-segregated private schools in which girls' academic preparation was inferior to that of boys. Few youngsters secured full-time employment until after they had completed their formal education in their late teens or early twenties, although young boys and girls from well-off Midwestern farm families frequently worked part-time in their own gardens and marketed the produce they harvested.

By adolescence, the experience of white boys and girls from comfortably well-off families diverged most markedly. Parents sought to protect teenage daughters from premarital sex by confining them to home and school and discouraging their playing freely outdoors with their brothers and younger sisters. Teenage girls read a lot and favored books that featured girls like themselves undergoing the difficult transition from childhood to adolescence in the context of comfortable white family homes. Through adolescence, white middle-class girls cultivated long-lasting, same-sex friendships with other young women like themselves. Parents limited their daughters' social activities, but teenage girls were still able to engage in individual sports such as walking, ice skating, roller skating, and biking. Girls also participated in Sunday school and other religious activities that prepared girls for the future when they would teach moral values to their own children.

Adolescent boys from similar families enjoyed more freedom than their sisters. Boys spent much of their time outside the home, whether attending school, participating in boy culture with friends, or playing team sports such as baseball. Boys too developed close same-sex friendships, although theirs usually ended when they began their professional careers. Although prosperous white parents tried to protect their sons by enrolling them in character-building programs conducted by the YMCA and other religious organizations, boys enjoyed enough freedom from parental control to be sexually adventuresome. Yet the restrictions placed on them were onerous enough to attract boys most to books about young men like themselves, who enjoyed exciting adventures, out-of-doors, well beyond the purview of parents.

The second type of upbringing was that of white urban working-class youngsters, but to some extent, white boys and girls who grew up on farms or on the frontier experienced childhood similarly. Mothers were the prime caretakers of such youngsters in infancy, although homemaking responsibilities in small city, farm, and frontier homes precluded mothers from devoting all their energies to child care. Because urban working-class fathers labored for long hours in factories and frontier fathers often toiled far from home, neither had much time to participate in child rearing. Fathers on small farms in settled parts of the country were more often involved in raising their sons and daughters. Hardworking parents in cities and on farms expected children to obey promptly and punished disobedience swiftly and harshly. Parents also educated youngsters to honor and respect other family members, friends, and neighbors on whom they might need to call in time of need.

White urban working-class, farm, and frontier children grew up in small homes within which they enjoyed little privacy or play space. Of necessity, they played outside their homes and encountered dangers in city streets, barnyards, or lonely prairies. Their parents could not afford to purchase them many toys, so white urban working-class and farm youngsters made their own playthings.

All such youngsters had short childhoods. For most, schooling ended by their early teens, although the sons and daughters of skilled workers and of

Scots and Jewish immigrants often attended urban schools longer. A minority enrolled in Catholic parochial schools, and the poorest received their education in Protestant, Catholic, or Jewish orphan asylums. Because of work responsibilities, white farm boys often attended school just three months a year until their late teens, when they had mastered the basic academic skills their sisters, who attended six months a year, acquired earlier.

After about four to five years of schooling, most white urban working-class and farm children took full-time jobs. Their families were too poor to spare children from contributing to the family economy. A few children might stay in school longer if they had older employed brothers and sisters. Conversely, very young children in large urban families where parents and children were unemployed or earned little often ended up in orphan asylums or in foster care. Children were most likely to enter full-time employment as soon as they were physically able if their fathers were unemployed or absent. However, ethnicity played a part for Italian and Irish parents inclined to putting youngsters to work early regardless, but Jewish parents preferred to keep their sons and daughters in school as long as possible.

There were fewer and lower-paying jobs open to white working-class girls than to their brothers. Home manufacturing jobs went largely to Jewish and Italian girls, and employment in domestic service went largely to Irish and Scandinavian young women. Parents expected their daughters to contribute their pay to the family coffers, although most working girls kept some of their wages to spend in urban dance halls, theaters, and amusement parks. White working-class parents valued the sexual purity of their daughters, but economic necessity forced girls to go to work young and prevented parents from protecting their daughters from sexual advances by male bosses and workmates. In addition, the low wages of urban working girls necessitated their depending on young men to treat them to urban entertainments. Treating often placed young women in sexual danger. Parents who felt that their daughters' virginity was at risk sometimes placed them in juvenile reformatories for their own protection. Most girls avoided incarceration, but they were well aware of the problems they faced at work and in the larger urban world and especially enjoyed reading dime novels about young women like themselves who successfully avoided sexual assault and found true romance.

Urban working-class boys enjoyed more and higher-paying employment opportunities than their sisters in factories, street trades, and home manufacturing. Parents allowed boys to keep more of their earnings, which boys spent in the free and easy, sporting, and sexual world of saloons and music halls, as well as in dance halls and amusement parks in the company of young, respectable working women. Parental permissiveness with working-class sons ended when boys failed to contribute financially to their families or got into trouble with the law. Then parents willingly committed boys to juvenile reformatories. The fast-paced, exciting world of city streets inclined working-class boys to prefer dime-novel fiction about street-smart young men like themselves who worked in factories and knew how to defend themselves with their fists, or about outlaws who, throughout a series of exciting adventures, triumphed over working-class enemies such as railroads and banks.

The third and last mode of childhood experience was that of African-American boys and girls growing up as slaves and as freed persons. In slavery, infants remained in the care of their mothers for only a few short months. Thereafter, other older or younger slaves tended infants while their mothers worked in the fields or in plantation homes. Most slave youngsters knew their fathers, though many slave men lived apart from their families on neighboring plantations. In slave cabins, children had neither privacy nor much room to play. Instead they played outdoors in plantation yards with handmade or hand-me-down toys. Their playmates were usually other slave children and sometimes their white masters' children, who did not always treat young slaves equitably. Both west-African and slave experience led slave parents to emphasize interdependency—to encourage their children to respect black relatives and friends who might be called upon to take youngsters in should their natural families be separated by sale. Youngsters appropriated such values for their own and practiced them by collaborating in singing games and by altering traditional game rules to prevent any child from being eliminated from play. Parents also expected youngsters to obey them promptly without question or risk corporal punishment. Disobedient slave children put both themselves and their parents at risk of a whipping from white owners. Only through careful socialization could slave parents provide their children with some degree of protection from physical harm. Ultimately, however, the fate of both slave parents and their youngsters was in the hands of their white owners.

These owners forbade slave youngsters from receiving any education. Inevitably, young and old slaves depended on an oral culture. They admired clever speech. Young men and women courted though fast and witty speech making. Boys played the dozens, a game of ritual insult that taught them how to accept criticism and avoid violent response—practical necessities for slaves who were too often taunted by their all-powerful white owners.

African-American slave parents were much less likely to socialize their boys and girls differently than were whites of any social class. In childhood, slave boys and girls played together and, by the time they were six or seven, worked at just about the same tasks around plantations. Their childhoods were extremely short. Slave parents wanted to protect their daughters from sexual exploitation by whites but were not always able to do so. Parents were less inclined to frown on sexual alliances between their daughters and slave men, for a fecund young woman was usually able to remain within her family circle because her owner was unlikely to sell her.

Once freed from slavery, African-American children in the South gained the opportunity to live full-time with both their mothers and fathers. Freed-women now assumed complete responsibility for rearing their own children, and freedmen assumed responsibility for supporting them. Because most freed blacks earned low wages, they could provide their children with few material comforts. Most black youngsters, whether they lived in the country or the city, resided in small homes and played with toys they fashioned themselves. Partly because of their poverty, black parents continued to drum into their children the importance of interdependence, and partly because of continued threats of violence from whites, parents continued to insist that their children obey them without question. A troublesome black child and his or her parents were no longer under threat of sale, but in freedom, they could well be under threat of serious bodily harm.

The childhoods of free Southern black children were short. To help their impoverished families, children went to work early alongside their mothers and fathers on sharecropping farms or in Southern city streets. Many black children enrolled in the schools opened to them for the first time in Reconstruction, but few attended for long. For most, work was more important than receiving an education in a poorly funded, overcrowded, segregated Southern school.

However, the educational and work experiences of free black children in the North were somewhat different. There, black mothers and fathers earned more at wage-labor jobs than did most Southern blacks. Northern black parents labored long to permit their children to stay, until their late teens, in public schools, most of which were integrated after the Civil War. In the North, there were few employers that hired black children—all the more reason to keep them in school. Northern free black youngsters enjoyed childhoods as long as those of middle-class white boys and girls, although black children did not have nearly as many extracurricular recreational activities open to them as did their white classmates.

Wherever they lived, free black parents continued to socialize their daughters and sons similarly. Boys and girls played together and attended school together. There was no sex segregation in Southern black schools. However, once children entered the labor force, African-American girls customarily took jobs in domestic service and boys usually became day laborers.

Both in slavery and in freedom, black children and their parents enjoyed a unique folk literary tradition made up of moral tales and animal and human trickster stories. For black youngsters, the moral stories reinforced the importance of obedience to authority and the value of friendship. The animal and human trickster stories educated boys and girls in how to cope with white authority while at the same time covertly attacking that authority.

Between 1850 and 1890, the childhoods of American children of different social classes and races varied enormously. The three most crucial differences were the length of their childhoods, the duration of their schooling, and the age at which they began full-time employment. The length of childhood determined how long children would be free from major responsibilities and how long they would be dependent on parents. The duration of children's education and the age at which they went to work were related and affected whether they would become literate and whether they would gain an education that would improve their occupational opportunities.

The difference in opportunities and responsibilities between poor and more well-off children meant that the actions of the former privileged the latter. Because white working-class girls and African-American girls performed domestic service in white middle-class homes, white middle-class girls were free to play, read, and attend school well into their teens. Because slave children worked in plantation homes and fields, the sons and daughters of white slave owners enjoyed a comfortable existence and access to extended education. Because the sons and daughters of poor white Midwestern farmers hired out as farmhands, their employers' children worked less and attended school more.

While the variety of childhood experience in this period was great, there were some ways in which children's lives became more alike. The abolition of slavery ended a major inequality between youngsters and ensured that all American-born youngsters would be citizens. The end to slavery also meant that all youngsters, regardless of race, could be raised by their mothers and fathers. In this period, mothers were the chief caretakers of children. Public schooling, although not as universal as it is today, was nonetheless accessible to most children after Reconstruction, and schools throughout the nation trumpeted the values of obedience to authority, self-control, and competitiveness. At the same time, other, less positive features of public education, such as the emphasis on boring, rote memorization of racist textbook material, ensured that most pupils did not relish prolonging their education, and prejudice against blacks persisted among white youths.

Middle-class parents also tried to make youngsters of all social classes more alike by imposing middle-class values on not only their own but other people's children. Thus, well-off parents created public schools in cities partly to socialize immigrant and impoverished youngsters to middle-class values. These parents also tried to bring an end to certain forms of child labor so that all youngsters, not just those of the middle class, would spend more time in public schools. Last, middle-class child savers built orphan asylums and created home placing-out programs to reeducate needy children who lacked comfortable, stable families of their own. In these efforts, middle-class reformers were only partially successful. They were not able to make over most needy children into middle-class look-alikes because so many of the parents of impoverished youngsters objected. Some working-class and immigrant parents contested the imposition of middle-class values in public schools by withdrawing their youngsters from them at an early age or by enrolling youngsters in parochial schools instead. At home, working-class parents taught their youngsters to value interdependence over individual, personal advancement. Poor parents who required their children's labor for family survival lied about their youngsters' ages to officials who enforced child-labor laws. And many poor parents whose children ended up in orphan asylums, reformatories, or foster care fought to have their children released as soon as family financial circumstances improved.

Childhood between 1850 and 1890 appears strikingly different from childhood in the late twentieth century. In the 1990s, young people throughout the country have much more in common than their nineteenth-century counterparts. A high percentage of children in the 1990s attend public schools until their late teens; play with the same toys, which parents purchase at chain toy stores; listen to the same music on the radio; watch the same sitcoms on television; and view the same Disney movies in mall multiplex theaters. These changes are substantial, although even in the nineteenth century, there were signs of the common youth culture that would develop much later. These signs include the increasing opportunities for education for children of all races; the development of gender-integrated and racially integrated schools, at least in the North; the growing popularity everywhere in the country of games such as baseball; and the increasing desire of youngsters who had both money and access to toy stores to possess the same sorts of playthings.

The three very different childhood patterns of the late nineteenth century no longer exist, but certain features of each persist even into the late twentieth century. In the 1990s, virtually all parents would agree with the white middle-class nineteenth-century commitment to extending the length of childhood, providing youngsters with time to play and access to manufactured toys, and prolonging children's education through high school. At the same time, most parents today would concur with the belief of nineteenth-century working-class parents that adolescent children should work some outside the home to earn money, if not to support their families, at least to pay for their own leisure-time activities. In addition, teens today expect the same freedom to control their social lives that urban working-class nineteenth-century boys and girls possessed. Unfortunately, most of today's parents, like working-class parents of the past, lack the power to protect their youngsters fully from dangers in the larger world, which now include exposure to drugs, alcohol, and guns. Finally, most parents today would endorse the practice of African-American parents of the last century of socializing boys and girls with some degree of equality. Parents today, like black parents in the past, realize that young people of both genders will eventually be employed outside the home and, by adulthood, will be economically responsible for raising their own sons and daughters.

Chronology

1840–1860	Public schools founded in North, Midwest, and Far West.
1841–1856	Catharine Beecher's *Treatise on Domestic Economy*.
1847–1854	1.2 million Irish immigrants to U.S.
1850s	Baseball becomes popular sport.
	YMCAs founded.
1850–1880	Age grading introduced in urban schools.
1853	Charles Loring Brace, New York Children's Aid Society.
1854	Massachusetts State Industrial School for Girls, first cottage-style institution in United States.
	Newsboys' Lodging House, New York City.
1855–1859	Depression.
1854–1884	Sixty thousand poor children placed in West by New York Children's Aid Society.
1860s	Commercial baby formulas first available.
	Boys organize high school sports.
	Beadle's dime novels appear.
1860	Kindergarten introduced, Boston.
1862	Girls' Lodging House, New York City.
1863	Draft riots, New York City.
1861–1865	Civil War.
	Farm machinery introduced in North and West.
1865	Civil War ends, Freedman's Bureau founded.
	Thirteenth Amendment.
1865–1870	Public schools founded in South.

1866   State laws passed to exclude children from almshouses.

          Horace Bushnell, *Christian Nurture.*

1868   Fourteenth Amendment.

          Hampton Institute.

          Horatio Alger, *Ragged Dick.*

          Louisa May Alcott, *Little Women.*

1869   New York Foundling Hospital.

1869–1890 Commercial training introduced in some high schools.

1870   Fifteenth Amendment.

          U.S. census reports one in eight children, age 10–15, employed.

          Thomas Bailey Aldrich, *Story of a Bad Boy.*

1870–1900 Eleven million immigrants to United States chiefly from southern and eastern Europe.

          Female teachers become norm in public schools.

          Twenty-eight states pass anti-child labor laws.

1872   Freedman's Bureau ends.

1873   Edward Clarke, *Sex in Education.*

1873–1879 Depression.

1875   Insurance companies begin insuring children.

          Society for the Prevention of Cruelty to Children.

1877   Anthracite Coal Strike, Molly Maguires.

          National railroad strikes.

          Deadwood Dick stories begin.

          Mark Twain, *Tom Sawyer.*

1880s   Tenancy and sharecropping prevail in South.

          Manual training introduced in some high schools.

          One in three children, age 10–15, employed.

          Tennis and roller skating become popular.

          First city playgrounds built.

          Joel Chandler Harris publishes African-American animal trickster stories.

1880   Louisa May Alcott, *Jack and Jill.*

1881   Tuskegee Institute.

1882	Daniel Carter Beard, *American Boys Handy Book.*
1885–1887	Depression.
1885	Mark Twain, *Huckleberry Finn.*
1886	Haymarket Square Riot, Chicago.
	American Federation of Labor.
1887	Lina and Adelia Beard, *American Girls Handy Book.*
	Safety bicycle introduced.
1889	Jane Addams, Hull House, Chicago.
	First physical education program, Boston schools.
1890s	Coney Island becomes popular.
1891	Basketball invented.
	First record of "dozens" play.
1893–1897	Depression.

Notes

Chapter 1

1. United States Bureau of the Census, *Historical Statistics of the United States, Colonial Times to 1970*, 2 vols. (Washington, D.C.: Government Printing Office, 1975), I:15–17.

2. Samuel P. Hays, *The Response to Industrialism, 1885–1914* (Chicago: University of Chicago Press, 1957); Robert L. Heilbroner and Aaron Singer, *The Economic Transformation of America, 1600 to the Present*, 2d ed. (San Diego: Harcourt, Brace Jovanovich, 1984); Robert Wiebe, *The Search for Order, 1860–1910* (New York: Hill and Wang, 1967).

3. Alfred D. Chandler Jr., *The Visible Hand: The Managerial Revolution in American Business* (Cambridge, Mass.: Belknap Press, 1977); Richard C. Wade, *The Urban Frontier: The Rise of Western Cities, 1790–1830* (Cambridge, Mass.: Harvard University Press, 1959); Olivier Zunz, *Making America Corporate, 1870–1929* (Chicago: University of Chicago Press, 1990).

4. Oscar Handlin, *Boston's Immigrants, A Study in Acculturation, Revised and Enlarged Edition* (Cambridge, Mass.: Harvard University Press, 1959); Alan M. Kraut, *The Huddled Masses: The Immigrant in American Society, 1880–1921* (Arlington Heights, Ill.: Harlan Davidson, 1982); Kerby A. Miller, *Emigrants and Exiles: Ireland and the Irish Exodus to North America* (New York: Oxford University Press, 1985).

5. Stephanie Coontz, *The Social Origins of Private Life: A History of American Families, 1600–1900* (London, New York: Verso, 1988), 290–91.

6. Sarah Deutsch, *No Separate Refuge: Culture, Class, and Gender on an Anglo-Hispanic Frontier in the American Southwest, 1880–1940* (New York: Oxford University Press, 1987), 7.

7. Samuel Rezneck, "Distress, Relief, and Discontent in the United States during the Depression of 1873–78," *Journal of Political Economy* 58

(December 1950): 494–512; ———, "Patterns of Thought and Action in an American Depression, 1882–1886," *American Historical Review* 61 (January 1956): 284–306; ———, "Unemployment, Unrest, and Relief in the United States during the Depression of 1893–97," *Journal of Political Economy* 61 (August 1953): 324–25; Alan Trachtenberg, *The Incorporation of America: Culture and Society in the Gilded Age* (New York: Hill and Wang, 1982), 39.

8. Harold Aurand, *From the Molly Maguires to the United Mine Workers: The Social Ecology of an Industrial Union, 1869–1897* (Philadelphia: Temple University Press, 1971); Paul Avrich, *The Haymarket Tragedy* (Princeton: Princeton University Press, 1984); Philip S. Foner, *The Great Labor Uprising of 1877* (New York: Monad Press, 1977); Nell Irvin Painter, *Standing at Armageddon: The United States, 1877–1919* (New York: W. W. Norton, 1987), 14–50.

9. Stuart M. Blumin, *The Emergence of the Middle Class: Social Experience in the American City, 1760–1900* (Cambridge: Cambridge University Press, 1989); Alice Kessler-Harris, *Out to Work: A History of Wage-Earning Women in the United States* (New York: Oxford University Press, 1982); Sam B. Warner Jr., *Streetcar Suburbs: The Process of Growth in Boston, 1870–1900* (Cambridge, Mass.: Harvard University Press, 1962).

10. Stuart Bruce, *Samuel Gompers and the Origins of the American Federation of Labor, 1848–1896* (Westport, Conn.: Greenwood Press, 1973); David Montgomery, *Fall of the House of Labor: The Workplace, the State, and American Labor Activism, 1865–1925* (New York: Cambridge University Press, 1987); W. J. Rorabaugh, *The Craft Apprentice: From Franklin to the Machine Age in America* (New York: Oxford University Press, 1986).

11. Alexander Keyssar, *Out of Work: The First Century of Unemployment in Massachusetts* (Cambridge: Cambridge University Press, 1986), 50, 54, 58.

12. Quoted in Gary B. Nash and Julie Roy Jeffrey, *The American People: Creating a Nation and a Society*, 2d ed., vol. 2 (New York: Harper and Row, 1990), 635.

13. Kessler-Harris, *Out to Work*, 123–24; Keyssar, *Out of Work*, 97.

14. John Higham, *Strangers in the Land: Patterns of American Nativism, 1860–1925* (New Brunswick, N.J.: Rutgers University Press, 1955).

15. Claudia Goldin, "Female Labor Force Participation: The Origin of Black and White Differences, 1870 to 1880," *Journal of Economic History* 37 (March 1977): 87–108; Jacqueline Jones, *Labor of Love, Labor of Sorrow: Black Women, Work, and the Family from Slavery to the Present* (New York: Basic Books, 1985), 111, 124–25, 137–41.

16. John A. Garraty, *The New Commonwealth, 1877–1890* (New York: Harper and Row, 1968), 33–77; Fred A. Shannon, *The Farmer's Last*

Frontier: Agriculture, 1860–1897 (New York: Holt, Rinehart, Winston, 1945).

17. Jay Mandle, *The Roots of Black Poverty: The Southern Plantation after the Civil War* (Durham, N.C.: Duke University Press, 1978); Howard N. Rabinowitz, *The First New South, 1865–1920* (Arlington Heights, Ill.: Harlan Davidson, 1992), 10–17; Roger L. Ranson and Richard Sutch, *One Kind of Freedom: The Economic Consequences of Emancipation* (New York: Cambridge University Press, 1977).

18. Garraty, *The New Commonwealth*, 36–37; Sally McMurry, *Families and Farmhouses in Nineteenth-Century America: Vernacular Design and Social Change* (New York: Oxford University Press, 1988), 90–91.

Chapter 2

1. The best one-volume history of the Civil War and its causes is James M. McPherson, *Battle Cry of Freedom: The Civil War Era* (New York: Oxford University Press, 1988). See also Bruce Collins, *The Origins of America's Civil War* (New York: Holmes and Meir, 1981); James McPherson, *Ordeal by Fire: The Civil War and Reconstruction*, 1st ed. (New York: Knopf, 1982); David Potter, *The Impending Crisis, 1848–1861* (New York: Harper and Row, 1976). On women's attitudes toward the war, see especially LeeAnn Whites, "The Civil War as a Crisis of Gender," in *Divided Houses: Gender and the Civil War,* ed. Catherine Clinton and Nina Silber (New York: Oxford University Press, 1992), 3–21.

2. The best one-volume history of Reconstruction is Eric Foner, *Reconstruction: America's Unfinished Revolution, 1863–1877* (New York: Harper and Row, 1988). See also John Hope Franklin, *Reconstruction after the Civil War*, 2d ed. (Chicago: University of Chicago Press, 1994); Kenneth Stampp, *The Era of Reconstruction, 1865–1877* (New York: Vintage Books, 1965).

3. McPherson, *Battle Cry of Freedom*, 608.

4. Reid Mitchell, *The Vacant Chair: The Northern Soldier Leaves Home* (New York: Oxford University Press, 1992), 4.

5. Bell Irvin Wiley, *The Life of Billy Yank, The Common Soldier of the Union* (New York: Doubleday, 1971; originally published in 1952), 298–99. There were perhaps four hundred women who served in the Civil War by passing themselves off as men. For an interesting discussion of one such young woman, who, at the age of 19, enlisted in the Union Army, see Sarah Rosetta Wakeman, *An Uncommon Soldier: The Civil War Letters of Sarah Rosetta Wakeman, alias Private Lyons Wakeman, 153rd Regiment, New York State Volunteers,* ed. Lauren Cook Burgess (Pasadena, Md.: Minerva Center, 1994).

6. Jim Murphy, *The Boy's War: Confederate and Union Soldiers Talk About the Civil War* (New York: Clarion Books, 1990), 10, 40, 72, 73; Wiley, *Life of Billy Yank*, 297–300.

7. Elizabeth Daniels, "The Children of Gettysburg," *American Heritage* 40, no. 4 (May/June 1989): 97–107.

8. Mitchell, *Vacant Chair*, 29–30, 34.

9. J. Matthew Gallman, *Mastering Wartime: A Social History of Philadelphia during the Civil War* (New York: Cambridge University Press, 1990), 71–74, 79, 80–81; Nancy Grey Osterud, "Rural Women during the Civil War: New York's Nanticoke Valley, 1861–1865," *New York History* 62, no. 4 (1990), 357–85; Mitchell, *Vacant Chair*, 76–77.

10. Anne C. Rose, *Victorian America and the Civil War* (New York: Cambridge University Press, 1992), 184–87.

11. Mitchell, *Vacant Chair*, 15–16, 116–17.

12. Robert Bremner, *The Public Good: Philanthropy in the Civil War Era* (New York: Knopf, 1980), 74.

13. McPherson, *Battle Cry of Freedom*, 564–65, 600–606, 788–89.

14. Quote from Sally McMurry, *Transforming Rural Life: Dairying Families and Agricultural Change, 1820–1885* (Baltimore: Johns Hopkins University Press, 1995), 129–33. See also Paul Wallace Gates, *Agriculture and the Civil War* (New York: Knopf, 1965).

15. Quote from Phillip Shaw Paludan, *"A People's Contest": The Union and the Civil War, 1861–1865* (New York: Harper and Row, 1988), 182–84; Gallman, *Mastering Wartime*, 242–45; McPherson, *Battle Cry of Freedom*, 447–48.

16. First quote from Bremner, *The Public Good*, 74–76; Paludan, *"A People's Contest,"* 182. Last quote from Marilyn Irwin Holt, *The Orphan Trains: Placing Out in America* (Lincoln: University of Nebraska Press, 1992), 74.

17. Lee Soltow and Edward Stevens, *The Rise of Literacy and the Common School in the United States: A Socioeconomic Analysis to 1870* (Chicago: University of Chicago Press, 1981), 119.

18. Calculated from Adrian Cook, *The Armies of the Streets: The New York City Draft Riots of 1863* (Lexington: University of Kentucky Press, 1974), 256–66.

19. Theda Skocpol, *Protecting Soldiers and Mothers: The Political Origins of Social Policy in the United States* (Cambridge: Harvard University Press, 1992), 106–7, 115–16.

20. Gallman, *Mastering Wartime*, table 8.4, p. 202; Paludan, *"A People's Contest,"* 220, 222.

21. Bell Irwin Wiley, *The Life of Johnny Reb, The Common Soldier of the Confederacy* (New York: Doubleday, 1971; originally published 1943), 330–31. Drew Gilpin Faust, "Altars of Sacrifice: Confederate Women

and the Narratives of War," in *Divided Houses: Gender and the Civil War*, ed. Catherine Clinton and Nina Silber (New York: Oxford University Press, 1992), 182–92.

22. Murphy, *The Boys' War*, 10, quote 40; Wiley, *The Life of Johnny Reb*, 333–34.

23. George Rable, *Civil Wars: Women and the Crisis of Southern Nationalism* (Urbana: University of Illinois Press, 1989), 163, 169.

24. McPherson, *Battle Cry of Freedom*, 860–61, 430–32; Donna Rebecca Dondes Krug, "The Folks Back Home: The Confederate Homefront During the Civil War" (Ph.D. diss., University of California at Irvine, 1990), 231–36; Rable, *Civil Wars*, 66–67, 82.

25. "Poverty" in *Encyclopedia of the Confederacy*, ed. Richard N. Current, 4 vols. (New York: Simon and Schuster, 1993), 3:1244; McPherson, *Battle Cry of Freedom*, 447; Rable, *Civil Wars*, 78, 96–99; Krug, "The Folks Back Home," 257–58.

26. Krug, "The Folks Back Home," 239–41, 280–82, 329–30; quote from Rable, *Civil Wars*, 104–5; also see 108–10.

27. Rable, *Civil Wars*, 182–83, 187; Krug, "The Folks Back Home," 305, 312, 316; Mary Elizabeth Massey, *Refugee Life in the Confederacy* (Baton Rouge, La.: Louisiana State University Press, 1964), 152, quote 244.

28. Rable, *Civil Wars*, 160–61, 171–73; Reid Mitchell, *Civil War Soldiers: Their Expectations and Their Experiences* (New York: Viking Penguin, 1988), quote 117.

29. Faust, "Altars of Sacrifice," 193–95; Mitchell, *Vacant Chair*, 160–63.

30. Skocpol, *Protecting Soldiers and Mothers*, 139–40; LeeAnn Whites, "The Charitable and the Poor: The Emergence of Domestic Politics in Augusta, Georgia, 1860–1880," *Journal of Social History* 17 (Summer 1984): 601–16.

31. First quote from Steven Hahn, *The Roots of Southern Populism: Yeoman Farmers and the Transformation of the Georgia Upcountry, 1850–1890* (New York: Oxford University Press, 1983), 140. Second quote from Krug, "The Folks Back Home," 366.

32. Foner, *Reconstruction*, 129 (quote), 393–94, 399–400; Rable, *Civil Wars*, 241.

33. Krug, "The Folks Back Home," 392.

34. Peter Bardaglio, "The Children of Jubilee: African American Childhood in Wartime," in *Divided Houses: Gender and the Civil War*, ed. Catherine Clinton and Nina Silber (New York: Oxford University Press, 1992), 219.

35. "Slave Children," in *Encyclopedia of the Confederacy*, ed. Richard N. Current, 4 vols. (New York: Simon and Schuster, 1993), 1:307.

36. Ira Berlin, Barbara Jeanne Fields, Steven F. Miller, Joseph P. Reidy, and Leslie S. Rowland, *Slaves No More: Three Essays on Emancipa-

tion and the Civil War (New York: Cambridge University Press, 1992), 15–16.

37. First quote from Leon Litwack, *Been in the Storm So Long: The Aftermath of Slavery* (New York: Knopf, 1979), 33. Second quote from Bardaglio, "Children of Jubilee," 221.

38. Berlin, *Slaves No More*, 23, 41, 44–45, 49, 53–54, 57–59, 95, 112, 118–19, 131, 205, 214; Litwack, *Been in the Storm So Long*, 82–83. I have been unable to locate any figures on the ages of blacks in the Union Army, so I cannot explain how many young black men and boys served and in what capacities (i.e., drummer boys).

39. Bardaglio, "Children of Jubilee," 222–23 (quotes), 224; Berlin, *Slaves No More*, 23, 62–67, 70–71.

40. Quote from Mitchell, *Civil War Soldiers*, 122–23; Mitchell, *Vacant Chair*, 106–8.

41. Paludan, *"A People's Contest,"* 214.

42. Quotes from Litwack, *Been in the Storm So Long*, 230–37; Herbert Gutman, *The Black Family in Slavery and Freedom, 1750–1925* (New York: Pantheon, 1976), 141–42.

43. Barbara Fields, *Slavery and Freedom on the Middle Ground* (New Haven: Yale University Press, 1985), 35, 79, 138–40; Rebecca Scott, "The Battle over the Child: Child Apprenticeship and the Freedmen's Bureau in North Carolina," *Prologue* 10 (1978): 101–13; Barry A. Crouch, *The Freedmen's Bureau and Black Texans* (Austin: University of Texas Press), 58–59; Peter Kolchin, *First Freedom: The Responses of Alabama's Blacks to Emancipation and Reconstruction* (Westport, Conn.: Greenwood Press, 1972), 63–67.

44. First quote from Litwack, *Been in the Storm So Long*, 191; second quote from Fields, *Slavery and Freedom on the Middle Ground*, 139–41.

45. Bremner, *The Public Good*, 115–17; Fields, *Slavery and Freedom on the Middle Ground*, 153–56; Scott, "The Battle over the Child"; Crouch, *The Freedmen's Bureau and Black Texans*, 58–59; Kolchin, *First Freedom*, 63–67; Foner, *Reconstruction*, 20–21, 96, 151–52, 372; Litwack, *Been in the Storm So Long*, 238.

46. Howard N. Rabinowitz, "From Exclusion to Segregation: Health and Welfare Services for Southern Blacks, 1865–1890," *Social Service Review* 48, no. 3 (September 1974): 327–54.

47. Skocpol, *Protecting Soldiers and Mothers*, 138.

48. Ronald E. Butchart, *Northern Schools, Southern Blacks and Reconstruction: Freedmen's Education, 1862–1875* (Westport, Conn.: Greenwood Press, 1980), 176–77.

49. Samuel L. Horst, *Education for Manhood: The Education of Blacks in Virginia During the Civil War* (Lenham, Md.: University Press of America,

1987), 1; Foner, *Reconstruction*, 96–98; Butchart, *Northern Schools, Southern Blacks*, 170–71; Kolchin, *First Freedom*, 86.

50. Jacqueline Jones, *Soldiers of Light and Love: Northern Teachers and Georgia Blacks, 1865–1873* (Chapel Hill: University of North Carolina Press, 1980), 18, 31, 76, 90, 110.

51. Butchart, *Northern Schools, Southern Blacks*, 135–36, 140–43, 152–54.

52. Jones, *Soldiers of Light and Love:* 117, 120–22, 130–33, 203, quote from 138–39.

53. Robert Charles Morris, *Reading, 'riting, and Reconstruction: The Education of Freedmen in the South, 1861–1870* (Chicago: University of Chicago Press, 1981), 91–92; Butchart, *Northern Schools, Southern Blacks*, 173.

54. Jones, *Soldiers of Light and Love*, 80–82; Morris, *Reading, 'riting, and Reconstruction*, 224; Crouch, *The Freedmen's Bureau and Black Texans*, 62; Foner, *Reconstruction*, 428.

55. Foner, *Reconstruction*, 366–67; Jones, *Soldiers of Light and Love*, 205; quoted in Litwack, *Been in the Storm So Long*, 490.

56. Foner, *Reconstruction*, 589, 592; Jones, *Soldiers of Light and Love*, 192–99, 203; Butchart, *Northern Schools, Southern Blacks*, 195; Litwack, *Been in the Storm So Long*, 488; Kolchin, *First Freedom*, 99.

57. Foner, *Reconstruction*, 104–5; 158–62, 167, 171–74, 408–9.

Chapter 3

1. Jay Mechling, "Advice to Historians on Advice to Mothers," *Journal of Social History* 9 (Fall 1975): 44–63; Nancy F. Cott, "Notes toward an Interpretation of Antebellum Childrearing," *Psychohistory Review* 6, no. 4 (1978): 4–20.

2. Stuart M. Blumin, *The Emergence of the Middle Class: Social Experience in the American City, 1760–1900* (Cambridge: Cambridge University Press, 1989), 298–310.

3. Stephanie Coontz, *The Social Origins of Private Life: A History of American Families, 1600–1900* (London, New York: Verso, 1988), 167, 188.

4. Blumin, *The Emergence of the Middle Class*, 121; Coontz, *The Social Origins of Private Life*, 192.

5. Carl N. Degler, *At Odds: Women and the Family in America from the Revolution to the Present* (New York: Oxford University Press, 1980), 67–69.

6. Steven Mintz, *A Prison of Expectations: The Family in Victorian Culture* (New York: New York University Press, 1983), 28–29.

7. Karin Calvert, *Children in the House: The Material Culture of Early Childhood, 1600–1900* (Boston: Northeastern University Press, 1992), 97.

8. Josephine Gear, "The Baby's Picture: Woman as Image Maker in Small-Town America," *Feminist Studies* 13, no. 2 (1987): 419–42.

9. Cott, "Notes toward an Interpretation of Antebellum Childrearing," 9; Jeanne Boydston, *Home and Work: Housework, Wages, and the Ideology of Labor in the Early Republic* (New York: Oxford University Press, 1990), 77–81.

10. Robert L. Griswold, *Fatherhood in America, A History* (New York: Basic Books, 1993), 15. See also Robert L. Griswold, *Family and Divorce in California, 1850–1890: Victorian Illusions and Everyday Realities* (Albany: State University of New York Press, 1982), 164.

11. John Demos, *Past, Present and Personal: The Family and the Life Course in American History* (New York: Oxford University Press, 1986), 49–50, 52; Cott, "Notes toward an Interpretation of Antebellum Childrearing," 9.

12. E. Anthony Rotundo, *American Manhood: Transformations in Masculinity from the Revolution to the Modern Era* (New York: Basic Books, 1993), 225–26, 230–34; Griswold, *Family and Divorce in California,* 166.

13. Michael Grossberg, "Who Gets the Child? Custody, Guardianship, and the Rise of Judicial Patriarchy in Nineteenth-Century America," *Feminist Studies* 9 (1983), 235–60. See also Griswold, *Family and Divorce in California,* 153–69.

14. Joseph P. Kett, *Rites of Passage: Adolescence in America, 1790 to the Present* (New York: Basic Books, 1977), 115. See also Robert V. Wells, *Revolutions in Americans' Lives: A Demographic Perspective on the History of Americans, Their Families, and Their Society* (Westport, Conn.: Greenwood Press, 1982).

15. Degler, *At Odds,* 178–248; Mary P. Ryan, *The Cradle of the Middle Class: The American Family in Oneida County, New York, 1790–1865* (New York: Cambridge University Press, 1981), 156.

16. John D'Emilio and Estelle Freedman, *Intimate Matters: A History of Sexuality in America* (New York: Harper and Row, 1988), 174.

17. Steven Mintz and Susan Kellogg, *Domestic Revolutions: A Social History of American Family Life* (New York: Free Press, 1989), 52.

18. Kathryn Kish Sklar, *Catharine Beecher* (New Haven, Conn.: Yale University Press, 1973), 151–53.

19. Cott, "Notes toward an Interpretation of Antebellum Childrearing," 6; Bernard Wishy, *The Child and the Republic: The Dawn of Modern Child Nurture* (Philadelphia: University of Pennsylvania Press, 1968), 22–24.

20. Nancy M. Theriot, *The Biosocial Construction of Femininity: Mothers and Daughters in Nineteenth-Century America* (Westport, Conn.: Greenwood Press, 1988), 142–43.

21. First quote from Wishy, *The Child and the Republic*, 37; Samuel H. Preston and Michael R. Haines, *Fatal Years: Child Mortality in Late Nineteenth Century America* (Princeton: Princeton University Press, 1991), 27. Last quote from Sally G. McMillen. *Motherhood in the Old South: Pregnancy, Childbirth, and Infant Rearing* (Baton Rouge: Louisiana State University Press, 1990), 112.

22. Richard A. Meckel, *Save the Babies: American Public Health and the Prevention of Infant Mortality, 1850–1929* (Baltimore: Johns Hopkins University Press, 1990), 53.

23. Wishy, *The Child and the Republic*, 38–40; Theriot, *The Biosocial Construction of Femininity*, 143; Calvert, *Children in the House*, 97–99.

24. Sylvia D. Hoffert, *Private Matters: American Attitudes toward Childbearing and Infant Nurture in the Urban North, 1800–1860* (Urbana: University of Illinois Press, 1989), 152–54.

25. First quote from Cott, "Notes toward an Interpretation of Antebellum Childrearing," 10; other quotes from Mintz, *A Prison of Expectations*, 31; Coontz, *The Social Origins of Private Life*, 214, 267.

26. Degler, *At Odds*, 91; Ryan, *Cradle of the Middle Class*, 159–61.

27. Quote from Mintz, *A Prison of Expectations*, 32; Peter N. Stearns and Timothy Haggerty, "The Role of Fear: Transitions in American Emotional Standards for Children, 1850–1950," *American Historical Review* 96 (February 1991), 63–94. Of course, some persons continued to use religion as a justification for corporal punishment, and some still do. See Philip Greven, *Spare the Child: The Religious Roots of Punishment and the Psychological Impact of Physical Abuse* (New York: Alfred A. Knopf, 1991), 46–96.

28. Cott, "Notes toward an Interpretation of Antebellum Childrearing," 13–14.

29. Mintz, *A Prison of Expectations*, 14, 35 (quote); Blumin, *The Emergence of the Middle Class*, 151, 155, 276.

30. Quotes from Coontz, *The Social Origins of Private Life*, 269; Ryan, *Cradle of the Middle Class*, 168; Mintz and Kellogg, *Domestic Revolutions*, 59.

31. Calvert, *Children in the House*, 97–109.

32. Quote from Coontz, *The Social Origins of Private Life*, 214; Peter N. Stearns, "Girls, Boys, and Emotions: Redefinitions and Historical Change," *Journal of American History* 80, no. 1 (June 1993): 36–74. See also Carol Z. and Peter N. Stearns, *Anger: The Struggle for Emotional Control in American History* (Chicago: University of Chicago Press, 1986).

33. Demos, *Past, Present and Personal*, 57; Ryan, *Cradle of the Middle Class*, 175.

34. Calvert, *Children in the House*, 109–10; Stearns, "Girls, Boys, and Emotions," 37, 42–45.

35. Rotundo, *American Manhood*, 33–52, 96–98, quotes from 44, 52.

36. Quotes from Anne Scott MacLeod, "The *Caddie Woodlawn* Syndrome: American Girlhood in the Nineteenth Century," in *A Century of Childhood, 1820–1920,* ed. Mary Lynn Stevens Heininger (Rochester, N.Y.: The Margaret Woodbury Strong Museum, 1984), 99–105; Rotundo, *American Manhood,* 94.

37. First quote from D'Emilio and Freedman, *Intimate Matters,* 77, see also 70, 75; second quote from Ellen K. Rothman, *Hands and Hearts: A History of Courtship in America* (New York: Basic Books, 1984), 214, see also 119–22.

38. Karen Lystra, *Searching the Heart: Women, Men, and Romantic Love in Nineteenth-Century America* (New York: Oxford University Press, 1989), 78–79; Stephen Seidman, "The Power of Desire and the Danger of Pleasure: Victorian Sexuality Reconsidered," *Journal of Social History* 24, no. 1 (Fall 1990): 47–67; Rothman, *Hands and Hearts,* 113.

39. Carroll Smith-Rosenberg, "Puberty to Menopause: The Cycle of Femininity in Nineteenth-Century America," in *Disorderly Conduct: Visions of Gender in Victorian America* (New York: Oxford University Press), 182–96.

40. Joan Jacobs Brumberg, *Fasting Girls: The Emergence of Anorexia Nervosa as a Modern Disease* (Cambridge: Harvard University Press, 1988), 126, 135, 176, 178–79, 182. See also by the same author, "Chlorotic Girls, 1870–1920: A Historical Perspective on Female Adolescence," *Child Development* LIII (1982): 1468–77.

41. Theriot, *The Biosocial Construction of Femininity,* 120–21, 123; quotes from Brumberg, *Fasting Girls,* 129, 136, 138.

42. Carroll Smith-Rosenberg, "The Female World of Love and Ritual: Relations between Women in Nineteenth-Century America," in *Disorderly Women,* 53–76.

43. Linda W. Rosenzweig, "The Anchor of My Life: Middle-Class American Mothers and College-Educated Daughters, 1880–1920," *Journal of Social History* 25 (Fall 1991): 5–27. Also see her book *The Anchor of My Life: Middle-Class American Mothers and Daughters, 1880–1920* (New York: New York University Press, 1993).

44. Ryan, *Cradle of the Middle Class,* 62, 164, 168; Stearns, "Girls, Boys, and Emotions," 45.

45. Rotundo, *American Manhood,* 225–26, 229–41; ———, "Body and Soul: Changing Ideals of American Middle-Class Manhood, 1770–1920," *Journal of Social History* 16 (1983): 23–38.

46. Quotes from D'Emilio and Freedman, *Intimate Matters,* 76, 182; see also 68, 72, 179, 181; Rotundo, *American Manhood,* 124–26.

47. E. Anthony Rotundo, "Romantic Friendship: Male Intimacy and Middle-Class Youth in the Northern United States, 1800–1900," *Journal of Social History* 23 (Fall 1989): 1–26.

48. On the eighteenth century, see Daniel Blake Smith, "Autonomy and Affection: Parents and Children in Chesapeake Families," in *The American Family in Social-Historical Perspective*, 3d ed., ed. Michael Gordon (New York: St. Martin's Press, 1983), 209–29.

49. Catherine Clinton, *The Plantation Mistress: Women's World in the Old South* (New York: 1982), 155; Elizabeth Fox-Genovese, *Within the Plantation Household: Black and White Women of the Old South* (Chapel Hill: University of North Carolina Press, 1988), 280; McMillen, *Motherhood in the Old South*, 111–14, 118, 122 (quote), 127, 170 (quote); Jane Turner Censer, *North Carolina Planters and Their Children, 1800–1860* (Baton Rouge: Louisiana State University Press, 1984), 37 (quote).

50. Clinton, *The Plantation Mistress*, 47–49.

51. Censer, *North Carolina Planters and Their Children*, 26–27, 36–40; McMillen, *Motherhood in the Old South*, 120, 140; Clinton, *The Plantation Mistress*, 39–40.

52. Joan E. Cashin, "The Structure of Antebellum Planter Families: The Ties That Bound Us Was Strong," *Journal of Southern History* 56, no. 1 (1990): 55–70, first quote 63; second quote from Censer, *North Carolina Planters and Their Children*, 20; last quote from Clinton, *The Plantation Mistress*, 39, 50–53.

53. Censer, *North Carolina Planters and Their Children*, 40, 48 (quote), 51.

54. For a somewhat different perspective on Southern child rearing than that described here, see Bertram Wyatt-Brown, *Southern Honor: Ethics and Behavior in the Old South* (New York: Oxford University Press, 1982).

55. First quote from Censer, *North Carolina Planters and Their Children*, 51; second quote from Kett, *Rites of Passage*, 35; last quotes from Fox-Genovese, *Within the Plantation Household*, 212–13.

56. Clinton, *The Plantation Mistress*, 45–46, 56–57; Fox-Genovese, *Within the Plantation Household*, 113, 207–8; quote from Censer, *North Carolina Planters and Their Children*, 52.

57. Anne C. Rose, *Victorian America and the Civil War* (New York: Cambridge University Press, 1992), 191–92.

58. First quote from Griswold, *Fatherhood in America*, 43. Second quote from Robert Anthony Orsi, *The Madonna of 115th Street: Faith and Community in Italian Harlem, 1880–1950* (New Haven: Yale University Press, 1985), 120.

59. First quote from Griswold, *Fatherhood in America*, 37; Elizabeth Ewen, *Immigrant Women in the Land of Dollars: Life and Culture on the Lower East Side, 1890–1925* (New York: Monthly Review Press, 1985), 190, 208–11. Second quote from Peter N. Stearns, *Be a Man! Males in Modern Society* (New York: Holmes and Meier Publishers, 1979), 61–62.

60. Griswold, *Fatherhood in America*, 44–49; Coontz, *The Social Origins of Private Life*, 296; quote from Ewen, *Immigrant Women in the Land of Dollars*, 112, 136.

61. Louise Lamphere, *From Working Daughters to Working Mothers: Immigrant Women in a New England Industrial Community* (Ithaca, N.Y.: Cornell University Press, 1987), 149; Degler, *At Odds*, 220–22; quote from Ewen, *Immigrant Women in the Land of Dollars*, 133.

62. Ewen, *Immigrant Women in the Land of Dollars*, 138, 142, 166; quote from Orsi, *The Madonna of 115th Street*, 113.

63. First quote from Christine Stansell, *City of Women: Sex and Class in New York, 1789–1860* (Urbana: University of Illinois Press, 1987), 313. Second quote from Ewen, *Immigrant Women in the Land of Dollars*, 98–99. See also Michael J. Eula, *Between Peasant and Urban Villager: Italian-Americans of New Jersey and New York, 1880–1980: The Structures of Counter-Discourse* (New York: Peter Lang, 1993), 92–95.

64. Sarah Deutsch, *No Separate Refuge: Culture, Class, and Gender on an Anglo-Hispanic Frontier in the American Southwest, 1880–1940* (New York: Oxford University Press, 1987), 7; quote from Stansell, *City of Women*, 313.

65. First quote from Stansell, *City of Women*, 203; second quote from Ewen, *Immigrant Women in the Land of Dollars*, 191.

66. Coontz, *The Social Origins of Private Life*, 297, 308; Ewen, *Immigrant Women in the Land of Dollars*, 104, 161–62; Boydston, *Home and Work*, 127.

67. Jacquelyn Dowd Hall, James Leloudes, Robert Korstad, Mary Murphy, Lu Ann Jones, and Christopher B. Daly, *Like a Family: The Making of a Southern Mill World* (Chapel Hill: University of North Carolina Press, 1987), 169–70.

68. Richard Griswold del Castillo, *La Familia: Chicano Families in the Urban Southwest, 1848 to the Present* (Notre Dame, Ind.: University of Notre Dame Press, 1984), 50–55, 78, 82; Deutsch, *No Separate Refuge*, 44, 49; Orsi, *The Madonna of 115th Street*, 113.

69. First quote from Eula, *Between Peasant and Urban Villager*, 101–2; second quote from Ewen, *Immigrant Women in the Land of Dollars*, 98; Linda Gordon, *Heroes of Their Own Lives: The Politics and History of Family Violence, Boston, 1880–1960* (New York: Viking, 1988), 177–80. See also Sherri Broder, " 'Informing the Cruelty': The Monitoring of Respectability in Philadelphia's Working-Class Neighborhoods in the Late Nineteenth Century," *Radical America* 21, no. 4 (1987): 34–47.

70. First quote from Ewen, *Immigrant Women in the Land of Dollars*, 211; second quote from D'Emilio and Freedman, *Intimate Matters*, 184–85.

71. Kathy Peiss, *Cheap Amusements: Working Women and Leisure in Turn-of-the-Century New York* (Philadelphia: Temple University Press, 1986), 53–55, 69–72, 90–93, 109, 118–19, 122–23; Stansell, *City of Women*, 89, 98 (on Caroline Wood).

72. Quotes from Peiss, *Cheap Amusements*, 109–14; Stansell, *City of Women*, 81–82.

73. Quotes from Peiss, *Cheap Amusements*, 59–60, 68, 90–93, 118–19, 127, 142, 145; D'Emilio and Freedman, *Intimate Matters*, 185–86; Stearns, *Be a Man!*, 63.

74. Richard A. Meckel, "Educating a Ministry of Mothers: Evangelical Maternal Associations, 1815–1860," *Journal of the Early Republic* 2, no. 4 (1982): 403–23; quote from Boydston, *Home and Work*, 81.

75. First quote from Elliott West, *Growing Up with the Country: Childhood on the Far Western Frontier* (Albuquerque: University of New Mexico Press, 1989), 158. Second quote from Sally McMurry, *Families and Farmhouses in Nineteenth-Century America: Vernacular Design and Social Change* (New York: Oxford University Press, 1988), 91.

76. Lee A. Craig, *To Sow One Acre More; Childbearing and Farm Productivity in the Antebellum North* (Baltimore: Johns Hopkins University Press, 1993), 10–11.

77. John Mack Faragher, *Sugar Creek: Life on the Illinois Prairie* (New Haven: Yale University Press, 1986), 205; Craig, *To Sow One Acre More*, 92–100.

78. Demos, *Past, Present and Personal*, 47, 58; West, *Growing Up with the Country*, 153–58; Griswold, *Fatherhood in America*, 25–26.

79. All quotes from West, *Growing Up with the Country*, 125 (Wallace Wood), 151 (Lizzie Moore), 150 (Jessie Newton), 55–56 (privacy, housing); see also 149, 158, 254.

80. First quote from Farragher, *Sugar Creek*, 100; second quote from Liahna Babener, "Bitter Nostalgia: Recollections of Childhood on the Midwestern Frontier," in *Small Worlds: Children and Adolescents in America, 1850–1950*, ed. Elliott West and Paula Petrick (Lawrence, Kansas: University Press of Kansas, 1992), 313.

81. Quotes from West, *Growing Up with the Country*, 152, 159, 224–25; Hall et al., *Like a Family*, 20–22.

82. McMurry, *Families and Farmhouses in Nineteenth-Century America*, 90, 100, 192–93, 196, 198, 201–3.

83. Christie Farnham, "Sapphire? The Issue of Dominance in the Slave Family, 1830–1865," in *"To Toil the Livelong Day": America's Women at Work, 1780–1980*, ed. Carol Groneman and Mary Beth Norton (Ithaca, N.Y.: Cornell University Press, 1987), 74; Herbert G. Gutman, *The Black Family in Slavery and Freedom, 1750–1925* (New York: Vintage Books, 1976), 10–11, 190–91.

84. First quote in Deborah Gray White, *Ar'n't I a Woman? Female Slaves in the Plantation South* (New York: W. W. Norton, 1985), 159. Second quote in Brenda Stevenson, "Distress and Discord in Virginia Slave Families, 1830–1860," in *In Joy and in Sorrow: Women, Family, and Marriage in the Victorian South, 1830–1900,* ed. Carol Bleser (New York: Oxford University Press, 1991), 108.

85. First quote in Farnham, "Sapphire?" 81; second quote in Thomas L. Webber, *Deep Like the Rivers: Education in the Slave Quarter Communities, 1831–1865* (New York: Norton, 1978), 169–70.

86. Eugene D. Genovese, *Roll, Jordan, Roll: The World the Slaves Made* (New York: Pantheon, 1972), 498; Richard Steckel, "A Peculiar Population: The Nutrition, Health, and Mortality of American Slaves from Childhood to Maturity," *Journal of Economic History* 46, no. 3 (September 1986): 721–41; and Steckel, "A Dreadful Childhood: The Excess Mortality of American Slaves," *Social Science History* 10, no. 4 (Winter 1986): 427–66.

87. Lester Alston, "Children as Chattel," in *Small Worlds, Children and Adolescents in America, 1850–1950,* ed. Elliott West and Paula Petrik (Lawrence: University Press of Kansas, 1992), 211; Webber, *Deep Like the Rivers,* 14–15; quote from Genovese, *Roll, Jordan, Roll,* 507; Steckel, "A Peculiar Population," 733–38.

88. Genovese, *Roll, Jordan, Roll,* 528–29; quote from Webber, *Deep Like the Rivers,* 160–63; Norrece T. Jones Jr., *Born a Child of Freedom, Yet a Slave: Mechanisms of Control and Strategies of Resistance in Antebellum South Carolina* (Middletown, Conn.: Wesleyan University Press, 1990), 22.

89. Alston, "Children as Chattel," 220–21; first quote in Stevenson, "Distress and Discord in Virginia Slave Families," 111; N. Jones, *Born a Child of Freedom,* 53; second quote in Genovese, *Roll, Jordan, Roll,* 514.

90. Quotes from Farnham, "Sapphire?" 70, 72, 81; Gutman, *The Black Family,* 217–19; N. Jones, *Born a Child of Freedom,* 52.

91. First quote from Jones, *Born a Child of Freedom,* 52; second quote from Genovese, *Roll, Jordan, Roll,* 512; Alston, "Children as Chattel," 215; Stevenson, "Distress and Discord in Virginia Slave Families," 115; Webber, *Deep Like the Rivers,* 165.

92. White, *Ar'n't I a Woman?* 94 (quote), 92, 95–96; Webber, *Deep Like the Rivers,* 13–14; Farnham, "Sapphire?" 82; Gutman, *The Black Family,* 60–75, 76 (quote).

93. Jacqueline Jones, *Labor of Love, Labor of Sorrow: Black Women, Work, and the Family from Slavery to the Present* (New York: Basic Books, 1985), 61–62.

94. Quote in Andrew Billingsley, *Climbing Jacob's Ladder: The Enduring Legacy of African-American Families* (New York: Simon and Schuster, 1992), 128; Gutman, *The Black Family,* 448.

95. Coontz, *The Social Origins of Private Life,* 316; James Borchert, *Alley Life in Washington: Family, Community, Religion and Folklife in the City, 1850–1970* (Urbana: University of Illinois Press, 1980), 86–87.

96. Elizabeth Hafkin Pleck, *Black Migration and Poverty, Boston, 1865–1900* (New York: Academic Press, 1979), 165–78, 182, 194.

97. Gutman, *The Black Family,* 449; Borchert, *Alley Life in Washington,* 73–85.

98. Griswold, *Fatherhood in America,* 52–54; quote from Jones, *Labor of Love, Labor of Sorrow,* 60.

99. Jones, *Labor of Love, Labor of Sorrow,* 88, 129.

100. Jones, *Labor of Love, Labor of Sorrow,* 65, 91, 126–28.

101. West, *Growing Up with the Country,* 232.

102. Preston, Haines, *Fatal Years,* 6–7, 13, 38, 74, 81, 94–95, 98–99, 121; Meckel, *Save the Babies,* 42. See also Charles R. King, *Children's Health in America: A History* (New York: Twayne Publishers, 1993).

103. Meckel, *Save the Babies,* 20, 22, 26, 30, 35–36, 41, 46–49, 62; McMillen, *Motherhood in the Old South,* 136.

104. Meckel, *Save the Babies,* 65–89.

105. Quote from Hoffert, *Private Matters,* 148; Janet Golden, " 'Raised to the Dignity of a Specialty': Pediatrics and Infant Feeding, 1870–1920," unpublished paper; Ewen, *Immigrant Women in the Land of Dollars,* 138.

106. First quote from McMillen, *Motherhood in the Old South,* 116–17, see also 154, 156; second quote from Hoffert, *Private Matters,* 150; Preston and Haines, *Fatal Years,* 12; Ewen, *Immigrant Women in the Land of Dollars,* 143.

107. Quote from Hoffert, *Private Matters,* 183, see also 171, 186; Preston and Haines, *Fatal Years,* 31; West, *Growing Up with the Country,* 236–39.

108. Viviana A. Zelizer, *Pricing the Priceless Child: The Changing Social Value of Children* (New York: Basic Books, 1985), 115–31.

109. Griswold del Castillo, *La Familia,* 77; quote from Gutman, *The Black Family,* 192–93.

110. In his influential book *The Lonely Crowd; A Study of the Changing American Character* (New Haven: Yale University Press, 1950), Riesman argued that *inner-direction* was characteristic of nineteenth-century Americans, whereas *other-direction,* or paying attention to the needs of contemporaries, is characteristic of the twentieth.

Chapter 4

1. David Tyack and Elizabeth Hansot, *Managers of Virtue: Public School Leadership in America, 1820–1980* (New York: Basic Books, 1982), 29.

2. John W. Meyer, David Tyack, Joane Nagel, and Audri Gordon, "Public Education as Nation-Building in America: Enrollments and Bureaucra-

tization in the American States, 1870–1930," *American Journal of Sociology* 85 (1979): 591–613.

3. Carl F. Kaestle, *Pillars of the Republic: Common Schools and American Society, 1780–1860* (New York: Hill and Wang, 1983), 76–78; Tyack and Hansot, *Managers of Virtue,* 21, 46–48, 52, 63. See also David Tyack, *The One Best System: A History of American Urban Education* (Cambridge, Mass.: Harvard University Press, 1974); David Nasaw, *Schooled to Order: A Social History of Public Schooling in the United States* (New York: Oxford University Press, 1979); and three books by Lawrence Cremin, *American Education: The National Experience, 1783–1876* (New York: Harper and Row, 1980); *The Transformation of the School: Progressivism in American Education, 1876–1957* (New York: Knopf, 1961); and *American Education: The Metropolitan Experience, 1876–1980* (New York: Harper and Row, 1988).

4. Anne N. Boylan, *Sunday School: The Formation of an American Institution, 1790–1880* (New Haven: Yale University Press, 1988), 9–10, 16–19, 21, 59; Tyack and Hansot, *Managers of Virtue,* 21, 24, 34–35, 54.

5. Michael B. Katz, *Reconstructing American Education* (Cambridge, Mass.: Harvard University Press, 1987), 14–15; Meyer et al., "Public Education as Nation-Building," 600; Kaestle, *Pillars of the Republic,* 83, 90, 94.

6. Kaestle, *Pillars of the Republic,* 79–80, 190–92; Katz, *Reconstructing American Education,* 16–19; Tyack and Hansot, *Managers of Virtue,* 54.

7. Ira Katznelson and Margaret Weir, *Schooling for All: Class, Race, and the Decline of the Democratic Ideal* (New York: Basic Books, 1985), 45, 50–54; Kaestle, *Pillars of the Republic,* 138–41; Katz, *Reconstructing American Education,* 21–22. See also Samuel Bowles and Herbert Gintis, *Schooling in Capitalist America* (New York: Basic Books, 1976); James D. Anderson, *The Education of Blacks in the South, 1860–1935* (Chapel Hill: University of North Carolina Press, 1988), 28.

8. Marvin Lazerson, "Understanding American Catholic Educational History," *History of Education Quarterly* 17, no. 3 (1977): 297–317.

9. David Tyack and Elizabeth Hansot, *Learning Together: A History of Coeducation in American Public Schools* (New Haven: Yale University Press, 1990),100–12.

10. Kaestle, *Pillars of the Republic,* 172; Vincent P. Franklin, "Continuity and Discontinuity in Black and Immigrant Minority Education in Urban America: A Historical Assessment," in *Educating an Urban People: The New York City Experience,* ed. Diane Ravitch and Ronald K. Goodenow (New York: Columbia Teachers College Press, 1981), 51; Anderson, *Education of Blacks in the South,* 16–19. This argument and that

which follows in this and the next paragraphs will be elaborated when schools in the South and urban North are discussed in more detail.

11. Tyack and Hansot, *Managers of Virtue*, 85; Roger L. Ransom and Richard Sutch, *One Kind of Freedom: The Economic Consequences of Emancipation* (Cambridge: Cambridge University Press, 1977), 17–19.

12. Kaestle, *Pillars of the Republic*, 107; Lee Soltow and Edward Stevens, *The Rise of Literacy and the Common School in the United States: A Socioeconomic Analysis to 1870* (Chicago: University of Chicago Press, 1981), 120 (quote), 121, table 4.6 (statistics).

13. Tyack and Hansot, *Learning Together*, 63–69; Myra H. Strober and Audri Gordon Lanford, "The Feminization of Public School Teaching: Cross-Sectional Analysis, 1850–1880," *Signs: Journal of Women in Culture and Society* 11, no. 2 (Winter 1986): 213–35.

14. William Bullough, *Cities and Schools in the Gilded Age: The Evolution of an Urban Institution* (Port Washington, N.Y.: Kennikat Press, 1974), 32–35.

15. Elliott West, *Growing Up with the Country: Childhood on the Far Western Frontier* (Albuquerque: University of New Mexico Press, 1989), 197–98, 207; Tyack and Hansot, *Learning Together*, 63–64; Tyack, *The One Best System*, 60.

16. Barbara Finkelstein, *Governing the Young: Teacher Behavior in Popular Primary Schools in Nineteenth-Century United States* (London: The Falmer Press, 1989), 45. See also Carl Kaestle, *Literacy in the United States: Readers and Reading Since 1880* (New Haven: Yale University Press, 1991).

17. Soltow and Stevens, *The Rise of Literacy*, 113; quote from West, *Growing Up with the Country*, 200; Finkelstein, *Governing the Young*, 41–57.

18. Finkelstein, *Governing the Young*, 67–81.

19. Ruth Miller Elson, *Guardians of Tradition: American Schoolbooks of the Nineteenth Century* (Lincoln, Nebr.: University of Nebraska Press, 1964), 10, 25–34.

20. Elson, *Guardians of Tradition*, 46–54, 67, 69, 88, 92, 104, 124–26, 143–44, 147–49.

21. Barbara Finkelstein, "Dollars and Dreams: Classrooms as Fictitious Message Systems, 1790–1830," *History of Education Quarterly* 31 (Winter 1991): 476–77; quotes from Finkelstein, *Governing the Young*, 96–106, 119, 124–26.

22. Tyack and Hansot, *Managers of Virtue*, 33.

23. Wayne E. Fuller, *The Old Country School: The Story of Rural Education in the Midwest* (Chicago: University of Chicago Press, 1982), 4, 29–41, 47–48; West, *Growing Up with the Country*, 186–89; Kaestle, *Pillars of the Republic*, 190–92.

24. Soltow and Stevens, *The Rise of Literacy*, table 4.7, 121.

25. Carl F. Kaestle and Maris A. Vinovskis, *Education and Social Change in Nineteenth Century Massachusetts* (New York: Cambridge University Press, 1980), 82; Pamela Barnhouse Walters and Phillip J. O'Connell, "The Family Economy, Work, and Educational Participation in the United States, 1890–1940," *American Journal of Sociology* 93 (March 1988): 1116–52. See also Avery M. Guest and Stewart E. Tolnay, "Agricultural Organization and Educational Consumption in the United States in 1900," *Sociology of Education* 58 (1985): 201–12; Bruce Fuller, "Youth Job Structure and School Enrollment, 1890–1920," *Sociology of Education* 56 (1983): 145–56; Meyer et al., "Public Education as Nation-Building in America"; Soltow and Stevens, *The Rise of Literacy*, 122.

26. W. Fuller, *The Old Country School,* 3; Walters and O'Connell, "The Family Economy," 1135.

27. Soltow and Stevens, *The Rise of Literacy*, 121; Jeremy Atack and Fred Bateman, *To Their Own Soil: Agriculture in the Antebellum North* (Ames: Iowa State University Press, 1987), 47; Tyack and Hansot, *Learning Together,* 45.

28. Soltow and Stevens, *The Rise of Literacy,* 129; Guest and Tolnay, "Agricultural Organization and Educational Consumption," 201–12.

29. Atack and Bateman, *To Their Own Soil,* 48; Soltow and Stevens, *The Rise of Literacy*, table 4.1, 138.

30. Tyack and Hansot, *Managers of Virtue*, 79.

31. On the power of farm owners over rural schools and the problems of tenant farmers, see Paul Theobald, "Country School Curriculum and Governance: The One-Room School Experience in the Nineteenth-Century Midwest," *American Journal of Education* 101 (February 1993): 116–39. On the number of farm owners in 1860, see Lee A. Craig, *To Sow One Acre More: Childbearing and Farm Productivity in the Antebellum North* (Baltimore: Johns Hopkins U. Press, 1993), 50. Quote from Mary Hurlburt Cordier, *Schoolwomen of the Prairies and Plains: Personal Narratives from Iowa, Kansas, and Nebraska, 1860s–1920s* (Albuquerque: University of New Mexico Press, 1992), 111.

32. W. Fuller, *The Old Country School,* 7, 8, 72–76; Cordier, *Schoolwomen of the Prairies,* 112, 114, 125; Tyack and Hansot, *Learning Together,* 59, 60, 70, 75; Kaestle, *Pillars of the Republic,* 13–14, 23.

33. Barbara Finkelstein, "In Fear of Childhood: Relationships between Parents and Teachers in Popular Primary Schools in the Nineteenth Century," *History of Childhood Quarterly* 3 (Winter 1976): 321–326.

34. W. Fuller, *The Old Country School,* 159–61, 208–9; Strober and Lanford, "The Feminization of Public School Teaching," 212–235; Kaestle, *Pillars of the Republic,* 22.

35. West, *Growing Up with the Country*, 200–201; W. Fuller, *The Old Country School*, 93–95; Cordier, *Schoolwomen of the Prairies*, 116–17; Tyack and Hansot, *Learning Together*, 58–59; Kaestle, *Pillars of the Republic*, 15–17.

36. Tyack and Hansot, *Learning Together*, 60, 73; Finkelstein, "In Fear of Childhood," 322–24; Kaestle, *Pillars of the Republic*, 18–19.

37. Quote from West, *Growing Up with the Country*, 199–200; Theobald, "Country School Curriculum and Governance," 130; Tyack and Hansot, *Learning Together*, 117; W. Fuller, *The Old Country School*, 22–23; Cordier, *Schoolwomen of the Prairies*, 118.

38. Kaestle, *Pillars of the Republic*, 193–95; Jane Turner Censer, *North Carolina Planters and Their Children, 1800–1860* (Baton Rouge: Louisiana State University Press, 1984), 44–46, 54–58.

39. Kaestle, *Pillars of the Republic*, 203, 205–6; Anderson, *The Education of Blacks in the South*, 16–17; Ransom and Sutch, *One Kind of Freedom*, 15–19.

40. Quote from Tyack and Hansot, *Managers of Virtue*, 84; William A. Link, *A Hard Country and a Lonely Place: Schooling, Society, and Reform in Rural Virginia, 1870–1920* (Chapel Hill: University of North Carolina Press, 1986), 7; Kaestle, *Pillars of the Republic*, 214.

41. Ransom and Sutch, *One Kind of Freedom*, 15; quotes from Anderson, *The Education of Blacks in the South*, 17, 33.

42. Robert Margo, *Race and Schooling in the South, 1880–1950: An Economic History* (Chicago: University of Chicago Press, 1990), 11; Anderson, *The Education of Blacks in the South*, 19; Ransom and Sutch, *One Kind of Freedom*, 26.

43. Quote from Margo, *Race and Schooling in the South*, 20; Soltow and Stevens, *The Rise of Literacy*, 119; Walters and O'Connell, "The Family Economy," table 1.

44. James D. Anderson. "Ex-Slaves and the Rise of Universal Education in the New South, 1860–1880," in *Education and the Rise of the New South*, ed. Ronald K. Goodenow and Arthur O. White (Boston: G. K. Hall, 1981), 9–10, 14–19; Anderson, *The Education of Blacks in the South*, 26–27.

45. John Rury, *Education and Women's Work: Female Schooling and the Division of Labor in Urban America, 1870–1930* (Albany: State University of New York Press, 1991), 38–41; Tyack and Hansot, *Learning Together*, 96–97.

46. Link, *A Hard Country and a Lonely Place*, 20–23, 29–30, 34, 50–51, 54, 57; Elson, *Guardians of Tradition*, 8.

47. Walters and O'Connell, "The Family Economy," table 1; Margo, *Race and Schooling in the South*, 10–11; first quote from Link, *A Hard Coun-*

try and a Lonely Place, 52; second quote from Ransom and Sutch, *One Kind of Freedom*, 179.

48. Jacquelyn Dowd Hall, James Leloudis, Robert Korstad, Mary Murphy, Lu Ann Jones, and Christopher B. Daly, *Like a Family: The Making of a Southern Cotton Mill World* (Chapel Hill: University of North Carolina Press, 1987), 127–28; Cathy L. McHugh, "Schooling in Post-Bellum Southern Cotton Mill Villages," *Journal of Social History* 20, no. 1 (1986): 149–61.

49. Tyack and Hansot, *Learning Together*, 56; Link, *A Hard Country and a Lonely Place*, 39–42, 51–52; Ransom and Sutch, *One Kind of Freedom*, 27–29; Paul E. Peterson, *The Politics of School Reform, 1870–1940* (Chicago: University of Chicago Press, 1985), 99.

50. Tyack and Hansot, *Managers of Virtue*, 92–93.

51. Anderson, *The Education of Blacks in the South*, 197–98, 67–75.

52. Anderson, *The Education of Blacks in the South*, 28, 34–42, 51, 62–64; chapter by James Anderson in *Work, Youth and Schooling: Historical Perspectives on Vocationalism in American Education*, ed. Harvey Kantor and David Tyack (Stanford: Stanford University Press, 1982), 185–89.

53. Tyack and Hansot, *Managers of Virtue*, 87; Ransom and Sutch, *One Kind of Freedom*, 27–28, table 2.3, 29, 177–78; Margo, *Race and Schooling in the South*, 6–9, 11.

54. Margo, *Race and Schooling in the South*, 11, table 2.2, 10; Tyack and Hansot, *Learning Together*, 88–89; Link, *A Hard Country and a Lonely Place*, 58.

55. This argument had been made by many historians beginning with Michael B. Katz, *The Irony of Early School Reform: Educational Innovation in Mid-Nineteenth Century Massachusetts* (Cambridge, Mass.: Harvard University Press, 1968); ———, *Class, Bureaucracy, and Schools: The Illusion of Educational Change in America* (New York: Praeger, 1971); Michael B. Katz, Michael J. Doucet, and Mark J. Stern, *The Social Organization of Early Industrial Capitalism* (Cambridge, Mass.: Harvard University Press, 1982). See also Stanley K. Schultz, *The Culture Factory: Boston Public Schools, 1789–1860* (New York: Oxford University Press, 1973); Selwyn K. Troen, *The Public and the Schools: Shaping the St. Louis School System, 1838–1920* (Columbia: University of Missouri Press, 1975); Diane Ravitch, *The Great School Wars, New York City, 1805–1973: A History of Public Schools as Battlefields of Social Change* (New York: Basic Books, 1974); Colin Greer, *The Great School Legend: A Revisionist Interpretation of American Public Education* (New York: Basic Books, 1972); Joel Spring, *Education and the Rise of the Corporate State* (Boston: Beacon Press, 1972); and Bowles and Gintis, *Schooling in Capitalist America*. For a critique of

this interpretation see Richard Rubinson, "Class Formation, Political Organization, and Institutional Structure: The Case of Schooling in the United States," *American Journal of Sociology* 92 (1986): 519–548.

56. Reed Ueda, *Avenues to Adulthood: The Origins of the High School and Social Mobility in an American Suburb* (New York: Cambridge University Press, 1987), 76; Katz, *Restructuring American Education*, 21–22; Finkelstein, "Dollars and Dreams," 474.

57. Tyack and Hansot, *Learning Together*, 82; Marvin Lazerson, *The Origins of the Urban School: Public Education in Massachusetts, 1870–1915* (Cambridge, Mass.: Harvard University Press), 11; Bullough, *Cities and Schools in the Gilded Age,* 22–23, 26–27.

58. Walters and O'Connell, "The Family Economy," 1129–35; Soltow and Stevens, *The Rise of Literacy*, table 4.6, 121.

59. Rury, *Education and Women's Work,* 14; Kaestle, *Pillars of the Republic,* 172–74; David M. Ment, "Education and the Black Community in Nineteenth-Century Brooklyn," in *Educating an Urban People: The New York City Experience,* ed. Diane Ravitch and Ronald K. Goodenow (New York: Columbia Teachers College Press, 1981), 31–35; Kenneth Kusmer, *A Ghetto Takes Shape: Black Cleveland 1870–1930* (Urbana: University of Illinois Press, 1976), 6–10, 17.

60. Peterson, *The Politics of School Reform,* 104, 111, 115; quotes from Franklin, "Continuity and Discontinuity in Black and Immigrant Minority Education," 51–53; Walter Licht, *Getting Work: Philadelphia, 1840–1950* (Cambridge, Mass.: Harvard University Press, 1992), 83–84.

61. Tyack, *The One Best System,* 109–25; Ment, "Education and the Black Community in Nineteenth-Century Brooklyn," 36; Kusmer, *A Ghetto Takes Shape,* 61–62.

62. Bullough, *Cities and Schools in the Gilded Age,* 44–46; Tyack, *The One Best System,* 30–32; Tyack and Hansot, *Managers of Virtue,* 94–103; Katz, *Class, Bureaucracy, and Schools,* 56–104.

63. Tyack, *The One Best System,* 30–32; 44–45; Bullough, *Cities and Schools in the Gilded Age*, 45.

64. William W. Cutler III, "Cathedral of Culture: The Schoolhouse in American Educational Thought and Practice since 1820," *History of Education Quarterly* 29, no. 1 (1989): 1–40; Bullough, *Cities and Schools in the Gilded Age,* 26–27.

65. Ravitch, *The Great School Wars,* 92–99; Finkelstein, "In Fear of Childhood," 321–36, 330, quote from 328.

66. Tyack and Hansot, *Learning Together*, 83–87; Strober and Lanford, "The Feminization of Public School Teaching," 212–35.

67. Emily Cahan, *Past Caring: A History of U.S. Preschool Care and Education for the Poor, 1820–1965* (New York: National Center for Children

in Poverty, Columbia University, 1989), 11–19; Caroline Winterer, "Avoiding a 'Hothouse System of Education': Nineteenth Century Early Childhood Education from the Infant Schools to the Kindergartens," *History of Education Quarterly* 32, no. 3 (Autumn 1992): 289–314; Kaestle and Vinovskis, *Education and Social Change*, 58–66.

68. Quote from David John Hogan, *Class and Reform: School and Society in Chicago, 1880–1930* (Philadelphia: University of Pennsylvania Press, 1985), 80–82; Margaret O'Brien Steinfels, *Who's Minding the Children? The History and Politics of Day Care in America* (New York: Simon and Schuster, 1973), 37–49; Winterer, "Avoiding a 'Hothouse System of Education,' " 301–7.

69. Sheila M. Rothman, *Woman's Proper Place: A History of Changing Ideals and Practices, 1870 to the Present* (New York: Basic Books, 1978), 99–100.

70. Edward A. Krug, *The Shaping of the American High School, 1880–1920*, vol. 1 (Madison: University of Wisconsin Press, 1969); David F. Labaree, *The Making of an American High School: The Credentials Market and the Central High School of Philadelphia, 1838–1939* (New Haven, Conn.: Yale University Press, 1988); Ueda, *Avenues to Adulthood*, 91; Tyack and Hansot, *Learning Together*, 136; Peterson, *The Politics of School Reform*, 10, 22.

71. Quote from Cutler, "Cathedral of Culture," fig. 7, 23; Tyack and Hansot, *Learning Together*, 122, 136.

72. Rury, *Education and Women's Work*, 35–44; Tyack and Hansot, *Learning Together*, 114–38; Ravitch, *The Great School Wars*, 100; Labaree, *The Making of an American High School*.

73. Daniel T. Rodgers and David B. Tyack, "Work, Youth, and Schooling," in *Work, Youth, and Schooling: Historical Perspectives on Vocationalism in American Education*, ed. Harvey Kantor and David B. Tyack (Stanford: Stanford University Press, 1982), 274; Joseph F. Kett, *Rites of Passage: Adolescence in America, 1790 to the Present* (New York: Basic Books, 1977), 153–55; Licht, *Getting Work*, 96.

74. Licht, *Getting Work*, 62–87, 89; first quotes from Hogan, *Class and Reform*, 154, 159; Peterson, *The Politics of School Reform*, 65–70; last quotes from Rury, *Education and Women's Work*, 137.

75. Ileen A. De Vault, *Sons and Daughters of Labor: Class and Clerical Work in Turn-of-the-Century Pittsburgh* (Ithaca: Cornell University Press, 1990), 28–29; quotes from Ueda, *Avenues to Adulthood*, 89–91.

76. Lynn Y. Weiner, *From Working Girl to Working Mother: The Female Labor Force in the United States, 1820–1980* (Chapel Hill: University of North Carolina Press, 1985); Margery W. Davies, *Woman's Place is at the Typewriter: Office Work and Office Workers, 1870–1930* (Philadelphia: Temple University Press, 1982); Ellyce Rotella, *From*

Home to Office: U.S. Women at Work, 1870–1930 (Ann Arbor, Mich.: UMI Research Press, 1981); De Vault, *Sons and Daughters of Labor,* 13–21.

77. De Vault, *Sons and Daughters of Labor,* 36–37; Licht, *Getting Work,* 91 (quote), 72.

78. Kaestle and Vinovskis, *Education and Social Change,* 90; Katz et al., *The Social Organization of Early Industrial Capitalism,* 270–72; Troen, *The Public and the Schools,* 126; Soltow and Stevens, *The Rise of Literacy,* 128; Licht, *Getting Work,* 88.

79. Joel Perlmann, *Ethnic Differences: Schooling and Social Structure among the Irish, Italians, Jews, and Blacks in an American City, 1880–1935* (New York: Cambridge University Press, 1988), 23; Soltow and Stevens, *The Rise of Literacy,* 145.

80. Soltow and Stevens, *The Rise of Literacy,* 129; Kaestle and Vinovskis, *Education and Social Change,* 90; Katz et al., *The Social Organization of Early Industrial Capitalism,* 271–72; Troen, *The Public and the Schools,* 127.

81. Ueda, *Avenues to Adulthood,* 55, 157–59; Perlmann, *Ethnic Differences,* 28, 37, 39.

82. Ueda, *Avenues to Adulthood,* 170–71; Rury, *Education and Women's Work,* 69–88, quote from 82 .

83. Ueda, *Avenues to Adulthood,* 56; Rury, *Education and Women's Work,* 25–34.

84. Katz, *The Irony of Early School Reform,* 27–50; Bowles and Gintis, *Schooling in Capitalist America*; De Vault, *Sons and Daughters of Labor,* 26–27; quote from Ueda, *Avenues to Adulthood,* 89–94.

85. Ueda, *Avenues to Adulthood,* 107; Kaestle and Vinovskis, *Education and Social Change,* 122–24.

86. De Vault, *Sons and Daughters of Labor,* 91–129; Ueda, *Avenues to Adulthood,* 76, 102, 104.

87. Quote from Walters and O'Connell, "The Family Economy," 1145. On urban black fertility see Claudia Goldin, "Family Strategies and the Family Economy in the Late Nineteenth Century: The Role of Secondary Workers," in *Philadelphia: Work, Space, Family, and Group Experience in the 19th Century,* ed. Theodore Hershberg (New York: Oxford University Press, 1981), 297. See also Perlmann, *Ethnic Differences,* 170–79, 193; Tyack, *The One Best System,* 109–25.

88. On black newspapers see Frankie Hutton, *The Early Black Press in America, 1827–1860* (Westport, Conn.: Greenwood Press, 1993); and Roland Edgar Wolseley, *The Black Press, USA,* 2d ed. (Ames: Iowa State University Press, 1990). On black women's organizations, see Dorothy C. Salem, *To Better Our World: Black Women in Organized Reform, 1890–1920* (Brooklyn: Carlson Publishers, 1990); on the NAACP, see

Charles Flint Kellogg, *NAACP, A History of the National Association for the Advancement of Colored People* (Baltimore: Johns Hopkins University Press, 1967).

89. Soltow and Stevens, *The Rise of Literacy*, 138; quote from Leonard Dinnerstein, "Education and the Advancement of American Jews," in *American Education and the European Immigrant, 1840–1940*, ed. Bernard J. Weiss (Urbana: University of Illinois Press, 1982), 44–49; Perlmann, *Ethnic Differences*, 123–24, 132–39, 161–62.

90. Perlmann, *Ethnic Differences*, 61; Ueda, *Avenues to Adulthood*, 168.

91. Quotes from Selma Berrol, "Immigrant Children at School, 1880–1940: A Child's Eye View," in *Small Worlds: Children and Adolescents in America, 1850–1950*, ed. Elliott West and Paula Petrik (Lawrence: University Press of Kansas), 44–45, 47–48, 55; Katz et al., *The Social Organization of Early Industrial Capitalism*, 270; Elizabeth Ewen, *Immigrant Women in the Land of Dollars: Life and Culture on the Lower East Side, 1880–1925* (New York: New York University Press, 1985), 197.

92. Tyack, *The One Best System*, 106–8; quote from Tyack and Hansot, *Managers of Virtue*, 78–80.

93. James W. Sanders, "Roman Catholics and the School Question in New York City, Some Suggestions for Research," in *Educating an Urban People: The New York City Experience*, ed. Diane Ravitch and Ronald K. Goodenow (New York: Columbia Teachers College Press, 1981), 122–24; Vincent P. Lannie, *Public Money and Parochial Education: Bishop Hughes, Governor Seward, and the New York School Controversy* (Cleveland: Press of Case Western University, 1968); Jay P. Dolan, *The Immigrant Church: New York's Irish and German Catholics, 1815–1865* (Baltimore: Johns Hopkins University Press, 1975), 107–8.

94. James W. Sanders, *The Education of an Urban Minority: Catholics in Chicago, 1833–1865* (New York: Oxford University Press, 1977), 40–41, 57–60; Marvin Lazerson, "Understanding American Catholic Educational History," *History of Education Quarterly* 17, no. 3 (1977): 297–317; Sanders, "Roman Catholics and the School Question in New York City," 119–21.

95. Sanders, "Roman Catholics and the School Question in New York City," 119–21.

96. Quotes from Dolan, *The Immigrant Church*, 114–18; Sanders, *The Education of an Urban Minority*, 46, 87.

97. Mary J. Oates, "Organized Volunteerism: The Catholic Sisters in Massachusetts, 1870–1940," *American Quarterly* 30 (1978): 652–80; Licht, *Getting Work*, 76; Perlmann, *Ethnic Differences*, 73–74; Glen Gabert Jr., *In Hoc Signo? A Brief History of Catholic Parochial Education in America* (Port Washington, N.Y.: Kennikat Press, 1973), 31; James

Hennessey, *American Catholics: A History of the Roman Catholic Community in the United States* (New York: Oxford University Press, 1981), 187.

98. Quoted in Salvatore J. LaGumina, "American Education and the Italian Immigrant Response," in *American Education and the European Immigrant, 1840–1940,* ed. Bernard J. Weiss (Urbana: University of Illinois Press, 1982), 68, see also 62–69; Sanders, *The Education of an Urban Minority,* 67; Hogan, *Class and Reform,* 132–33; Licht, *Getting Work,* 76.

99. Virginia Yans-McLaughlin, *Family and Community: Italian Immigrants in Buffalo, 1880–1930* (Ithaca: Cornell University Press, 1971), 185–197; Michael J. Eula, *Between Peasant and Urban Villager; Italian-Americans of New Jersey and New York, 1880–1980: The Structures of Counter-Discourse* (New York: Peter Lang, 1993), 99; Perlmann, *Ethnic Differences,* 83–121.

Chapter 5

1. Jacquelyn Dowd Hall, James Leloudis, Robert Korstad, Mary Murphy, Lu Ann Jones, and Christopher B. Daly, *Like a Family: The Making of a Southern Cotton Mill World* (Chapel Hill: University of North Carolina Press, 1987), 16.

2. B. O. Flower in *The American City: A Documentary History,* ed. Charles N. Glaab (Homewood, Ill.: Dorsey Press, 1963), 282.

3. Viviana A. Zelizer, *Pricing the Priceless Child: The Changing Social Value of Children* (New York: Basic Books, 1985), 77.

4. Lee A. Craig, *To Sow One Acre More: Childbearing and Farm Productivity in the Antebellum North* (Baltimore: Johns Hopkins University Press, 1993), 50–51.

5. Elliott West, *Growing Up with the Country: Childhood on the Far Western Frontier* (Albuquerque: University of New Mexico Press, 1989), 74–75, 83–84.

6. Craig, *To Sow One Acre More,* 32, 38–39; West, *Growing Up with the Country,* 76–78, 86–88.

7. West, *Growing Up with the Country,* 93–94; quotes from Craig, *To Sow One Acre More,* 36–37, 83.

8. Carol Coburn, *Life at Four Corners: Religion, Gender, and Education in a German-Lutheran Community, 1868–1945* (Lawrence: University Press of Kansas, 1992), 87; West, *Growing Up with the Country,* 142–43.

9. First quote from Coburn, *Life at Four Corners,* 122; other quotes from David E. Schob, *Hired Hands and Plowboys: Farm Labor in the Midwest, 1815–60* (Urbana: University of Illinois Press, 1975), 188, 189, 201, 205; Sally McMurry, *Families and Farmhouses in Nineteenth-Century America: Vernacular Design and Social Change* (New York: Oxford University Press, 1988), 184–85.

10. Faye E. Dudden, *Serving Women: Household Service in Nineteenth-Century America* (Middletown, Conn.: Wesleyan University Press, 1983), 33, 36–40.

11. First quote from Lester Alston, "Children as Chattel," in *Small Worlds: Children and Adolescents in America, 1850–1950,* ed. Elliott West and Paula Petrik (Lawrence: University Press of Kansas, 1992), 226; other quotes from Deborah Gray White, *Ar'n't I a Woman? Female Slaves in the Plantation South* (New York: W. W. Norton, 1985), 92–94; Marie Jenkins Schwartz, " 'Me an' My Mammy's Gonna Pick a Bale of Cotton': Slave Child Labor in the Alabama Black Belt," paper presented at the Southern Historical Association, Atlanta, Ga., November 6, 1992. See also Wilma King, *Stolen Childhood: Slave Youth in Nineteenth-Century America* (Bloomington: Indiana University Press, 1995), which was published too late to be used in this study.

12. Eugene Genovese, *Roll, Jordan, Roll: The World the Slaves Made* (New York: Vintage Books, 1976), 517.

13. Schwartz, "Me an' My Mammy's Gonna Pick a Bale of Cotton"; quote from Alston, "Children as Chattel," 227.

14. Quote from Willie Lee Rose, *Slavery and Freedom,* ed. William W. Freehling (New York: Oxford University Press, 1982), 37–38; Alston, "Children as Chattel," 228.

15. Jacqueline Jones, *Labor of Love, Labor of Sorrow: Black Women, Work, and the Family from Slavery to the Present* (New York: Basic Books, 1985), 61–62, 87–88, 91, 94.

16. Robert Margo, *Race and Schooling in the South, 1880–1950: An Economic History* (Chicago: University of Chicago Press, 1990), 10.

17. Dudden, *Serving Women,* 33.

18. Albert Camarillo, *Chicanos in a Changing Society: From Mexican Pueblos to American Barrios in Santa Barbara and Southern California, 1848–1930* (Cambridge, Mass.: Harvard University Press, 1979), 6–14, 27, 34–37, 87, 91–93.

19. Liahna Babener, "Bitter Nostalgia: Recollections of Childhood on the Midwestern Frontier," in *Small Worlds: Children and Adolescents in America, 1850–1950,* ed. Elliott West and Paula Petrik (Lawrence: University Press of Kansas, 1992), 303, 311–13.

20. West, *Growing Up with the Country,* 73, 122, 124–26, 133, 225.

21. McMurry, *Families and Farmhouses in Nineteenth-Century America,* 89–91.

22. Craig, *To Sow One Acre More,* 40–41, 83, 92; Lee Soltow and Edward Stevens, *The Rise of Literacy and the Common School in the United States: A Socioeconomic Analysis to 1870* (Chicago: University of Chicago Press, 1981), 129.

23. McMurry, *Families and Farmhouses in Nineteenth-Century America,* 187, 189, 201.

24. Mary P. Ryan, *Womanhood in America from Colonial Times to the Present* (New York: New Viewpoints, 1975), 86, 91, 113. See also Nancy F. Cott, *The Bonds of Womanhood: "Woman's Sphere" in New England, 1780–1835* (New Haven: Yale University Press, 1977); and Barbara Welter, "The Cult of True Womanhood, 1820–1860," *American Quarterly* 18, 2 (Summer 1966): 151–74.

25. Joel Perlmann, "After Leaving School: The Jobs of Young People in Providence, R.I., 1880–1915," in *Schools in Cities: Consensus and Conflict in American Educational History,* ed. Ronald Goodenow and Diane Ravitch (New York: 1983), 8, 10, 16.

26. W. J. Rorabaugh, *The Craft Apprentice: From Franklin to the Machine Age in America* (New York: Oxford University Press, 1986), 131–32, 137.

27. Walter Licht, *Getting Work: Philadelphia, 1840–1950* (Cambridge, Mass.: Harvard University Press, 1992), 102–9.

28. David John Hogan, *Class and Reform: School and Society in Chicago, 1880–1930* (Philadelphia: University of Pennsylvania Press, 1985), 103.

29. Stephan Thernstrom, *Poverty and Progress: Social Mobility in a Nineteenth Century City* (New York: Athenenum, 1971), 22.

30. Joseph Kett, *Rites of Passage: Adolescence in America, 1790 to the Present* (New York: Basic Books, 1977), 169; Hogan, *Class and Reform,* 104.

31. Patrick M. Horan and Peggy G. Hargis, "Children's Work and Schooling in the Late Nineteenth-Century Family Economy," *American Sociological Review* 56, no. 5 (October 1991): 590.

32. Linda Gordon, *Heroes of Their Own Lives: The Politics and History of Family Violence, Boston, 1880–1960* (New York: Viking, 1988), 127.

33. Ileen A. De Vault, *Sons and Daughters of Labor: Class and Clerical Work in Turn-of-the-Century Pittsburgh* (Ithaca: Cornell University Press, 1990), 74; Michael Katz, Michael J. Doucet, and Mark J. Stern, *The Social Organization of Early Industrial Capitalism* (Cambridge, Mass.: Harvard University Press, 1982), 273; Claudia Goldin, "Family Strategies and the Family Economy in the Late Nineteenth Century: The Role of Secondary Workers," in *Philadelphia: Work, Space, Family, and Group Experience in the 19th Century, Essays Toward an Interdisciplinary History of the City,* ed. Theodore Hershberg (New York: Oxford University Press, 1981), 289; Perlmann, "After Leaving School," table 6, p. 17.

34. Soltow and Stevens, *The Rise of Literacy,* 134; Frances H. Early, "The French-Canadian Family Economy and Standard of Living in Lowell, Massachusetts, 1870," *Journal of Family History* 7, no. 2 (1982): 186–87; Goldin, "Family Strategies and the Family Economy," 292.

35. Gordon, *Heroes of Their Own Lives*, 126–27, 181.

36. Joel Perlmann, *Ethnic Differences: Schooling and Social Structure among the Irish, Italians, Jews, and Blacks in an American City, 1880–1935* (New York: Cambridge University Press, 1988), 48, 50.

37. Virginia Yans-McLaughlin, *Family and Community: Italian Immigrants in Buffalo, 1880–1930* (Ithaca: Cornell University Press, 1971), 172–73. Quote from Michael J. Eula, *Between Peasant and Urban Villager; Italian-Americans of New Jersey and New York, 1880–1980: The Structures of Counter-Discourse* (New York: Peter Lang, 1993), 95.

38. Perlmann, *Ethnic Differences*, 130–62.

39. Alice Kessler-Harris, *Out to Work: A History of Wage-Earning Women in the United States* (New York: Oxford University Press, 1982), 123–24; Alexander Keyssar, *Out of Work: A Social History of Unemployment in Massachusetts* (New York: Cambridge University Press, 1983), 97.

40. All quotes from Early, "The French-Canadian Family Economy," 185; Soltow and Stevens, *The Rise of Literacy*, 138.

41. David Nasaw, *Children of the City at Work and at Play* (Garden City, N. Y.: Anchor Press Doubleday, 1985), 88–91, 95, 98, 105–7.

42. Goldin, "Family Strategies and the Family Economy," 285, 289; Horan and Hargis, "Children's Work and Schooling," 590–91; Reed Ueda, *Avenues to Adulthood: The Origins of the High School and Social Mobility in an American Suburb* (New York: Cambridge University Press, 1987), 117; Soltow and Stevens, *The Rise of Literacy*, 136.

43. De Vault, *Sons and Daughters of Labor*, 87–88; Hogan, *Class and Reform*, 114–20, 125; Ueda, *Avenues to Adulthood*, 114–17. Joel Perlmann interprets the evidence on children's labor, schooling, and home ownership differently in his "Working Class Homeownership and Children's Schooling in Providence, Rhode Island, 1880–1925," *History of Education Quarterly* 23, no. 2 (1983): 175–93.

44. Joel Perlmann, "The Schooling of Blacks in a Northern City: Providence, R.I., 1880–1925," *Perspectives in American History* 2 (1985): 125–82; Goldin, "Family Strategies and the Family Economy," 298–99; Jones, *Labor of Love, Labor of Sorrow*, 75, 113.

45. Claudia Goldin, "Female Labor Force Participation: The Origin of Black and White Differences, 1870 to 1880," *Journal of Economic History* 37 (March 1977): 87–108; Jones, *Labor of Love, Labor of Sorrow*, 111, 124–25, 137–41.

46. Donald O. Parsons and Claudia Goldin, "Parental Altruism and Self-Interest: Child Labor among Late Nineteenth-Century American Families," *Economic Inquiry* 27, no. 4 (1989): 637–59; quote from Walter I. Trattner, *Crusade for the Children: A History of the National Child Labor Committee and Child Labor Reform in America* (Chicago: Quadrangle Books, 1970), 38.

47. Hall et al., *Like a Family*, 52, 56, 66.
48. August Kohn, *The Cotton Mills of South Carolina* (Columbia, S.C., 1907), reprinted in *Children and Youth in America, A Documentary History*, vol. 2, ed. Robert H. Bremner (Cambridge, Mass.: Harvard University Press, 1971), 616.
49. Daniel J. Walkowitz, chapter in *Workers in the Industrial Revolution: Recent Studies of Labor in the United States and Europe*, ed. Peter N. Stearns and Daniel J. Walkowitz (New Brunswick, N.J.: Transaction Books, 1974), 268.
50. LeeAnn Whites, "The De Graffenried Controversy: Class, Race, and Gender in the New South," *Journal of Southern History* 54, no. 33 (1988): 460–61.
51. Tamara K. Hareven, *Family Time, Industrial Time: The Relationship between the Family and Work in a New England Industrial Community* (New York: Cambridge University Press, 1982), 211, 213; Early, "The French-Canadian Family Economy," 181; Hall et al., *Like a Family*, 33–34.
52. Parsons and Goldin, "Parental Altruism and Self-Interest," 655. Quote from Hareven, *Family Time, Industrial Time*, 190.
53. Hareven, *Family Time, Industrial Time*, 74; Hall et al., *Like a Family*, 61 (quote), 68–72, 77, 93 (quote); Jones, *Labor of Love, Labor of Sorrow*, 135–36.
54. First quote from Hall et al., *Like a Family*, 94–95; second quote from Jeremy Felt, *Hostages of Fortune: Child Labor Reform in New York State* (Syracuse: Syracuse University Press, 1965), 29.
55. David L. Angus and Jeffrey Mirel, "From Spellers to Spindles: Work-Force Entry by the Children of Textile Workers, 1888–1890," *Social Science History* 9, no. 2 (1985): 123–44; quote from Hareven, *Family Time, Industrial Time*, 193.
56. Quotes from Thomas J. Keil and Wayne M. Usei, "The Family Wage System in Pennsylvania's Anthracite Region: 1850–1900," *Social Forces* 67, no. 1 (1988): 186, 187–89; Francis H. Nichols, "Children of the Coal Shadow," *McClure's Magazine*, February 1903, reprinted in *Children and Youth in America, A Documentary History*, vol. 2, ed. Robert H. Bremner (Cambridge, Mass.: Harvard University Press, 1971), 624–25.
57. Keil and Usei, "The Family Wage System," 187, 205; John E. Bodnar, "Socialization and Adaptation: Immigrant Families in Scranton, 1880–1890," in *Growing Up in America: Historical Experiences*, ed. Harvey J. Graff (Detroit: Wayne State University Press, 1987), 387–93.
58. Felt, *Hostages of Fortune*, 6–10; Christine Stansell, *City of Women: Sex and Class in New York, 1789–1860* (New York: Alfred A. Knopf, 1986), 140.

59. Nasaw, *Children of the City*, 51–55 (quotes), 62–81, 101; West, *Growing Up with the Country*, 91.

60. Jones, *Labor of Love, Labor of Sorrow*, 125; Laurence A. Glasco, "The Life Cycles and Household Structure of American Ethnic Groups: Irish, Germans, and Native-born Whites in Buffalo, New York, 1855," in *A Heritage of Her Own: Toward a New Social History of American Women*, ed. Nancy F. Cott and Elizabeth H. Pleck (New York: Simon and Schuster, 1979), 279–85; David M. Katzman, *Seven Days a Week: Women and Domestic Service in Industrializing America* (New York: Oxford University Press, 1978), 69, 110–11; Stansell, *City of Women*, 140, 160; Dudden, *Serving Women*, 46–47.

61. Steven Mintz and Susan Kellogg, *Domestic Revolutions: A Social History of American Family Life* (New York: Free Press, 1988), 103.

62. Glasco, "The Life Cycles and Household Structure of American Ethnic Groups," 270, 274; Dudden, *Serving Women*, 235; Katzman, *Seven Days a Week*, 87; Jones, *Labor of Love, Labor of Sorrow*, 124.

63. Nasaw, *Children of the City*, 131, 133; Hall et al., *Like a Family*, 162; Jones, *Labor of Love, Labor of Sorrow*, 124, 142.

64. Parsons and Goldin, "Parental Altruism and Self-Interest," 641, 652; Nasaw, *Children of the City*, 132, 136 (quote); Elizabeth Ewen, *Immigrant Women in the Land of Dollars: Life and Culture on the Lower East Side, 1880–1925* (New York: New York University Press, 1985), 105–6.

65. Soltow and Stevens, *The Rise of Literacy*, 134; Perlmann, "After Leaving School," 12; Hogan, *Class and Reform*, 285, n. 27; Licht, *Getting Work*, 88; James D. Anderson, *The Education of Blacks in the South, 1860–1935* (Chapel Hill: University of North Carolina Press, 1988), 149.

66. Trattner, *Crusade for the Children*, 32–33.

67. Gordon, *Heroes of their Own Lives*, 125–26; Zelizer, *Pricing the Priceless Child*, 77, 83.

68. Trattner, *Crusade for the Children*, 41; Felt, *Hostages of Fortune*, 7–8 (quotes), 14–15, 20–22.

69. Trattner, *Crusade for the Children*, 39–40.

70. Craig, *To Sow One Acre More*, 90–91; Parsons, Goldin, "Parental Altruism and Self-Interest," 638.

Chapter 6

1. Sally McMurry, *Families and Farmhouses in Nineteenth-Century America: Vernacular Design and Social Change* (New York: Oxford University Press, 1988), 184–92.

2. Mary Lynn Stevens Heininger, *A Century of Childhood, 1820–1920* (Rochester, N.Y.: Margaret Woodbury Strong Museum, 1984), 19;

Bernard Mergen, *Play and Playthings, A Reference Guide* (Westport, Conn.: Greenwood Press, 1982), 82.

3. Bernard Mergen, "Children's Play in American Autobiographies, 1820–1914," in *Hard at Play: Leisure in America, 1840–1940,* ed. Kathryn Grover (University of Massachusetts Press, 1993), 164.

4. Mergen, "Children's Play in American Autobiographies," 166–67; D. D. Bruce Jr., "Play, Work, and Ethics in the Old South," *Southern Folklore Quarterly* 41 (1977): 33–52; Larcom, *A New England Girlhood* (New York: Cornerhouse Publishers, 1977; reprint of 1889 ed.), 30–33.

5. First quote from Anne Scott MacLeod, "The *Caddie Woodlawn* Syndrome: American Girlhood in the 19th Century," in *A Century of Childhood, 1820–1920,* ed. Mary Lynn Stevens Heininger (Rochester, N.Y.: Margaret Woodbury Strong Museum, 1984), 100–101. Second quote from Andrew Gulliford, "Fox and Geese in the School Yard: Play and American's Country Schools, 1870–1940," in *Hard at Play: Leisure in America, 1840–1940,* ed. Kathryn Grover (University of Massachusetts Press, 1993), 193. The Crosswell study is reprinted in Brian Sutton-Smith, *The Folkgames of Children* (Austin: University of Texas Press, 1972), 282–94; Mergen, "Children's Play in American Autobiographies," 163, 169. Also on play see Iona and Peter Opie, *Children's Games in Street and Playground* (London: Oxford University Press, 1969).

6. Wayne E. Fuller, *The Old Country School: The Story of Rural Education in the Midwest* (Chicago: University of Chicago Press, 1982), 20 (quote); Larcom, *A New England Girlhood,* 109–10, 114–16; Brian Sutton-Smith, "The Play of Girls," in *Becoming Female,* ed. Claire B. Knapp and Martha Kirkpatrick (New York: Plenum, 1979), 232, 235.

7. William B. Waits, *The Modern Christmas in America: A Cultural History of Gift Giving* (New York: New York University Press, 1993), 16; Gary Cross, ms. of "The Coming of the Toy Box," chap. 2 in *Toys in the Making of American Childhood* (forthcoming); quote from Gulliford, "Fox and Geese in the School Yard," 191.

8. Mergen, "Children's Play in American Autobiographies," 178–79, 165.

9. Cross, *Toys in the Making of American Childhood.*

10. Waite, *The Modern Christmas,* 25, 127–29; Brian Sutton-Smith, *Toys as Culture* (New York: Gardner Press, 1986), 26–27, 120. Also on toys see Iona and Robert Opie and Brian Alderson, *The Treasures of Childhood, Books Toys, and Games from the Opie Collection* (London: Pavilion Books, 1989).

11. Kenneth W. Goings, *Mammy and Uncle Mose: Black Collectibles and American Stereotyping* (Bloomington: Indiana University Press, 1994), 8–9, plate 4, figure 33.

12. Heininger, *A Century of Childhood, 1820–1920,* 8; Mergen, *Play and Playthings,* 105–6.

13. Miriam Formanek-Brunell, *Made to Play House: Dolls and the Commercialization of American Girlhood, 1830–1930* (New Haven: Yale University Press, 1993), 28.

14. Elliott West, *Growing Up with the Country: Childhood on the Far Western Frontier* (Albuquerque: University of New Mexico Press, 1989), 116. Money-oriented board games were probably intended for boys as well. Cross, ms. of "Training for the Future: Boys' Machines and Girls' Dolls," chap. 3 of *Toys in the Making of American Childhood.*

15. Karin Calvert, *Children in the House: The Material Culture of Early Childhood, 1600–1900* (Boston: Northeastern University Press, 1992), 111–13; Cross, *Toys in the Making of American Childhood.*

16. Formanek-Brunell, *Made to Play House,* 8–23, 28, 30, 32–33.

17. First quote from Daniel Carter Beard, *The American Boys Handy Book* (Boston: David R. Godine, 1983; reprint of 1882 ed.), xvii; Lina Beard and Adelia B. Beard, *The American Girls Handy Book* (Boston: David R. Godine, 1987; reprint of 1887 ed.), xxiii.

18. West, *Growing Up with the Country,* 104, 107; Larcom, *A New England Girlhood,* 126.

19. Quoted in MacLeod, "*Caddie Woodlawn,*" 105.

20. Ellen K. Rothman, *Hands and Hearts: A History of Courtship in America* (New York: Basic Books, 1984), 208–9.

21. Douglas A. Noverr and Lawrence E. Ziewacz, *The Games They Played: Sports in American History, 1865–1980* (Chicago: Nelson Hall, 1983), 32; Steven A. Riess, *City Games: The Evolution of American Urban Society and the Rise of Sports* (Urbana: University of Illinois Press, 1989), 41–46, 62; Roy Rosenzweig, *Eight Hours for What We Will: Workers and Leisure in an Industrial City, 1870–1920* (Cambridge: Cambridge University Press: 1983), 128–29; Stephen Hardy, *How Boston Played: Sport, Recreation and Community 1865–1915* (Boston: Northeastern University Press, 1982), 68–80.

22. Dwight W. Hoover, "Roller-Skating Toward Industrialism," in *Hard at Play: Leisure in America, 1840–1940,* ed. Kathryn Grover (Amherst: University of Massachusetts Press, 1993), 65–72.

23. Hardy, *How Boston Played,* 110–11; Martha H. Verbrugge, *Able-Bodied Womanhood: Personal Health and Social Change in Nineteenth-Century Boston* (New York: Oxford University Press, 1988), 137–38.

24. Robert A. Smith, *A Social History of the Bicycle* (New York: 1972), 14, 64–109.

25. Joseph F. Kett, *Rites of Passage: Adolescence in America, 1790 to the Present* (New York: Basic Books, 1977), 190–91; Anne Boylan, *Sunday*

School: The Formation of An American Institution, 1790–1880 (New Haven: Yale University Press, 1988), 114–19, 133 (quote), 161–64.

26. David I. MacLeod, *Building Character in the American Boy: The Boy Scouts, YMCA, and their Forerunners, 1870–1920* (Madison: University of Wisconsin Press, 1983), 37, 44–51; quote from Guilliford, "Fox and Geese in the School Yard," 196; Riess, *City Games,* 16–19.

27. Riess, *City Games,* 33–36, 66–67, 132; Noverr and Ziewacz, *The Games They Played,* 18–19.

28. James Wilder and Robyn Hansen, compilers, "A Glossary of Outdoor Games," in *Hard at Play: Leisure in America, 1840–1940,* ed. Kathryn Grover (Amherst: University of Massachusetts Press, 1993), 227–50; quote from West, *Growing Up with the Country,* 111–12.

29. Guilliford, "Fox and Geese in the School Yard," 191–96; Hardy, *How Boston Played,* 111–20; Noverr and Ziewacz, *The Games They Played,* 26–30; Riess, *City Games,* 56.

30. MacLeod, *Building Character,* 9, 17–18, 33–34, 72–82.

31. Nina Mjagkij, *Light in the Darkness: African-Americans and the YMCA, 1852–1946* (Lexington: University Press of Kentucky, 1994), 1–38; Riess, *City Games,* 158.

32. MacLeod, *Building Character,* 77, 86–89; Kett, *Rites of Passage,* 190.

33. Paula Petrik, "The Youngest Fourth Estate: The Novelty Toy Printing Press and Adolescence, 1870–1886," in *Small Worlds: Children and Adolescents in America, 1850–1950,* ed. Elliott West and Paula Petrik (Lawrence: University Press of Kansas, 1992), 125–42.

34. Anne Scott MacLeod, *American Childhood: Essays on Children's Literature of the 19th and 20th Centuries* (Athens: University of Georgia Press: 1994), 91 (quote), 114–19; Mergen, "Children's Play in American Autobiographies," 183. See also Anne Scott MacLeod, *A Moral Tale: Children's Fiction and American Culture, 1820–1860* (Hamden, Conn.: Shoe String Press, 1975).

35. MacLeod, *American Childhood,* 89–98, 144–46; Daniel T. Rodgers, "Socializing Middle-Class Children: Institutions, Fables, and Work Values in Nineteenth Century America," *Journal of Social History* 13 (1980): 354–67; ———, *The Work Ethic in Industrial America, 1850–1920* (Chicago: University of Chicago Press, 1978), 127–32.

36. R. Gordon Kelly, *Mother was a Lady: Self and Society in Selected American Children's Periodicals, 1865–1890* (Westport, Conn.: Greenwood Press, 1974), 3–4; Macleod, *American Childhood,* 153–54, 155 (quote); Rodgers, "Socializing Middle-Class Children."

37. Rodgers, *Work Ethic,* 133; Jerry Griswold, *Audacious Kids: Coming of Age in America's Classic Children's Books* (New York: Oxford University Press, 1992), 20.

38. Elizabeth Lennox Keyser, "'The Most Beautiful Things in the World'? Families in *Little Women,*" in *Stories and Society: Children's Literature in*

Its Social Context, ed. Dennis Butts (New York: Macmillan, 1992), 50–64. See also Elizabeth Lennox Keyser, *Whispers in the Dark: The Fiction of Louisa May Alcott* (Knoxville: University of Tennessee Press, 1993).

39. Griswold, *Audacious Kids,* 157–60; Macleod, *American Childhood,* 75; MacLeod, *"Caddie Woodlawn"* 106–12, 110, 111 (quotes).

40. Albert E. Stone, *The Innocent Eye: Childhood in Mark Twain's Imagination* (New Haven: Yale University Press, 1961), 61, 86–87; quotes from MacLeod, *American Childhood,* 72–75; Griswold, *Audacious Kids,* 46. For more on *Huckleberry Finn,* see notes 68–71.

41. Petrik, "The Youngest Fourth Estate," 127–30; Rodgers, *Work Ethic,* 136–39; MacLeod, *American Childhood,* 81–83.

42. David Nasaw, *Children of the City at Work and at Play* (Garden City, N. Y.: Anchor Press Doubleday, 1985), 19–22, 30.

43. Quote from Mergen, *Play and Playthings,* 62–63; Wilder and Hansen, "A Glossary of Outdoor Games," 242.

44. Kathy Peiss, *Cheap Amusements: Working Women and Leisure in Turn-of-the-Century New York* (Philadelphia: Temple University Press, 1986), 58; Cary Goodman, *Choosing Sides: Playground and Street Life on the Lower East Side* (New York: Schocken Books, 1979), xxii; Nasaw, *Children of the City,* 26–30, 33 (quote).

45. Hardy, *How Boston Played,* 87, 92; Rosenzweig, *Eight Hours for What We Will,* 130–36; Dominick Cavallo, *Muscles and Morals: Organized Playgrounds and Urban Reform, 1880–1920* (Philadelphia: University of Pennsylvania Press, 1981); Mark A. Kadzielski, " 'As a Flower Needs Sunshine': The Origins of Organized Children's Recreation in Philadelphia, 1886–1911," *Journal of Sport History* 4, no. 2 (1977): 169–88; Riess, *City Games,* 134.

46. Cavallo, *Muscles and Morals,* 25, 28, 31–32; Riess, *City Games,* 134, 168; Rosenzweig, *Eight Hours for What We Will,* 137–39, 149–50; Hardy, *How Boston Played,* 105.

47. Nasaw, *Children of the City,* 30, 118 (quote); Mergen, *Play and Playthings,* 107.

48. Peiss, *Cheap Amusements,* 88–91, 96–107, 115–27, 140–41.

49. Foster Rhea Dulles, *A History of Recreation: America Learns to Play* (Englewood Cliffs, N.J.: Prentice Hall, 1965), 100–121.

50. Peiss, *Cheap Amusements,* 60–62, 96, 141–42; Riess, *City Games,* 17–20, 73–75.

51. Peiss, *Cheap Amusements,* 59, 92; Riess, *City Games,* 95–100; quote from Michael J. Eula, *Between Peasant and Urban Villager; Italian-Americans of New Jersey and New York, 1880–1980: The Structures of Counter-Discourse* (New York: Peter Lang, 1993), 134–35.

52. MacLeod, *Building Character,* 63–71.

53. Michael Denning, *Mechanic Accents: Dime Novels and Working-Class Culture in America* (New York: Verso, 1987), 10–12, 19, 24–25, 30–41.

54. Denning, *Mechanic Accents*, 51–52, 157–63, 119, 145–46, 168–72, 188–95.
55. Eugene D. Genovese, *Roll, Jordan, Roll: The World the Slaves Made* (New York: Pantheon, 1972), 505; David K. Wiggins, "The Play of Slave Children in the Plantation Communities of the Old South, 1820–1860," in *Growing Up in America, Children in Historical Perspective,* ed. N. Ray Hiner and Joseph M. Hawes (Urbana: University of Illinois Press: 1985), 175–76; Mergen, *Play and Playthings*, 39. See also Scott Walcott Howlett, "'My Child, Him is Mine': Plantation Slave Children in the Old South" (Ph.D. diss., University of California, Irvine, 1993), 177–86.
56. Mergen, *Play and Playthings*, 53; Wiggins, "The Play of Slave Children," 177; quote in Genovese, *Roll, Jordan, Roll*, 506.
57. Wiggins, "The Play of Slave Children," 181; Charles W. Joyner, *Down By the Riverside, A South Carolina Slave Community* (Urbana: University of Illinois Press, 1984), 61.
58. Genovese, *Roll, Jordan, Roll*, 505–6; quote from Wiggins, "The Play of Slave Children," 178. Mergen believes whipping games among slaves were rare, *Play and Playthings*, 43.
59. Genovese, *Roll, Jordan, Roll*, 506; Wiggins, "The Play of Slave Children," 178; Mergen, *Play and Playthings*, 42.
60. Sutton-Smith, "Play of Girls," 249; quote from Mergen, *Play and Playthings,* 45–46; Wiggins, "The Play of Slave Children," 179–80, 186.
61. Genovese, *Roll, Jordan, Roll*, 518–19; first quote from Wiggins, "The Play of Slave Children," 183–85; second quote from Mergen, *Play and Playthings*, 49.
62. Lawrence Levine, *Black Culture and Black Consciousness* (New York: Oxford University Press, 1977), 5–55.
63. Mary Frances Berry and John W. Blassingame, *Long Memory: The Black Experience in America* (New York: Oxford University Press, 1982), 28.
64. Levine, *Black Culture*, 346–58; Claudia Mitchell-Kernan, "Signifying," and Roger D. Abrahams, "Playing the Dozens," in *Mother Wit from the Laughing Barrel: Readings in the Interpretation of Afro-American Folklore,* ed. Alan Dundes (Jackson: University Press of Mississippi: 1990), 310–28; 298–309.
65. Jacqueline Jones, *Labor of Love, Labor of Sorrow: Black Women, Work, and the Family from Slavery to the Present* (New York: Basic Books, 1985), 88.
66. James Borchert, *Alley Life in Washington: Family, Community, Religion and Folklife in the City, 1850–1970* (Urbana: University of Illinois Press, 1980), 156–57, 294; Riess, *City Games*, 113–14, 146–47 (quote).
67. Beryle Banfield, "Racism in Children's Books: An Afro-American Perspective," in *The Black American in Books for Children: Readings in*

Racism, 2d ed., comp. Donnarae MacCann (Metuchen, N.J.: Scarecrow Press: 1985), 28.

68. Carmen Subryan, "Mark Twain and the Black Challenge," in *Satire or Evasion? Black Perspectives on Huckleberry Finn,* ed. James S. Leonard, Thomas A. Tenney, and Thadious M. Davis (Durham, N.C.: Duke University Press, 1992), 94, 99.

69. John H. Wallace, "The Case Against *Huck Finn,*" Peaches Henry, "The Struggle for Tolerance: Race and Censorship in *Huckleberry Finn,*" and David L. Smith, "Huck, Jim, and American Racial Discourse," in *Satire or Evasion? Black Perspectives on Huckleberry Finn,* ed. James S. Leonard, Thomas A. Tenney, and Thadious M. Davis (Durham, N.C.: Duke University Press, 1992), 16–48, 103–23.

70. Fredrick Woodard and Donnarae MacCann, "*Huckleberry Finn* and the Tradition of Blackface Minstrelsy," in *The Black American in Books for Children, Readings in Racism,* 2d ed., comp. Donnarae MacCann (Metuchen, N.J.: Scarecrow Press: 1985), 76–78. See also Bernard W. Bell, "Twain's 'Nigger' Jim: The Tragic Face behind the Minstrel Mask," in *Satire or Evasion? Black Perspectives on Huckleberry Finn,* ed. James S. Leonard, Thomas A. Tenney, Thadious M. Davis (Durham, N.C.: Duke University Press, 1992), 124–40.

71. Shelley Fisher Fishkin, *Was Huck Black? Mark Twain and African-American Voices* (New York: Oxford University Press, 1993), 21 (quote), 13–40, 53–64, 93–106, 107 (quote). Note also that David L. Smith in "Huck, Jim, and American Racial Discourse" argues that Jim, far from suffering from his superstitions, actually profited from them (108–9).

72. Bernard Wolfe, "Uncle Remus and the Malevolent Rabbit," in Alan Dundes, *Mother Wit from the Laughing Barrel, Readings in the Interpretation of Afro-American Folklore* (Jackson: University Press of Mississippi: 1990), 527.

73. Levine, *Black Culture,* 86–89, 88 (quote).

74. Levine, *Black Culture,* 93, 105–6.

75. Levine, *Black Culture,* 109–15.

76. Levine, *Black Culture,* 116–20.

77. Levine, *Black Culture,* 126–32.

Chapter 7

1. Christine Stansell, *City of Women: Sex and Class in New York, 1789–1860* (Urbana: University of Illinois Press, 1987), 52–54.

2. Viviana A. Zelizer, *Pricing the Priceless Child: The Changing Social Value of Children* (New York: Basic Books, 1985), 11, 70–72.

3. Joan Gittens, *Poor Relations: The Children of the State in Illinois, 1818–1880* (Urbana: University of Illinois Press, 1994), 21–22.

4. Priscilla Ferguson Clement, *Welfare and the Poor in the Nineteenth Century City: Philadelphia, 1800–1854* (Rutherford, N.J.: Fairleigh Dickinson University Press, 1985), 118–40.

5. Homer Folks, *The Care of Destitute, Neglected, and Delinquent Children* (New York: Johnson Reprint Co., 1970; reprint of 1901 ed.), 4–7, 12, 37–39, 72–149.

6. Robert Bremner, *The Public Good: Philanthropy in the Civil War Era* (New York: Knopf, 1980), 159, 161; Priscilla Ferguson Clement, "With Wise and Benevolent Purpose: Poor Children and the State Public School at Owatonna, 1885–1915," *Minnesota History* 49, no. 1 (Spring 1984): 12–13.

7. Michael B. Katz, *In the Shadow of the Poor House: A Social History of Welfare in America* (New York: Basic Books, 1986), 86–87.

8. Priscilla Ferguson Clement, "Nineteenth-Century Welfare Policy, Programs and Poor Women: Philadelphia as a Case Study," *Feminist Studies* 18, no. 1 (Spring 1992): table 2, 40.

9. Raymond A. Mohl, "The Abolition of Public Outdoor Relief, 1870–1900: A Critique of the Piven and Cloward Thesis," in *Social Welfare or Social Control? Some Historical Reflections on Regulating the Poor,* ed. Walter I. Trattner (Knoxville: University of Tennessee Press, 1983), 40–42.

10. Nancy Cott, *The Bonds of Womanhood: "Woman's Sphere" in New England, 1780–1835* (New Haven: Yale University Press, 1977), 35, 46, 84.

11. Bethesda Home of Philadelphia, *Annual Report*, 1871.

12. Timothy Andrew Hacsi, " 'A Plain and Solemn Duty': A History of Orphan Asylums in America" (Ph.D. diss., University of Pennsylvania, 1993), 111–12.

13. Calculated from U.S. Bureau of the Census, *Benevolent Institutions, 1910* (Washington, D.C.: U.S. Government Printing Office, 1913).

14. Peter C. Holloran, *Boston's Wayward Children: Social Services for Homeless Children, 1830–1930* (Rutherford, N.J.: Fairleigh Dickinson University Press, 1989), 137–39, 144–45.

15. Priscilla Ferguson Clement, "The Incorrigible Child: Juvenile Delinquency in the United States from the 17th through the 19th Centuries," in *History of Juvenile Delinquency: A Collection of Essays on Crime Committed by Young Offenders in Selected Countries,* vol. 2, ed. Albert Hess and Priscilla F. Clement (Aalen, Germany: Scientia Verlag Press, 1993), 477–78.

16. Quoted in Hyman Bogen, *The Luckiest Orphans: A History of the Hebrew Orphan Asylum of New York* (Urbana: University of Illinois Press, 1992), 57–58.

17. Hacsi, "A Plain and Solemn Duty," 98; Nurith Zmora, *Orphanages Reconsidered: Child Care Institutions in Progressive Era Baltimore* (Philadelphia: Temple University Press, 1994), 73–77.

18. Steven L. Schlossman, *Love and the American Delinquent: The Theory and Practice of "Progressive" Juvenile Justice, 1825–1920* (Chicago: University of Chicago Press, 1976), 37–40.

19. Gary Edward Polster, *Inside Looking Out: The Cleveland Jewish Orphan Asylum, 1868–1924* (Kent, Ohio: Kent State University Press, 1990), 13; Holloran, *Boston's Wayward Children*, 84–86; Clement, "The Incorrigible Child," 464.

20. Quote from Polster, *Inside Looking Out*, 43; Reena Sigman Friedman, "'These Are Our Children': Jewish Orphanages in the United States, 1880–1925" (Ph.D. diss., Columbia University, 1991), 445. Published in 1994 by the University Press of New England.

21. First quote from Clement, "The Incorrigible Child," 465; second quote from Eric C. Schneider, *In the Web of Class: Delinquents and Reformers in Boston, 1810s–1930s* (New York: New York University Press, 1992), 103.

22. Bogen, *The Luckiest Orphans*, 82; Polster, *Inside Looking Out*, 159–61.

23. Polster, *Inside Looking Out*, 48, 99–100.

24. Hacsi, "A Plain and Solemn Duty," 265–68; Bogen, *The Luckiest Orphans*, 58 (quote), 69.

25. Hacsi, "A Plain and Solemn Duty," 237–42; Schneider, *In the Web of Class*, 39; Bogen, *The Luckiest Orphans*, 93–94.

26. Quote from Schneider, *In the Web of Class*, 114; Clement, *Welfare and the Poor in the Nineteenth Century City*, 253; Polster, *Inside Looking Out*, 52–57, 83–85.

27. Hacsi, "A Plain and Solemn Duty," 249–55; Polster, *Inside Looking Out*, 18–20, 39; Zmora, *Orphanages Reconsidered*, 98–105. On nineteenth-century Southern child-welfare programs, see Gail S. Murray, "Poverty and its Relief in the Antebellum South: Perceptions and Realities in Three Selected Cities: Charleston, Nashville, and New Orleans" (Ph.D. diss., Memphis State University, 1991).

28. Polster, *Inside Looking Out*, 33–36; Bogen, *The Luckiest Orphans*, 99–100; Hacsi, "A Plain and Solemn Duty," 248; Clement, "The Incorrigible Child," 471 (quote), 472–73.

29. Bogen, *The Luckiest Orphans*, 40, 47; Polster, *Inside Looking Out*, 16.

30. Marilyn Irvin Holt, *The Orphan Trains: Placing Out in America* (Lincoln: University of Nebraska Press, 1992), 44–45.

31. Charles Loring Brace, *The Dangerous Classes of New York and Twenty Years' Work among Them* (New York: Wynkeep and Hallenbeck, 1872), 80–82, 84, 88.

32. Thomas Bender, *Toward an Urban Vision: Ideas and Institutions in 19th Century America* (Lexington: University Press of Kentucky, 1975), 143.

33. Paul Boyer, *Urban Masses and Moral Order in America, 1820–1920* (Cambridge, Mass.: Harvard University Press, 1978), 96–100; Holt, *The Orphan Trains*, 21, 71–72.

34. Joseph M. Hawes, *Children in Urban Society: Juvenile Delinquency in Nineteenth-Century America* (New York: Oxford University Press, 1971), 100–101.

35. Holt, *The Orphan Trains*, 31, 36, 49, 54–55, 58.

36. Hawes, *Children in Urban Society*, 102–3; Holloran, *Boston's Wayward Children*, 92; Holt, *The Orphan Trains*, 116 (quote), 147–50.

37. Quote in Hawes, *Children in Urban Society*, 94–95; Stansell, *City of Women*, 213.

38. Quote from Hawes, *Children in Urban Society*, 96–98; Holloran, *Boston's Wayward Children*, 53; Ruth Shackelford, "To Shield Them from Temptation: 'Child-Saving' Institutions and the Children of the Underclass in San Francisco, 1850–1910" (Ph.D. diss., Harvard University, 1991), 431–52.

39. Priscilla Ferguson Clement, "Families and Foster Care: Philadelphia in the Late Nineteenth Century," *Social Service Review* 53, no. 3 (September 1979): 412, 415; Schneider, *In the Web of Class*, 70; Zelizer, *Pricing the Priceless Child*, 185.

40. Linda Gordon, *Heroes of Their Own Lives: The Politics and History of Family Violence, Boston, 1880–1960* (New York: Viking, 1988), 27–29, 34, 37–38, 47, 51–52, 55.

41. Hawes, *Children in Urban Society*, 139 (quote), 141–42; Gordon, *Heroes of Their Own Lives*, 39–41, 43–45; Zelizer, *Pricing the Priceless Child*, 176–77.

42. Sherri Broder, "Child Care or Child Neglect? Baby Farming in Late Nineteenth-Century Philadelphia," *Gender and Society* 2, no. 2 (June 1988): 128–50.

43. Virginia Anne M. Quiroga, "Poor Mothers and Babies: A Social History of Childbirth and Child Care Institutions in Nineteenth Century New York City" (Ph.D. diss., State University of New York at Stony Brook, 1984), 130–33.

44. Charles E. Rosenberg, *The Care of Strangers: The Rise of America's Hospital System* (New York: Basic Books, 1987), 114; Holt, *The Orphan Trains*, 109–10.

45. Schneider, *In the Web of Class*, 47, 80; Gordon, *Heroes of their Own Lives*, 84; Zmora, *Orphanages Reconsidered*, 54, 63.

46. Philadelphia, Northern Home for Friendless Children, *First Annual Report* (Philadelphia, 1852), 9.

47. David M. Katzman, *Seven Days a Week: Women and Domestic Service in Industrializing America* (New York: Oxford University Press), 110–14.

48. Alice Kessler-Harris, *Out to Work: A History of Wage-Earning Women in the United States* (New York: Oxford University Press, 1982), 46–47; Suzanne Lebsock, *The Free Women of Petersburg: Status and*

Culture in a Southern Town, 1784–1860 (New York, Norton, 1984), 181–87; quotes from Stansell, *City of Women*, 70, 73.

49. Broder, "Child Care or Child Neglect?" 136.

50. Quiroga, "Poor Mothers and Babies," 58, 144, 146 (quote).

51. Quiroga, "Poor Mothers and Babies," 92; Broder, "Child Care or Child Neglect?" 139–40; Gordon, *Heroes of Their Own Lives*, 44.

52. Bruce Bellingham, " 'Little Wanderers': A Socio-Historical Study of the Nineteenth Century Origins of Child Fostering and Adoption Reform, Based on Early Records of the New York Children's Aid Society" (Ph.D. diss., University of Pennsylvania, 1984), 87, 94 .

53. Bellingham, "Little Wanderers," 75, 108 (quote); Holt, *The Orphan Trains*, 64.

54. Clement, "The Incorrigible Child," 476.

55. Quote from Schneider, *In the Web of Class*, 80; Bellingham, "Little Wanderers," 101.

56. Polster, *Inside Looking Out*, 135–36 (first quote), 142 (second quote). Clement, "The Incorrigible Child," 474.

57. Barbara Lawrence Bellows, "Tempering the Wind: The Southern Response to Urban Poverty, 1850–1865" (Ph.D. diss., University of South Carolina, 1983), 101–2. See also by the same author, *Benevolence among Slaveholders: Assisting the Poor in Charleston, 1670–1860* (Baton Rouge: Louisiana State University Press, 1993), 120–59.

58. Robert Bremner, "Other People's Children," *Journal of Social History* 16 (Spring 1983): 85.

59. James Laughery Paul, *Pennsylvania's Soldiers' Orphan Schools*, 3d ed. (Harrisburg: Lane S. Hart, 1877), 46, 52–53.

60. Urban Archives Center, Temple University Library (Philadelphia), Church Home for Children, Box 3, Register 1878–1894; Case of Mrs. M. on Feb. 13, 1884; case of Mrs. H. on May 20, 1886.

61. Bellingham, "Little Wanderers," 129, 138–40, table 8, 329.

62. Gordon, *Heroes of Their Own Lives*, 92–94.

63. Bellingham, "Little Wanderers," 76, 130; Clement, "Families and Foster Care," 414.

64. Priscilla Ferguson Clement, "Children and Charity: Orphanages in New Orleans, 1817–1914," *Louisiana* History 27, no. 4 (Fall 1986): 345–49.

65. Bellows, "Tempering the Wind," 98–99.

66. Clement, "With Wise and Benevolent Purpose," 9–10.

67. Clement, "The Incorrigible Child," 475–77.

68. Josiah Flynt Willard, *My Life,* (New York: The Outing Publishing Co., 1908), 92–98; Clement, "The Incorrigible Child," 472; Schneider, *In the Web of Class*, 49.

69. Bellingham, "Little Wanderers," 205, 209–10; Clement, "With Wise and Benevolent Purpose," 9.

70. Quote from Holt, *The Orphan Trains*, 49; Bellingham, "Little Wanderers," 140–41.

71. Flynt, *My Life*, 90; Schneider, *In the Web of Class*, 48 (quote), 104; Bogen, *The Luckiest Orphans*, 45.

72. Polster, *Inside Looking Out*, 136–37 (first quote), 157 (second quote).

73. First quote in Schneider, *In the Web of Class*, 104; second quote in Shackelford, "To Shield Them from Temptation," 556.

74. Zmora, *Orphanages Reconsidered*, 134–35; Polster, *Inside Looking Out*, 17, 137–38 (quote); Friedman, "These Are Our Children," 83.

75. Polster, *Inside Looking Out*, 150 (quote), 152; Zmora, *Orphanages Reconsidered*, 129–30.

76. First quote from Holloran, *Boston's Wayward Children*, 76; second quote from Polster, *Inside Looking Out*, 111.

77. Bogen, *The Luckiest Orphans*, 37–38; Clement, "With Wise and Benevolent Purpose," 6; Zmora, *Orphanages Reconsidered*, 86–87.

78. Clement, "The Incorrigible Child," 466; Bogen, *The Luckiest Orphans*, 142–43; Zmora, *Orphanages Reconsidered*, 168–69; Holloran, *Boston's Wayward Children*, 88 (quote); Polster, *Inside Looking Out*, 191.

79. First quote from Polster, *Inside Looking Out*, 100; second quote from Bogen, *The Luckiest Orphans*, 82.

80. First quote from Polster, *Inside Looking Out*, 190; second quote from Friedman, "These Are Our Children," 453–54.

81. Polster, *Inside Looking Out*, 50, 56–57, 85–87.

82. Zelizer, *Pricing the Priceless Child*, 178–81; quotes from Holt, *The Orphan Trains*, 139.

Bibliographical Essay

General

There are few histories of the 1850–1890 era that deal exclusively with children. Among the few are Elliott West, *Growing Up with the Country: Childhood on the Far Western Frontier* (Albuquerque: University of New Mexico Press, 1989); Viviana Zelizer, *Pricing the Priceless Child: The Changing Social Value of Children* (New York: Basic Books, 1985); Joseph P. Kett, *Rites of Passage: Adolescence in America, 1790 to the Present* (New York: Basic Books, 1977); David Nasaw, *Children of the City, At Work and at Play* (Garden City, N.Y.: Anchor Press/Doubleday, 1985).

There are two good collections of articles on various aspects of the history of children, including N. Ray Hiner and Joseph Hawes, eds., *Growing Up in America: Children in Historical Perspective* (Urbana: University of Illinois Press, 1985) and Elliott West and Paula Petrik, eds., *Small Worlds: Children and Adolescents in America, 1850–1950* (Lawrence: University Press of Kansas, 1992). There are useful bibliographical essays on various aspects of the history of children in Joseph M. Hawes and N. Ray Hiner, eds., *American Childhood: A Research Guide and Historical Handbook* (Westport, Conn.: Greenwood Press, 1985).

While histories of children are scarce, histories of families are plentiful. Among those that best cover children are Steven Mintz and Susan Kellogg, *Domestic Revolutions: A Social History of American Family Life* (New York: Free Press, 1988); and Stephanie Coontz, *The Social Origins of Private Life: A History of American Families, 1600–1900* (New York: Verso, 1988).

Civil War

For brief descriptions of adolescent boys who fought in the Civil War, see two books by Bell Irvin Wiley, *The Life of Billy Yank, The Common Soldier of the Union* (New York: Doubleday, 1971) and *The Life of Johnny Reb, The Common Soldier of the Confederacy* (New York: Doubleday, 1971). Also helpful on the life of young soldiers and on how Northern families confronted the war are two books by Reid Mitchell, *Civil War Soldiers: Their Expectations and their Experiences* (New York: Viking Penguin, 1988) and *The Vacant Chair: The Northern Soldier Leaves Home* (New York: Oxford University Press, 1993). See also Phillip Shaw Paludan, *"A People's Contest": The Union and the Civil War, 1861–1865* (New York: Harper and Row, 1988).

A unique and useful article on how children experienced invasion and war is Elizabeth Daniels, "The Children of Gettysburg," *American Heritage* 40, no. 4 (May/June 1989): 97–107.

There are two excellent sources on the experiences of Confederate women and children: Donna Rebecca Dondes Krug, "The Folks Back Home: The Confederate Homefront During the Civil War" (Ph.D. diss., University of California at Irvine, 1990) and George Rable, *Civil Wars: Women and the Crisis of Southern Nationalism* (Urbana: University of Illinois Press, 1993). On African-American children in wartime, see Peter Bardaglio, "The Children of Jubilee: African American Childhood in Wartime," in *Divided Houses: Gender and the Civil War*, ed. Catherine Clinton and Nina Silber (New York: Oxford University Press, 1992), and Herbert Gutman, *The Black Family in Slavery and Freedom, 1750–1925* (New York: Vintage Books, 1976). *The Encyclopedia of the Confederacy* also contains several interesting articles on children and the Civil War.

As for Reconstruction and children, most has been written on African-American children, including Barbara Fields, *Slavery and Freedom on the Middle Ground* (New Haven: Yale University Press, 1985); Ronald E. Butchart, *Northern Schools, Southern Blacks and Reconstruction, Freedmen's Education, 1862–1875* (Westport, Conn.: Greenwood Press, 1980); Jacqueline Jones, *Soldiers of Light and Love: Northern Teachers and Georgia Blacks, 1865–1873* (Chapel Hill: University of North Carolina Press, 1980); and Robert Charles Morris, *Reading, 'riting, and Reconstruction: The Education of Freedmen in the South, 1861–1870* (Chicago: University of Chicago Press, 1981).

Child Rearing

A great deal has been written about middle-class methods of child rearing in the nineteenth century. Among the most helpful sources are Karen Calvert, *Children in the House: The Material Culture of Early Childhood, 1600–1900* (Boston: Northeastern University Press, 1992); Nancy F. Cott, "Notes toward an Interpretation of Antebellum Childrearing," *Psychohistory Review* 6, no. 4 (1978): 4–20; Carl Degler, *At Odds: Women and the Family in America from the Revolution to the Present* (New York: Oxford University Press, 1980); Robert L. Griswold, *Fatherhood in America, A History* (New York: Basic Books, 1993); Steven Mintz, *A Prison of Expectations: The Family in*

Victorian Culture (New York: New York University Press, 1983); E. Anthony Rotundo, *American Manhood: Transformations in Masculinity from the Revolution to the Modern Era* (New York: Basic Books, 1993); Mary P. Ryan, *The Cradle of the Middle Class: The American Family in Oneida County, New York, 1790–1865* (New York: Cambridge University Press, 1981); Peter N. Stearns, "Girls, Boys, and Emotions: Redefinitions and Historical Change," *Journal of American History* 80, no. 1 (June, 1993): 36–74; and Bernard Wishy, *The Child and the Republic: The Dawn of Modern American Child Nurture* (Philadelphia: University of Pennsylvania Press, 1968).

On child rearing among antebellum Southern white planters, the best work is by Sally G. McMillen, *Motherhood in the Old South: Pregnancy, Childbirth, and Infant Rearing* (Baton Rouge: Louisiana State University Press, 1990). Also useful are Jane Turner Censer, *North Carolina Planters and Their Children, 1800–1860* (Baton Rouge: Louisiana State University Press, 1984); Catherine Clinton, *The Plantation Mistress: Women's World in the Old South* (New York, 1982); and Elizabeth Fox-Genovese, *Within the Plantation Household: Black and White Women of the Old South* (Chapel Hill: University of North Carolina Press, 1988).

On white urban working-class patterns of child rearing see Elizabeth Ewen, *Immigrant Women in the Land of Dollars: Life and Culture on the Lower East Side, 1880–1925* (New York: New York University Press, 1985); Robert Anthony Orsi, *The Madonna of 115th Street: Faith and Community in Italian Harlem, 1880–1950* (New Haven: Yale University Press, 1985); Kathy Peiss, *Cheap Amusements: Working Women and Leisure in Turn-of-the-Century New York* (Philadelphia: Temple University Press, 1986); Christine Stansell, *City of Women: Sex and Class in New York, 1789–1860* (Urbana: University of Illinois Press, 1987).

On rural child rearing in the North, Midwest, and West, see Lee A. Craig, *To Sow One Acre More: Childbearing and Farm Productivity in the Antebellum North* (Baltimore: Johns Hopkins University Press, 1993); Sally McMurry, *Families and Farmhouses in Nineteenth-Century America: Vernacular Design and Social Change* (New York: Oxford University Press, 1988); and Elliott West, *Growing Up with the Country: Childhood on the Far Western Frontier* (Albuquerque: University of New Mexico Press, 1989).

On African-American styles of child rearing there are many good studies, including Lester Alston, "Children as Chattel," in *Small Worlds: Children and Adolescents in America, 1850–1950,* ed. Elliott West and Paula Petrik (Lawrence: University Press of Kansas, 1992); Eugene D. Genovese, *Roll, Jordan, Roll: The World the Slaves Made* (New York: Pantheon Books, 1972); Herbert Gutman, *The Black Family in Slavery and Freedom, 1750–1925* (New York: Vintage Books, 1976); Jacqueline Jones, *Labor of Love, Labor of Sorrow: Black Women, Work, and the Family from Slavery to the Present* (New York: Basic Books, 1985); Norrece T. Jones, *Born a Child of Freedom,*

Yet a Slave: Mechanisms of Control and Strategies of Resistance in Antebellum South Carolina (Middletown, Conn.: Wesleyan University Press, 1990); Brenda Stevenson, "Distress and Discord in Virginia Slave Families, 1830–1860," in *In Joy and in Sorrow: Women, Family, and Marriage in the Victorian South, 1830–1900,* ed. Carol Bleser (New York: Oxford University Press, 1991); Thomas L. Webber, *Deep Like the Rivers: Education in the Slave Quarter Communities, 1831–1865* (New York: Norton, 1978); Deborah Gray White, *Ar'n't I a Woman? Female Slaves in the Plantation South* (New York: W. W. Norton, 1985).

The most useful works on child health in the late nineteenth century are Charles R. King, *Children's Health in America: A History* (New York: Twayne Publishers, 1993); Samuel H. Preston and Michael R. Haines, *Fatal Years: Child Mortality in Late Nineteenth Century America* (Princeton: Princeton University Press, 1991); and Richard A. Meckel, *Save the Babies: American Public Health and the Prevention of Infant Mortality, 1850–1929* (Baltimore: Johns Hopkins University Press, 1990).

Education

Much has been written on nineteenth-century schooling. In fact, of all aspects of the history of late-nineteenth-century children, this is the area most intensively studied.

The best general studies of schooling in the era are David Tyack and Elizabeth Hansot, *Managers of Virtue: Public School Leadership in America, 1820–1980* (New York: Basic Books, 1982); David Tyack, *The One Best System, A History of American Urban Education* (Cambridge, Mass.: Harvard University Press, 1974); Carl F. Kaestle, *Pillars of the Republic: Common Schools and American Society, 1780–1860* (New York: Hill and Wang, 1983); Michael B. Katz, *Reconstructing American Education* (Cambridge, Mass.: Harvard University Press, 1987); and Ira Katznelson and Margaret Weir, *Schooling for All: Class, Race, and the Decline of the Democratic Ideal* (New York: Basic Books, 1985).

On Sunday schools, the finest single study is Anne N. Boylan, *Sunday School: The Formation of an American Institution, 1790–1880* (New Haven: Yale University Press, 1988).

On who enrolled in and attended public schools in various parts of the United States, see Pamela Barnhouse Walters and Phillip J. O'Connell, "The Family Economy, Work, and Educational Participation in the United States 1890–1940," *American Journal of Sociology* 93 (March 1988): 1116–52; and Lee Soltow and Edward Stevens, *The Rise of Literacy and the Common School in the United States: A Socioeconomic Analysis to 1870* (Chicago: University of Chicago Press, 1981).

On teaching style, there are several excellent works by Barbara Finkelstein including *Governing the Young: Teacher Behavior in Popular Primary*

Schools in Nineteenth-Century United States (London: The Falmer Press, 1989); "Dollars and Dreams: Classrooms as Fictitious Message Systems, 1790–1830," *History of Education Quarterly* 31 (Winter 1991): 463–87; and "In Fear of Childhood: Relationships between Parents and Teachers in Popular Primary Schools in the Nineteenth Century," *History of Childhood Quarterly* 3 (Winter 1976): 321–26.

An excellent source on nineteenth-century schoolbooks is Ruth Miller Elson, *Guardians of Tradition: American Schoolbooks of the Nineteenth Century* (Lincoln: University of Nebraska Press, 1964).

On education of young women, see David Tyack and Elizabeth Hansot, *Learning Together: A History of Coeducation in American Public Schools* (New Haven: Yale University Press, 1990); and John Rury, *Education and Women's Work: Female Schooling and the Division of Labor in Urban America, 1870–1930* (Albany: State University of New York Press, 1991).

On Midwestern and Western rural schools, see Wayne E. Fuller, *The Old Country School: The Story of Rural Education in the Midwest* (Chicago: University of Chicago Press, 1982); Avery M. Guest and Stewart E. Tolnay, "Agricultural Organization and Educational Consumption in the United States in 1900," *Sociology of Education* 58 (1985): 201–12.

On Southern schooling, see the aforementioned book by Jane Turner Censer on planter education, as well as William A. Link, *A Hard Country and a Lonely Place: Schooling, Society, and Reform in Rural Virginia, 1870–1920* (Chapel Hill: University of North Carolina Press, 1986). On education of African-Americans, there are several superior studies including James D. Anderson, *The Education of Blacks in the South, 1860–1935* (Chapel Hill: University of North Carolina Press, 1988); Robert Margo, *Race and Schooling in the South, 1880–1950: An Economic History* (Chicago: University of Chicago Press, 1990); and Roger L. Ransom and Richard Sutch, *One Kind of Freedom: The Economic Consequences of Emancipation* (Cambridge: Cambridge University Press, 1977).

On the function of Northern urban schools to control poor and working-class and immigrant children, see Michael B. Katz, *The Irony of Early School Reform: Educational Innovation in Mid-Nineteenth Century Massachusetts* (Cambridge, Mass.: Harvard University Press, 1968); Michael B. Katz, *Class, Bureaucracy, and Schools: The Illusion of Educational Change in America* (New York: Praeger, 1971); Stanley K. Schultz, *The Culture Factory: Boston Public Schools, 1789–1860* (New York: Oxford University Press, 1973); Selwyn K. Troen, *The Public and the Schools: Shaping the St. Louis School System, 1838–1920* (Columbia: University of Missouri Press, 1975); and Colin Greer, *The Great School Legend: A Revisionist Interpretation of American Public Education* (New York: Basic Books, 1972). For an interesting study of who attended one city's public schools, see Joel Perlmann, *Ethnic Differences: Schooling and Social Structure Among the Irish, Italians, Jews, and Blacks in an American City, 1880–1935* (New York: Cambridge University Press, 1988). And for a fine analysis of a suburban high school, see Reed Ueda, *Avenues to Adulthood: The Origins of the High School and Social Mobility in an American Suburb* (New York: Cambridge University Press, 1987).

On the development of vocational education in late-nineteenth-century urban schools, see Ileen A. De Vault, *Sons and Daughters of Labor: Class and Clerical Work in Turn-of-the-Century Pittsburgh* (Ithaca: Cornell University Press, 1990); Walter Licht, *Getting Work: Philadelphia, 1840–1950* (Cambridge, Mass.: Harvard University Press, 1992); and David John Hogan, *Class and Reform: School and Society in Chicago, 1880–1930* (Philadelphia: University of Pennsylvania Press, 1985).

On Catholic schools, the best studies are James W. Sanders, "Roman Catholics and the School Question in New York City: Some Suggestions for Research," in *Educating an Urban People: The New York City Experience,* ed. Diane Ravitch and Ronald K. Goodenow (New York: Columbia Teachers College Press, 1981); James W. Sanders, *The Education of an Urban Minority: Catholics in Chicago, 1833–1865* (New York: Oxford University Press, 1977); Marvin Lazerson, "Understanding American Catholic Educational History," *History of Education Quarterly* 17, no. 3 (1977).

Work

On children's labor on farms, see previously mentioned books by Sally McMurry, Elliott West, and Lee A. Craig.

On child labor in cities among various ethnic groups, see David Nasaw, *Children of the City At Work and At Play* (Garden City, N.Y.: Anchor Press Doubleday, 1985); Virginia Yans-McLaughlin, *Family and Community: Italian Immigrants in Buffalo, 1880–1930* (Ithaca: Cornell University Press, 1971); Michael J. Eula, *Between Peasant and Urban Villager; Italian-Americans of New Jersey and New York, 1880–1980: The Structures of Counter-Discourse* (New York: Peter Lang, 1993); Laurence A. Glasco, "The Life Cycles and Household Structure of American Ethnic Groups: Irish, Germans, and Native-Born Whites in Buffalo, New York, 1855," in *A Heritage of Her Own: Toward a New Social History of American Women,* eds. Nancy F.Cott and Elizabeth H. Pleck (New York: Simon and Schuster, 1979), 279–85; Joel Perlmann, "After Leaving School: The Jobs of Young People in Providence, R.I., 1880–1915," in *Schools in Cities: Consensus and Conflict in American Educational History,* ed. Ronald Goodenow and Diane Ravitch (New York: 1983).

On child labor in textile mills, see Jacquelyn Dowd Hall, James Leloudis, Robert Korstad, Mary Murphy, Lu Ann Jones, and Christopher B. Daly, *Like a Family: The Making of a Southern Cotton Mill World* (Chapel Hill: University of North Carolina Press, 1987), and Tamara K. Hareven, *Family Time, Industrial Time: The Relationship between the Family and Work in a New*

England Industrial Community (New York: Cambridge University Press, 1982).

On child labor in mines, see Thomas J. Keil and Wayne M. Usei, "The Family Wage System in Pennsylvania's Anthracite Region: 1850–1900," *Social Forces* 67, no. 1 (1988): 185–207.

On young women's labor in domestic service see Faye E. Dudden, *Serving Women: Household Service in Nineteenth-Century America* (Middletown, Conn.: Wesleyan University Press, 1983) and David M. Katzman, *Seven Days a Week: Women and Domestic Service in Industrializing America* (New York: Oxford University Press, 1978).

On child labor among African-Americans, see previously mentioned works by Lester Alston, Jacqueline Jones, and Eugene Genovese, as well as several excellent articles by Claudia Goldin including "Family Strategies and the Family Economy in the Late Nineteenth Century: The Role of Secondary Workers," in *Philadelphia: Work, Space, Family, and Group Experience in the 19th Century, Essays Toward an Interdisciplinary History of the City*, ed. Theodore Hershberg (New York: Oxford University Press, 1981); "Female Labor Force Participation: The Origin of Black and White Differences, 1870 to 1880," *Journal of Economic History* 37 (March 1977): 87–108; and with Donald O. Parsons, "Parental Altruism and Self-Interest: Child Labor Among Late Nineteenth-Century American Families," *Economic Inquiry* 27, no. 4 (1989), 637–59.

On child-labor reform, the two most useful works are Walter I. Trattner, *Crusade for the Children: A History of the National Child Labor Committee and Child Labor Reform in America* (Chicago: Quadrangle Books, 1970); and Jeremy Felt, *Hostages of Fortune: Child Labor Reform in New York State* (Syracuse: Syracuse University Press, 1965).

Play, Toys, and Children's Literature

There are several excellent articles on play, including that of children, in Kathryn Grover, ed., *Hard at Play: Leisure in America, 1840–1940* (University of Massachusetts Press, 1993). Other broad surveys of interest include Mary Lynn Stevens Heininger, *A Century of Childhood, 1820–1920* (Rochester, N.Y.: Margaret Woodbury Strong Museum, 1984); Bernard Mergen, *Play and Playthings, A Reference Guide* (Westport, Conn.: Greenwood Press, 1982); Brian Sutton-Smith, *The Folkgames of Children* (Austin: University of Texas Press, 1972).

A fascinating history of Christmas gift giving to children (and others) is William B. Waits, *The Modern Christmas in America: A Cultural History of Gift Giving* (New York: New York University Press, 1993). On toys see Gary Cross, *Toys in the Making of American Childhood* (forthcoming); Miriam Formanek-Brunell, *Made to Play House: Dolls and the Commercialization of American Girlhood, 1830–1930* (New Haven: Yale University Press, 1993);

Karin Calvert, *Children in the House: The Material Culture of Early Child-hood, 1600–1900* (Boston: Northeastern University Press, 1992); Brian Sut-ton-Smith, *Toys as Culture* (New York: Gardner Press, 1986).

There are several excellent histories that touch on the sports that children (especially boys) played in this era. They include Douglas A. Noverr and Lawrence E. Ziewacz, *The Games They Played: Sports in American History, 1865–1980* (Chicago: Nelson Hall, 1983); Steven A. Riess, *City Games: The Evolution of American Urban Society and the Rise of Sports* (Urbana: University of Illinois Press, 1989); Roy Rosenzweig, *Eight Hours for What We Will: Workers and Leisure in an Industrial City, 1870–1920* (Cambridge: Cambridge University Press: 1983); and Stephen Hardy, *How Boston Played: Sport, Recreation and Community 1865–1915* (Boston: Northeastern University Press, 1982).

On the play of working-class children, especially useful are David Nasaw, *Children of the City At Work and At Play* (Garden City, N.Y.: Anchor Press Doubleday, 1985); and Kathy Peiss, *Cheap Amusements: Working Women and Leisure in Turn-of-the-Century New York* (Philadelphia: Temple University Press, 1986).

On African-American children and play in slavery and freedom, see Eugene D. Genovese, *Roll, Jordan, Roll: The World the Slaves Made* (New York: Pantheon, 1972); and David K. Wiggins, "The Play of Slave Children in the Plantation Communities of the Old South, 1820–1860," in *Growing Up in America: Children in Historical Perspective,* eds. N. Ray Hiner and Joseph M. Hawes (Urbana: University of Illinois Press: 1985).

The best study of character-building organizations for middle- and work-ing-class youth in this era is David I. MacLeod, *Building Character in the American Boy: The Boy Scouts, YMCA, and their Forerunners, 1870–1920* (Madison: University of Wisconsin Press, 1983).

On children's literature, there are two fine books by Anne Scott MacLeod: *American Childhood: Essays on Children's Literature of the 19th and 20th Centuries* (Athens: University of Georgia Press, 1994) and *A Moral Tale: Children's Fiction and American Culture, 1820–1860* (Hamden, Conn.: Shoe String Press, 1975). Two other important works on children's reading by Daniel T. Rodgers are "Socializing Middle-Class Children: Institutions, Fables, and Work Values in Nineteenth Century America," *Journal of Social History* 13 (1980): 354–67; and *The Work Ethic in Industrial America, 1850–1920* (Chicago: University of Chicago Press, 1978). Also useful are Jerry Griswold, *Audacious Kids: Coming of Age in America's Classic Children's Books* (New York: Oxford University Press, 1992) and Michael Denning, *Mechanic Accents: Dime Novels and Working-Class Culture in America* (New York: Verso: 1987). On African-American folk stories for children and adults, the classic study is Lawrence Levine, *Black Culture and Black Consciousness* (New York: Oxford University Press, 1977). Also useful are various chapters in Donnarae MacCann, comp., *The Black American in Books for Children: Readings in Racism,* 2d ed. (Metuchen, N.J.: Scarecrow Press, 1985), and Alan Dundes, ed., *Mother Wit from the Laughing Barrel: Readings in the Interpretation of Afro-American Folklore* (Jackson: University Press of Mississippi, 1990). The literature on Mark Twain and *Huckleberry Finn* is immense. Of most use to me were James S. Leonard, Thomas A. Tenney, and Thadious M. Davis, eds., *Satire or Evasion? Black Perspectives on Huckleberry Finn* (Durham, N.C.: Duke University Press, 1992), and Shelley Fisher Fishkin, *Was Huck Black? Mark Twain and African-American Voices* (New York: Oxford University Press, 1993).

Dependent and Delinquent Children

There are several general studies of welfare to children in cities and states, including Peter C. Holloran, *Boston's Wayward Children: Social Services for Homeless Children, 1830–1930* (Rutherford, N.J.: Fairleigh Dickinson University Press, 1989); Joan Gittens, *Poor Relations: The Children of the State in Illinois, 1818–1880* (Urbana: University of Illinois Press, 1994); Homer Folks, *The Care of Destitute, Neglected, and Delinquent Children* (New York: Johnson Reprint Co., 1970; reprint of 1901 ed.); Ruth Shackelford, "To Shield Them from Temptation: 'Child-Saving' Institutions and the Children of the Underclass in San Francisco, 1850–1910" (Ph.D. diss., Harvard University, 1991).

Broader studies of urban welfare that include some information on child welfare include Priscilla Ferguson Clement, *Welfare and the Poor in the Nineteenth Century City: Philadelphia, 1800–1854* (Rutherford, N.J.: Fairleigh Dickinson University Press, 1985); Barbara Bellows, *Benevolence Among Slaveholders: Assisting the Poor in Charleston, 1670–1860* (Baton Rouge: Louisiana State University Press, 1993); Gail S. Murray, "Poverty and its Relief in the Antebellum South: Perceptions and Realities in Three Selected Cities: Charleston, Nashville, and New Orleans" (Ph.D. diss., Memphis State University, 1991).

For an overall view of orphan asylums, see Timothy Andrew Hacsi, " 'A Plain and Solemn Duty': A History of Orphan Asylums in America" (Ph.D. diss., University of Pennsylvania, 1993). Among the many new and interesting studies of orphan asylums are Hyman Bogen, *The Luckiest Orphans: A History of the Hebrew Orphan Asylum of New York* (Urbana: University of Illinois Press, 1992); Priscilla Ferguson Clement, "With Wise and Benevolent Purpose: Poor Children and the State Public School at Owatonna, 1885–1915," *Minnesota History* 49, no. 1 (Spring 1984), 2–13; Priscilla Ferguson Clement, "Children and Charity: Orphanages in New Orleans, 1817–1914," *Louisiana History* 27, no. 4 (Fall 1986): 337–52; Reena Sigman Friedman, *These Are Our Children: Jewish Orphanages in the United States, 1880–1925* (University Press of New England, 1994); Gary Edward Polster,

Inside Looking Out: The Cleveland Jewish Orphan Asylum, 1868–1924 (Kent, Ohio: Kent State University Press, 1990); Nurith Zmora, *Orphanages Reconsidered: Child Care Institutions in Progressive Era Baltimore* (Philadelphia: Temple University Press, 1994).

On juvenile reformatories, see Priscilla Ferguson Clement, "The Incorrigible Child: Juvenile Delinquency in the United States from the 17th through the 19th Centuries," in *History of Juvenile Delinquency: A Collection of Essays on Crime Committed by Young Offenders in Selected Countries,* vol. 2, ed. Albert Hess and Priscilla F. Clement (Aalen, Germany: Scientia Verlag Press, 1993), 453–90; Joseph M. Hawes, *Children in Urban Society: Juvenile Delinquency in Nineteenth-Century America* (New York: Oxford University Press, 1971); Steven L. Schlossman, *Love and the American Delinquent: The Theory and Practice of "Progressive" Juvenile Justice, 1825–1920* (Chicago: University of Chicago Press, 1976); Eric C. Schneider, *In the Web of Class: Delinquents and Reformers in Boston, 1810s-1930s* (New York: New York University Press, 1992).

A fine study of the Society for the Prevention of Cruelty to Children is Linda Gordon, *Heroes of Their Own Lives: The Politics and History of Family Violence, Boston, 1880–1960* (New York: Viking, 1988).

On placing out poor children in families, see Bruce Bellingham, " 'Little Wanderers': A Socio-Historical Study of the Nineteenth Century Origins of Child Fostering and Adoption Reform, Based on Early Records of the New York Children's Aid Society" (Ph.D. diss., University of Pennsylvania, 1984); Priscilla Ferguson Clement, "Families and Foster Care: Philadelphia in the Late Nineteenth Century," *Social Service Review* 53, no. 3 (September 1979): 406–20; and Marilyn Irvin Holt, *The Orphan Trains: Placing Out in America* (Lincoln: University of Nebraska Press, 1992).

Index

Abbott, Jacob, 164
abolition movement, 11, 24, 97, 106
Adams, William T. *See* Optic, Oliver
Addams, Jane, 58, 109
adoption, informal, 191
adolescents: African-American, 129,
    145; on farms, frontier, 65–66,
    92–94, 125–26, 130; female,
    45–49, 59–60, 92–93, 113, 125,
    141, 145–46, 157–60, 163–64,
    170–71, 173, 206–7, 220–22; male,
    45, 48–49, 59–60, 92–94, 106,
    125, 141, 160–64, 171–75, 206,
    212, 221–23; middle-class, 45–49,
    157–64, 220; slave, 70–74, 127; in
    Southern planter families, 51–54;
    working-class, 59–61, 135, 145,
    170–75, 184, 206–7, 222–23, 226
African-Americans, 6–7, 50, 154, 156,
    162–64, 225; child labor, 68,
    70–71, 114, 123–29, 136–37,
    144–45, 224; child rearing, 34, 36,
    66–74, 226; and Civil War, 9,
    11–12, 14, 17, 22–27, 219; and
    education, 85, 89, 96–97, 100–103,
    106, 112, 114–15, 129, 219, 224;

fathers, 5, 24–26, 29, 33–34, 137,
    224; folk tales, 179–82, 184; kin
    networks, 69, 72; mothers, 5,
    24–27, 33–34, 136–37, 224; play,
    175–78, 224; and Reconstruction,
    27–35, 219
age (of population), 1
agriculture, 5–6, 100; machinery and, 6,
    15, 66, 93, 131–32
Alcott, Louisa May, 165–66; *Jack and
    Jill*, 165–66; *Little Women*, 165–66
Aldrich, Thomas Bailey, 166; *Story of a
    Bad Boy*, 166
Alger, Horatio, 167, 174; *Ragged Dick*,
    167
almshouses, 186–90, 202–3, 205; Civil
    War, 16–17
anorexia nervosa, 46
apprenticeship, 132–33; of African-
    American children, 27–29, 219
Armstrong, Samuel Chapman, 101
Atlanta, 20, 29, 101, 138

baby farming, 202, 204
Barnard, Henry, 82
Beard, Adelia, 157

The Author

Priscilla Ferguson Clement is Associate Professor of History and Women's Studies at Penn State University, Delaware County Campus, where she has taught since 1967. She is the recipient of the Lindback Award for Distinguished Teaching at Penn State. Her fields of specialty are social welfare history, women's history, and the history of children and the family. In 1994–1995 she was a Commonwealth Speaker with the Pennsylvania Humanities Council. She has received grants from the National Endowment for the Humanities, the Schlesinger Library, and the Indiana Center on Philanthropy. Clement is the author of *Welfare and the Poor in the Nineteenth Century City: Philadelphia, 1800–1854* and the co-editor (with Albert Hess) of the two-volume *History of Juvenile Delinquency: A Collection of Essays on Crime Committed by Young Offenders in Selected Countries*. She has published articles and chapters in books on children, the homeless, orphanages, foster care programs, and on women and welfare in nineteenth-century America.

The Editors

Joseph M. Hawes is Professor of History at the University of Memphis. His most recent book is *The Children's Rights Movement: A History of Advocacy and Protection* (Twayne, 1991). He is also the author of the forthcoming *American Children Between the Wars, 1920–1940* (Twayne).

N. Ray Hiner is Chancellors' Club Teaching Professor of History and Education at the University of Kansas. He has published widely on the history of children and education in the United States and is coeditor (with Joseph M. Hawes) of *Growing up in America* (1985), *American Childhood* (1985), and *Children in Historical Perspective* (1991). He is currently writing a book on children in the life and thought of Cotton Mather.